149,00

colecção **BIBLIOTECA DIPLOMÁTICA**

Filipe Ribeiro de Meneses

Correspondência diplomática irlandesa sobre Portugal, o Estado Novo e Salazar

(1941-1970)

Ficha técnica

Título
Correspondência diplomática irlandesa sobre Portugal, o Estado Novo e Salazar (1941-1970)

Coordenação Editorial
IDI - MNE

Edição
Colecção Biblioteca Diplomática do MNE – Série A
Ministério dos Negócios Estrangeiros, Portugal

Design Gráfico
Risco, S.A.

Paginação, Impressão e Acabamento
Europress, Lda.

Tiragem
1000 exemplares

Data
Outubro de 2005

Depósito Legal
235905/05

ISBN
972-98906-5-X

Índice

Prefácio	7
Agradecimentos	11
Introdução	13
Parte I (1941-1946)	21
Parte II (1947-1955)	135
Parte III (1956-1961)	245
Parte IV (1962-1970)	421

ANEXOS

Ministros dos Negócios Estrangeiros irlandeses, 1932-1971	543
Secretários Gerais (*Secretaries*) do *Department of External Affairs*, 1927-1974	545
Processos consultados	547

Prefácio

O título deste magnífico livro de compilação e análise do Doutor Filipe Ribeiro de Meneses, *Correspondência diplomática irlandesa sobre Portugal, o Estado Novo e Salazar (1941-1970)*, diz-nos muito sobre o seu conteúdo, mas não nos diz tudo. Não tem apenas o interesse que caracteriza uma qualquer troca formal de correspondência entre dois Estados europeus soberanos que decidem contracenar nos palcos da diplomacia internacional. A alçada intelectual do trabalho que ora se publica vai muito para além disso.

Para a Irlanda – e o facto de a correspondência aqui reproduzida e minuciosamente comentada e contextualizada ser a do acervo documental oriunda dos arquivos de lá e não se ater apenas aos de cá é por si só intrinsecamente interessante – tratava-se do estabelecimento de uma relação com um potencial político-constitucional forte. A jovem República via-se fascinada pela figura de Salazar e pelo corporativismo que o Estado Novo tentou então instaurar em Portugal, à imagem de que no entre-Guerras se verificou um pouco por toda a Europa. A posição, paralela, de neutralidade, tão árdua quanto nominal, face a um conflito devastador como a Segunda Guerra Mundial e as suas sequelas, acrescentava decerto inspiração a uma convergência programática ambicionada e com raízes históricas nos contactos já então longos e com alguma robustez.

Os paralelismos dos dois Países justificavam comparações, uma vez acordado o interesse político irlandês no regime salazarista. Tal como o Doutor Filipe Ribeiro de Meneses sublinha logo na sua introdução (e este é um tema-refrão que percorre os comentários que vai fazendo à documentação que nos apresenta), essa dimensão política dá a tónica ao relacionamento bilateral que em grande parte a correspondência cartografa: aquilo que sobressai da sua leitura é que de um pico de curiosidade inicial com a opção portuguesa, a diplomacia irlandesa foi progressiva e inexoravelmente perdendo interesse num regime que, considerava com óbvio fundamento, não lograva cumprir o programa que para si próprio gizara. A narrativa macro é fascinante. Senhora de uma Constituição datada de 1937, com uma componente corporativista que lhe dava uma semelhança de família com a portuguesa de 1933, a Irlanda sentia, de início, uma natural afinidade electiva com o Portugal do Estado Novo. O entusiasmo com uma experiência paralela, amparado numa proximidade histórica resultante do facto de que desde há muito Portugal albergava refugiados irlandeses, foi porém sol de pouca dura. A pouco e pouco o desencanto irlandês foi-se instalando, alterando a par e passo as coordenadas e a intensidade de um relacionamento político bilateral cada vez por isso mesmo mais normalizado e menos atípico. Assim sendo, não é de estranhar que as diferenças surgidas em torno da questão colonial portuguesa a partir de 1956 se aprofundassem tão rapidamente. Estamos assim perante mais do que um mero estudo sobre diplomacia. Estamos face a um trabalho de utilidade para investigadores interessados em pesquisas de fundo relativas a processos político-constitucionais de *state-building* (de que sabemos pouco e que por isso tendemos a compreender mal) e também úteis a investigadores que se queiram debruçar sobre mecanismos de *policy transfer* e polinização cruzada, que hoje em dia tão mais comuns se mostram do que na época aqui esmiuçada.

Num balanço geral, trabalhos como o de Filipe Ribeiro de Meneses são decisivos não só para um melhor conhecimento dos relacionamentos diplomáticos bilaterais portugueses no passado histórico recente. Dão-nos também a conhecer facetas até aqui mal conhecidas do enquadramento internacional em que vivia e respirava o Estado Novo.

Parece-me de realçar uma característica estrutural do livro que tenho o gosto de prefaciar. Ao comentar longa e incisivamente a correspondência que transcreve e apresenta, o Doutor Ribeiro de Meneses ergue alto uma fasquia que nem sempre assim tem estado. A figura "clássica" da colectânea ou compilação vê-se em consequência transmutada num verdadeiro trabalho de autor, de natureza em simultâneo marcadamente empírica e ensaística, no qual a documentação emerge como uma espécie de conjunto alargado de citações que vão dando corpo e vida a uma linha interpretativa que as domestica, enquadrando-as.

Seguramente que, num eventual estudo levado a cabo de acordo com uma formatação mais tradicional, outras contextualizações, mais amplas, nos disponibilizariam um rendilhado mais denso e nos permitiriam delinear em maior pormenor uma conjuntura decerto muitíssimo complexa em diversos planos. Desde logo a inclusão da dimensão comercial, aqui dispensada, viria reconfigurar a moldura de análise de maneiras decerto não-despiciendas. Mas, com o formato utilizado, tornam-se mais nítidas tanto as tendências de curta-média duração como as linhas de força de um relacionamento diplomático que se vê assim realçado contra o pano de fundo de um quadro maior de que constitui parte e parcela.

Mais ainda, ajudam a valorizar o acervo de trabalhos que o Instituto Diplomático quer publicar na sua colecção.

Professor Doutor Armando Marques Guedes
Presidente do Instituto Diplomático

Agradecimentos

A elaboração deste volume foi possível apenas graças ao contributo de várias instituições e pessoas a quem devo agradecer: o Instituto Diplomático; os *National Archives of Ireland,* em Dublin; o *Irish Research Council for the Humanities and Social Sciences,* cuja *Research Fellowship* me permitiu ter o tempo necessário para redigir a versão final do texto; o Instituto de Ciências Sociais da Universidade de Lisboa, na qual sou, neste momento, Investigador Visitante; as Embaixadas da Irlanda em Lisboa e de Portugal em Dublin (na qual nunca deixei de me sentir em casa); Miriam Tiernan, *Archivist* do *Department of Foreign Affairs,* em Dublin, e a Dra. Maria Helena Neves Pinto, Directora do Serviço de Biblioteca e Documentação Diplomática do Ministério dos Negócios Estrangeiros; o meu compadre, Cormac Ó Cléirigh, pela ajuda com o irlandês; os meus pais; o meu irmão; a Alison. Este livro é dedicado à Sofia.

Introdução

As origens deste projecto encontram-se numa exploração inicial dos *National Archives of Ireland*, em Dublin, em 2000. Entre projectos, e com algum tempo nas mãos, abordei a sua colecção diplomática, no que dizia respeito a Portugal, pouco sabendo da natureza da correspondência que iria encontrar. Em boa verdade, não sabia nem quando a Legação irlandesa em Lisboa tinha sido aberta, nem quando o primeiro diplomata português acreditado em Dublin iniciou as suas funções. Desde então, porém, tenho-me familiarizado com o conteúdo de uma correspondência diplomática que traça, entre 1941 e 1970, o lento afastamento dos dois países, apesar de frequentes expressões de amizade e da invocação do acolhimento dado por Portugal, ao longo dos séculos, a refugiados irlandeses. A importância desta correspondência reside, parece-me, em dois factos essenciais. Em primeiro lugar, a relação Irlanda-Portugal foi marcada por um interesse genuíno, da parte de Dublin, no Estado Novo e nas fórmulas corporativas supostamente encontradas por Salazar para dar "vida nova" à nação portuguesa. Parte do desencanto irlandês com Portugal, que se acentuou de ano para ano ao longo desta correspondência, residiu não necessariamente na natureza ditatorial de Salazar, mas na sua incapacidade – ou falta de vontade – de criar um regime corporativo genuíno. Em segundo lugar, esta correspondência demonstra de forma clara as dificuldades práticas causadas, quer à Irlanda, quer a Portugal, pelas suas causas ditas sagradas – as questões da Irlanda do Norte e das "Províncias Ultramarinas" – em que por tanto tempo e tão intransigentemente se empenharam, sem sucesso, e a grande custo.

Foi uma neutralidade comum durante a Segunda Guerra Mundial que ditou a abertura da Legação irlandesa em Lisboa, no início de 1942. Quando essa decisão foi estudada e tomada, o futuro da Europa era impossível de prever. Se uma derrota inglesa se tornava cada dia mais difícil, então a derrota da Alemanha parecia de todo impossível. A maior parte dos observadores atentos previam um longo e extenuante conflito entre gigantes. Sabemos agora, claro, que em fins de

1941 a posição dos Aliados melhorou, graças à resistência soviética em Moscovo e à entrada no conflito dos Estados Unidos: mas na época era impossível quantificar a importância destes acontecimentos de forma a calcular os anos que faltavam para o fim da guerra. Os exércitos do Eixo, embora com enormes dificuldades, suportaram o Inverno russo e os ataques do exército vermelho: e no Oriente os primeiros meses de guerra foram marcados exclusivamente por vitórias japonesas, começando pelo ataque surpresa à esquadra americana em Pearl Harbour. Num curto espaço de tempo o Japão pareceu ter colmatado todas as deficiências materiais que o impediam, em teoria, de travar uma longa guerra. Controlando as Filipinas, as Índias Orientais Holandesas, a Malásia e a Birmânia, e tendo humilhado a Grã-Bretanha em Singapura, a esquadra e o exército japonês pareciam ter todos os trunfos na mão, aguardando serenamente um ataque Aliado.

Porquê, neste cenário de guerra sem fim, a decisão irlandesa de abrir sem demoras uma Legação em Lisboa, especialmente tendo em conta o reduzido tamanho dos quadros da sua diplomacia? São três as respostas. Em primeiro lugar encontra-se a necessidade de acompanhar o movimento no porto de Lisboa, subitamente crucial para a Irlanda. Forçada a adquirir uma marinha mercante durante a guerra, pôde a Irlanda apenas comprar navios antigos de porte e raio de acção limitados, aos quais estava vedada a travessia do Atlântico. Importações tinham de ser feitas através de Lisboa, porto não ocupado e no limite do raio de acção dos navios da *Irish Shipping Ltd*. O volume de correspondência relacionada com o movimento de entradas e saídas de mercadorias em Lisboa (e com as tentativas de adquirir mais navios para a *Irish Shipping Ltd*) manteve-se elevado durante a guerra, sendo sempre superior a qualquer outro assunto. Creio, porém, que para uma audiência portuguesa, este é um tópico de menor interesse, e é por isso posto de parte neste estudo. Em segundo lugar estava a necessidade de recolher informações sobre a guerra e futuros desenvolvimentos europeus e mundiais – e, ao mesmo tempo, de disseminar o ponto de vista irlandês e defender a sua política de neutralidade dos ataques desferidos, de tempos em tempos, pelos Aliados (e seus defensores na imprensa portuguesa da época). Portugal, país continental não ocupado onde nenhum dos beligerantes exercia uma influência preponderante, era o palco ideal para estas acções. Um jornalista do *Irish Times*, a 23 de Outubro de 1941, escreveu:

> I have often wondered, by the way, why Mr. de Valera has not established an Irish Diplomatic Mission of some sort in Portugal, and I can imagine no more interesting job – except possibly my own – than that of an envoy to the Portuguese capital.
>
> Lisbon at present is the hub of the western universe, and it must be the most fascinating place in the world. Just imagine every day passenger aircraft arrive from Berlin, London, Rome, Marseilles and Paris, and the event of the week must be the arrival of the Clipper from the United States.
>
> I believe that in Lisbon's fashionable cafés and restaurants British, Germans, Frenchmen and Italians, to say nothing of the inevitable Americans, may be seen cheek by jowl with one another enjoying a short respite from the belligerent atmosphere of their own countries.
>
> From the diplomatic, as well as from the commercial, point of view, I should imagine that an Irish Legation – or, at least, a Consulate-General – in Lisbon would be of decided value to our State.

Em vários documentos reunidos neste volume se encontra a preocupação irlandesa em corrigir um juízo negativo sobre a política internacional traçada e seguida por Eamon de Valera, e, igualmente, em entender o porquê da boa vontade Aliada para com a neutralidade portuguesa, manifestada várias vezes após o fim da guerra. Por fim, a terceira razão prende-se com a natureza do Estado Novo e com o que a Irlanda poderia aprender com este regime.

A Constituição irlandesa, publicada em 1937 e ainda hoje em vigor, tem uma componente corporativista importante. A câmara alta, o *Seanad Éireann*, é tida como o ponto de encontro entre os mundos político, económico, social e cultural. Subordinado à câmara baixa (*Dáil Éireann*) e à vontade do Governo, era o Senado tido, no final da década de 30 e durante a Segunda Guerra Mundial, por certos grupos conservadores como uma instituição cuja importância iria, forçosamente, crescer com o passar do tempo. Um forte movimento corporativista (*vocationalist*, na linguagem política irlandesa da época), liderado por algumas figuras de peso no mundo intelectual ligado à Igreja Católica, defendia o abandono gradual da democracia parlamentar: e para estes, Portugal era um modelo a seguir. Tendo em conta as fortes possibilidades, em 1941, de uma vitória alemã, um melhor entendimento dos processos governativos e administrativos do Estado Novo português podia ser visto como um trunfo destinado a assegurar a independência do jovem Estado irlandês. A imagem tida de Salazar por este núcleo de intelectuais católicos não podia ser melhor: professor universitário, defensor da Igreja, opositor do totalitarismo e no poder apenas por resposta ao pedido urgente da nação e não, como outros ditadores, graças ao recurso à violência. Segundo um documento distribuído pelo Governo irlandês em Março de 1940,

[...] it is to be hoped that Salazar's work and ideas will be closely examined and carefully pondered by those responsible for building up the New Ireland which is slowly emerging above the waters after a tragic shipwreck and a long submersion.[1]

É a observação irlandesa do funcionamento das instituições portuguesas que forma o núcleo central da primeira parte desta compilação.

Os documentos que integram esta obra estão divididos em quatro períodos. O primeiro vai desde a chegada a Lisboa do primeiro encarregado de negócios irlandês, em Dezembro de 1941, até ao fim de 1946. É um período em que Portugal, pelas razões que acima mencionei, exerceu alguma importância nas considerações de Dublin. Estavam os dois países ligados por interesses comerciais e pela sua neutralidade (embora estas neutralidades e suas causas fossem bem distintas, como cedo se viu) e pelas consequências, no pós-guerra, desse

---

[1] "Salazar and his work", da autoria do Jesuíta P. J. Gannon. Distribuido aos outros membros do Governo pelo Ministro da Indústria e do Comércio irlandês em Março de 1940. National Archives of Ireland, Department of the Taoiseach, S 11601^A Portugal – Economic and Financial Policy.

posicionamento diplomático. É de salientar, neste período de adaptação, a ausência de referências às principais preocupações diplomáticas do Governo de Salazar, o que demonstra que estas, de facto, se discutiam num círculo bastante restrito. Só no pós-guerra é que a natureza da neutralidade portuguesa, e as dificuldades enfrentadas pelo país, começaram a ser discutidas pelos diplomatas irlandeses, espantados pelas palavras de apreço de figuras britânicas e americanas. Em relação à política interna de Portugal, porém, estes diplomatas rapidamente compreenderam que o regime corporativo português, tantas vezes descrito na Irlanda como um modelo a seguir, não existia, estando eles perante uma ditadura altamente centralizada e incapaz – ou desinteressada – de responder às necessidades materiais da população. O juízo feito pelo primeiro Encarregado de Negócios irlandês, Colman O'Donovan, aquando da sua partida, não deixa margens para dúvida: o regime tinha os dias contados, pois Salazar, sem colaboradores à sua altura, via-se forçado a adiar sucessivamente as reformas necessárias para dar vida própria às instituições corporativas.

O segundo período, até à entrada dos dois países na ONU, em finais de 1955, é marcado pela estagnação das relações entre os dois países. A Irlanda conhecendo já os limites reais do Estado Novo, e tendo-se entretanto desinteressado do corporativismo, os diplomatas de Dublin limitavam-se a comentar a evolução dos acontecimentos em Portugal sem grande entusiasmo. Não havia, segundo eles, alternativa a Salazar, e com este no poder nada se alteraria. A natureza da representação irlandesa em Portugal durante este período, e nos anos que se lhe seguiram, mostra como Lisboa tinha caído em importância aos olhos de Dublin. Ficou a Legação irlandesa entregue, a partir de Agosto de 1948, ao Conde O'Kelly de Gallagh, peça importante da primeira geração de diplomatas ao serviço do governo irlandês. Tendo servido como Ministro em Paris, O'Kelly de Gallagh abandonou o serviço activo em 1935, sendo "repescado" para Lisboa em face de uma falta de vontade nítida em enviar um funcionário do quadro activo. Permaneceu este diplomata à frente da Legação irlandesa em Lisboa, com algumas importantes interrupções, até 1967. Quer isto dizer que a atitude de simpatia por Salazar (e de hostilidade à oposição portuguesa) e por certos aspectos do seu regime, que O´Kelly de Gallagh desde cedo demonstrou, sobreviveu na correspondência diplomática irlandesa mais anos do que seria de esperar, tendo em conta, como veremos, a evolução do posicionamento internacional da Irlanda. O momento alto das relações dos dois países neste período foi a visita particular, e discreta, de Eamon de Valera a Portugal, em Setembro de 1953, detalhada nesta colecção. É de salientar, porém, que já neste período existiam sinais de desconfiança entre os dois países, motivados em grande parte pelas causas que, em cada país, eram tidas como sagradas, mas que no outro não eram entendidas. A participação de navios de guerra portugueses num exercício da NATO conduzido a partir de Londonderry, na Irlanda do Norte, em 1952, foi mal vista por Dublin, enquanto que, no seu posicionamento face à questão do Estado Português da Índia, a Irlanda procurava manter-se neutra, para desgosto de Lisboa.

O terceiro período, de 1956 até ao fim de 1961, é marcado pela crescente crispação das relações entre os dois países. Irlanda e Portugal encararam a ONU, a partir de 1956, de uma maneira completamente diferente. Para a Irlanda, uma participação activa na ONU era absolutamente necessária, pois esta organização representava um palco essencial para a defesa dos interesses dos pequenos países. A ONU (e mesmo, antes dela, a Sociedade das Nações, que De Valera tinha apoiado com todas as suas forças) permitia a Dublin sair da sombra de Londres e defender perante um público global causas que lhe eram queridas: a neutralidade (que Portugal tinha entretanto abandonado) e a "Irlanda irredenta" do Ulster. Desde cedo, e graças à questão da neutralidade, a Irlanda começou a estabelecer contactos com os países não-alinhados e, através dele, a manifestar a sua oposição à política colonial de várias potências europeias. A posição portuguesa na ONU, porém, era radicalmente diferente, sendo uma de contenção; o seu principal objectivo era levar a comunidade internacional a aceitar a posição portuguesa sobre a indivisibilidade do território nacional e, por isso mesmo, a inaplicabilidade ao território nacional dos poderes de fiscalização colonial da ONU – algo que depressa se demonstrou ser impossível. Assim sendo, as divergências entre os dois países surgiram rapidamente, começando pela questão do Estado Português da Índia que, como vimos, estava já em aberto. A União Indiana e a Irlanda, ambas tendo negociado a sua independência do Reino

Unido após uma guerra mundial, e ambas tendo visto o território que consideravam seu dividido como o preço dessa mesma independência, tinham interesses em comum que tornavam a sua relação mais forte do que os laços entre Dublin e Lisboa. O apelo português ao sentimento católico irlandês cedo se esgotou, com o *Department of External Affairs* a optar pela posição de Nova Delhi na questão de Goa, que foi seguida atentamente. Embora os antecedentes históricos fossem completamente diferentes, os irlandeses eram incapazes de olhar para Goa e os outros enclaves portugueses na Índia e não se lembrar dos seis condados do Ulster ainda sob soberania britânica. Todas as tentativas feitas por diplomatas portugueses para interessar Dublin no ponto de vista de Lisboa foram recebidas com uma indiferença calculada.

O fosso cavado em torno da questão de Goa foi depois alargado pela posição portuguesa de intransigência em relação a África. Um exemplo óbvio desta divergência terá sido o encontro entre Salazar e o *Taoiseach* Séan Lemass, herdeiro de de Valera à frente do partido *Fianna Fáil* e do Governo, no Palace Hotel do Buçaco, em 1960. Estando o Primeiro-Ministro irlandês a caminho do Nigéria, para assistir às cerimónias da independência daquela ex-colónia britânica (de grande importância simbólica para a Irlanda, cujas ordens missionárias nela tinham desempenhado um enorme papel), não se coibiu Salazar de empregar argumentos francamente racistas para o demover do seu optimismo em relação a África – optimismo demonstrado, aliás, pela presença de tropas irlandesas no Congo ex-belga ao serviço da ONU naquela que foi a primeira de muitas participações irlandesas em missões de manutenção de paz. Como fica demonstrado nas páginas que se seguem, foram numerosas as tentativas portuguesas para reconquistar a boa vontade de Dublin em relação à política ultramarina portuguesa, mas sempre sem sucesso.

O quarto período, de 1962 à morte de Salazar, é marcado pela oposição aberta da Irlanda, nas Nações Unidas, à política colonial portuguesa, não tendo os irlandeses ilusões sobre os problemas que as futuras ex-colónias portuguesas certamente iriam encontrar. A frustração de Dublin com a falta de evolução na posição portuguesa, mesmo após a perda de Goa e do início das guerras coloniais em África, ditou o congelamento das relações formais entre os dois países. Toda a correspondência relativa ao desejo português de promover a sua Legação em Dublin a Embaixada, e de ver a Irlanda fazer o mesmo em Lisboa, ou pelo menos nomear um Ministro Plenipotenciário, não sendo representada por um Encarregado de Negócios interino, reflecte o mau momento que as relações entre os dois países estavam a atravessar. É de salientar, porém, que a opinião do *Department of External Affairs* sobre o império colonial português não foi construída com base nos ofícios que lhe chegavam de Lisboa, pois estes (e não só os do Conde O'Kelly de Gallagh) eram geralmente favoráveis à presença portuguesa em África.

Esta colecção acaba com a morte de Salazar, ignorando, nos anos 1969 e 1970, a correspondência relativa ao Governo de Marcello Caetano. A razão é simples; a documentação aberta ao público, que avança no tempo de ano para ano, não chegou ainda ao 25 de Abril, ficando uma investigação do período marcelista necessariamente incompleta. Achei que haveria por isso mais coerência em restringir o volume aos Governos de Salazar, e ao acompanhamento de sua doença e morte. Não resisti, porém, a incluir a chamada de atenção do *Department of External Affairs* ao *Taoiseach*, Jack Lynch, após a sua conversa, em Novembro de 1969, com o Embaixador português António Rocha Fontes.

Nota:

Na documentação diplomática irlandesa do período coberto por este livro, títulos, datas e instituições são escritos em irlandês, enquanto o texto dos ofícios e restante correspondência é escrito em inglês. Assim sendo, e como este livro se destina a um público português, traduzi o que estava em irlandês directamente para português, aproveitando para simplificar e uniformizar a aparência dos documentos seleccionados.

Parte I
(1941-1946)

A documentação contida na primeira parte deste volume começa com o estabelecimento da Legação irlandesa em Lisboa e acaba no final de 1946, sendo por isso dominada pela experiência comum de neutralidade durante a Segunda Guerra Mundial e pelas impressões de Portugal, do Estado Novo e de Salazar colhidas pelos três primeiros diplomatas irlandeses acreditados em Lisboa, Colman O'Donovan,[1] Patrick O'Byrne,[2] e Cornelius C. Cremin,[3] que reaparecerá mais tarde como Secretário-Geral do Department of External Affairs. É de realçar que, como foi escrito na Introdução, estas impressões são de algum valor histórico já que a visão tida na Irlanda, em 1942, do Estado Novo era geralmente positiva e que as impressões dos diplomatas irlandeses em Lisboa estava a ser enviadas para um ministério extremamente conservador, dominado pelas figuras de Eamon de Valera, *Taoiseach* (Primeiro Ministro) e Ministro dos Negócios Estrangeiros, e de Joseph P. Walshe, Secretary (Secretário-Geral). Este conservadorismo está bem patente, por exemplo, no documento N.º 8, "The duties of our representatives abroad", no qual é recomendada aos diplomatas irlandeses a observância religiosa de acordo com os preceitos da Igreja Católica.

---

[1] Colman J. O'Donovan nasceu em Dublin em 1895. Após um ano ao serviço da Brigada de Dublin do IRA durante a guerra da independência, transitou para a função pública, entrando no carreira diplomática em 1930. Serviu como Primeiro Secretário em Washington (1930-1933), Berlim (1933-1935), Londres (1935-1938) e em Roma, junto da Santa Sé (1938-1942, sendo Encarregado de Negócios *ad interim* a partir de 1940). Depois da sua estadia em Lisboa, abandonou a carreira diplomática, passando para o Ministério do Governo Local e da Saúde Pública.

[2] Patrick J. O´Byrne nasceu em 1893. Entrou para a função pública irlandesa pouco depois da independência, primeiro no Ministério da Defesa e depois no DEA, servindo no estrangeiro a partir de 1926, embora em funções estritamente administrativas. Em Março de 1942 foi enviado para Lisboa como assistente do Encarregado de Negócios (O'Donovan), sendo promovido a Segundo Secretário em Fevereiro de 1944. Em 1948 partiu para a Legação em Roma, ainda como Segundo Secretário.

[3] Cornelius Cremin é geralmente considerado o melhor da primeira geração de diplomatas irlandeses. Educado em Cork e Oxford, entrou para o DEA em Dezembro de 1935, tendo ficado em primeiro lugar no concurso do ano anterior. Foi colocado em Paris em 1937, e em Berlim, como Encarregado de Negócios *ad interim*, em 1943. De Berlim viajou de carro para Lisboa em 1945, regressando a Dublin no ano seguinte. Foi depois Embaixador em Paris, junta da Santa Sé, em Londres (por duas vezes), Secretário-Geral do DEA, e Representante Permanente junto das Nações Unidas.

Como foi também mencionado na Introdução, a correspondência diplomática enviada de Lisboa para Dublin durante a guerra foi dominada por questões comerciais, já que o porto de Lisboa era um ponto de paragem e transbordo essencial para mercadorias importadas pela Irlanda. O documento N.º 18 dá conta da importância vital de Lisboa para o bem estar económico da Irlanda, bem como a compreensão irlandesa pelas dificuldades portuguesas em abrir uma Legação em Dublin. É de salientar, em relação a este ponto, que Colman O´Donovan, antes da sua partida para Lisboa, foi convidado a passar uma semana no *Department of Supplies*.

Uma análise mais completa da documentação contida nesta Parte encontra-se no meu artigo "Um olhar irlandês sobre Portugal, Salazar e o Estado novo", em *Política Internacional*, N.º 22, Vol. 3, Outono-Inverno 2000.

Não seria este autor o primeiro a apontar agumas as semelhanças entre de Valera e Salazar (ver Documento N.º 14). Quer pela longevidade política, quer pela visão que tinham do país ideal, sonhado, que queriam (re)construir (dotando-o para alcançar esse fim de uma constituição e das instituições que acreditavam ser necessárias), quer pelos seus nacionalismo e catolicismo acerbados, torna-se óbvio que havia pontos em comum entre os dois homens. Havia, também, diferenças importantes. Tendo criado na Irlanda instituições democráticas, estava de Valera disposto a sujeitar a sua obra ao eleitorado, aceitando as derrotas a que este, por vezes, lhe impunha; e a ideia de um jovem Salazar, de arma em punho, a bater-se contra um exército estrangeiro, como o fez de Valera em 1916, é, no mínimo, inverosímil. Mas os dois estudavam-se e admiravam-se à distância. No Arquivo Oliveira Salazar encontra-se o rascunho de uma carta enviada por Salazar a de Valera em 1939:

Excellency,
The Rev. O'Sullivan on his return from Ireland, delivered me a perfect copy of the Irish Constitution signed by Your Excellency, courtesy that I heartily acknowledge.
I also thank you for the kind words of esteem and sympathy that were transmitted to me, and you may be sure that the same sentiments are felt by

the Portuguese people and its Government for Ireland and its rulers (?) – especially for Your Excellency,

The kind description that the Rev. O'Sullivan made to Your Excellency of Portugal and its traditional sympathy for Irish Catholics, would revive in Your Excellency the wish of visiting my country, though not officially, and in pilgrimage to Fatima.

It would be a great pleasure for me to make Your Excellency's personal acquaintance and to express to Your Excellency how much we appreciate our good relations with the Irish Nation, to which Your Excellency so superiorly presides.

Believe me Yours Sincerely,

Encontra-se também a resposta de de Valera, datada de 16 de Maio de 1939:

Your Excellency

I was very pleased on my return from Rome to find your letter awaiting me.

I am afraid that I must postpone my visit to Portugal to another time. My recent absence in Rome and my proposed tour of America, as well as a visit which I must again pay to my doctor in Zurich in September, will already have taken me too long in one year away from my duties.

I regret very much that I shall not be able to visit Portugal. The great work which your Excellency has been doing in reorganising the economic life of your nation is known to me from books and from friends who have seen it and told me of it, but I should like to see it for myself.

Ireland and Portugal having in the main the same philosophy of life any solutions which one finds for social affairs ought with the necessary adaptations be available, at least in the broad outline, for the other. We are struggling here with problems to which you appear to have found solutions. I am anxious to study whether these solutions can be adapted to our State, which is differently constituted to yours.

Will all good wishes for yourself and for the Portuguese people.

Yours very sincerely,

Eamon de Valera[4]

---

[4] Ambas as cartas se encontram no Arquivo Oliveira Salazar, Torre do Tombo, AOS/CP/272.

Este convite a de Valera será repetido várias vezes ao longo dos anos seguintes, até à visita particular do Taoiseach em 1953, parte de uma peregrinação que o levou a Lurdes e ao País Basco. Como a correspondência contida nesta Parte demonstra, porém, este interesse irlandês nas «soluções» portuguesas (ver Documento N.º 7) cedo desapareceu. O Documento N.º 14 contem uma primeira indicação de que nem tudo estava bem em Portugal, com uma figura eclesiástica conhecida de John Charles McQuaid, Arcebispo de Dublin e colaborador próximo de de Valera, a afirmar que os irlandeses nada tinham a aprender em Portugal, dado o nível de pobreza que aqui prevalecia, único no mundo. As queixas e críticas de O´Donovan são constantes: sobre a lentidão da administração pública portuguesa (Documentos N.º 22 e 26), a falta de um sistema de racionamento de bens essenciais (Documento N.º 25), a doutrina (ou falta dela) por trás do Estado Novo (Documentos N.º 27 e 45), e a União Nacional (Documento N.º 38). A conclusão de O'Donovan, em vésperas de partir (Documento N.º 49), não deixa margem para dúvidas: o regime tinha os dias contados. São de salientar as críticas do Cardeal Patriarca e do Núncio Apostólico, feitas, sem dúvida, em virtude do estatuto especial da Irlanda, nação Católica na qual a Igreja detinha um enorme poder. Para leitores atentos em Dublin, esta última comunicação portuguesa de O´Donovan terá sido, provavelmente, devastadora. Nos ofícios de Patrick J. O'Byrne, que sucedeu interinamente a O'Donovan, voltando a chefiar interinamente a Legação em Lisboa na primavera de 1946, encontram-se sobretudo críticas ao sistema de distribuição de produtos alimentares, que causava situações aflitivas: em Novembro de 1946, O'Byrne informou o DEA de que o contínuo da Legação estava a sofrer os efeitos de uma constante má alimentação, não sendo ele um caso único entre o pessoal português ao serviço das várias missões diplomáticas estrangeiras acreditadas em Lisboa.[5] E embora o DEA mostrasse pouco interesse pelo caso, não terá este deixado uma boa impressão em Dublin.

Cornelius (Con) C. Cremin, Encarregado de Negócios interino a partir de Junho de 1945, acompanhou o fim da guerra e são de sua autoria alguns ofícios

---

[5] National Archives of Ireland, Department of External Affairs, Embassy Lisbon, 6/29A, Secret and confidential matters, 1945-1947.

de grande interesse sobre o posicionamento português nesse período tão agitado. Pouco ou nada teve a dizer sobre o sistema corporativo; a sua atenção dirigiu-se sobretudo para a interpretação retrospectiva feita pelos portugueses da sua própria neutralidade (Documentos N.º 64 e 78), as adaptações do regime português às realidades do pós-guerra (Documentos N.º 56 e 67), e a importância para Salazar da sobrevivência de Franco, acossado pelos Aliados, destacando-se entre estes a Grã-Bretanha, governada a partir do verão de 1945 pelo partido Trabalhista (Documentos N.º 59 e 60). Cremin acompanhou com cuidado as eleições de 1945 (a partir do Documento N.º 68), manifestando sempre alguma surpresa pelo desenrolar dos acontecimentos (especialmente pelo convite à participação da oposição) e ainda alguma hostilidade para com o MUD, incapaz, segundo ele, de apresentar propostas para lá da conquista do poder. São de sua autoria o relato de dois encontros com Salazar. O primeiro destes encontros foi uma conversa a sós, a 17 de Dezembro de 1945, que durou 20 minutos (Documento N.º 86), e ficou marcado sobretudo pelo tópico da neutralidade, manifestando Salazar a sua admiração por de Valera, que tinha conseguido, apesar das ligações constitucionais entre a Irlanda e o Reino Unido (abolidas formalmente apenas em 1949), manter o seu país fora da guerra. O segundo foi um jantar na Embaixada britânica (Documento N.º 96), tendo Cremin sido sentado ao lado de Salazar. Nas duas conversas Salazar mencionou a possibilidade de de Valera vir a Portugal.

Tenta-se, por fim, nesta parte ilustrar foi o esforço dos diplomatas irlandeses para defender, perante a opinião pública portuguesa e por isso perante o mundo, a linha política determinada por de Valera, intervindo junto das autoridades para contrariar qualquer crítica que a imprensa aliadófila fizesse à neutralidade de Dublin. Assim, em Março de 1944, O'Donovan entrou em contacto directo com a imprensa portuguesa e com o SPN para assegurar uma cobertura positiva da crise nas relações da Irlanda com os Aliados, aberta pela exigência americana do fecho das representações oficiais alemã e japonesa em Dublin. O'Donovan distribuiu pela imprensa o texto de telegramas recebidos de Dublin que demonstravam como toda a opinião pública irlandesa apoiava a neutralidade cuidadosamente observada por de Valera. Não teve O'Donovan um sucesso completo. O mais hostil de todos os artigos publicados na altura em Portugal surgiu a 16 de

Março no *Jornal do Comércio*, intitulado 'Persistência irlandesa, tolerância britânica'. Segundo o seu autor,

[...]

Ainda no começo desta guerra vimos como foram tomadas precauções, do lado alemão, para prevenir o Reich contra possíveis ataques através de países neutros. A Grã-Bretanha, em face, não de um país neutro, mas de uma parte do seu território que se arvorou em Domínio e impôs pela força, pela resistência revolucionária, um estatuto político que a Inglaterra aceitou para evitar derramamento de sangue, não só tem respeitado a proclamada neutralidade irlandesa, como levou, pelo seu exemplo, os Estados Unidos e os outros Domínios a tomarem atitude semelhante.

Parece ter chegado o momento em que a situação da Irlanda terá de modificar-se.

[...]

Os termos em que se exprimiu Churchill permitem-nos concluir que De Valera não encontrará ambiente moral nem condições materiais para defender os direitos teóricos do Domínio a que preside contra os interesses da segurança do Império e seus aliados na guerra.

A 29 de Março, tendo entretanto surgido alguns artigos favoráveis à posição irlandesa no jornal *A Voz* (26 e 27 de Março), O´Donovan deu-se por satisfeito com a situação; intervenções junto do SPN, da Censura, do Secretário-Geral do Ministério dos Negócios Estrangeiros e do próprio *Jornal do Comércio* (que tinha publicado a 22 de Março os telegramas enviados por O'Donovan, mas com traduções que lhes alteravam subtilmente o sentido) tinham levado a um melhor conhecimento da posição irlandesa. Mais tarde Cremin (Documento N.º 81) dar--se-ia igualmente por satisfeito com o tom da imprensa portuguesa para com Portugal. O'Byrne foi apanhado de surpresa em Maio de 1946 (Documento N.º 98) por um artigo em *A Voz* ridicularizando a posição constitucional irlandesa, mostrando até alguma apreciação pelo humor contido no artigo; por esse facto foi repreendido pelo SubSecretário-Geral (Documento N.º 99); rapidamente, porém, obteve uma audiência com o director daquele jornal, após a qual uma clarificação da posição irlandesa foi publicada.

1941

1
Carta, Eamon de Valera a António de Oliveira Salazar:
Dublin, 27 de Agosto de 1941[6]

Cher Monsieur Salazar,

J'ai chargé Monsieur Sean Murphy, notre Ministre Plenipotentiaire en France, de vous faire parvenir cette lettre.

Depuis longtemps déjà j'ai voulu établir les relations amicales qui existent entre nos deux pays sur une base diplomatique. Le Gouvernement Irlandais a observé avec sympathie et admiration la grande oeuvre de reconstruction que vous avez accomplie en Portugal, et il a naturellement desiré pouvoir suivre les details de plus près. Les temps actuels mettent nos deux pays en présence de problèmes qui comportent des difficultés semblables. En outre, la représentation de l'Irlande à Lisbonne devient une nécessité pour faciliter nos nationaux que passent par votre pays et en même temps pour accélérer les communications entre nos Légations en Europe et l'Irlande.

Pour le moment j'ai l'intention avec votre permission bienveillante d'envoyer un Chargé d'Affaires à Lisbonne et de remettre à la fin de la guerre l'accreditation d'un Ministre Plénipotentiaire. Je voudrais envoyer comme notre représentant M. Colman O'Donovan actuellement Chargé d'Affaires près le Saint Siège. Je suis sur que vous le trouverez digne de l'aide que vous pourrez lui donner pour bien accomplir sa mission.

Le Gouvernement Irlandais sera très heureux de recevoir un représentant du Portugal quand vous croirez le moment propice pour prendre une action

---

[6] National Archives of Ireland (NAI), Department of External Affairs (DEA), 317/40 Appointment of a Chargé d'Affaires at Lisbon, 1941-1948.

réciproque mais il comprendra qu'un delai appréciable puisse s'imposer du côté de votre Gouvernment pour lequel le besoin n'est pas si urgent.

Je vous prie, cher Monsieur Salazar, d'agréer mes souhaits les plus sincères pour vous et le bonheur et la prosperité de votre pays.

de Valera

2
Carta, António de Oliveira Salazar a Eamon de Valera: Lisboa, 27 de Setembro de 1941[7]

J'ai eu l'honneur de recevoir la lettre que Votre Excellence a eu l'obligeance de m'addresser par l'entremise de Monsieur Sean Murphy. Malheureusement il ne m'a pas été possible de voir Monsieur Murphy lors de son passage à Lisbonne. Je vais tâcher de vous faire parvenir ma réponse ayant encore recours à l'amabilité de Votre Ministre Plénipotentiaire en France.

Il ne pouvait pas manquer de m'être très agréable ainsi qu'au Gouvernement Portugais, la résolution prise par Votre Excellence de faire accréditer un Chargé d'Affaires d'Irlande au Portugal et le choix que Vous avez fait de Mr Colom [sic] O'Donovan pour lui faire confier cette mission. Je suis convaincu que cette représentation diplomatique servira à resserrer davantage les rapports très amicaux déjà existants entre nos deux pays et donnera comme résultat une plus grande rapidité dans la résolution des questions qui puissent nous intéresser.

Comme Votre Excellence si justement prévoyait, il ne nous est pas possible de correspondre avec une entière réciprocité au geste amical avec lequel l'Irlande vient de distinguer notre pays. Néanmoins, je tiens à assurer Votre Excellence que je ne manquerai pas de profiter de la première opportunité pour accréditer un Chargé d'Affaires du Portugal en Irlande, en comptant comme assuré, dès maintenant, Votre bienvaillant accord.

---

[7] NAI, DEA, 317/40 Appointment of a Chargé d'Affaires at Lisbon, 1941-1948.

Je vous envoie mes meilleurs remerciements pour votre lettre et je vous prie de croire, Monsieur le Président, à la parfaite sincerité des voeux que je formule pour les prospérités personnelles de Votre Excellence et de Son Gouvernement, ainsi que pour la paix et la prosperité de Son pays.

Oliveira Salazar

3
Telegrama, Legação irlandesa em Vichy (Eireann) ao *Department of External Affairs* (Estero): Vichy, 7 de Outubro de 1941[8]

422 Personal. Portuguese Government welcome establishment of diplomatic relations, and accept the appointment of O'Donovan. Letter to this effect follows in bag.

Eireann

4
Artigo, *Irish Times*: Dublin, 6 de Novembro de 1941
Diplomatist for Lisbon
Mr. Colm [sic] O'Donovan Appointed

The Irish Government have decided to have a diplomatic representative at Lisbon. This was disclosed in the following official communication last night:

Following an agreement with the Portuguese Government, it has been decided to appoint a Chargé d'Affaires to look after Irish interests in Lisbon.

The post will be filled by Mr. Colm [sic] O'Donovan, who was until recently Chargé d'Affaires at the Holy See. He will take up his duties early in December.

Mr. O'Donovan, who is a brother of Mr. D.J. O'Donovan, recently appointed Commissioner for Co. Dublin, has been connected with the Eire Legation at the Vatican – first as Secretary and later in the absence of the late Minister, Mr. W.J.B. Macaulay, as Chargé d'Affaires.

---

[8] NAI, DEA, 317/40 Appointment of a Chargé d'Affaires at Lisbon, 1941-1948.

It may be recalled that, in the *Irish Times* of 23 October, the desirability of an Irish Legation at Lisbon was suggested owing to the importance of that city as 'the hub of the Western Universe' at the present time.

Hitherto the Irish Government has not had any representative, consular or otherwise, at Lisbon. Mr. Kevin J. Kenny is honorary consul at Dublin for Portugal.

5
Telegrama, Estero à Legação irlandesa em Madrid (Legirlanda): Dublin, 11 de Novembro de 1941[9]

111. It is rumoured that smallpox and typhus prevalent in Lisbon. Can you say whether this is so.

Estero

6
Telegrama, Legirlanda a Estero: Madrid, 13 de Novembro de 1941[10]

147. Your telegram 111. We have no knowledge of epidemics in Lisbon neither has the Portuguese Embassy.

Legirlanda

7
Texto de declaração de Eamon de Valera ao Comité de Finanças do Parlamento irlandês (Dáil Éireann): Dublin, 4 de Dezembro de 1941[11]

1. This estimate provides for the new Legation which it is proposed to establish at Lisbon. The provision proposed is on almost exactly the same lines as

---

[9] NAI, DEA, 317/40 Appointment of a Chargé d'Affaires at Lisbon, 1941-1948.
[10] NAI, DEA, 317/40 Appointment of a Chargé d'Affaires at Lisbon, 1941-1948.
[11] NAI, DEA, 317/40 Appointment of a Chargé d'Affaires at Lisbon, 1941-1948. Esta declaração, e a discussão que suscitou, pode ser lida no Volume 85 dos debates do Dáil Éireann, ou no website do mesmo.

that made in the case of our Legation in Switzerland. I don't think it presents any special feature to which I need draw the attention of Deputies […]

2. I am sure that there will be general satisfaction that we are to have this direct contact with Portugal. Portugal is a neighbouring country. Her geographical situation and her attitude in relation to the present conflict, are very similar to our own and no doubt the problems which confront the two countries, particularly at the present time, have also many points of resemblance. We have all heard of the great advances which Portugal has made under the leadership of her present Premier, Dr. Salazar. The progressive and Christian outlook of the Portuguese Government in handling its economic and other domestic problems has attracted attention and admiration throughout the world and, not least I think, in this country.

3. I am sure that people here will consider it right and proper that these two countries should be in direct diplomatic relations, and I have no doubt that the closer contact will prove useful and valuable to us.

4. At the present time, there are special reasons why this should be so. Lisbon is now a main junction with our communications with the outside world. It is the terminus of the air service from Foynes, some of our boats are calling there fairly frequently and even at the present moment we have a number of our nationals stranded there awaiting the making of arrangements for their return to this country. Lisbon is also important in connection with our supplies. Deputies are aware, I think, that some of our cargoes from overseas are shipped to Portugal in the first instance and are then loaded into those of our ships which are not in a position to face Atlantic crossings. All this makes it desirable and indeed necessary that we should have a representative in Portugal. Especially under present conditions, travel and shipping depend to a great extent on consular services, and wherever there is a large body of Irish interests requiring such services as there is in Portugal at the moment, it is fitting that we should provide a representative of our own to whom our nationals can turn for protection and assistance when they require it.

5. In these various ways, I am sure that the new Legation in Portugal will amply justify itself and I therefore ask the House to vote this supplementary estimate.

1942

8
Ofício, Secretário-Geral do *Department of External Affairs* (DEA)
ao Encarregado de Negócios irlandês em Lisboa:
Dublin, 28 de Janeiro de 1942[12]

<u>THE DUTIES OF OUR REPRESENTATIVES ABROAD</u>

During the present period of crisis, the duties of our Representatives abroad call for the very highest degree of care and self-sacrifice. The main purpose of an Irish Representative is to uphold the good name and the right to independence of his country in the official circles of the Government to which he is accredited. Irish independence so long as it remains incomplete in territory and character, can easily be lost again in a clash between the Great Powers such as that which is now only beginning. The Representative's whole energies must be concentrated all the time on securing the goodwill and strong support of the receiving Government for the completion and maintenance of Ireland's status in the community of nations.

The Taoiseach requires from all our Representatives idealism and a spirit of genuine selflessness in their work. He exhorts them to be completely representative of every thing that is best in Irish life and to practise openly the teachings of our traditional religion. Moreover, he requires our Representatives to have a profound interest in the Irish language, and literature, because he believes that, without this qualification, it is impossible for a Representative to have whole-hearted zeal for Ireland.

The Representative should keep his Department constantly informed of everything which affects the welfare of Ireland, however remote. Apart from watching and reporting on matters of direct Irish interest, those, e.g., dealing with the protection of our citizens, our trade, etc., he should send home constant

---

[12] NAI, DEA, Embassy Lisbon, Miscellaneous Files (Unnumbered), Confidential communications from DEA, 1942-1963.

reports on every aspect of the life of the country to which he is accredited which might in any way be helpful in the building up of the Irish State.

The Representative should cultivate good relations with all the members of the diplomatic corps. He should take the greatest possible care to avoid giving offence to anyone. His conversation amongst his colleagues must be completely representative of his country's policy. Any expression of opinion contrary to his country's policy would not merely be a betrayal of a very high office. It could easily lead to the Representative acquiring a reputation for putting his personal feelings before his country's interests and he might in the end render himself unfit for further service.

The Taoiseach hopes that all our Representatives will acquire for themselves the highest reputation for charity towards the Representatives of all nations. He does not think that we can afford to take part in the quarrels of the Great Powers. He urges all our Representatives to make their friends as far as possible amongst the Representatives of the smaller peoples akin to ourselves.

J. P. Walshe

9
Ofício, Secretário-Geral do DEA ao Encarregado de Negócios irlandês em Lisboa: Dublin, 27 de Janeiro de 1942[13]

SECRET

The following is the text of a secret circular telegram that was sent to all our Legations in Europe at the end of last February:

'Following instructions are precautionary and do not imply immediate danger.

1. In case of invasion here, send formal note to Foreign Minister in terms which will be wired to you shortly. Be sure report of invasion is correct before taking action. Issue text to press and secure maximum publicity. Regard your

---

[13] NAI, DEA, Embassy Lisbon, Miscellaneous Files (Unnumbered), Confidential communications from DEA, 1942-1963.

primary task in new circumstances as propaganda. Use utmost efforts to foster sympathy and counter invader's publicity justifying the attack.

2. Act on instructions received from us through Washington Legation and send telegrams for Department to Washington for re-transmission here if direct communication is interrupted. With necessary assistance listen to medium-wave transmission day and night on effective receiver. If Athlone fails try 16.82 and 48.47 metres.

3. Further instructions regarding same eventuality will be sent to you from time to time. Inform Department if any special points occur to you. If necessary observe instructions of 11th May 1940 […]'

J. P. Walshe

10
Ofício, Secretário-Geral do DEA ao Encarregado de Negócios irlandês em Lisboa: Dublin, 27 de Janeiro de 1942[14]

In view of the recent developments in the Far East, it has been decided to ask Portugal to take over the protection of Irish interests in the area.

We desire that you should approach the Portuguese authorities with a view to ascertaining whether they would be prepared to accept responsibility in the matter, and I am accordingly sending you herewith an Aide Mémoire on the subject, which I should be glad if you would taken an early opportunity of presenting to the Portuguese Foreign Office.

J. P. Walshe

AIDE MÉMOIRE[15]

In areas, such as the Far East, in which Ireland has no diplomatic or consular representatives, the protection of Irish interests has hitherto been undertaken by the British Government.

---

[14] NAI, DEA, Embassy Lisbon, Miscellaneous Files, A.7/42 Irish nationals and interests in the war area, 1942.

[15] Cópia deste documento foi entregue a António de Oliveira Salazar a 26 de Fevereiro de 1942.

2. Owing to the recent developments in the Far East, the protection of Irish interests by British diplomatic and consular representatives is no longer practicable in certain areas there, and the Irish Governemnt accordingly desires to ascertain whether the Portuguese Government could see their way to take over the protection of Irish interests in those areas.

3. The services that it would be necessary to provide for Irish citizens resident in the areas referred to would be limited to the following:

(i) The issue and renewal of passports;

(ii) the making and transmission of inquiries regarding whereabouts and welfare;

(iii) intervention with the Japanese authorities concerning any cases of wrongful internment; and

(iv) in exceptional cases, the transmission of funds required in cases of destitution.

While information regarding the number of Irish citizens concerned is not available, it is improbable that the number would exceed a few hundred.

4. Should the Portuguese Government be prepared, in principle, to assume the limited responsibility indicated above, details of the necessary administrative arrangements might form the subject of subsequent negotiations.

11
Telegrama, Legação irlandesa em Madrid (Legirlanda) a Estero: Madrid, 23 de Fevereiro de 1942[16]

P26

24. Franco and Salazar on February 12th agreed:

(1) If Portuguese islands or colonies are invaded, Spain, without prior consultation, would assist Portugal with her armed forces;

(2) full anti-communistic collaboration;

(3) economic agreement aiming at establishing price levels for imported colonial goods and securing import facilities by joint action;

(4) co-operation in spreading Iberic influence by the means of Hispanidad.

---

[16] NAI, DEA, Secretary's Office Files, P12/4 Madrid Legation, 1939-1948.

This information is from Axis colleague who consulted Italian and German Ambassadors and considered point (1) as directed more especially against Americans and English.

American naval attaché, whom I believe to be Intelligence officer, says that he was present at meeting of Spanish Ambassador at Lisbon and Portuguese Ambassador at Madrid, when idea of meeting was conceived, but Suñer was then hostile. Developments at Rio de Janeiro and naval attaché's assurance to Portuguese representative that Churchill's mistaken optimism about North Africa could be relied upon brought decision to have meeting.

Ambassadors hoped growing strength of Allies would induce Spanish adoption of neutral attitude and benevolent neutrality. Events have not justified these expectations, and my belief is strengthened that present Spanish régime will never move towards neutrality.

Legirlanda

12
Telegrama, Legação irlandesa em Lisboa (Hibernia) a Estero: Lisboa, 26 de Fevereiro de 1942[17]

13. Presented credentials to Salazar this evening. Reception most cordial. He appeared to be genuinely glad at establishment of Legation, and said that they would fully reciprocate as soon as possible.

He sent warm greetings to the Minister and said he followed his work with great interest and sympathy. He said that he has heard of his intention to visit the Shrine of Our Lady of Fatima, and twice during the interview he begged me to tell him that visit would be most welcome.

When repeating this at the end of the interview, he said – "Even on a private visit, he would be most welcome whenever he would consider it opportune".

Continuation follows shortly.

Hibernia

---

[17] NAI, DEA, 317/40 Appointment of a Chargé d'Affaires at Lisbon, 1941-1948.

13
Telegrama, Hibernia a Estero: Lisboa, 26 de Fevereiro de 1942[18]

14. Despa. Continuation of my telegram 13.

Salazar asked about our relations with Britain and America and asked how we managed to make certain whether Britain accepts our remaining out of the war.

With reference to our representation in the Far East, he said the request would be examined with great good will and sympathy, but he did not know whether matters might not be complicated or made inopportune; most strongly urged Timor which was still under discussion with Japan. I also gathered that he wishes to find out how the British would regard it.

Hibernia

14
Ofício, Encarregado de Negócios irlandês em Lisboa ao Secretário-Geral do DEA: Lisboa, 4 de Março de 1942[19]

My contacts with the Ministry for Foreign Affairs have been marked by the greatest goodwill and friendliness on the part of all whom I have met. I get the impression that decisions on all matters, even of no special importance, are made at the top. My reception by Dr. Salazar was most cordial. He said he welcomed the establishment of the Legation because it would enable closer relations to be created between the two countries, and that they would reciprocate fully as soon as possible. He referred to the Taoiseach as a fine Catholic, and when I indicated the Taoiseach's interest in his reforms in the financial and social spheres he assured me that I could count on all the Departments concerned to provide me with any facts or information which I might require for my reports. In reply to his question I told him that our relations with the British and the American Governments were very friendly and were perhaps better at the present moment

---

[18] NAI, DEA, 317/40 Appointment of a Chargé d'Affaires at Lisbon, 1941-1948.

[19] NAI, DEA, 219/81 Confidential reports from Lisbon Legation, 1942-1945.

owing to assurances given by the latter in regard to American troops in the North. I referred to the question of the North as being the only one in the way of complete understanding with the British. He was particularly pressing in his questions as to how we succeeded in getting the British to accept our non--participation in the war. My answer that the British realised that opinion in the country was practically unanimous against entry into the war did not appear to make much impression and he proceeded to enquire if there was much pro-German feeling to which I replied that the feeling of most of the extreme elements was not pro-German but rather anti-British. It was only when I said that participation would inevitably produce civil war that he registered enlightenment. On the subject of the difficulties which the war created for us I mentioned the shortage of wheat as being the most serious and said that in regard to some other things such as petrol and coal I thought that the British were making available to us as much as we could expect in view of their own difficulties.

It is well known that Dr. Salazar does not give much of his time to the Diplomatic Corps and I have been told that some of my colleagues have never met him. Even the British Ambassador regretted to me that he could not see him more often. It was therefore the more gratifying, and not, I think, due to a national affability, that he appeared to be interested in our interview which came to an end on my initiative after I had been with him nearly twenty minutes. I had been told that he had aged very much recently, but he appeared to me to be very well-preserved, spruce and alert though his hair was greyer than I had expected from his photographs.

It is of course not possible to attempt at this early stage a report on the situation here but first impressions have perhaps enough value to be worth recording. Well-wishers of the régime, and these are be far the most numerous among the contacts I have so far made, praise Salazar and excuse failures and shortcomings as due to the times and to the difficulties of his task in a very backward country. Others maintain reserve, whilst still others are disapproving. When I remarked to a Reverend confrere of the Archbishop to whom His Grace had given me a letter of introduction before I left Dublin, that we were very interested in what was being attempted here, he replied that we had nothing to learn here, that there was no country in the world where there was so much poverty, and more in that strain even including derogatory references to Salazar. I understand however that he was the reputation of being a bit of a crank on the subject. When I made the same remark to the Nuncio he gave me no reaction though he did say at another point in our conversation, and with evident approval, that he thought there were many points of resemblance between Salazar and the Taoiseach. This has also been said to me by a dozen people since I came here and is also very much my own opinion. The Nuncio is a great friend of Ireland and showed himself to be very well informed on the subject during my interview of three-quarters of an hour with him.

In the shops and newspaper kiosks one sees evidence of German propaganda thoroughness. British propaganda activity is also considerable though on a less expensive scale. There is a fair amount of Italian and Japanese propaganda but so far I have observed little from America. On the streets one hears quite a lot of German spoken and also much English. Newspapers give pride of place to the German communiqués and appear to be at pains to give no cause for Axis complaint but generally they seem to give a neutral presentation of the news except for perhaps an anti-Soviet tendency. There is no comment on the war news [...]

Without knowledge of the language, and without staff or premises, my first weeks here have been difficult ones. My most urgent need is premises and in this matter I trust the Department will fall in with my recommendations [...]

Colman O'Donovan

15
Ofício, Subsecretário-Geral (Assistant Secretary) do DEA ao Encarregado de Negócios irlandês em Lisboa: Dublin, 14 de Abril de 1942[20]

There is a passage in your report 1/42 of the 4th March which we found rather intriguing. It is the passage in which you refer to assurances given by the United

---

[20] NAI, DEA, 219/81 Confidential reports from Lisbon Legation, 1942-1945.

States Government as to the American troops in the North. We are not clear as to what you mean by 'assurances' and as to what assurances you had in mind. Perhaps you would drop me a note about this.

We found the report very interesting.

F. H. Boland

16
Ofício, Encarregado de Negócios irlandês em Lisboa ao Secretário-Geral do DEA: Lisboa, 26 de Maio de 1942[21]

May 13th being the 25th anniversary of the miracle of Fatima, my wife and I made the pilgrimage to the shrine. We left Lisbon on the afternoon of the 12th instant, returning the following evening. In spite of restrictions on motoring and of rather inclement weather, there was a very large attendance of pilgrims, perhaps a quarter of a million, and the ceremonies were most impressive. The great majority were drawn from the poorest classes and many had come long distances barefoot from the surrounding countryside. I have not heard that any miracle is claimed to have occurred on this occasion.

I should have preferred to make the pilgrimage on a later occasion but it was suggested to me by Fr. O'Sullivan that in view of the great devotion to Our Lady of Fatima in Ireland it would be regrettable if I were not present on this 25th anniversary [...]

Colman O'Donovan

---

[21] NAI, DEA, 219/81 Confidential reports from Lisbon Legation, 1942-1945.

17
Ofício, DEA ao Encarregado de Negócios irlandês em Lisboa:
Dublin, 3 de Novembro de 1942[22]

The attached copy of a leading article in the *Irish Independent* of the 30th September should be of use to you when discussing our neutrality with unsympathetic foreigners.

18
Ofício, Subsecretário-Geral do DEA a T. J. Flynn, Secretário-Geral do
Departament of Industry and Commerce:
Dublin, 4 de Novembro de 1942[23]

The following is the text of an 'immediate' message which was received this morning from the Legation in Lisbon:

Serious social unrest and strikes developing here. I have sent report by 'hyleclare' and further report will follow by airmail tomorrow. Please warn ship owners that dockyard labourers are on strike.

We are writing O'Donovan telling him we assume his message is understood as meaning that ship owners would be advised not to send their vessels to Lisbon for the present, that action in this sense is being taken but that, as the dislocation to traffic means serious loss, he should wire us at once when conditions seem to him to justify the resumption of sailings.

F. H. Boland

---

[22] NAI, DEA, Embassy Lisbon, Miscellaneous Files (Unnumbered), Irish neutrality, 1945. Este editorial, intitulado 'Neutrality is not a party issue', afirmava que 'all parties present in this State are of one mind on the question of neutrality. Nobody has the right to make it a party issue […] No Minister has any more right than the humblest citizen to claim that he kept us out of the war. It was the will of the Irish people which settled our neutrality, not the will of any political leader or of any political party […]'

[23] NAI, DEA, 219/81 Confidential reports from Lisbon Legation, 1942-1945.

19
Telegrama, Hibernia a Estero: Lisboa, 9 de Novembro de 1942[24]

192. Dispa. Docks and labourers have returned to work my tel. 191.

Hibernia

20
Ofício, Encarregado de Negócios irlandês em Lisboa ao Secretário-Geral, DEA: Lisboa, 26 de Novembro de 1942[25]

In confirmation of my telegram N°203 I beg to report that the Diário do Governo of the 24th inst, published today, contains a decree creating Legations in Dublin, Cairo, Caracas, Lima and Mexico, all of the second class. The announcement was also carried in this morning's papers.

With a view of obtaining further information I telephoned to the Chef du Protocol this afternoon to arrange an interview (officials at the Ministry are not available before 4 p.m.) but he told me there was nothing he could add to what was contained in the decree. I managed, however, to elicit the surmise that nothing would be done before the 1st January when the budgetary year begins [...]

I informed him that my Government would be very gratified with the news that Portugal was now to have a Legation in Dublin and added that I would be glad to be in a position to inform them as soon as possible as to the person designated for the post.

I presume I am correct in supposing that the request for the agrément will in due course be made through this Legation. If you wish me to see the Secretary General in the matter of the appointment perhaps you would instruct me by telegram. Things move very slowly in this country, and if we are interested in

---

[24] NAI, DEA, 219/81 Confidential reports from Lisbon Legation, 1942-1945.

[25] NAI, DEA, 318/79 Establishment of a Portuguese Legation in Dublin and appointment of a Chargé d'Affaires, 1947-1964.

seeing the Legation in being at an early date it might be advisable to make special representations to that end.

Colman O'Donovan

21
Ofício, Subsecretário-Geral do DEA ao Encarregado de Negócios irlandês em Lisboa: Dublin, 21 de Dezembro de 1942[26]

With reference to the final paragraph of your minute of the 26th November regarding the establishment of a Portuguese Legation in Dublin, I am directed to say that it is considered better to let matters take their course and not to make any special representations about the appointment of the head of the new mission to the Secretary General of the Portuguese Foreign Office.

F. H. Boland

1943

22
Ofício, Encarregado de Negócios irlandês em Lisboa ao Secretário-Geral do DEA: Lisboa, 13 de Maio de 1943[27]

With reference to your cable N.º 38 of 21st April I should be glad to be informed by cable what is the latest date by which the report asked for must be furnished. The collection of necessary data has been much delayed by the slowness of the departments concerned here and certain sections of the report have on that account not yet been touched.

---

[26] NAI, DEA, 318/79 Establishment of a Portuguese Legation in Dublin and appointment of a Chargé d'Affaires, 1947-1964.

[27] NAI, DEA, Embassy Lisbon, 6/3 Report of economic and social conditions in Portugal, 1943--1946.

The Department doubtless appreciates the difficulties of furnishing a realistic critical and comprehensive report on economic and social conditions in Portugal at the present time. Most of the material which I have to use is obtained from official sources and my own experience and opportunities for observation are unfortunately very limited both in time and scope. To depict in detail both the present situation and the results achieved would entail a vast amount of study and enquiry. The material on which I am working is very voluminous and is all in Portuguese, and where possible I am converting trade and financial statistics into sterling values, so that much time and labour are involved [...]

Colman O'Donovan

23
Ofício, Encarregado de Negócios irlandês em Lisboa ao Secretário-Geral do DEA: Lisboa, 18 de Maio de 1943[28]

I should be glad to receive urgently a copy of "The Irish Monthly" of March containing an article by John J. M. Lyon on relations between Ireland and Portugal.[29] The article has been given a good deal of publicity here and I may wish to deal in my Report on Economic and Social Conditions with some matters touched upon in it.

Colman O'Donovan

---

[28] NAI, DEA, Embassy Lisbon, 6/3 Report of economic and social conditions in Portugal, 1943--1946.

[29] John M. Ryan MA, 'Ireland and Portugal', *The Irish Monthly*, Março de 1943, pp.93-99. Ryan era um admirador incondicional de Salazar, escrevendo, neste artigo, 'above all, social and economic life in Portugal has been rebuilt on a corporative, functional basis, with the result that those of us in Ireland who ambition the vocational organisation of our country are provided with a splendid exemplar, the working of which will amply repay attentive study.'

24
Ofício, Encarregado de Negócios irlandês em Lisboa ao Secretário-Geral do DEA: Lisboa, 29 de Julho de 1943[30]

I regret that pressure of work makes it necessary to send, untranslated, the enclosed leading articles from the 'Diário da Manhã' and the 'A Voz' of yesterday on the subject of the Italian crisis. As you will see the 'Voz' argues that it is not Fascist doctrine which has failed. The 'Diário da Manhã' emphasizes that the Portuguese régime is not borrowed from outside but on the contrary is based on Portuguese history and traditions. The passage that runs 'we Portuguese, at least among Europeans, have the best reasons of any people for receiving with serenity the departure of the Fascist Chief' is not convincing and seems to cloak a very real uneasiness as to the effect on opinion here of what has happened in Italy. There is no doubt that the news was received here with great satisfaction by the populace, probably because of the prospect it seemed to offer of the shortening of the war rather than because of any effect that it might be thought to have on the régime here. However that may be the authorities appear to be disturbed at the manner in which the topic was discussed in the streets, trams, cafés, etc and for two nights the cafés and bars were closed by the police at an early hour.

The inconspicuousness of the announcement of the resignation of Mussolini in the 'Diário da Manhã' last Monday exceeded all possible requirements of neutrality, the news appearing at the bottom of the first page under a single--column caption which did not even mention his name.

Colman O'Donovan

---

[30] NAI, DEA, 219/81 Confidential reports from Lisbon Legation, 1942-1945.

25
Ofício, Encarregado de Negócios irlandês em Lisboa ao Secretário-Geral do DEA: Lisboa, 20 de Setembro de 1943[31]

The official note of which I enclose a translation was issued on the 2nd September by the office of the President of the Council, with the object of allaying the general excitement caused by the circulation of the various rumours referred to in my recent reports. In fact this object has by no means been achieved and many people see in the note a confirmation of their fears as to the internal and external situation. Where no official information is vouchsafed regarding happenings of vital importance for the country it is but natural that rumour will distort and enlarge them, but there would seem to be a solid substratum of truth in many of the stories which have been in circulation.

It is not true that the Governor of Macau has been shot by the Japanese [...] no mention has been made in the press of anything untoward having happened at Macau, but it is common knowledge here that the Japanese some days ago seized a British ship which had taken refuge there after the capture of Hong Kong. It is said that shooting took place and that about 25 people were killed. Following on this and other incidents it was reported that Salazar would make an important speech on the radio a fortnight ago last Wednesday, and it was generally stated that he was going to announce the breaking off of relations with Japan. In the event he made no speech and I have heard that pressure from Spain was responsible for his change of plan. It is widely believed, however, that the large-scale military exercises announced for the end of this month or the beginning of October may be a cover for mobilisation and that Portugal will shortly participate in conjunction with British and American troops in an attack on the island of Timor. A great quantity of war material has recently been imported from England and a military mission is at present in that country, though no announcement of the visit has been made in the Press [...] of the fact. No secret is made in official quarters that relations with Japan are severely strained.

---

[31] NAI, DEA, 219/81 Confidential reports from Lisbon Legation, 1942-1944.

The position of Snr Monteiro in London has been for some time the subject of many rumours but his recall nevertheless caused some surprise as it had been said that General Carmona was opposed to it and that the British Ambassador had also made strong representations against it, even threatening that his Government would not give their agrément to a new incumbent. Monteiro was very pro-British and had been speaking a good deal on public occasions and over the radio, boosting the British war effort and Anglo-Portuguese ties, but it seems that what decided the matter was a lunch given by him at which a Soviet representative was present [...]

The internal position continues to be bad and there are no signs of a serious attempt being made to cope with the supply situation. There have been many arrests and punishments of firms found to have been hoarding but these measures, though popular, do not tackle the root of the trouble, which lies in the failure of the Government to introduce an effective system of rationing. The position of Salazar is weaker at the present moment than it has ever been and unless there is some improvement in the food situation there is a strong probability of further and perhaps more serious disorders in the near future. Daily in the press grumblers and unruly elements are denounced and the enclosed official note of the President of the Council, as you will have seen, also threatened that they would be dealt with. A printed circular which has been issued through the post and a copy of which has come into my possession calls on the people and the Army to to get rid of Salazar. The circular opens with a violent denunciation of the régime and its failures. A translation of the concluding paragraph is enclosed.[32]

This circular is probably the work of Communist elements, and it would therefore be a mistake to attach too great importance to it. The Administration likes to make out that all the disorders are organised by the Communists but

---

[32] O'Donovan incluiu com este ofício uma tradução do documento aqui referido, segundo o qual '[...] Salazar is no longer capable of coping with events. His bloody hands have no strength to control with firmness the helm of Government. His exit is imperative, and quickly, to avoid a catastrophic solution which will perhaps bring a horrific civil war of the Spanish kind.

On the Army devolves the duty of intervening promptly inspired only by the supreme national interest [...]'

many Portuguese with whom I have talked with do not credit them with much strength in this country.

If it should happen that Portugal enters the war in the near future doubtless her supply difficulties would be surmounted with the assistance of Britain and America. That eventuality is now considered by the Portuguese to be extremely probable and to be necessary if she is to retain her possessions in the Pacific and to have a say at the Peace Conference. (As I have remarked in previous reports Portugal is the only neutral which has colonies, and she has moreover offered no resistance to the occupation of one of them by an Axis power.) There are also many indications that some such development is pending. Within the past few weeks large numbers have been called to the colours; intensive training in the use of the armaments bought from England has been going on, and I have heard that 300 British instructors are at present in Portugal [...]

Colman O'Donovan

26
Ofício, Encarregado de Negócios irlandês em Lisboa ao Secretário-Geral do DEA: Lisboa, 21 de Dezembro de 1943[33]

CONFIDENTIAL

With reference to your minute of 16th July N°233/201 I regret that I have been prevented by illness from making a study which I had proposed to make of the question of censorship in this country. As I see no prospect of being able to undertake such a task for some time to come I think it as well to transmit such material as I have collected together with a few observations on certain aspects of the question.

I accordingly send you herewith the following decree laws governing the relations of the State with the Press:

Decree-law N.° 12,000, dated 29th July 1926 (the exercise of the right of freedom of the press);

---

[33] NAI, DEA, 233/201 Censorship in Portugal, 1943-1945.

Decree-law N.º 22,469, dated 11th April 1933 (the previous censorship of newspapers and periodicals);

Decree-law N.º 22,756, dated 29th June 1933 (Censorship of Communism);

Decree-law N.º 23,054, dated 25th September 1933 (Secretariat of National Propaganda)

Decree-law N.º 26,589, dated 14th May, 1936 (number of pages in daily papers, foreign publications in Portugal);

Decree-law N.º 30,320, dated 19th March 1940 (office of co-ordination of propaganda and information services);

Decree-law N.º 33,015 dated 30th August 1943 (control of book-publishing firms).

The Censorship of the Press has, I am informed by the official in charge, always been a mild one. My own observation tends to bear this out. The papers are given considerable latitude in regard to war news and views and up to some time ago the Government organ "Diário da Manhã" seemed to have a definite pro-Axis complexion. No doubt this was partly attributable to a desire to off-set the opposite tone of the other papers and to give no cause for complaint to the Germans. It followed naturally from the entry of Brazil into the war, that the press generally adopted a more pro-Allied attitude, and with the conclusion of the Azores agreement a still more marked change in that direction is observable, as was to be expected. The "Diário da Manhã" has taken to daily commentaries on the war, which are by the nature of things favourable to the Allies, and has even spoken well of the Moscow conference. It has also ceased to publish a notice which has appeared daily in its columns for the past year or so to the effect that the paper did not take sides and always endeavoured to give an impartial and neutral presentation of the news as it did not wish to depart from the loyal and honest neutrality which the Government has defined and maintained. However it cannot yet be said that the Portuguese press has abandoned all pretence of neutrality.

No written orders or directions are given to the Press but from time to time the Editors are summoned to a conference with the Censorship officer and, on the occasion of the Azores agreement, with Dr. Salazar, with the purpose of guiding them in their comments on events.

The newspapers and periodicals of both sides of belligerents are on sale in the shops though they are first scrutinised by the censorship auxiliaries and occasionally a particular issue is suppressed. For instance the 'Observer' of 17th October was suppressed because of the enclosed leading articles on Salazar. The Germans have a special Portuguese edition of their propaganda periodical which goes by the name of "Signal" ("Sinal" in Portuguese) and they also subsidise a Portuguese weekly called the "Esfera" which is an undisguised organ of Nazi propaganda. It was in this paper that the articles appeared which brought forth the condemnation by the Cardinal Patriarch of the writings of Dr. Alfredo Pimenta to which I referred in my minute of 9th August N.º P9/43.

Books are not subject to censorship in the sense of having to be submitted to the Censorship authorities in advance as is the case with newspapers and periodicals. Cable despatches from Lisbon of foreign newspaper correspondents have to be submitted beforehand to the Censorship office and I understand that there is much complaint amongst such correspondents about the practical working of this control. The complaints relate not so much to any very drastic interference with their despatches as to the delay in issuing the approvals necessary to the release of the despatches. In other words it would seem to be largely a question of the incorrigible dilatoriness normal to Government offices here causing exasperation to the correspondents who are naturally eager to get their material through to their papers in the shortest possible time.

In conclusion a brief reference to the question of films may be of interest. There appears to be no attempt at maintaining a neutral position, the matter being left to the laws of supply and demand. At one time, I understand, a number of German films were shown but owing to the pressure which the British and American film interests were able to bring to bear they have long since disappeared from the Portuguese cinemas. The German film industry was not in a position to supply sufficient films to maintain fully any cinema which wished to show them with the result that all the cinemas ceased to show German films because if they did so they would not be supplied with British or American films. All the best--known British and American war films are shown in Lisbon cinemas. I do not know whether they are cut before showing but they are certainly not seriously interfered with and I have seen a few which must have been highly offensive to the Axis powers. The British and American newsreels are also a prominent feature of nearly all cinema performances. Before they are put on a notice appears on the screen calling on the audience to make no manifestation and this injunction is very well obeyed not only by the Portuguese but (and even especially) by the British and American members of the audience. Thus I have seen large numbers of British sit quite impassively when the figure of Churchill or the Union Jack is flashed dramatically on the screen and listen in silence to words which elsewhere would stir them to enthusiastic applause.

Colman O'Donovan

1944

27
Ofício, Encarregado de Negócios irlandês em Lisboa ao Secretário-Geral do DEA: Lisboa, 8 de Janeiro de 1944[34]

Within the past few months many things have happened to strengthen Dr. Salazar's position and others again have flowed from that result. The Azores agreement, with its counterpart of substantial food and other supplies for Portugal, the withdrawal (or dismissal) of Armindo Monteiro, the late Portuguese Ambassador in London, the announcement of the Second Congress of the União Nacional for next May, the publication of Eggerton's book, the increase of salaries of civil servants including the Army following on a general increase of wages in offices and factories, the recent amnesty of political prisoners, the development of the Timor incident – these are examples of one or the other.

Details of the agreements reached with the British have not been published but it seems clear that Salazar drove a hard bargain [...] There is no doubt that the concession of the facilities in the Azores was popular in itself and there is still

---

[34] NAI, DEA, 219/81 Confidential reports from Lisbon Legation, 1942-1944.

less doubt that the substantial supplies that are coming to Portugal as a result of the concession have greatly relieved many of the country's pressing social and economic difficulties. That these have been agreed to apparently without any insistence on the introduction of a strict system of rationing is the measure of Dr. Salazar's success in the negotiations. Perhaps it was recognised that any such control was unattainable in this country where two thirds of the people cannot read or write. In a later report examples will be given of the wide range of articles which can still be freely purchased on the shops in Lisbon by anyone who can afford to pay for them. This state of affairs and the notoriously considerable smuggling out of the country of goods which found their way to Germany were no doubt in large part responsible for the friction with the British Blockade authorities to which Dr. Salazar referred to in his speech [...]

The historical introduction[35] is well done and reveals great admiration for Portuguese achievements and ideals and great affection for Portugal and her people. The main portion of the book, dealing with the present régime, consists very largely of quotations from Salazar's speeches and official reports, interspersed with comments which do not appear to be based on actual knowledge of the facts of the situation. It is greatly to be regretted that a good objective account of the Portuguese experiment has not yet been written. Probably the most efficient Department of the Government is the Propaganda Secretariat, which has enlisted or inspired writers all over the world, and especially in Catholic countries, to write up this country from material issued by the Secretariat. For instance none of the writers of articles on Portugal in Irish periodicals appears to have any direct personal knowledge of the country. If they merely wrote of Salazar's political, social and economic thought nothing bad could come of it but unfortunately they sometimes appear to write in praise of a system of government the workings of which they know nothing except what is selected for their edification by the Propaganda Service of that Government. Dr. Salazar has repeatedly insisted that he is not a doctrinaire, and there is nothing to show that

---

[35] Do livro *Salazar: Rebuilder of Portugal* do Coronel F.C.C. Egerton, sobre quem O'Donovan escreveu, neste mesmo ofício, que nenhum britânico em Portugal se lembrava dele.

is main achievements could not equally have been gained under any other type of government directed by a man of his genius and character. Indeed, as will be seen from the next paragraph, reports are current that important changes in the system of government and in Portuguese internal and external policy generally are not far off.[36] [...]

It may now be said that the great majority of the working population of Portugal have had their incomes increased by at least 20%. These concessions were wrung from the Government virtually at the point of the pistol, the twice-repeated rioting and strikes of the past twelve months and open revolt among the troops in the Azores having forced them to take action. The increases in fact amount to a mere palliative and there will undoubtedly be further unrest if something effective is not done to keep down the prices [...]

There can no longer, I think, be any doubt that the Portuguese Government is merely awaiting a suitable moment to declare war on Japan. Salazar's reference to Timor in his speech to the National Assembly fell little short of an ultimatum, and an inspired article in the *Jornal do Comércio* of the 23rd December brought matters to a stage further. No doubt the Government would wish that Germany should be out of the war before taking the plunge but events in the Southern Pacific are moving in such a way that she may not be able to wait if she wishes, as she must, to take part in the operations for the recovery of the Island from the Japanese [...] it is difficult to gauge public opinion in this country but I imagine that such a step would be popular if it did not bring the German planes over Lisbon, and there are good reasons for believing that it would not have that result. Except for the sticking up of papers on windows there have been no A.R.P. measures in Lisbon and there are no shelters [...]

Colman O'Donovan

---

[36] Referência ao Segundo Congresso da União Nacional, que se avizinhava.

28
Ofício, Encarregado de Negócios irlandês em Lisboa ao Secretário-Geral do DEA: Lisboa, 18 de Janeiro de 1944[37]

[...] I said[38] that our neutrality could seem strange only to those who did not know our history, that we had seven hundred years of fighting and disturbance, that we had started twenty years ago to try to build up the country in peaceful relations with the whole world, that the country was divided against our will, that we were too weak to prevent out country from being devastated if we got involved in the war, that our participation could not in any case affect the course of the war, and that we saw no reasons why we should seek the distinction of being the only country in the world to enter the war since 1939 without being forced into it in resistance to aggression [...]

Colman O'Donovan

29
Ofício, Encarregado de Negócios irlandês em Lisboa ao Secretário-Geral do DEA: Lisboa, 11 de Fevereiro de 1944[39]

I have been informed by my French colleague that he has heard that the Japanese have agreed:
1) To allow a Portuguese Mission from Macau to visit Timor, examine the situation, and proceed to Portugal to report and
2) to allow the Portuguese troops, which were on their way two years ago but were turned back en route, to proceed to Timor and take over from the Japanese occupying troops.

Monsieur Monier's information was to the effect that such an agreement had actualy been signed and that an announcement regarding Timor would be made

---

[37] NAI, DEA, 219/81 Confidential reports from Lisbon Legation, 1942-1944.

[38] Relato de conversa tida com o Embaixador do Brasil em Lisboa, Dr. Neves de Fontoura, na qual este perguntou se a Irlanda estaria interessada em abrir uma representação diplomática no Brasil.

[39] NAI, DEA, 219/81 Confidential reports from Lisbon Legation, 1942-1944.

by Dr. Salazar before the National Assembly due to meet in the next couple of weeks. When he referred to the rumour in conversation with a Japanese colleague here he was told that it might be abut 85% correct.

Since my minute of 19th January N.º P5/44 the press outcry about Timor seems to have been discontinued.

Colman O'Donovan

30
Ofício, Encarregado de Negócios irlandês em Lisboa ao Secretário-Geral do DEA: Lisboa, 9 de Março de 1944[40]

By a decree published a couple of weeks ago the Propaganda Secretariat, tourist services, press service including censorship, national and international exhibitions not specially attributed to some other organism, and broadcasting, are integrated into a single organism called the National Secretariat of Information and Popular Culture, dependent on the President of the Council. As well as conveniently joining together a variety of services of a related kind the decree, as will be noted, discontinues the use of the word propaganda, a term which Dr. Salazar is said never to have liked. [...]

Colman O'Donovan

31
Ofício, Encarregado de Negócios irlandês em Lisboa ao Secretário-Geral do DEA: Lisboa, 11 de Março de 1944[41]

It may be of interest to our tourist authorities to learn that the Portuguese are actively preparing to meet a very considerable development of tourist traffic

---

[40] NAI, DEA, Embassy Lisbon, 6/2, Various enquiries and information regarding conditions, practices, organizations, etc, 1944-1945.

[41] NAI, DEA, Embassy Lisbon, 6/2, Various enquiries and information regarding conditions, practices, organizations, etc, 1944-1945.

after the war. The preparations include a good deal of work in roads, national monuments etc. (which also gives considerable employment), the re-organisation of the hotel industry (see my minute of 2nd December last N.º D2/43) and the production of tourist literature of the highest artistic quality.

There is no doubt that the beauties of Portugal became known for the first time to a large number of people as a consequence of the war. In addition to this, it is apparently expected that when the war is over people from England and many other countries who have been prevented from spending their holiday abroad will come in large numbers to Portugal which according to present signs will be one of the few countries where more or less normal holiday amenities will be available.

The Portuguese are also planning an air service to the colonies and Brazil and a purely Portuguese company with a capital of £500,000 is being formed by certain shipping and air companies, to operate such a service after the war.

Colman O'Donovan

32
Telegrama, Estero a Hibernia: Recebido pela Legação em Lisboa a 12 de Março de 1944[42]

23. Texts have been published here of note handed to Taoiseach by American Minister on 21st February regarding removal of German and Japanese representation in Dublin and Irish reply of 7th March confirming Taoiseach's verbal reply to US Minister refusing the request. American note bases request in danger of espionage activities here to success of forthcoming military operations and lives of American and British soldiers involved. Irish reply affirms that Taoiseach's statement in 1935 that our territory would never be permitted to be used as a base for attack on neighbours applies also to the US, points to efficacy of our

---

[42] NAI, DEA, Embassy Lisbon, Miscellaneous files, E.1/44 United States request for withdrawal of Axis representatives in Ireland, 1944.

anti-espionage measures, notes that no specific instances of injury to American interests are adduced in American note and states that German Minister's wireless transmitter has been in our custody for several months and that he had for long time been debarred from using it. Reply also refers to uniformly friendly character of our neutrality in relation to US and improvement in relations with Britain due to respect for our neutrality. It recites specific assurances given by American Minister on 29th February that US Government did not contemplate quote military or other measures unquote on account of our refusal.

Estero

33
Telegrama, Estero a Hibernia: Dublin, 12 de Março de 1944[43]

24. PDG We should be glad to receive urgently a summary of comments in Portuguese press on the subject of our exchange of notes with the US Government, as well as quotations of extracts likely to be of interest. Your telegram may be done in the clear.

Estero

34
Telegrama, Hibernia a Estero: Lisboa, 16 de Março de 1944[44]

32. Dearg. Comment of Press is increasing and is generally fair to us, while admitting British tolerance and comprehension.

Do you wish me to send in clear extracts most of which may be on balance favourable to Britain though showing understanding of our position?

---

[43] NAI, DEA, Embassy Lisbon, Miscellaneous files, E.1/44 United States request for withdrawal of Axis representatives in Ireland, 1944.

[44] NAI, DEA, Embassy Lisbon, Miscellaneous files, E.1/44 United States request for withdrawal of Axis representatives in Ireland, 1944.

Official who controls Press is keeping me informed all papers in whatever way comment is made, and has assured me of sympathetic handling of matter. At same time, you will appreciate that Anglo-Portuguese relations largely govern comments here.

Government organ has so far made no comment.

Estero

35
Ofício, Encarregado de Negócios irlandês em Lisboa ao Secretário-Geral do DEA: Lisboa, 18 de Março de 1944[45]

From the enclosed cuttings you will see that considerable publicity has been given to the fact that selections from the writings of Antonio Botto have been adopted by the Irish educational authorities for use in school-books. No doubt the tales selected are unobjectionable, but I can only regard the choice of this author as extremely unfortunate. As a man and as a writer his reputation is most unsavoury, and the last place one would expect to find his writings is in Catholic schools.

It is true that a volume of Botto's tales for children (doubtless the ones from which the selections were taken) received the 'Imprimatur' of the Cardinal Patriarch of Lisbon. It would be going too far to say that this was obtained by a trick; at any rate the 'Imprimatur' was given in ignorance of the other writings and of the personal notoriety of the author. His Eminence, whose censors apparently lead isolated lives, was caught napping and has regretted his action ever since.[46]

Colman O'Donovan

---

[45] NAI, DEA, 414/10 Press comments in Portugal re Ireland, 1942-1947.

[46] Cópia deste ofício foi enviado pelo Secretário-Geral do DEA, sob instruções de de Valera, ao seu equivalente no Ministério da Educação, a 28 de Abril de 1943. A 14 de Maio veio a resposta: *O Livro das Crianças*, de Botto, tinha sido traduzido para irlandês por iniciativa do Ministério da Educação, mas não constava dos livros de leitura escolar.

36
Carta, Encarregado de Negócios irlandês em Lisboa aos Directores dos principais jornais portugueses: Lisboa, 20 de Março de 1944[47]

The Irish Legation has the honour to furnish the following information in connection with the situation arising from the refusal of the United States request for the removal of the Axis diplomatic and consular missions in Dublin. It will be seen that the Irish people, parliament and press are solidly united in support of the Governent's attitude.[48]

Colman O'Donovan

37
Ofício, Encarregado de Negócios irlandês em Lisboa ao Secretário-Geral do DEA: Lisboa, 21 de Março de 1944[49]

I enclose for your information the text of a circular which I have issued to the Portuguese press. I am also sending copies to the Secretariat of National Propaganda, the Censor's Office, the Ministry of Foreign Affairs, the office of the President of the Council, the office of the President as well as to Corpo Santo, Bom Sucesso and some of our nationals here.

Since the beginning of the recent crisis I have kept in touch with the officer in the Secretariat of National Propaganda who has charge of the press and he has been very useful to me. At an early stage he had told me that I could be sure the matter would receive sympathetic handling in the Portuguese press, but when later I drew his attention to some things which were not very fair to us he informed me that in fact the press is not told what to write nor interfered with very much. Some of the papers had long-standing British associations but even

---

[47] NAI, DEA, Embassy Lisbon, Miscellaneous files, E.1/44 United States request for withdrawal of Axis representatives in Ireland, 1944.

[48] Este documento foi acompanhado de um resumo de vários telegramas recebidos por O'Donovan dedicados ao incidente Hiberno-Americano. Ver a Introdução à Parte I deste volume.

[49] NAI, DEA, Embassy Lisbon, Miscellaneous files, E.1/44 United States request for withdrawal of Axis representatives in Ireland, 1944.

these, as Portuguese, would feel sympathy for us. The trouble in many cases was that the Agencies supplying the material were British or American. It was for this reason that I decided to issue the circular. I shall also try to see as many of the editors as I can within the next few days especially those likely to be best disposed towards us. It would, I think, be a mistake for me to engage in polemics here and I shall confine myself to simple statements of our position.

The "Novidades" is a Catholic paper and it should only be necessary to see the editor to ensure that we get a fair show. You will have seen from my telegram N.º 27 that an article in that paper on 12th inst. gave the main points of the American note whilst giving none from ours. The "Jornal do Comércio" is strongly British in its associations and I am by arrangement leaving it to the Press officer to suggest to them that their article of 16th inst. in which they more or less say that Ireland will have to change its tune is not a proper one for one neutral to write about another small and friendly fellow neutral which finds its neutrality menaced by two great Powers.

From the original cuttings which I sent you with my special airmail bag N.º 11 you will have seen that a few papers "splashed", with large captions, the Agency despatch which suggested that the plans for the Dieppe raid had been revealed to the Germans in advance through espionage in Ireland. I told the press officer that there was not the smallest foundation for that suggestion which was not made at the time and which was now made for purely propaganda purposes without any evidence in support. If the Portuguese press chose to use such material, I suggested that at least he should see that it was not given more prominence than it deserved. He said that he would do what he could.

I am trying to see the Secretary General of the Ministry for Foreign Affairs, as a word from above would perhaps be more effective than individual approaches to the various editors. I shall report on my interview in due course.

[…Carta enviada ao director de *A Voz*, Pedro Correia Marques, a 23 de Março de 1944…]:

[…]
Irish neutrality represents the united will of the people and parliament and is the logical consequence of Irish history and of the forced partition of the

national territory. That neutrality has been scrupulously observed all through the present war. To have conceded to the British forces the use of the Irish ports would have immediately involved Ireland in the war with all the consequences of ruin and destruction which are now but too familiar. And it cannot even be claimed that such facilities were vital to British defence, as it was later shown that the mastery over the U-Boats could be achieved without the advantage which the Irish ports would undoubtedly have offered. Similarly to request the removal of the representatives of the Axis powers in Dublin is to ask Ireland to take the first step towards war. Ireland can and does take every possible precaution that the presence of these missions does not result in injury to the United Nations and there is every evidence that these measures have been effective.

After seven hundred years of turmoil and strife the present generation of Irishmen has seen its ambition of freedom realised for a large part of the national territory. For the past twenty years they have for the first time been able to devote all their energies to the development and reconstruction of their country in peaceful relations with all other nations. They have perhaps the most democratic constitution in the world and every shade of opinion in the country has voiced its determination to keep out of the war. Their right to do this cannot be, and has not been, questioned by any belligerent.[50]

Colman O'Donovan

[...Carta enviada ao director de *A Voz*, Pedro Correia Marques, a 30 de Março de 1944...]

[...]

I wish now to thank you more formally for what I feel to be a very valuable contribution not only to the understanding of Ireland's case in Portugal but also to the larger cause of general international unity and understanding.

Colman O'Donovan

---

[50] Os efeitos desta carta são visíveis em *A Voz*, 27 de Março de 1944. É interessante notar que no artigo em causa, basicamente uma tradução da carta de O'Donovan, a Constituição irlandesa, embora descrita como uma das mais democráticas do mundo, é tida como estando nos seus pontos essenciais de inteiro acordo com a portuguesa.

38
Ofício, Encarregado de Negócios irlandês em Lisboa ao Secretário-Geral do DEA: Lisboa, 31 de Março de 1944[51]

With references to previous reports on the forthcoming 2nd Congress of the União Nacional (see page 2 of my minute of 8th January N.º P2/44 and my minute of 11th February N.º P11/44) it seems now to be the general view in circles which should know what is going on that the Congress will be more or less devoted to window dressing. Although the work of the various committees is given a great deal of publicity in the papers and in the radio talks the general impression seems to be that nothing of great consequence will emerge from the Congress. I have heard of a number of cases in which people who had been invited to speak or present papers had, through lack of interest, declined to so.

Colman O'Donovan

39
Ofício, Encarregado de Negócios irlandês em Lisboa ao Secretário-Geral do DEA: Lisboa, 29 de Maio de 1944[52]

[...] The result[53] is not a masterpiece of elegant prose and you will, I am afraid, find it hard to get the sense of a good deal of it. For this the involved language of the original is largely responsible. A cultured Portuguese friend once said to me that Dr. Salazar's speeches will be read as models of literature long after their present political interest has disappeared. I have no doubt that this is true, but in the meantime they are the despair of those who have to try to translate them into another language, especially of one whose knowledge of Portuguese is as imperfect as mine is [...]

Colman O'Donovan

---

[51] NAI, DEA, 219/81 Confidential reports from Lisbon Legation, 1942-1944.
[52] NAI, DEA, 219/81 Confidential reports from Lisbon Legation, 1942-1944.
[53] Da tradução do discurso de Salazar ao Congresso da União Nacional, 25 de Maio de 1944.

40
Ofício, Encarregado de Negócios irlandês em Lisboa ao Secretário-Geral do DEA: Lisboa, 2 de Junho de 1944[54]

With reference to your minute 234/40 of October last, I should be glad of you would be good enough to send me a copy of a further article by Mr. J. L. M. Ryan dealing with Portugal which, according to the Lisbon papers, appeared in the March number of "THE IRISH MONTHLY".[55] The article in question, which is stated to be concerned with the Portuguese Corporative Organisation, has been reviewed at some length. The Swedish Minister has just telephoned me to the Legation enquiring where he could procure a copy [...]

Colman O'Donovan

41
Ofício, Secretário-Geral do DEA ao Encarregado de Negócios irlandês em Lisboa: Dublin, 1 de Julho de 1944[56]

CONFIDENTIAL

Looking back over your reports, I see that you ask for an instruction in reply to your account (18th January) of your conversation with the Brazilian Ambassador. I am afraid it would be sometime before representation in Brazil can become a

---

[54] NAI, DEA, Embassy Lisbon, 6/2, Various enquiries and information regarding conditions, practices, organisations, etc, 1944-1945.

[55] John M. Ryan MA, 'Portuguese corporativism now', *The Irish Monthly*, Março de 1944, pp.105-111. Este artigo era uma defesa do sistema corporativo português, modelo a seguir, segundo Ryan, numa altura em que surgiam as primeiras críticas. Escreveu Ryan, 'few in Portugal have anything but praise and respect for their leader. Rightly or wrongly, whatever disaffection there exists is directed against the corporative system itself. Much of this is due to an incomplete popular understanding of what corporativism really is. Its real enemies are easily able to deceive those who are ignorant of its full significance. From which it would appear that intensive education of the people is a necessary preliminary to the full success of an economic system with a functional basis.'

[56] NAI, DEA, 219/81 Confidential reports from Lisbon Legation, 1942-1944.

practicable proposition. Australia, South Africa, the Argentine, and possibly New Zealand and Russia, would take precedence of Brazil. In that country there are few Irish people, and not withstanding the Ambassador's 50 millions (most of whom are Indians), Brazil is very far from being as developed as the Argentine.

Of course, it is possible that we shall have a more developed trade with Brazil after the war, and it may be necessary in the course of time to appoint a Consul there. But that will be all.

J. P. Walshe

42
Ofício, Encarregado de Negócios irlandês em Lisboa ao Secretário-Geral do DEA: Lisboa, 7 de Setembro de 1944[57]

I am not yet in a position to say whether there is any special significance in the formation of a new Government by Dr. Salazar at the present moment. He has made such changes on four previous occasions and the cabinet which went out yesterday has been in office for nearly nine years, a longer period than any Government since the establishment of the Republic.

Of the twenty members of the new Government only two fill their former posts, viz. Dr. Salazar himself and the Minister for Finance. Dr. Salazar, however, gives up the War Ministry.

One Under-Secretary, War, becomes Minister of the same Department. Another, Finance, becomes Minister in another Department, viz Economy. Three of the Under-Secretaries keep that category, but change Departments.

The last Minister to Vichy, Dr. Caeiro da Matta, becomes Minister for Education. He had formerly been Minister for Foreign Affairs on more that one occasion. Except for him (61) and Dr. Salazar (57) all of the members are in their thirties or forties.

---

[57] NAI, DEA, 219/81 Confidential reports from Lisbon Legation, 1942-1944.

I shall comment further in the changes in a later report. In the meantime I enclose a translation of a speech made by Dr. Salazar at the ceremony of installation of the new Minister of War.

Colman O'Donovan

43
Carta, Encarregado de Negócios irlandês em Lisboa ao Secretário-Geral do DEA: Lisboa, 12 de Outubro de 1944[58]

I should be grateful if you could be as good as to obtain a fresh butter licence for me from the Department of Supplies and ask Messrs Findlaters to resume supplies exactly as before.

A rough and ready rationing of traders here was introduced recently which led me to hope that I could obtain supplies here but it has completely broken down. The traders are supposed to look after their permanent clients but in fact they sell the butter where they like and there is no prospect of getting one's ration from them.

Colman O'Donovan

44
Ofício, Encarregado de Negócios irlandês em Lisboa ao Secretário-Geral do DEA: Lisboa, 17 de Outubro de 1944[59]

[...]
I place myself at the disposal of the Department of Education if they should, when the time comes, desire suggestions or advice in the matter of the translation

---

[58] NAI, DEA, Embassy Lisbon, 6/2, Various enquiries and information regarding conditions, practices, organisations, etc, 1944-1945.

[59] NAI, DEA, Embassy Lisbon, 6/2, Various enquiries and information regarding conditions, practices, organisations, etc, 1944-1945. Um ofício de 29 de Junho de 1944 instruiu O'Donovan a elaborar uma lista de obras literárias portuguesas – romances, biografias, e peças de teatro – para

of any chosen Portuguese books into Irish. It would naturally be of help to me to know what rates they would be prepared to pay. I shall in the meantime try to find out whether one of the Corpo Santo priests who knows both Portuguese and Irish well and is also a very cultured and competent person [...] would regard himself as qualified for the work [...]

To return to the enclosed list for a moment, I think it shows very bad taste on the part of the "Propaganda Secretariat" (which has only recently assumed the other name – see my minute of 9th March last) to include the biography of Salazar of their own production. I am not personally able to assess its literary merit but such enquiries as I have made do not suggest that it is a work of any special literary distinction or significance and the author as far as I know is of little account. All things considered, I think it would be well to wait for the list of the Institute of High Culture before making a selection.

Colman O'Donovan

---

serem traduzidas para irlandês. A 28 de Agosto O'Donovan pediu a colaboração do MNE na elaboração da dita lista, e a 12 de Outubro chegou a resposta inicial do MNE, que tinha por seu turno consultado o Instituto para a Alta Cultura e o Secretariado Nacional de Informação e Cultura Popular. Este último tinha sugerido as seguintes obras: Carlos Selvagem, *Dulcineia ou a última aventura de D. Quixote*; Alfredo Cortez, *Zilda*; Vasco de Mendonça Alves, *O meu amor é traiçoeiro*; Vitoriano Fraga, *A caraça encarnada*; Vitorino Nemésio, *Mau tempo no canal*; Eça de Queiroz, *A cidade e as serras*; Júlio Dinis, *Uma família inglesa*; José de Oliveira, *O romance de Garrett*; Luiz Teixeira, *Perfil de Salazar*; e Oliveira Martins, *A vida de Nun'Alvares ou Os filhos de D. João I*. A 4 de Dezembro o MNE enviou a O'Donovan as sugestões do Instituto para a Alta Cultura: Trindade Coelho, *Os meus amores*; Júlio Dinis, *Uma família inglesa*; Eça de Queiroz, *A cidade e as serras*; Ferreira de Castro, *A selva*; e Alfredo Cortez, *Tá mar*.

45
Ofício, Encarregado de Negócios irlandês em Lisboa ao Secretário-Geral do DEA: Lisboa, 27 de Novembro de 1944[60]

CONFIDENTIAL

I beg to suggest that copies of all important reports of commissions set up by the Government especially on matters of general interest be sent to our Legations abroad as a matter of course immediately on publication.

With regard to the report of the Committee on Vocational Organisation, which I had to write especially to obtain, I shall, when I have leisure, have views to express and information to give, based on experience in this country, which may be of interest to the Government in its considerations of the report. In this connection I should be glad to be informed whether the report which I prepared last year on social and economic conditions in Portugal was intended for the use of the Commission in question. If that was the case I can only regret that I was not aware of the fact as I should then have addressed myself more particularly to the question of the vocational organisation of this country and its practical working.

With reference to paragraph 40 of the Commission's report I should be glad to know what material regarding Portugal was used by the Commission. Although their report was issued as recently as a month or so ago and the Legation has been in existence since February of 1942 I was at no time asked to assist their enquiries. They state in paragraph 54: 'The Commission is unable to give a complete description of the Corporations, the second stage of the Portuguese system; for as they were established only on 12th November 1938 we were not able owing to the outbreak of the war, to procure the text of the Decree and relevant official documents.' These documents could, of course, have been obtained at any time through the Legation.

It is, I think, regrettable, especially while this investigation was proceeding, that the Censorship authorities did not discourage the advocacy of the Portuguese corporative system in the periodical press by writers whose sole or main sources of information about the workings of the system appear to be derived from the

---

[60] NAI, DEA, 219/81 Confidential reports from Lisbon Legation, 1942-1944.

publications of the Propaganda Secretariat. I cannot claim that I am competent to pass judgement on the system but I know enough to be perturbed that a public opinion in favour of this type of corporativism should be allowed to be created by persons of apparently no special competence at a time when the whole question was, as it were, sub judice at home and had certainly not emerged from the trial stage here. For instance there has not yet been set up a Corporation for any industry or activity whatsoever.

In my opinion Salazar's main achievements, which are in the spheres of financial internal order, public works, and international affairs, have nothing whatever to do with the corporative system.

In spite of the authoritarian régime here criticism is becoming more vocal as serious defects in the system become evident.

I am aware that the Commission has not reported in favour of state corporativism but it is not at all unlikely that their views on vocational organisation generally may have been influenced by what they have been reading about this country. It is far from my intention to suggest that I have the smallest criticism to make of their proposals – indeed I have barely started reading them and in any case would not feel qualified to do so – but I have thought it right to say this much before the Government comes to any conclusion on this important question.

Colman O'Donovan

1945

46
Carta, Secretário-Geral do DEA ao Encarregado de Negócios irlandês em Lisboa: Dublin, 2 de Janeiro de 1945[61]

The Department understands that in the newspaper "A Voz" of the 18th October there was an article criticising the working of corporative bodies, particularly the Guilds.

---

[61] NAI, DEA, Embassy Lisbon, 6/26, Corporate system in Portugal, 1945.

We should be glad if you would be good enough to forward a copy – or if at all possible, a translation – of this article.

J. P. Walshe

47
Ofício, Encarregado de Negócios irlandês em Lisboa ao Secretário-Geral do DEA: Lisboa, 19 de Janeiro de 1945[62]

With reference to your unnumbered minute of the 2nd January, I enclose a translation of the article in the "Voz" of the 18th October to which you refer. An article of the previous day also indulged in strong criticism of the "Grémios" (Associations of employers) which were held responsible for the fact that potatoes were rotting in many parts of the country when there were none to be had in Lisbon.

It is hardly necessary to add that press criticism of the corporative organisations on general or fundamental grounds would not be permitted by the authorities here. But the public outcry against the unefficiency [sic] and corruption of the "Grémios" and certain official organisations during the present emergency was on such a scale that it was doubtless thought wise to assent to the limited criticism contained in these articles.

Colman O'Donovan

48
Carta, Eamon de Valera a António de Oliveira Salazar: Dublin, 1 de Fevereiro de 1945[63]

Excellency,

I have the honour to inform Your Excellency that Mr. Colman O'Donovan, who was represented Ireland since 1942 in the capacity of Chargé d'Affaires, has been transferred to Dublin and will shortly be leaving Portugal.

---

[62] NAI, DEA, Embassy Lisbon, 6/26, Corporate system in Portugal, 1945.
[63] NAI, DEA, 317/40 Appointment of a Chargé d'Affaires at Lisbon, 1941-1948.

Pending the appointment of Mr. O'Donovan's successor, the Legation will be in charge of Mr. Patrick J. O'Byrne, Secretary of the Legation, who will act as Chargé d'Affaires *ad interim*.

Accept, Excellency, the assurance of my highest consideration.

de Valera

49
Ofício, Encarregado de Negócios irlandês em Lisboa ao Secretário-Geral do DEA: Lisboa, 22 de Fevereiro de 1945[64]

Memorandum – SECRET

1 Visit to Dr. Salazar

At my farewell interview with Dr. Salazar on the 1st February I referred to the Commission on Vocational Organisation which has recently presented its Report and Recommendations and said I was sure that Mr. de Valera would ask me many questions about the practical workings of the corporative system in Portugal which I was afraid I would be unable to answer. He referred to the various official reports that had been issued and I said that I thought I had read most of them but that I had been too much taken up with the day-to-day work of the Legation to be able to move around the country as much as I should have wished and to observe and study things for myself. Risking an indiscretion and presuming on Dr. Salazar's known and expressed regard for the Taoiseach, I said that what Mr. de Valera would wish to know from me was how the system was working out and whether it was fulfilling the hopes with which it had been founded. Dr. Salazar then said that the corporative organisations had been set up with certain aims but that owing to the war they had to pursue other aims and that the two sets of aims had often been harmful to each other. It became a question of living rather than of living in a particular way. They had not made as much

---

[64] NAI, DEA, 313/11 Confidential reports from Lisbon Legation, 1945. Cópia deste ofício foi enviado a de Valera.

progress as they had hoped and as they would have were it not for the war. They had not, for instance, yet reached the stage of setting up the corporations which were to be the 'crowning' of the edifice. Speaking in a low voice he said: 'we continue in the conviction that the present system is the best (I am not sure if he said 'the only one') for our country. A régime of liberty would mean Bolshevism and chaos.' I could not but feel that his manner lacked enthusiasm.

I thanked Dr. Salazar for his exposé and said that although there was no question of setting up a Corporative State in Ireland where the people and the Government were attached to the democratic idea, great interest was taken in the possibilities of organisation on vocational lines and I knew that Mr. de Valera would be particularly interested to learn what had been the main difficulties encountered in the working of such organisations in Portugal. Dr. Salazar asked me to repeat my question and then said: 'The greatest danger we have encountered has been the monopolistic tendency of the organisations.' I cannot quote the exact words in which he continued from here but the sense of them was that they had found the corporative organisations to be actuated by selfish aims and a desire to exclude or obstruct new competing enterprises and to hamper other initiatives aimed at the general good. It was evident from the way he spoke that he was talking of something that was very serious, and it will be observed that he spoke of 'danger' when the word I used was 'difficulties'.

Before taking leave of him I told Dr. Salazar about the requisitioning last year of our 508 tonnes of palm kernels […] when saying goodbye he asked me to convey his sincerest compliments to Mr. de Valera and again expressed the hope that he would find it possible to visit Portugal and the shrine of Our Lady of Fatima. I am afraid that neither now or when he first expressed this wish on my arrival here did I note the exact words so that it will be necessary when the time comes to find out what kind of visit he has in mind.

2 Visit to Cardinal Patriarch of Lisbon

The Cardinal Patriarch was a fellow professor of Dr. Salazar at Coimbra University and is held in the highest popular affection and esteem. They have always been the close friends though I gather two years or so ago from a colleague that a coolness has developed between them owing to the absence of measures to relieve the miserable condition of the poor. I have had no confirmation of this from any other quarter but certainly the Cardinal did not give me the impression of being satisfied with the existing state of affairs in Portugal. I had no difficulty in getting him to talk, which he did very earnestly and choosing his words with slow deliberation. He said: ' There is grave discontent in the country – you know it.' I said that I had heard that that was the case. Laying emphasis on the opening words he continued: 'To a large extent it is due to the war.' Speaking very gravely he repeated the words 'to a large extent' in such a way as to convey that to a considerable extent it was due to something else. He said that economically conditions were worse and prices higher during the last war, but my own reading and hearing of those days of the chaotic Republican régime show this to be faint praise indeed. He said: 'It is charged that corruption is widespread – you know it, but how much if this is due to dishonest individuals in the organisations I cannot say'. It was clear that he implied that the trouble might be inherent in the system. He then went on to say: 'When he was introducing the system Dr. Salazar told me that his idea was that the State should not dominate everything but that it should have to intervene until such time as the corporative organisations learned to stand on their own legs.' He paused and repeated: 'that was his idea (sa pensée)', and it was clear that he was implying that the reality was far otherwise, as undoubtedly it is. He said that one great difficulty was the absence of trained officials. I asked 'How does one surmount such a difficulty: the organisations cannot work well without trained officials, but how to train officials until the organisations are there?' The Cardinal replied 'that is the problem'.

When I was leaving the Cardinal asked me to convey his respectful homage to Mr. de Valera whom he referred to as 'a fine Christian Statesman'.

3 Visit to the Apostolic Nuncio

The Nuncio has adopted the policy of keeping much to himself during the war and the only serious conversations I have had with him were two of about an hour's duration each on my arrival and on my departure. Though he is frequently criticised for cutting himself off from everybody in this way I cannot but think that he has been wise in doing so as he is a man of very outspoken mind. In my first conversation with him he did not say much about the régime in Portugal though it was evident that he was not enamoured of it. In our second conversation he spoke very plainly and more than once reminded me that he was speaking in the strictest confidence. He was moved to do so I think because of our interest in the subject of vocational organisation. He regarded the position of Portugal as desperate and said that the only hope for the country was that the British would intervene before it was too late and somebody else (Moscow) did so. He did not exclude intervention in support of Salazar, but I cannot imagine a person like Dr. Salazar in such a role. He regarded the corporative state in Portugal as a camouflage and an imposture and holds out that it will collapse without Salazar. It had not 'caught on' with the people, on whom it was imposed by force. It had nothing in common with the ideals behind the encyclicals though great propaganda had been made of them to put it over, and most of the men around Salazar were anti--clericals. It was only Salazar's personal prestige which kept the régime afloat. 'Dr. Salazar is the best of the Portuguese', he said, 'but he is an old Portuguese'. At the door when I was leaving he said 'If you wish to help Portugal, I'll give you an address: the Foreign Office, London'.

4. Visit to the British Ambassador

I saw the British Ambassador before I left and thanked him for the friendly assistance which I had always received from his Embassy and consular officers whenever I had needed it and said that I would not fail to mention this to Mr. de Valera on my return to Dublin […]

5. My Personal Impressions

I leave Portugal with a definite opinion that the present régime will not last. It may be that under any system government in Portugal would be inefficient and corrupt but it seems clear that the present over-organised and bureaucratic system lends itself particularly to the spread of these evils. There is already talk of a peaceful change-over to a democratic régime though of course such views are not expressed openly. Nevertheless public feeling against the *Grémios* has recently become so strong that a certain amount of criticism has had to be allowed in the Press. Within the past month a son of António Ferro, the propaganda chief of the régime, confessed to a priest friend of mine that a change-over was inevitable as there would be no place for the present system in an anti--Fascist world.

The condition of the poor is miserable beyond description and nothing effective is being done about it. Although seventeen years have passed since Dr. Salazar came into power a start has not yet been made in the immense problem of illiteracy. Neither has the problem of improving hospitals been tackled, whereas vast sums have been spent on making magnificent roads and public buildings, stadiums, centres of higher education and a host of other spectacular monuments to the régime. The ration of bread, which is the staple food of the working man, is 300 grammes whereas his normal consumption would be 1 kilo per day, and many cases have occurred of men leaving their work or slowing down in protest. There have been during the past two years three serious outbreaks of strikes which were put down only by strong military and police action, arrests, deportation etc. Within the past two months discontent in the Army led to a démarche amounting almost to an ultimatum to Salazar. I understand that it was made in an orderly and disciplined way, not by a deputation but by a single spokesman, a General who is a staunch friend of Dr. Salazar's and of General Carmona. As a result of this a further increase of up to 15% in the pay of the Army and Civil Service was granted (there had already been a 20% increase about a year ago.) Although bread, olive oil and a few other items on the poor man's diet have been rationed, life continues to be very easy for those who have money. Anyone who can afford to pay for them can get half-a-dozen suits of clothes at a time and the shops are full of luxury goods at exorbitant prices. About six months ago a Government order decreed that the prices of all goods were to be marked on them, but before long the Police were to be found requesting shopkeepers to withdraw the price tickets in the case of certain highly-priced articles as they were being found to be a provocation to the poor.

The war is of course the great alibi of the authorities in regard to everything that is amiss but I think that it cannot be doubted that a very large part of the difficulties arises from the system. In my own official business I have found that several different organisms are concerned in almost every question and that each takes a different view about it, so that endless time is lost in conferences and arguments and nothing is done. Public officials are so badly paid that they have no interest in their work and are prone to accept bribes which the public have got into the habit of paying in order to reduce the unconscionable delays that would otherwise ensue or to obtain some other advantage. The number of prosecutions for irregularities is enormous and these are not confined to traders but include officials, many of them highly placed, of the *Grémios* and other organisations and public departments.

In the course of my term in Portugal I have heard much praise of Dr. Salazar but not of his collaborators nor of the régime as such. It does not appear to have taken root as one might expect it to have after ten years of trial if it was a healthy plant. It is the State which is strong, and the corporative organisations are sustained not by their own strength but by the strength of the State. The Corporative Chamber which is the national consultative body (not very often consulted) is composed mostly of professors, lawyers and members of the learned professions, doubtless with some acquaintance with the various branches of industry etc, rather than of craftsmen and experts directly chosen by the branches they represent.

My impression on leaving Portugal is that Dr. Salazar's position at the present moment is very insecure and that already the minds of thoughtful Portuguese are concerned about finding other men and other methods. I cannot say whether any particular person, such as the late Ambassador to London, snr. Monteiro, is in view for such a task or whether an actual movement can be said to exist, but I have heard on many sides that unless a peaceful change-over can be brought about in the near future there will inevitably be a very violent revolution in the country.

Colman O'Donovan

50
Ofício, Encarregado de Negócios ad interim irlandês em Lisboa ao Secretário-Geral, DEA: Lisboa, 5 de Março de 1945[65]

The reply given in your minute 348/3 dated 26th January regarding facilities for the purchase of table and seed potatoes was duly communicated to the Junta Nacional das Frutas and to Messrs. Pinto & Baptista Ltd.

The potato is only one of the many articles of food that have been suddenly disappearing completely from the markets overnight at more or less regular intervals. There is now in Lisbon an acute shortage of both potatoes and meat. Fish disappeared a few days ago and is now gradually appearing again.

In the case of potatoes, it seems phenomenal how, in presence of acute shortage, large sacks of them come to light from no-one knows where to be sold under the noses of the authorities in the city of Lisbon itself at fancy prices. The lucky person with money to spend can obtain a sack with little difficulty at a price which is 70-90% above the official rate.

Patrick J. O'Byrne

51
Ofício, Encarregado de Negócios *ad interim* irlandês em Lisboa ao Secretário-Geral, DEA: Lisboa, 1 de Junho de 1945[66]

The "mystery" of the questions of supply and demand of essential commodities in Portugal goes on.

About ten days ago there appeared to be a plentiful supply of potatoes available for purchase by the public. Then, one of the usual notices by the competent organisation appeared in the papers: the price of potatoes was fixed at Esc. 1$90 per kilo. Twenty-four hours later there was not a potatoe [sic] to be had anywhere in Lisbon. In accordance with the usual practice, they were

---
[65] NAI, DEA, Embassy Lisbon, 6/10, Rationing, 1942-1945.
[66] NAI, DEA, Embassy Lisbon, 6/10, Rationing, 1942-1945.

withdrawn and then the "black-market" once more began to operate. But the next statistical element on prices to be issued by the Government will certainly be based, so far as potatoes are concerned, on a retail price of Esc. 1$90 per kilo.

Potatoes are not the only commodity so affected here. The system is now a long-standing joke with the public.

Patrick J. O'Byrne

52
Ofício, Encarregado de Negócios *ad interim* irlandês em Lisboa ao Secretário-Geral, DEA: Lisboa, 5 de Junho de 1945[67]

In celebration of the termination of the war in Europe, the Government displayed the National Flag on all its buildings and warships; the Head of Government made a special address to the National Assembly and he also called on the Ambassadors of Great Britain and the United States of America and the Minister of France to compliment them on the victory of the United Nations […]

In the popular rejoicings all sections of the people took part and for two days, 8th and 9th, work in the capital and throughout the country almost came to a standstill. The people gave full rein to their pro-ally feelings; only manifestations in favour of Russia, or the displaying of the Red Flag, were quietly forbidden by the police authorities wherever such demonstrations of feelings were attempted […]

The finale of the victory celebrations in Lisbon took the form of a great national manifestation of gratitude to the President of the Republic and the Head of the Government, for the manner in which foreign policy had been conducted during the war in Europe. The demonstration took place on Saturday 19th May […]

I have been told that the demonstration in the Praça do Comércio was the biggest ever held in Lisbon.

Patrick J. O'Byrne

---

[67] NAI, DEA, 313/11 Confidential reports from Lisbon Legation, 1945.

53
Ofício, Encarregado de Negócios *ad interim* irlandês em Lisboa ao Secretário-Geral, DEA: Lisboa, 8 de Junho de 1945[68]

[…A Rainha Dona Amélia…] is regularly referred to in the press as "Her Majesty". On the occasion of her arrival in Portugal and in her public appearances, she was attended by members of the Protocol of the Ministry for Foreign Affairs. She has been welcomed by the President of the Republic and the Head of the Government and is a very popular figure in the country.

Patrick J. O'Byrne

54
Carta, Eamon de Valera a António de Oliveira Salazar: Dublin, 28 de Junho de 1945[69]

Excellency,

I have the honour to inform Your Excellency that Mr. Patrick J. O'Byrne, Second Secretary of the Irish Legation at Lisbon, who has acted as Chargé d'Affaires *ad interim* since Mr. O'Donovan's transfer to Dublin, will shortly be leaving Portugal for a period of some months.

Pending the appointment of a successor to Mr. O'Donovan, the Legation will be in charge of Mr. Cornelius C. Cremin, First Secretary of the Legation […]

de Valera

55
Telegrama, Estero a Hibernia: Dublin, 30 de Junho de 1945[70]

88 O MALLEY The British Ambassador is particularly good friend stop he intends to live here when he retires his wife is Ann Bridges the novelist he is a

---
[68] NAI, DEA, 313/11 Confidential reports from Lisbon Legation, 1945.
[69] NAI, DEA, 317/40 Appointment of a Chargé d'Affaires at Lisbon, 1941-1948.
[70] NAI, DEA, Embassy Lisbon, 6/29A, Secret and confidential matters, 1945-1947

realist about the European situation and is strongly anti-Russian you will find him very friendly and useful as a source of information and comment use this code when requesting conversation with him.[71]

Estero

56
Ofício, Encarregado de Negócios *ad interim* irlandês em Lisboa ao Secretário-Geral do DEA: Lisboa, 6 de Julho de 1945[72]

On the 2nd inst. the National Assembly, meeting in extraordinary session, began the discussion of a bill submitted by the Government proposing certain amendments to the Constitution (of 1933). I hope shortly to be able to report concerning the provisions of this bill and the parliamentary debates thereon. As far as I can gather from a superficial examination of the question the main effect of the proposed amendments would be to give the Assembly a somewhat greater control over the acts of the Government. Some colleagues of mine with a considerable experience of Portugal say that the changes envisaged are not of immediately far-reaching importance and suggest that they may have for object, with an eye to the changed political situation in Europe and the world generally, to anticipate possible accusations from abroad against Portugal on the ground of the more or less authoritarian régime prevailing under the Constitution. This suggestion may have some element of truth as it is obvious that in so far as the system here is authoritarian it is to that extent open to the charge of representing an exception to the principle for which the Allies fought: on the other side, however, it would be contended that the internal political régime here, while not conforming to the democratic ideal, is not an international issue so that if in fact the proposed changes tend to make the system more democratic, the reasons for

---

[71] Este telegrama faz mais sentido se em vez de 'requesting' se ler 'reporting'; Cremin, como veremos, usará o código 88 para se referir a O'Malley.

[72] NAI, DEA, Embassy Lisbon, 6/2, Various enquiries and information concerning conditions, practices, organisations, etc, 1944-1945.

them arise from internal conditions rather than recent international events especially, as the present proposal apparently follows on a motion of April 1944 by which the Assembly decided "to anticipate the revision of the Constitution by five years but did not succeed in effecting revision in the legislative session of 1944-45" (report of the Corporative Chamber, dated 16th June).

It is probable, however, that there would normally be a tendency to criticize the continued existence of a system of a kind which has been condemned or destroyed elsewhere. Two articles which appeared in the press of the 4th inst. are interesting in this connection. The one, which appeared in the official organ "DIÁRIO DA MANHÃ", quotes with approval certain statements said to have been made by Monsieur Paul Reynaud to a Reuter correspondent in which he declared that the principal constitutional reforms which he regards as necessary in France are the strengthening of the executive power through giving the Government the power (a) to dissolve parliament [...], (b) while maintaining a strict parliamentary control, to promulgate laws not of a fundamental character, experience having shown that it was impossible in pre-war France to get Parliament to vote in time essential legislation. [...]

C. C. Cremin

57
Ofício, Encarregado de Negócios *ad interim* irlandês em Lisboa ao Secretário-Geral do DEA: Lisboa, 14 de Julho de 1945[73]

Recent press articles on international affairs, in so far as they indicate a particular trend, are characterised by distrust and hostility towards Russia [...]

It is natural that the Portuguese should take a special interest in the Tangiers problem although this country is not a party to the administration of that zone and that, in view of the anti-Russian standpoint taken here and the inevitability of events in Spain having repercussions here to a greater or lesser extent, the press should be sensitive to the development of Russian policy generally and in

---

[73] NAI, DEA, 313/11 Confidential reports from Lisbon Legation, 1945.

particular to any development likely to give her a foothold across the Straits of Gibraltar: the Russian request to participate in the Tangiers conference keeps intruding in fact in all press discussion of the wider European issues.

As far as I can gather it is hoped here that the elections in England will result in the formation of a Government under Conservative leadership, on the ground that such a Government would be more likely to restrain Russia, and "left" movements in the European countries including, of course, Spain [...]

C. C. Cremin

58
Telegrama, Hibernia a Estero: Lisboa, 24 de Julho de 1945[74]

106 Glad to receive information contained in your telegram 88 stop my visits to colleagues so far have given nothing of special interest stop [...] Head of Protocol did not react favourably to my suggestion to see President of Council and I could not of course insist [...]

Hibernia

59
Ofício, Encarregado de Negócios *ad interim* irlandês em Lisboa ao Secretário-Geral do DEA: Lisboa, 2 de Agosto de 1945[75]

CONFIDENTIAL

1. As I have already indicated the result of the British elections was a complete surprise here for official circles as well as the ordinary public. On the whole there has not been as much editorial comment on the subject as one might perhaps have expected and this fact may in itself constitute a comment of a negative character – in the sense that there is a certain feeling of uneasiness which counsels caution [...]

---

[74] NAI, DEA, Embassy Lisbon, 6/29A, Secret and confidential matters, 1945-1947.

[75] NAI, DEA, Embassy Lisbon, 6/5, Portuguese neutrality in the Second World War, 1945-1960.

2. You are aware that the position in Spain is of fundamental importance for Portugal and that good relations with Spain coupled with tranquillity in that country constitute one of the corner-stones of the foreign policy of Dr. Salazar. It is obvious on the other hand that if the results of the elections in England are likely to influence the political situation prevailing in different European countries (and the comment on the elections which appeared in the Portuguese press before the results were announced leaves no doubt that the Portuguese believed that the elections would exercise such an influence) the régime in Spain is one of those likely to be affected by the voting in Great Britain. In so far, therefore, as the continuation of the present régime in Spain (more or less but not radically modified) constitutes in the eyes of the Portuguese Government an essential guarantee for the continued maintenance of order and tranquillity in Spain a Labour victory in England can reasonably give rise to misgivings here.

3. Apart altogether from the possible repercussion on Portugal of events in Spain or elsewhere in Europe many people would of course be inclined to think that the results of the British elections may have a direct influence on Portugal which is governed by a more or less authoritarian régime. Such a view may be correct to some extent – there is no doubt that such Portuguese elements as are opposed to the present régime would hope that this is the case. It seems extremely doubtful, however, whether the present British Government would encourage in any way influences which would tend to upset the existing political situation here. As far as one can judge Britain has no particular quarrel with Portugal's behaviour under the régime operating here which, from the statements which have appeared during and since the war, observed the terms of the alliance with Great Britain to the extent to which the latter desired […]

C. C. Cremin

60
Ofício, Encarregado de Negócios *ad interim* irlandês em Lisboa ao Secretário-Geral do DEA: Lisboa, 11 de Agosto de 1945[76]

CONFIDENTIAL

1. Since my minute of the 2nd August was written the Potsdam communiqué has made more acute the problem of developments in Franco's Spain and consequently has rendered more immediate the question of possible repercussions here from events in that country.

2. I mentioned in the minute under reference that relations with Spain constitute one of the corner-stones of the foreign policy of Dr. Salazar. That this should be so is not in the least surprising considering that Spain is Portugal's only continental neighbour, is a much bigger state, and that the length of the Portuguese-Spanish frontier makes repercussions from Spain in Portuguese life, material and spiritual, easy and almost inevitable. The internal situation in Spain cannot, therefore, be a matter of indifference to the Portuguese Government especially as the régime here is of a particular kind. A perusal of Dr. Salazar's speeches over the past nine years (I am sending the most relevant extracts on this subject in the next bag) makes clear that, apart from the fundamental permanent importance attributed to good relations with Spain, he at one time at any rate quite definitely considered (1) Communism as a very real political menace; (2) the establishment of the Franco régime in Spain as desirable in the interests of Portugal. […] It is […] reasonable to assume that the present Portuguese Government is most anxious to avoid a return to the 'status quo ante' in Spain. On the other hand, however, it is most improbable that Dr. Salazar, concerned as he undoubtedly is with the welfare of Portugal only, would risk compromising matters here by assisting in perpetuating a system in Spain which is formally condemned by the 'Big Three' as well as by France and probably most of the Governments at present in power on the Continent and in South America. What is more likely is that he would use his influence with the Franco Government to

---

[76] NAI, DEA, Embassy Lisbon, 6/5, Portuguese neutrality in the Second World War, 1945-1960.

bring about a change in the structure which would make the Government in Spain more acceptable to the big powers.

3. It is of course difficult to assess the extent of Dr. Salazar's influence with the Spanish Government although it is often claimed that he was instrumental in keeping Spain quiet in June 1940 and November 1942 (at the time of the North African landing.) He stated himself in a speech of the 25th May 1944, that one of the three great claims made up to them by England on Portugal as her ally was the "maintenance of a zone of peace in the Peninsula," clearly implying he had much to do with this being achieved. In so far as Salazar does dispose of influence at Madrid and would prefer to see a peaceful rather than a violent change in the situation in Spain he might well be led to encourage Franco to go further and more rapidly along the road towards the restoration of the monarchy which in all circumstances might represent from the Portuguese view point the least undesirable solution that might be attainable with the consent of the big powers.

4. Colleagues whom I have seen are divided as to the reaction on Portugal of events in Spain. The Danish Minister, who has been here ten years and had previously served in Madrid, thinks that the reaction would be direct and considerable. The South African Minister, who has been here since 1939, is inclined to think that there would be no serious repercussions in Portugal: he is a sincere admirer of Dr. Salazar and holds that the system here is much better for Portugal and other countries (South Africa is, of course, directly interested by reason of the Portuguese Colonies) than the unstable régime prevailing prior to 1926. The Egyptian Minister, who served in Spain prior to coming here in May 1943, regards repercussions as probable but is not able to assess their extent. The Brazilian Chargé d'Affaires believes that there would be no reaction of consequence here: he takes the view that what all other countries and in particular Great Britain, whose attitude would be the most important, want here is peace and order as the Portuguese régime has not injured any foreign power […]

C. C. Cremin

61
Telegrama, Hibernia a Estero: Lisboa, 16 de Agosto de 1945[77]

118 By order 15th August Government has frozen Japanese property in terms of decree regarding German property my despatch 23 May stop The Government has congratulated all UN representatives at Lisbon on victory and has ordained that flags be flown public buildings etc to mark end of hostilities stop The Press frankly welcomes allied victory and because of Timor etc defeat of Japanese but this subject by no means monopolises attention of press.

Hibernia

62
Ofício, Encarregado de Negócios *ad interim* irlandês em Lisboa ao Secretário-Geral do DEA: Lisboa, 18 de Agosto de 1945[78]

As I have already indicated the Portuguese press has welcomed the end of the war and the defeat of Japan. On the whole, however, the amount of space devoted in the press to the end of hostilities has been relatively modest. This probably to be attributed to the fact that on the one hand the rumour of an imminent Japanese surrender has been current in a very actual form for over a week and that on the other hand the end of the war in the Far East does not really affect everyday Portuguese life immediately in a very great manner and the feeling of relief which it brings to the man in the street is not comparable to that felt when the war in Europe came to an end: there has been on this occasion none of the public demonstrations of rejoicing which apparently took place when Germany capitulated. The only specific way in which the surrender of Japan immediately affects Portugal is in relation to Timor which the press has emphasized will now be liberated.

The Government's organ, the 'Diário da Manhã', in its issue of 15th August, said that the defeat of Japan represents the redemption of Western Civilisation

---
[77] NAI, DEA, 313/11 Confidential reports from Lisbon Legation, 1945.
[78] NAI, DEA, 313/11 Confidential reports from Lisbon Legation, 1945.

and expressed satisfaction that victory has come to Great Britain, Portugal's ally, and Brazil, her sister country [...] an article in 'A Voz' maintained that Portuguese neutrality was beneficial to England both in Europe and in the Far East where Macau (a Portuguese possession on the China coast) served as a refugee centre [...]

C. C. Cremin

63
Ofício, Encarregado de Negócios *ad interim* irlandês em Lisboa ao Secretário-Geral do DEA: Lisboa, 23 de Agosto de 1945[79]

CONFIDENTIAL

[...]

Danish Minister, whom I called on in the first week of July, when the proposed amendment to the Constitution was being debated, told me that he regarded this amendment only as a political device to be used as an argument of the Democratic form of the Portuguese régime in the event of accusations from abroad as to Portugal being under a Dictator system.

Both during my visit to him and his return visit to me early in the present month, he expressed his opinion that Spain represents a danger point for Portugal: he was of the view that some kind of trouble in Spain is inevitable and felt that developments there could not fail to have a direct influence here [...]

Brazilian Chargé d'Affaires – in his view there is no likelihood of any unrest in Portugal (see par. 4 my minute 11th August.) He believes that 'democracy' is a very relative conception – for him it means the ability of any man to achieve the highest post in the State: and he does not share the view of those who think the Portuguese system is likely to be a subject of attack by the Allies by reason of not being a democracy in e.g. the French sense [...]

C. C. Cremin

---

[79] NAI, DEA, 313/11 Confidential reports from Lisbon Legation, 1945.

64

Ofício, Encarregado de Negócios *ad interim* irlandês em Lisboa ao Secretário-Geral do DEA: Lisboa, 27 de Agosto de 1945[80]

[...]

5. Since the conclusion of the war in Europe official speakers and the press have availed themselves of every occasion to emphasize that Portugal's neutrality was, in Salazar's words on the 18th May past, a 'collaborationist neutrality' with England [...]

6. It must be admitted that the Portuguese Government can find corroboration elsewhere for its view of the utility to Great Britain of its neutrality during the war [...] General Franco, in his speech of the middle of July (as apparently in that pronounced towards the 18th June) gave the protocol of 29th July 1940 to the Spanish-Portuguese Treaty of March, 1939, as a fundamental element for the consolidation of Spanish neutrality. Portuguese writers, who regard this protocol as having been provoked by Lisbon (fulfilling the role attributed to Portugal by Salazar and Churchill) hold that the Government here was responsible not only for changing Spanish 'non-belligerency' into neutrality in the critical summer for England of 1940, but also for thereby ensuring the possibility of Allied landings in North Africa in November 1942.

7. The Portuguese, therefore, maintain that it is correct to say that Portugal did contribute (in other ways than by ceding the Azores) to an Allied victory. Insistence on the point may seem somewhat peculiar considering that on the purely formal plane the Portuguese Government was rather meticulous about observing the requirements of neutrality – you will recall that it decreed mourning on the announcement of Herr Hitler's death. Salazar said, however, in his speech of the 18th May last that 'when the strategic situation so completely altered the fundamental problem that a different position (from neutrality) was possible without great risk, time had already so consolidated the previous situation that, in the absence of great interests – and there were all sufficiently protected –

---

[80] NAI, DEA, Embassy Lisbon, 6/5, Portuguese neutrality in the Second World War, 1945-1960.

feelings of propriety, dignity and humanity opposed themselves to any change.' On the other hand it is worth noting that, in Salazar's view, 'ex post facto' statements about the direction of Portugal's neutrality in the war are unlikely to prejudice her position in the eventuality of a future war in Europe, as he also declared in the speech above cited that 'for reasons of a political and legal character it does appear to me that this is the last time when we could and should have been neutral in a European conflagration [...]

8. If one may generalise, therefore, from official, semi-official and press statements in recent months, the Portuguese Government proposes to stress in the peace (1) the alliance with Great Britain, (2) Portugal's contribution to the Allied victory, (3) her connection with Brazil, the latter country being regarded as especially important in the councils of the United Nations as having been an active belligerent on sea and land (in North Africa and Italy). Furthermore, the Portuguese Government will certainly strive to cultivate close relations with the USA, whose role in the post-war world will, in Salazar's view, be preponderant, especially for countries bordering on the Atlantic.

C. C. Cremin

65
Ofício, Encarregado de Negócios *ad interim* irlandês em Lisboa ao Secretário-Geral do DEA: Lisboa, 14 de Setembro de 1945[81]

The Netherlands Chargé d'Affaires when he returned my call some days ago told me that he has been very busy for the last couple of months in connection with the efforts to recover what he described as property stolen by the Germans and transferred to various neutral countries including Portugal. He said that the Allies are having great difficulty in recovering this property mainly, it would seem, money which they believe was in many cases transferred to the name of "men of straw" in the neutral countries. He said that they know there is a certain

---

[81] NAI, DEA, Embassy Lisbon, 6/5, Portuguese neutrality in the Second World War, 1945-1960.

amount of Allied property concealed in Portugal in this moment. He implied that the Swiss are making great difficulties about the restitution of the property transferred there by the Germans.

C. C. Cremin

66
Ofício, Encarregado de Negócios *ad interim* irlandês em Lisboa ao Secretário-Geral do DEA: Lisboa, 21 de Setembro de 1945[82]

At the beginning of the month there was a parade here of 1,200 Brazilian troops returning to Brazil from Italy and who spent 48 hours here to enable the parade to take place. The Government was very anxious that this parade should take place so that the Lisbon population could show the Brazilians that they are, in the words of Dr. Salazar, regarded as brothers by the Portuguese. The parade was originally to have taken place on the 14th August, which is observed here as the 'day of the Portuguese infantry' being the anniversary of the battle of Aljubarrota in which the Portuguese defeated the Spaniards six centuries ago. As the Brazilians, however, did not arrive by that date the celebration of the day by the Portuguese army was postponed and fixed for the day on which the parade took place. About 12,000 Portuguese troops participated. The Government decreed that on the morning of September 3rd business houses should be shut so as to enable the population to acclaim the Brazilians. All the population was exhorted to do so as a national duty and was again exhorted, for the same reason, to acclaim the Brazilian troops and the departure of the vessel which was to bring them to Brazil the following day.

This gesture, although perhaps natural in view of this historical ties which bind Brazil to Portugal, was probably given a greater importance than would be the case in normal instances because of the tendency of the Government to emphasize the community of interest with Brazil (see my minute 6/5 of 27th August).

C. C. Cremin

---

[82] NAI, DEA, Embassy Lisbon, 6/5, Portuguese neutrality in the Second World War, 1945-1960.

67
Ofício, Encarregado de Negócios *ad interim* irlandês em Lisboa ao Secretário-Geral do DEA: Lisboa, 21 de Setembro de 1945[83]

The possibility of a restoration of the Monarchy in Spain (whether or not this comes within the realm of practical politics) lends a certain interest to the question of the Portuguese monarchy. Mr O'Byrne reported in his minute of 10th June on the excellent reception accorded to D. Amelia de Orleans e Bragança during her visit here in the early part of the Summer. Before her departure in the beginning of July she was present at several big receptions and herself gave a very important reception in the Hotel Aviz.

It has been suggested that her visit on this occasion was at the express request of the Government. Whether this is correct or not it is obvious that she came with the consent of the Government and that she was granted all possible facilities for her journey and stay here. As far as I can gather people here do not think that a restoration of the Monarchy is a very likely eventuality but some people think that it might well be likely if there were a restoration in Spain. In so far as the present Government and system are dominated by the personality of Salazar it is obvious that the question of the succession will one day arise. A good friend of mine in the Foreign Office who has a great admiration for Salazar and was himself at one time on the teaching staff of Coimbra University tells me that Salazar is at heart a royalist – he was indeed during the last war accused of monarchist activities. My friend, therefore, holds that far from being opposed to a restoration, Salazar would be inclined to favour it if such a step seemed the best solution for the régime and all the more so as he is strongly of the opinion that continuity is one of the greatest virtues of any political system [...]

C. C. Cremin

---

[83] NAI, DEA, 313/11 Confidential reports from Lisbon Legation, 1945.

68

Ofício, Encarregado de Negócios *ad interim* irlandês em Lisboa ao Secretário-Geral do DEA: Lisboa, 11 de Outubro de 1945[84]

[…]

As regards the contents of the article the statement in regard to the system of election here and the presentation of candidates is now no longer valid (at least in theory) since the proclamation of the electoral law of the 22nd September. Dr. Salazar's speech of the 7th October and the fact that a meeting of political opposition candidates has been held suggests that a definite movement away from the exclusive character of previous elections is being made. As for the remainder of the article it is clear that the writer does not like the system here and consequently tends to exaggerate certain aspects of it; but there is no doubt a fundamental justification for his criticism if one starts from the viewpoint that all non-democratic systems are condemned without qualification. I will report later in regard to the suggestion in the last paragraph that the Army is dissatisfied and anxious for a fundamental change […][85]

C. C. Cremin

---

[84] NAI, DEA, Embassy Lisbon, 6/14, Elections, 1945. Ofício acompanhado do recorte de um artigo publicado a 7 de Outubro no jornal britânico *The Observer*, comprado por Cremin em Lisboa apesar de conter duras críticas a Salazar.

[85] Nota escrita à mão neste ofício:

'D.T…88 on 12/10/45

1. Article probably written by Jew named Deutscher.
2. Wrote F.O. to say this type of article harmful and spoils atmosphere required for his business. C.C.C.' 88 era o código que designava o Embaixador britânico (embora nascido na Irlanda) Owen O'Malley (ver Documento N.º 55).

69
Ofício, Encarregado de Negócios *ad interim* irlandês ao Secretário-Geral do DEA: Lisboa, 13 de Outubro de 1945[86]

[…]

5. The main claims of the "opposition" as represented at the above meeting (former active politicians in the pre-1926 period and sons and relatives of deceased "republicans" – this use of the word, current here, is not of course strictly correct, as the Portuguese State is still a Republic – Ministers, etc.) […]

6. It is impossible at this stage to forecast with any degree of accuracy the course of events in the political sphere in the immediate future. It seems very improbable that the Government will not dispose of a very big majority in the new Assembly, though apparently some people think that there may be a fair opposition challenge. What seems to me more important in the long run is the new element introduced into internal Portuguese politics. I think we can take it as a fact that the changes announced have been made at this stage mainly because of international tendencies – Salazar himself alluded to these tendencies and the opposition statements bear ample witness that they at any rate regard the prevailing current abroad as responsible for what has happened here. One must count with the possibility in the near or more distant future of an opposition party here – it is not easy to see how, if one admits an opposition, one can hope (as Salazar seems to do) to go without the ordinary parliamentary system. It is also another question how far the new liberties which are promised will go. In view, however, of the obvious interest which the new departure will arouse abroad and of the existence already in some countries of some opposition to the Portuguese system, it would seem very dangerous for Salazar to apply incompletely and *a fortiori* suppress the concessions announced: he took this step of his own accord and presumably in full knowledge of its implications, and any withdrawal would inevitably imply at the least a serious misjudgement of the

---

[86] NAI, DEA, Embassy Lisbon, 6/14, Elections, 1945. Ofício acompanhado do discurso de Salazar à União Nacional, 11 de Outubro de 1945.

Portuguese situation on his part. The opposition will doubtless not fail to make full use of the interest which they will almost certainly find in some sections of foreign press opinion. On the other hand, Salazar, who should know conditions, may be quite satisfied that he can easily maintain control of the country in which case he would, of course, have considerably strengthened his hand vis-à-vis foreign democratic criticism.

C. C. Cremin

70
Ofício, Encarregado de Negócios *ad interim* irlandês ao Secretário-Geral do DEA: Lisboa, 19 de Outubro de 1945[87]

[...]

3. The main points of the opposition propaganda are taken from the declaration approved at the first meeting on the 8th October [...] and the strongest emphasis has been on the necessity for an adjournment of the elections and the opening of a new electoral register. As regards the former point the argument used is that which I mentioned already – the inability of the opposition to conduct a campaign in the limited time available if the elections take place on the 18th of November. As regards the second point the extreme contention of the opposition is that the present electoral register only includes the names of voters favourable to the régime on the grounds that as, since 1926, abstentions in the elections for the National Assembly were counted as votes in favour of the only list (Government) submitted to the electorate, all those opposed to the Government took good care that they would not be registered and thereby increase the magnitude of the Pro-Government vote [...]

4. It must be admitted that the opposition has not hitherto come forward with anything in the nature of a positive programme. Briefly stated, their programme is the restoration of individual liberty and the abolition of certain

---

[87] NAI, DEA, Embassy Lisbon, 6/14, Elections, 1945.

features of the present régime – the "grémios" and corporative system generally, and all measures restricting individual freedom [...] Apart from extolling this mission the opposition press is much concerned with proving that the contention of the Government press and spokesmen that their adversaries have no political experience or ability is false; and the main argument they employ here is that having been excluded from power for 20 years it is natural that many of the active opponents of the régime should not have the training they might otherwise have had but that they cannot be said to be more inexperienced than was the present Head of Government and most of his collaborators when they first came to power. They point out that they have in their ranks professors, barristers, physicians, surgeons, scientists, educationalists and men of letters and that, therefore, their movement must be taken as being that of people with a sense of discipline, order and responsibility and not of irresponsible critics or trouble-makers [...]

5. [...]

6. The campaign in the opposition papers is on the whole being conducted with restraint and with little of the scurrility which apparently used to characterise the Portuguese press in the old Republican days, (it may be noted that the "A Voz" published an apology at the end of last week for the article for which an action was threatened against it.) The opposition press also stresses the point that the adversaries of the régime intend to work for their goal in an orderly and dignified manner [...]

7. As stated above, the Government case as so far exposed, is based mainly on the Government's record in the spheres of finance, public works, foreign affairs and internal political stability. In all these spheres the Government has, of course, an excellent record: it is obvious that on a purely objective consideration of the material situation in Portugal from most points of view it would be very difficult to make a case for overthrowing the Government, and although there are some chinks in the Government's armour (e.g. the matter of the standard of living of the mass of the population) the opposition could not seriously challenge the Government on this head nor, as already indicated, it is doing so but concentrating on the less tangible, but electorally, probably more potent issue of personal liberties. The Government answer is that the alternative to the present

régime is disorder and chaos and the "Diário da Manhã" for some days past has been developing this line strongly [...]

8. You are probably aware that the Government informed the opposition leaders on the 16th of the rejection of their demands and that the latter brought the matter to General Carmona on the following day. He replied that he did not wish to interfere with the Government's decisions. In these circumstances, the opposition should, consistently with their published statements, refrain from putting up candidates. The final date for submitting candidates is today but it would seem that the opposition leaders have not yet given up all hope of having the elections adjourned [...]

9. [...]

10. The strength of the opposition is difficult to gauge [...] there is certainly a potentially strong opposition, particularly among the classes subject to foreign ideas and influence, and it is probable that the lower classes (whose lot has not been markedly improved by the "New State") would provide a big number of recruits. As for the Army, it is alleged that many of the higher officers are anti--Salazar but that a great number of middle-rank officers are strongly in favour of the régime. It is likely, in any event, that General Carmona could carry a very big section of the Army with him and it is not considered likely that any disturbing movement from that quarter is to be anticipated immediately.

C. C. Cremin

71
Ofício, Encarregado de Negócios *ad interim* irlandês ao Secretário-Geral do DEA: Lisboa, 31 de Outubro de 1945[88]

I enclose herewith, for your information, copy of a note of some statements made to me a few days ago by an acquaintance here who is, I think, extremely well informed in regard to the opposition movement in this country.

---

[88] NAI, DEA, Embassy Lisbon, 6/14, Elections, 1945.

1. The "opposition" has several underground papers including a Communist organ ("Terra") described as particularly good and which has been published uninterruptedly for three years at frequently changing addresses. These papers are regularly sent to Moscow through X [sic] and used in Russian propaganda.

2. The opposition leaders are all worthy men but rather idealistic and it is doubtful whether they have the "tough" mentality which might be required to upset the régime here.

3. There is a considerable section of the Army which is in favour of a change of Government but they do not want to do away with the present Government until they are sure that they have another capable of replacing it immediately and without a period of disorder and anarchy. The present opposition leaders are not of the metal required and the Army are not going to move until they are sure that the transition can be made in an orderly manner. There was a definite possibility last July of a coup d'état on the part of the Army but it was not put through for the reason just mentioned. Two Generals were said to have been at the head of the movement then and one of them was arrested in Oporto some weeks ago.

4. The "opposition" intends to go underground once more if their demand for an adjournment of the elections is not conceded. There is little likelihood that it will be conceded.

C. C. Cremin

72
Ofício, Encarregado de Negócios *ad interim* irlandês ao Secretário-Geral do DEA: Lisboa, 2 de Novembro de 1945[89]

[…]

5. I mentioned in a previous report (par. 9 of my minute of the 19th October) that there was a theory in some circles here that the elections are the result of direct

---

[89] NAI, DEA, Embassy Lisbon, 6/14, Elections, 1945.

pressure from England (and possibly also the USA). My contacts with members of the British and American Embassies make me doubt whether there is any truth in this opinion. As far as I can gather the official British attitude is that the present régime suits the British interests quite well, as it enables them quietly to transact their business satisfactorily and in the knowledge that an agreement reached today will be observed tomorrow: as far as I can see, too, the claims of the opposition have not been strongly taken up in England and, at the least there seems to be no influential persistent propaganda in England against the present Government here: I believe that the absence of such propaganda conforms with official wishes. As for the USA who are, of course, (in the absence of Russia which is not represented in Lisbon) the most important mission here after Great Britain, from a wide international point of view (Spain is in a special category) I think that they are of the view that Portugal is an English preserve and do not feel like taking, at this stage at any rate, any political initiative to change that position […]

C. C. Cremin

73
Ofício, Encarregado de Negócios *ad interim* irlandês ao Secretário-Geral do DEA: Lisboa, 3 de Novembro de 1945[90]

[…]

In document N.º 3 you will find a phrase ("para inglês ver") which is interesting in throwing a light on Portuguese mentality and on the historical character of their relations with England. I understand that the phrase, of frequent current use, is several centuries old dating from the time that the only foreigners it was worth impressing were the English. It, of course, means that one is expected to put up a good façade to mislead the foreigner. The philosophy behind it seems to be that the foreigner would not like the Portuguese or their institutions if they saw them as they really are and should, therefore, be indulged. On the practical

---

[90] NAI, DEA, Embassy Lisbon, 6/14, Elections, 1945. Este ofício acompanha o texto de declarações feitas por figuras do MUD, tais como Mário de Lima Alves, e as respostas do Governo.

side this comes to mean that the foreigner is somewhat of a simpleton and can easily be taken in and by extension exploited: it is for instance a common practice to ask foreigners to pay more than the Portuguese and consequently one is generally well advised to use a Portuguese as a cover even for the simplest commercial transactions [...]

C. C. Cremin

74
Ofício, Encarregado de Negócios *ad interim* irlandês ao Secretário-Geral do DEA: Lisboa, 10 de Novembro de 1945[91]

You may be interested to know that I understand from a Foreign Office friend (whom I have already often quoted, and who is one of the Heads of Section in the Ministry with, in that capacity, direct and frequent access to the Minister) that Salazar some days ago expressed discontent with he fact that the Dublin post is not yet occupied and said that if the man appointed did not get there soon another appointment would have to be made. As a result, it appears that Dr. Rocheta is now due to leave Roumania by air next week, abandoning most of his luggage [...]

C. C. Cremin

75
Ofício, Encarregado de Negócios *ad interim* irlandês ao Secretário-Geral do DEA: Lisboa, 10 de Novembro de 1945[92]

[...]

2. [...] Another statement made to me by another source (whose value I cannot control) is to the effect that both Salazar and the opposition leaders were

---

[91] NAI, DEA, Embassy Lisbon, 6/3, Portuguese Legation in Dublin, 1942-1965.
[92] NAI, DEA, Embassy Lisbon, 6/14, Elections, 1945.

surprised with the strength of the opposition and that Salazar feels that he is the victim of some ingratitude. If this should be correct it might explain what some colleagues have found rather puzzling from the beginning, viz. the reasons which prompted Salazar to open the gates to the opposition at all, especially if he was not prepared to concede to them full facilities (including an adjournment) to enable them to organise and put their case, or in other words, why he appears to give with one hand and refuse with the other: the Swedish Minister, for instance, who like, I think, most colleagues here has a great admiration for Salazar and believes his disappearance would be a bad thing for Portugal, expressed the view to me a few days ago that the methods adopted here for the elections would, if applied there, provoke an immediate and violent outcry in his country […]

C. C. Cremin

76
Ofício, Encarregado de Negócios *ad interim* irlandês ao Secretário-Geral do DEA: Lisboa, 16 de Novembro de 1945[93]

1. There have been rumours here during the past week of the possibility of disturbances or demonstrations on the part of the opposition to express publicly and in a striking manner their discontent with the way in which the Government has dealt with the elections […]

2. As far as I can judge from reading the papers the censorship was effectively lifted to permit the most outspoken kind of criticism of the Government's policy in all domains and I can see no evidence that this concession has not been fully maintained: at all events the articles still appearing in the opposition press seem to be as frank as any election party could desire […] the question of public meetings is in a different category. Here the opposition has probably been at a disadvantage from he beginning as it would be quite unlikely, in the nature of things, that say the authorisation for an opposition meeting should be granted with as much rapidity as for a pro-Government meeting.

---

[93] NAI, DEA, Embassy Lisbon, 6/14, Elections, 1945.

3. [...]

4. [...]

5. At their meeting here on the 10th the opposition passed a resolution advising their followers to abstain from voting on Sunday in the ground that the minimum conditions which they regarded as essential to ensure "free" elections (i.e. adjournment of election day and new register) have not been fulfilled. The voting may perhaps furnish some negative evidence as to the possible strength of the electorate opposed to the Government [...]

C. C. Cremin

77
Ofício, Encarregado de Negócios *ad interim* irlandês ao Secretário-Geral do DEA: Lisboa, 16 de Novembro de 1945[94]

[...]

In his letter on the Cardinal's Pastoral, [Rocha] Martins approves the condemnation of totalitarianism (Par. 3 of the Translation) but says that he finds that Portugal has such a system, being ruled by a single party and with no possibility of forming others, and continuing to impose a censorship which has been abolished 'in every other country'; he asserts that most of the magnates of the New State came from the Academic Centre of Christian Democracy (in Coimbra) 'in which Your Eminence predominated with Dr. Oliveira Salazar', that 'all the members of that student organisation are placed in high positions and not only they but those who adhered to them, and that in the single party which has ruled here many Catholics predominate.' The author also asserts that whereas the Cardinal has laid it down that the Church as such should not participate in the election campaign an Arch-Deacon [...] had spoken at a meeting of the governmental 'União Nacional' exhorting Catholics to vote for the Government. Two references in Martins' letter have provoked a reaction in

---

[94] NAI, DEA, 313/11 Confidential reports from Lisbon Legation, 1945.

the Catholic press ('A Voz' and 'Novidades') here. The one is his implication that the Cardinal has seen fit to condemn totalitarianism only now when it has been destroyed in Germany and elsewhere. To this the 'Voz' and 'Novidades' reply that the Cardinal condemned the totalitarian régimes in Pastorals and statements made as long ago as 1938 and 1939. The second reference [...] is one to the money which the Cardinal collected during a visit to the African colonies some years ago. Martins assumes that 'Your Eminence certainly distributed (in alms etc) all he brought home'. The Catholic press funds a suggestion here that the Cardinal has not in fact spent all the money on the purposes for which it was intended and accuses Martins of being guilty of calumny without the slightest foundation [...]

I understand that the general opinion of the Portuguese is that the Cardinal's Pastoral, although it is in the abstract rather neutral in tone and content, is a definite exhortation to Catholics to vote for the Government. One point in the Pastoral to which I did not allude in my earlier minute as possibly favouring the Government on the present occasion is the Cardinal's statement (e.g. end of par. 9) that Catholics have a duty to vote: seeing that the opposition has put forward no candidates (or only in one colony) this exhortation, if interpreted literally, would favour the Government [...]

C. C. Cremin

78
Ofício, Encarregado de Negócios *ad interim* irlandês ao Secretário-Geral do DEA: Lisboa, 22 de Novembro de 1945[95]

1. I enclose herewith a copy of a note containing a summary (with extracts) of the official statement regarding the press of the following day. You will recall (see my minute 6/9 of 21st August) that a declaration of this kind was promised last August. The choice of date was, according to the preamble to the note,

---

[95] NAI, DEA, Embassy Lisbon, 6/5, Portuguese neutrality in the Second World War, 1945-1960.

conditioned by the arrival of Portuguese troops in Timor, an event which took place at the beginning of October.

2. From the point of view of the history of Portuguese neutrality in the recent war the most interesting fact revealed in the note is perhaps the existence of an agreement for military action by Portugal in association with the Allies for the recovery of Timor. It would seem, however, that essential action under this agreement must have been either very limited in the strength or very closely circumscribed in aim as the Allies appear, in effect, to have said that they do not require it.

3. I understand that the failure of the Portuguese Government to take any military action for the recovery of Timor has long been a subject of reproach by many Portuguese who were pro-Ally in the war and felt that to tolerate the invasion of the colony without reacting in the accepted normal manner (by declaring war on Japan) was stretching the policy of neutrality very far or alternatively indicated that the Government attached a low value to the preservation of one of Portugal's few remaining colonies in the eastern hemisphere. The Government was, of course, conscious of the criticism, a fact which probably explains the full nature of the note in question with its detailed exposition of the situation and the course of action adopted, as well as the role in the Government's decisions attributed to Macau [...] I gather that the British exerted considerable pressure on Australia to induce her to allow the Portuguese Government to take the credit for the recovery of the colony and that for some weeks after the surrender of Japan this question was a source of considerable anxiety to the Ministry for Foreign Affairs here.

4. The Government can, of course, at this stage claim to have preserved Portugal's neutrality in the war and at the same time recovered Timor. Salazar's own feelings in regard to the colony were expressed in the first of the interviews he gave to Ferro last week when he declared: 'Nothing caused me more preoccupation to date than Timor and the full safeguarding of its sovereignty. I would die of grief if a part of the Empire were lost through me. I could never have forgiven myself, all the more so as they could have accused me – although quite unjustly – of not having defended it by force of arms' [...]

C. C. Cremin

79
Ofício, Encarregado de Negócios *ad interim* irlandês ao Secretário-Geral do DEA: Lisboa, 22 de Novembro de 1945[96]

[…]

'Communism continues to constitute a serious danger since its world organisation and the seduction of its principles are maintained. It now takes the insinuating form of parties integrated, under national colours, in the life of states and fighting also in the name of democracy with the conscious or unconscious connivance of the so-called democrats. It cannot de denied that the communists are clever and work well'[97] […]

5. Dr. Salazar's views on communism are, of course, not new. The main interest of the above quotation is that he should have seen fit at this stage to make what is in effect a public statement on the subject […] It is, of course, a fact that the underground opposition in Portugal is largely of Communist inspiration (see par. 7 of my minute of 16th inst.) In so far as the régime here is anti--Communist the present international conjuncture is rather favourable to it. This avowed aspect of the Government's policy may, however, constitute a source of weakness if and when a better understanding is reached between the Soviet Union and the Anglo-Saxon powers. What might be a recommendation to the latter in a period of discord with Russia might prove an embarrassment to them if they were seeking to appease her.

C. C. Cremin

---

[96] NAI, DEA, Embassy Lisbon, 6/5, Portuguese neutrality in the Second World War, 1945-1960.

[97] Tradução de parte de uma entrevista concedida por António de Oliveira Salazar a António Ferro e publicada no *Diário de Notícias* de 14 de Novembro de 1945.

80
Ofício, Encarregado de Negócios *ad interim* irlandês ao Secretário-Geral do DEA: Lisboa, 24 de Novembro de 1945[98]

[...]

4. [...] The opposition cannot by any means, on the published results, justify its claims to have with it 50% of the Lisbon electorate.

6. One important colleague here gave it as his opinion [...] that the opposition were foolish not to have put forward candidates – he considers that they were too ambitious in wanting to oust the Government at the first stroke and should have contented themselves with showing, at the polls, that they do dispose of a substantial following. He also said that the Communist element here cannot, he believes, be regarded as a really serious influence.

C. C. Cremin

81
Ofício, Encarregado de Negócios *ad interim* irlandês ao Secretário-Geral do DEA: Lisboa, 29 de Novembro de 1945[99]

With reference to your minute 305/13 of the 12th inst. concerning the manner in which British news agencies distort certain Irish news-items[100] you may wish to honour that as far as I can judge from my own readings of the newspapers and from the cuttings received there has been nothing relating to Ireland in the Portuguese press of the past few months to which serious exception could be taken and nothing whatever to be compared with the kind of propa-

---

[98] NAI, DEA, Embassy Lisbon, 6/14, Elections, 1945. Neste ofício, Cremin apresentou os resultados provisórios da eleição, tendo 60% do eleitorado votado; segundo Cremin, Salazar estaria satisfeito com o resultado, obtido num dia de temporal que terá afastado muitos eleitores.

[99] NAI, DEA, 414/10 Press comments in Portugal re Ireland, 1942-1947.

[100] A 10 e a 17 de Julho de 1945 de Valera, no Dáil Éireann, afirmou que a Irlanda era uma República; a reacção internacional a esta declaração foi seguida com o maior interesse pelo DEA.

ganda sent out by the Exchange Telegraph in October about Emergency Powers order N.º 362.

As I mentioned on a previous occasion practically all the news that appears about Ireland (as about other foreign countries) in the Portuguese press comes from Reuter. Of the various agency items relating to Ireland which are mentioned below only two are from Agency other than Reuter (viz. the United Press) and one of the items was sent from Washington. I understand that in pre-war days Havas had the bulk of the Portuguese service; the defeat of France changed this position [...] As for the attitude of the Portuguese press towards Ireland I could say that, while we figure very little in it and then mainly through Agency reports, the underlying tendency is rather sympathetic: at least, as I have said, none of the more objectionable material published in other countries has been printed here over the past few months although I take it that many of the Agency messages sent to other foreign subscribers must also have come here: you are, of course, aware that there is an internal censorship of the press here – the suspension of the censorship on criticism of the Government's acts etc. which was introduced in connection with elections did not affect news from abroad; and the authorities here probably see no reason why the Portuguese press should indulge in unnecessary propaganda attacks on us. The fact that we are predominantly a Catholic Nation might perhaps tend to call forth a sympathetic reaction on the part of the present authorities here. In this connection it is interesting to note that the new British Ambassador (Sir Owen O'Malley) when he received the press after his arrival here in August explained that although not a Catholic like most Irishmen he was fully Irish. Our weak spot as regards the Portuguese would, of course, be that they are allies of England and very much tied to her in many ways so that any of our activities that might seem to directly counter British interests or wishes would be likely to be regarded with a certain coolness here. In fact, however, as mentioned at the outset nothing which could be regarded as grossly unfair or unfavourable to us has been printed here in recent months [...]

C. C. Cremin

82
Ofício, Encarregado de Negócios *ad interim* irlandês ao Secretário-Geral do DEA: Lisboa, 4 de Dezembro de 1945[101]

[...]

Although the Foreign Office Note was not an invitation it was clear that as the Government intended to mark the opening of the new legislature in as striking a manner as possible it was expected that diplomats should attend. In fact the majority of the Missions here was represented in the tribune but the newspaper reports gave quite a false account of those who were presented. The list published (see, for instance, the *Diário da Manhã*) mentioned as being present at least a few Heads of Mission who were not there (e.g. Belgium, Argentina, Uruguay) and omitted a number who were (e.g. Greece, Yugoslavia, Siam, Roumania, Dominica, and Ireland) [...]

C. C. Cremin

83
Ofício, Encarregado de Negócios *ad interim* irlandês ao Secretário-Geral do DEA: Lisboa, 4 de Dezembro de 1945[102]

[...]

I understand that the opposition has held one or two public meetings in the past fortnight but these meetings have not been reported at all in most of the press and only in a very summary fashion in such organs as have dealt with them. There is no doubt that political life here is, on the surface at any rate, back to what it was before the elections were announced and the electional [sic] campaign does not seem to have provoked any remarkable change in the situation. Those who claimed that disturbances during election week were unlikely have been justified in the result and others left with the feeling that quite a lot of

---

[101] NAI, DEA, Embassy Lisbon, 6/14, Elections, 1945.
[102] NAI, DEA, Embassy Lisbon, 6/14, Elections, 1945.

talk can take place here without its involving the slightest action. Those who know Lisbon well, say that it has always been prolific of quite unfounded rumours which are nevertheless repeated with the most circumstancial detail. The rumours of disturbances in connection with the elections clearly belonged to this category.

You may be interested to know that the Yugoslav Chargé d'Affaires [...] invited a number of opposition leaders to a reception which he gave here on the 29th November (the new Yugoslav national day) and to which members of the Government and almost all the diplomatic corps were invited.

C. C. Cremin

84
Ofício, Encarregado de Negócios *ad interim* irlandês ao Secretário-Geral do DEA: Lisboa, 6 de Dezembro de 1945[103]

Further to my minute of the 10th ult. concerning the Portuguese Chargé d'Affaires in Dublin, I understand that Dr. Rocheta arrived in Portugal a few days ago and proposes to leave for Ireland towards the end of the present month or the beginning of next month [...]

I might perhaps mention that contemporaries of Dr. Rocheta in the Ministry have told me that he is regarded as one of the very best of their younger men. Dublin seems to be a rather coveted post – at least I have been told at various times, over the past two years, by four Portuguese colleagues who might have been in the running, how very glad each of them would be to be sent there.

C. C. Cremin

---

[103] NAI, DEA, Embassy Lisbon, 6/3, Portuguese Legation in Dublin, 1942-1965.

85
Carta, António de Oliveira Salazar a Eamon de Valera: Lisboa, 6 de Dezembro de 1945[104]

Tenho a honra de comunicar a Vossa Excelência que o Governo da República Portuguesa decidiu acreditar o Primeiro Secretário de Legação, Snr. Dr. Manuel Farrajota Rocheta, na qualidade de Encarregado de Negócios de Portugal junto do Governo Irlandês.

Espero que Vossa Excelência aceitará com agrado esta decisão, reconhecendo o Snr. Dr. Rocheta na dita qualidade e dando inteiro crédito a tudo o que lhe manifeste em meu nome, tendo por fim estreitar as relações entre Portugal e a Irlanda.

Aproveito o ensejo para manifestar a Vossa Excelência os protestos da minha mais alta consideração.

Oliveira Salazar

86
Ofício, Encarregado de Negócios *ad interim* irlandês ao Secretário-Geral do DEA: Lisboa, 21 de Dezembro de 1945[105]

I enclose herewith a note on my interview with Dr. Salazar on the 17th inst.

As I mentioned at an earlier stage (my telegram 106 of the 24th July) I told the Head of Protocol when I presented the letter enclosed with your minute (217/53) of the 28th June last, that I would like to be received by Dr. Salazar. Dr. Viana asked me if I had any special question to raise at an interview and, on my replying in the negative, said that the Minister was extremely busy. In the circumstances I could not very well insist although I felt at the time and subsequently that this was a

---

[104] NAI, DEA, 318/79 Establishment of a Portuguese Legation in Dublin and appointment of a Chargé d'Affaires, 1942-1964.

[105] NA, DEA, 313/11A Confidential reports from Lisbon Legation, 1946-1951.

very casual way of treating my request especially as the Foreign Ministry was then (and still is) so constituted that there is no-one except Dr. Salazar above the heads of the various sections, and also because I was bound to meet people here who would expect and assume that I had, as a matter of course, met him. I had frequently thought of raising the question with the Protocol again but felt it was not worth risking another refusal. A good friend of mine in the Ministry suggested, however, when I showed him a few weeks ago the sets of coins received with D.C. circular N.º 7/45 that it might be interesting to present a set to his Minister and that I should ignore the Protocol and go through Dr. Mathias of the political section. I, therefore, mentioned the matter to the latter at the beginning of the month and was informed last Saturday (15th) that I would be received at 5 p.m. on Monday. Dr. Salazar received me punctually at that hour.

My impression of Dr. Salazar was quite different from that of an aloof and rather cold personality which one might form from the current photographs of him and perhaps the rather severe style of his writings and speeches. He struck me as a reflective and friendly person with none of the bustle about him which one might expect from what Ministry officials say about his being always extraordinarily busy; but then, of course, his tendency to work long hours is rather unusual in Portugal and does not characterise his own Ministry with a few exceptions.

In connection with Dr. Salazar's reference to the greater difficulty for us, as compared with Portugal, of preserving neutrality, I might mention that an almost exactly similar remark was made to me a week previously by one of the assistant chiefs of the Information Secretariat (Sr. Pereira de Carvalho). You will note that he seemed to be impressed by the fact of a big number of Irishmen having been in the British forces during the war. I do not know what significance he attaches to this fact, but you are aware that since the war ended the Portuguese Government have taken every opportunity to stress their contribution to an allied victory, and considerable publicity has been given here to a few individual cases of Portuguese who served in the British and American forces.

C. C. Cremin

NOTE

Dr. Salazar said he was glad to see me, and that he had not had the occasion to do so already. I replied that I had asked to see him shortly after I came but had been told he was very busy and that I had not, therefore, insisted. He seemed to think that the excuse that he was busy as a reason for not granting an interview was a poor one. He then asked me when the Taoiseach was going to come to Portugal, stating that he had told him (Dr. Salazar) the he would do so after the war to visit Fatima. I said that I had no information but felt sure the Taoiseach would be very glad to have an opportunity of coming to Portugal both to visit Fatima and also because of the admiration in Ireland for Dr. Salazar's achievements as well as for sentimental reasons because of our long-standing relations with the country as illustrated concretely by the old Dominican foundation here.

Dr. Salazar next enquired about the present state of communications between Portugal and Ireland. When I mentioned that for the past few days the possibility again existed of going directly there by plane he asked me what was the position about maritime communications and whether we had a merchant fleet sufficient for all our needs. I replied that we had not but that the Government intended to pursue the policy adopted during the war of seeing to it that we had an adequate merchant marine of our own. He next referred to our neutrality in the war and said that the Taoiseach 'who is very much admired here' must be a very able man to have succeeded in keeping us out of the conflict; that Portugal was, of course, also neutral but that her task in that respect was much less difficult than that of Ireland because of her geographical position and 'as a member of the Commonwealth'. He added hat he understood that there had been quite a number of Irishmen as volunteers in the British forces. I said that this was so but that I had not seen any official figures although I had heard the number put at from 100,000 to 150,000. This fact (of the presence of Irishmen in the British forces) seemed to impress him very much. He then said he believed we speak our own language and that this must be a handicap to our people when they go abroad. I told him that the efforts made in the past with the direct object of suppressing the language had had a considerable success, but that Irish is still spoken exclusively in certain areas, that it has been a consistent policy of the Irish Government to revive it and that it was taught in all the schools while in many schools all the teaching is through Irish. At this stage I handed him the case of Irish coins which I had brought with me saying that I thought they might interest him as the designs are rather unusual on coinage nowadays. He examined each one with considerable attention and went through the representations in each (I had put in the case a sheet of paper containing in French a description of the metal of each coin and of the reverse designs.) When he had looked at the obverse of several of the coins he asked me what the letters on them were – "Eire" which he had not clearly deciphered. I explained that it was the old and present name of the country, occurs in the more commonly known form of Ireland, and that I understand that a similar word occurs in Portuguese (meaning 'further away'). He said that it is quite possible there may be certain similarities between Irish and Portuguese as there is also a celtic stratum here but that he supposed that no celtic language is nowadays widely spoken: I mentioned the case of Welsh. I also handed him the Note by the Department of Finance on the coinage and the text of the lecture by Professor Bodkin (who lectured here a couple of years ago). He glanced through the letter and read part of one paragraph quite correctly but with a rather pronounced accent – his spoken knowledge of English is obviously much less good than of French.

I took my leave at this stage: as he escorted me to the door Dr. Salazar asked me not to fail to send his cordial greetings to the Taoiseach.

The interview lasted twenty minutes.

Lisbon, 18th December 1945.

1946

87
Ofício, Encarregado de Negócios *ad interim* irlandês em Lisboa ao Secretário-Geral do DEA: Lisboa, 4 de Janeiro de 1946[106]

Further to the second paragraph of my minute of the 10th November concerning the Portuguese Embassy in Madrid it was announced here a few days ago that Dr. António Faria Carneiro de Pacheco, Ambassador to the Holy See since September 1940, has been appointed in Madrid. Dr. Pacheco, who is now 58 years of age, was at one time Professor of Law and Vice-Rector of the Lisbon University. He was a Deputy in the parliament of 1918 (Government of Sidónio Pais, regarded as the precursor of the "New State") and was again in the National Assembly from 1934-37 […]

I have every reason to believe that the new Portuguese Ambassador to the Holy See will be Count Tovar; his appointment has not yet been made public but is common knowledge. I think he is rather disappointed at not going to Madrid which he regards as politically a more important post. Apparently the Spanish Ambassador here (a brother of General Franco's) was all in favour of Tovar's appointment but a political nominee was chosen. Other political personalities (including the Minister of Economy and the Minister of Education, one-time Minister in Vichy) were, I gather, also in the running for a time. The Ministry is, I believe, very glad that Tovar, a career man, has been selected as Ambassador to the Holy See rather than some politician. The only other career Portuguese Ambassador at present is the man in Washington.

C. C. Cremin

---

[106] NAI, DEA, 313/11A Confidential reports from Lisbon Legation, 1946-1951.

88
Ofício, Encarregado de Negócios *ad interim* irlandês em Lisboa ao Secretário-Geral do DEA: Lisboa, 1 de Fevereiro de 1946[107]

1. I referred in my minutes of the 11th and 19th October to representations made by the Lisbon Chamber of Commerce to the British authorities about the removal of obstacles to international trade, and to the alleged reply to these representations. I am told by friends with business connections here that Portuguese business people are becoming very resentful of the continuation of the British control on international commerce. Their argument is that the controls were designed to prevent goods reaching the countries at war with Britain and that, now that the war is over and the conquered countries completely under Allied authority, the continuation of the controls in question can no longer be justified and can only be regarded as a gratuitous and unwarranted interference with other countries' trade; they feel that the control of trade between Portugal and her colonies is particularly unjustified. A secondary objection which they have to the navicert system is that it means that England obtains quite unusual information about transactions between business firms in other countries.

2. You are aware of the predominant role which England has played in the past in Portuguese commercial life. The alleged feeling of resentment at the continuance of the navicert regulation is not calculated to help her in the future in a market for which the USA will probably make a strong bid. While the Portuguese are sentimentally well disposed towards England and the English it is nevertheless unlikely that they would allow that fact to influence them strongly when it comes to business. On the other hand, there is at present here, as in many other countries, a shortage of goods (e.g. machinery, vehicles, coal, asphalt) which cannot be produced locally. This is coupled in Portugal's case with the capacity (represented by cash holdings) to pay for the goods with the result that prospective clients are impatient of delay and more concerned with meeting their immediate needs than with considering whether it might not be bad policy

---

[107] NAI, DEA, Embassy Lisbon, 6/11, Foreign Trade, 1945-1953.

in the long run to transfer their demands from the best traditional market (England) for Portuguese exports; or, in other words, the immediate problem for the individual businessman here is not that of being assured of a market for Portuguese producers in the future but of finding abroad the goods he requires. On present prospects the USA seem likely to be able to meet his needs sooner than England, so that there is a natural temptation to turn to the former. A second point of importance in Lisbon is that of shipping, as purely commercial and agency business occupies a considerable place in business life here. In this respect also the USA seems likely to play, if not a role bigger than that of England, at least a much bigger role than she did before the war. American ships have in fact been calling here regularly for some time past.

3. I mentioned on a previous occasion that the US Ambassador, Mr. Baruch, is very active here. He is in fact untiring in bringing his country before the public and not a day passes but that newspapers report (frequently with a photograph which is the more effective as he is a strikingly tall bearded figure) his attending some function or other. He seizes every possible occasion to make a speech which is, of course, also prominently reported. During the past few months he has attended several business functions and spoken at them (in Portuguese), and about three months ago he gave a dinner at the Embassy in honour of the Captains of the first American vessels to call here since the war at which he exhorted the shipping agents (mostly with British connections) who were invited, to favour American shipping. Last week he was at the airport to meet the 'Constellation' which made a record crossing from New York (and which subsequently, over a few days, took numbers of prominent Portuguese, including practically all the Ministers of State, on "sight-seeing" flights) and this week he invited here as his guests and entertained, with most of the prominent people in Portuguese aviation, the US commander of the Santa Maria air-base as well as the Portuguese officers in charge there. He is in fact extremely energetic and is certainly very much better known to the Portuguese in general that any other foreign representative, not excluding the British Ambassador […]

C. C. Cremin

89
Ofício, Encarregado de Negócios *ad interim* irlandês em Lisboa ao Secretário-Geral do DEA: Lisboa, 8 de Fevereiro de 1946[108]

Mr. Randolf Churchill, whose series of articles on various countries has been appearing in the 'Irish Times', was in Lisbon last week on his way to Spain where he is apparently going on a journalistic mission. While here he had an interview with Dr. Salazar. I have been told that he was also received by Dr. Lima Alves who was, as you will recall, spokesman for the 'opposition' (MUD) during the election campaign last autumn. Dr. Alves apparently suggested that the English Conservatives should express support for the opposition movements in Portugal. Mr R. Churchill is alleged to have said that such movements could expect little support until they show what they are capable of and that while Dr. Alves and his associates might think that they are being oppressed by a dictatorial régime in Portugal, 'they should realise that Dr. Salazar is a very mild kind of dictator compared with say Marshall Tito in Yugoslavia'.

C. C. Cremin

90
Ofício, Encarregado de Negócios *ad interim* irlandês em Lisboa ao Secretário-Geral do DEA: Lisboa, 13 de Fevereiro de 1946[109]

[…] There was a longish 'exclusive' article in the important 'Primeiro de Janeiro', of Oporto, of the 1st January by Jack Willington under the heading 'Dublin, the happiest city in Europe', in which he said that the food and supply situation there is outstandingly good, that there is much intellectual and theatrical activity, that the Irish people are very glad to have been neutral in the war and that partition is the great preoccupation […]

C. C. Cremin

---

[108] NAI, DEA, 313/11A Confidential reports from Lisbon Legation, 1946-1951.
[109] NAI, DEA, 414/10 Press comments in Portugal re Ireland, 1942-1947.

91
Ofício, Encarregado de Negócios *ad interim* irlandês em Lisboa ao Secretário-Geral do DEA: Lisboa, 13 de Fevereiro de 1946[110]

You may find it useful to have the following list of the principal Portuguese daily newspapers.

"Diário da Manhã", morning, Lisbon, which is the mouthpiece of the "New State" and may be regarded as the Government organ.

"A Voz", morning, Lisbon, which is the official monarchist organ and is also very strongly Catholic in outlook. In internal politics it supports the present Government but does not refrain from criticising aspects of the régime which it regards as functioning in an unsatisfactory or inadequate manner. In foreign politics it is outspokenly anti-Russian and its present editor-in-chief seizes every opportunity to criticise the new régime in Poland. This newspaper, probably because of its Catholic tendency, has always shown itself interested in and well disposed towards Ireland.

"Novidades", morning, Lisbon, can be regarded as the official Catholic organ. In internal politics it is pro-Government and in external politics anti-Russian.

"Diário de Notícias", morning, Lisbon, seems, with the next mentioned daily, to have the biggest circulation in Lisbon. Its general attitude in internal and external politics seems to be fairly neutral with a tendency to favour the Government in any given issue. It is well written, has good collaborators and is the most important advertising medium in the country. As an indication of its being widely read one may cite the fact that the two interviews granted by Dr. Salazar to António Ferro last November in connection with the election campaign were initially published with the "Diário de Notícias" and the "O Século" and not, as one might have expected, in the "Diário da Manhã".

"O Século", morning, Lisbon, is of more or less the same kind as the "Diário de Notícias" but has probably a smaller circulation, and much less importance as an advertising medium.

---

[110] NAI, DEA, 414/23/7 Press of Portugal, 1946.

"Jornal do Comércio", morning, Lisbon, is the best organ on commercial matters. It is regarded here as politically pro-British.

"Primeiro de Janeiro", morning, Oporto, is politically the most important provincial daily and is regarded as a very good newspaper. In politics it is "republican" and anti-Governmental in so far as circumstances allow.

"Diário de Lisboa", evening, Lisbon, is one of the most widely read evening papers and is more concerned with circulations and news than with taking part in active politics. Its political complexion, however, seems to be rather anti--Governmental and it makes rather a speciality of particular articles on deficiencies in administration and price and supply control, and is a forum for correspondence on such matters.

"Diário Popular", evening, Lisbon, shares with the "Diário de Lisboa" the position of being a widely read evening newspaper. This journal is primarily interested in circulation and makes a speciality of "reportages" and special contributions: e.g. it published long sections of Paul Reynaud's Memoirs.

"República", evening, Lisbon, might be called the official Lisbon opposition paper. Its circulation increased at the time of the elections.

"Vitória", evening, Lisbon, was acquired during the elections by the União Nacional (Governmental organisation) and is run on more or less the same lines as the "Diário da Manhã" but avoids giving the impression of being so exclusively governmental.

C. C. Cremin

92
Ofício, Encarregado de Negócios ad interim irlandês em Lisboa ao Secretário-Geral do DEA: Lisboa, 14 de Fevereiro de 1946[111]

[...]

There is nothing very new in the submission mentioned above as compared with the opposition case put forward last October. It is interesting, however, to

---

[111] NAI, DEA, 6/14, Elections, 1945. Inclui cópia de um documento enviado pelo Professor Barbosa de Magalhães, pela Comissão Central do MUD, ao Presidente Carmona.

note that the opposition has not become inactive and it is to be assumed that the next elections due normally in 1949 will find them better prepared and organized than they were last autumn.

C. C. Cremin

93
Ofício, Encarregado de Negócios *ad interim* irlandês em Lisboa ao Secretário-Geral do DEA: Lisboa, 15 de Fevereiro de 1946[112]

You will observe from my minute of the 14th inst., 6/14, that the opposition again demands the abrogation of the legal provision making it impossible for civil servants to be candidates in parliamentary elections without the prior consent of the Government [...]

I have no special information as to the political leanings of civil servants generally but I have been told that, for instance, a very considerable number of the members of the Foreign Ministry are opposed to the present régime. You are probably aware that there is a rather unusual system in force in the civil service here by which promotion to each higher grade is made dependent on having an examination. This system was apparently introduced in the early years of the present régime because it was found that the public administration was full of officials who were more or less incompetent and owed their position mainly to political influence [...] in the case of the Ministry of Foreign Affairs it appears that a number of officials recruited in the old days and who might normally attain the highest rank will never enter the next grade [...]

C. C. Cremin

---

[112] NAI, DEA, Embassy Lisbon, 6/14, Elections, 1945.

94
Ofício, Encarregado de Negócios *ad interim* irlandês em Lisboa ao Secretário-Geral do DEA: Lisboa, 19 de Fevereiro de 1946[113]

1. In my report in connection with the election campaign last Autumn I mentioned that much criticism was being directed against the "Grémios" – you will remember (par. 7(4) of my minute of the 19th October) that the Minister of the Interior in one of his electoral speeches said that the "Grémios" were really the only institution open to attack from the opposition but that the Government would find the right solution for their deficiencies. You are aware that the "Grémios" are the corporative or pre-corporative organisations of employers in various branches of industry and commerce. The substance of the criticism against them is that, whereas they control all supplies in their particular branch of business, they have not seen to it that prices be kept within reasonable limits and furthermore they have not ensured that the supplies they control be available at the prices officially fixed while supplies of a particular product not obtainable at the official price can easily be found at a higher ("black market") price. The inference drawn (logically on the premises) is that those in the "Grémios" are exploiting the organisation for their personal profit. The classical official reply to this criticism is that without the "Grémios" things would be much worse than they are [...] However, as indicated by the statement of the Minister of the Interior last October even the Government does not deny that there are weaknesses in the "Grémio" system.

2. In the National Assembly on the 5th inst., a Deputy, Sr. Mário de Figueiredo, called for a commission of enquiry of the Assembly to investigate "the working of the elements composing the corporative organisation". He said that responsible persons connected with the activity of the New State have recognised "the necessity to identify whether there are deficiencies in the functioning of the elements of the corporative organisation and to discover the causes which create a public atmosphere of distrust in many of those elements so that if deficiencies

---

[113] NAI, Embassy Lisbon, DEA, 6/26, Corporate system in Portugal, 1945-1947.

should prove to exist they may be corrected and the causes which give rise to them be eliminated. On the other hand, in representations to this Assembly or in communications in the newspapers, some of which in spite of their gravity remain inexplicably unanswered, the necessity of doing this has been urged." He added that the principle of the corporative organisation is not in question but only the functioning of its component parts and suggested that various committees should be heard as to the setting up of the proposed commission of enquiry. On the 12th inst. Dr. Salazar sent to the Assembly with a covering message a statement from the Minister of Economy relating to the interpellation of Sr. Figueiredo. In his covering message Dr. Salazar said that the Minister's statement would show "the constant and vigilant care with which the Ministry of Economy follows the functioning of the organisms depending in it, both in regard to the internal life of those organisms and their activity in the economy of the country." He added that similar statements had not been sought from other Ministries because there appeared to have been no criticism especially as directed against the organisms subordinated to them but that there was nothing to prevent the National Assembly giving the widest possible scope to the proposed enquiry [...]

C. C. Cremin

95

Ofício, Encarregado de Negócios *ad interim* irlandês em Lisboa ao Secretário-Geral do DEA: Lisboa, 28 de Fevereiro de 1946[114]

In my minute of 2nd November last I reported that the authorities decided to release the sale of potatoes from all control. The immediate result of this measure was that the retail price of potatoes increased considerably. Subsequently the price became stabilised for a number of weeks at around Esc.3$00 a kilo (say 3 1/2d. per lb.) About three weeks ago, however, prices again began to rise and potatoes cannot now be bought for less that about Esc.4$30 per kilo [...] As far

---

[114] NAI, DEA, 313/11A Confidential reports from Lisbon Legation, 1946-1951.

as I can see, from an official note issued by the Corporative Technical Council, the authorities are not very sorry that the establishment of the régime of free sale of the potato, which had been called for by certain sections of the press when the sale was controlled, has led to a very considerable rise in the price [...]

C. C. Cremin

96

Ofício, Encarregado de Negócios *ad interim* irlandês em Lisboa ao Secretário-Geral do DEA: Lisboa, 25 de Março de 1946[115]

I have the honour to inform you that Dr. Salazar, whose neighbour I was at the dinner given in honour of General Carmona at the British Embassy on the 22nd inst., mentioned that he had heard that the Taoiseach might be going to Geneva for the League of Nations meeting next month and said that he wondered, if that were so, whether the Taoiseach might not go to Lisbon. He again referred to the Taoiseach's "promise" to visit Portugal (see enclosure to my minute 5/18 of 21st December last) adding that he himself would be very pleased to have an opportunity of meeting him. I replied that I felt sure that the Taoiseach would very much like to be able to visit Portugal and to meet Dr. Salazar but that I doubted whether he could manage to come here on this occasion both because of the lack of rapid transport from here to Switzerland and because the present unsettled international situation might make a long absence from Ireland difficult. Dr. Salazar agreed that the international situation is rather uneasy and asked me about the absence of air communications with Switzerland, a point in which I was able to give him some information on the lines of my minute 6/8 of the 4th January. His comment was that Portugal was the "innocent victim", in this matter of transport, of French/Spanish differences. In this course of further conversation Dr. Salazar again expressed his admiration for the Taoiseach and mentioned the difficulties he must have encountered in preserving our neutrality. I asked him if he had seen Randolf Churchill's recent article suggesting a resemblance between

---

[115] NAI, DEA, Embassy Lisbon, 6/5, Portuguese neutrality in the Second World War, 1945-1960.

the two men. He said that he had and I formed the impression that he was pleased with the comparison.

I assume that it is unlikely that the Taoiseach would consider coming through Lisbon on his way to or from the League meeting (if he is to attend it) especially as it is due to take place in a fortnight's time. I have no doubt that he would be accorded an outstanding reception in Portugal, but it would, I think, be wise, if a visit should be anticipated in the future, to leave at least a few weeks for arrangements to be made especially as it is possible that the Taoiseach would find it interesting to see many things in Lisbon, and visit various parts of the country, of religious, historical and architectural interest.

C. C. Cremin

97
Ofício, Encarregado de Negócios *ad interim* irlandês em Lisboa ao Secretário-Geral do DEA: Lisboa, 25 de Março de 1946[116]

[...]

Cardinal Spellman's reception by the Portuguese authorities was on a very elaborate scale and he was followed everywhere by journalists, photographers and high officials, including the Head of the Information Secretariat and the Head of the Protocol. Quite obviously the Portuguese Government intended to give a political significance to his visit; and in their opinion they succeeded in doing so. The Cardinal's visit here, therefore, is taken as putting Portugal in the right position as far as the USA is concerned and the Ambassador's remarks certainly support this interpretation.

On the British side the visit of the Commander in Chief of the Home Fleet, with the battleship "Nelson" and 5 destroyers, is regarded by the Portuguese as a political event of the very first magnitude. There can be little doubt that the British Ambassador was anxious to have his visit arranged so as to 'show the flag'

---

[116] NAI, DEA, Embassy Lisbon, 6/5, Portuguese neutrality in the Second World War, 1945-1960.

and reaffirm the English position of primacy in Portugal where, as I reported on a previous occasion, the Americans have been making considerable headway. The Portuguese were, however, equally anxious that the visit should take place as all such gestures can only serve to strengthen the country's position internationally, especially at a time when régimes of the kind in force here are subject to attack from abroad, and such a gesture at this particular juncture is all the more valuable because of the attitude adopted by Great Britain towards Spain and the easy tendency to lump the two countries together by reason of the apparent similarity of the régime and the recent tradition of a community of interest within the framework of the 'peninsular bloc' policy. I know that the Ministry for Foreign Affairs regards this visit as almost epoch-making in the political sphere, and in application of that view the Government has spared no pains to render the ceremonies associated with the visit outstanding […]

C. C. Cremin

98
Ofício, Encarregado de Negócios *ad interim* irlandês em Lisboa ao Secretário-Geral do DEA: Lisboa, 6 de Maio de 1946[117]

[…O jornal *A Voz* a 14 de Abril, publicou…]

a somewhat humorous commentary on Ireland's relations with the British Commonwealth under the heading "Rei exterior…" (External King). The following is a translation:

'Some time ago Ireland proclaimed its full independence. De Valera declared in the Dublin Parliament that Eire is a Republic. But the position is not very clear. When the Irish Government sends a Minister or Ambassador to a foreign country, their credentials are signed by H.M. King George VI. And England has a Commissioner in Dublin who holds the title "Representative of the United Kingdom in Eire". He is not called 'Commissioner' because this denomination is given to the

---

[117] NAI, DEA, 414/10 Press comments in Portugal re Ireland, 1942-1947.

high administrative officials whom England maintains in Palestine and other places of the globe subject to and constituting the higher interests of Great Britain. But in addition he is not called Minister or Ambassador, because England considers that if she gave him such a title she would, ipso facto, be recognising that Ireland is a foreign country…

An Irish Deputy, noted for his "shawian" humour, the Honourable Dillon, defined the Irish position in regard to the régime as "the Royal Irish Republic of De Valera". The Chief of the State of Eire said that Ireland is an independent Republic, associated with the British Community of Nations. Its external political affairs carry the Royal seal as happens in the case of all the Nations associated in the "Commonwealth". An ingenious and witty Irishman has invented an "external anthem" for Eire written in the following way:

God save our neighbour's King
Bless our external King
God save the King
Send him victorious
Fighting the war for us
Exterior to us
God save the King.'

It must be agreed that this anthem is worthy of the definition of the excellent Dillon.

Patrick J. O'Byrne

99
Subsecretário-Geral do DEA ao Encarregado de Negócios *ad interim* irlandês em Lisboa: Dublin, 13 de Julho de 1946[118]

I am directed to refer to your minute 7/11 7/9 of the 6th May, and to inform you that to those who really understand the present constitutional position in

---
[118] NAI, DEA, 414/10 Press comments in Portugal re Ireland, 1942-1947.

this country, and appreciate the political realities with which it was framed to deal, the commentary published in "A Voz" of the 14th April is not at all humorous.

The article, which is to a large extent plagiarised, reflects the tendency of some people here to sneer and gibe at a position they do not, or pretend not to, understand.

F. H. Boland

100
Ofício, Encarregado de Negócios *ad interim* irlandês em Lisboa ao Secretário-Geral do DEA: Lisboa, 7 de Agosto de 1946[119]

In the course of a long chat yesterday with Dr. Correia Marques, the Editor of "A Voz", I referred to the article ("Rei Exterior") which appeared in the paper on 14th April last (your minute 414/10 of 13th July) and told him that I was aware that it had caused general amusement and comment among the reading public. He laughed. I said that this particular "echo" from my country caused me anything but amusement. I commented that there must inevitably be some people in most countries who occasionally use that sense of humour to "ultrapassar os limites razoáveis" when speaking of very serious matters affecting themselves. I expressed that this "joke" of one or more persons in Ireland, who should not be ignorant of our position, had found a column in a Portuguese paper.

I presented a copy of Miss McArdle's booklet "Without fanfares" to Dr. Marques together with a copy of each of the enclosures forwarded to the Legation with your minute 219/108 dated 28th June (i.e. the text of the form of the letter of credence at present in use and the texts of the External Relations Act and Article 29, section 4 (2) of the Constitution). I asked him to read Miss McCardle's booklet and the other texts very carefully and to suggest to his sub-editor that he might find in them material for a further "echo" which should not fail to catch the imagination of his readers.

---

[119] NAI, DEA, 414/10 Press comments in Portugal re Ireland, 1942-1947.

I refrained in the course of my conversation from making any remark about the Deputy mentioned in "Rei Exterior" beyond the brief comment that he was well known at home.

I have also presented copies of "Without fanfares" to the President of the Council, the Under-Secretary and the Director of the Political Section of the Ministry for Foreign Affairs, the Secretariat of National Propaganda, the Press Association of Portugal, the Press Censor's Office and to the Superior and Superioress of the Irish Dominican communities.

I have two copies in my office and should like to have a further supply of, say, a dozen copies for distribution among interested friends.

Patrick J. O'Byrne

101

Telegrama, Hibernia a Estero: Lisboa, 12 de Agosto de 1946[120]

58 Following is summary of article which appeared in "Voz" of 10th August:

Ireland and Portugal applied for admission to UNO on the same day: the advantages to UNO of having in it nations that knew how to remain peaceable and benefit devastated world is pointed out. Portugal finds herself with the same thoughts and intentions as Ireland: both are Catholic nations, lovers of peace, faithful towards high ideals and lofty principles. Portugal and Great Britain have been allies for centuries.

Ireland forms part of British Commonwealth of Nations through King who is authorised by Executive Council to act for purpose of notification of Irish diplomatic and consular representatives and so acts when requested. Text of letter of credence quoted. Letter is signed by King; thus, in each diplomatic act, Ireland confirms its fidelity to British Commonwealth of Nations.

Hibernia

---

[120] NAI, DEA, 414/10 Press comments in Portugal re Ireland, 1942-1947.

102
Ofício, Encarregado de Negócios *ad interim* irlandês em Lisboa ao Secretário-Geral do DEA: Lisboa, 16 de Setembro de 1946[121]

[...Envia tradução de parte de um artigo de António Ruas no jornal *Sol*...]

"England was quite alone at the most crucial moment of her history. She needed the bases of Southern Ireland, which was a member, however refractory, of the British Commonwealth. In spite of everything she respected her neutrality. Both America and England could have taken possession, by violence, of the bases which they needed so badly at the peek [sic] of the submarine warfare. However, they aimed at carrying on a defensive warfare. That "fair play" was the guarantee of their victory. If both countries had followed the example of Germany, invading neutral countries, they would have given Germany an enormous moral force, which was, so to speak, the only thing she needed in order to transform Europe into a solid and inexpugnable fortress and win the war."

The writer's argument would seem to be a corollary to the argument used by the Taoiseach in the opening paragraph of his radio reply on the 17th May, 1945, to Mr. Churchill's broadcast of 13th May.

Patrick J. O'Byrne

---

[121] NAI, DEA, 414/10 Press comments in Portugal re Ireland, 1942-1947. A 1 de Outubro de 1946 cópia deste telegrama foi enviado pelo DEA ao Director do *Government Information Bureau*, escrevendo o funcionário do primeiro, '"Sol" is unknown to Mr. Cremin, our former Chargé d'Affaires in Lisbon, so it cannot be of much importance. In spite of occasional lapses like this, the Portuguese press is, on the whole, beginning to show some understanding of our relations with Britain and the Commonwealth'. NAI, DEA, 414/10 Press comments in Portugal re Ireland, 1942-1947.

103

Ofício, Encarregado de Negócios *ad interim* **irlandês em Lisboa ao Secretário-Geral do DEA: Lisboa, 14 de Outubro de 1946**[122]

There has been considerable unrest in Portugal during the summer months on account of the growing scarcity of food and of the increasing cost of most articles of diet. The position has deteriorated to such an extent that close observers of conditions have been fearing and prophesying serious disturbances throughout the country. Supplies of meat are almost completely lacking; there is an acute shortage of fish, sugar, and fats of all kinds; fruit has been in very short supply and very dear – oranges, for example, were retailed during the summer months at 10/- and 12/- a dozen. Olive oil, which is produced in abundance, has almost completely disappeared from the shops. Bread is, of course, scarce and of poor quality; and there is an acute shortage of potatoes. Milk is very scarce and there is practically no butter to be had. Rice, which is also grown in Portugal, has been conspicuous for a long time past by its complete absence from the markets. Recently the authorities commenced an energetic drive against operators in the black market and arrests on a large scale are being operated throughout the country. Hoarders, especially of olive oil, have been given a date by which they are to declare their stocks to the authorities; failure to comply will attract severe penalties.

In today's newspapers is published a communication issued by the Ministry of National Economy on the problem of feeding the population. It is a lengthy and fairly comprehensive document dealing with crop failures in recent years, transport difficulties and supply problems created for Portugal by the general position in the world. In view of the last mentioned point in particular, the necessity for maintaining control of production and distribution is emphasized – surely the enunciation of a truism but, nevertheless, essential for the education of the people, not only from the economic but also from the political point of

---

[122] NAI, DEA, Embassy Lisbon, 6/3, Report of Economic and Social Conditions in Portugal, 1943-1946.

view. Rightly or wrongly, the chorus of protest against the activities of the official organisations (grémios, juntas and other associations) has gradually been developing to such pitch that many ardent supporters of the system have seriously been considering whether the 'grémios' should not be abolished and the business of the supply and distribution of goods should not be restored to free enterprise or organised on a different basis. In this connection it appears that the lesson of Italy, after the downfall of Fascism, has not widely been learned or appreciated. The experience of that country after foreign occupation, when the corresponding corporate bodies virtually ceased to function, and where the economic control of the country fell very largely into the hands of speculators owing to a sudden change of régime, does not appear to be properly understood in Portugal. Here the cry is for the abolition of the 'grémios', but no-one, so far, has suggested any system to replace the present one – not even the new democratic party (MUD), which is credited with such growing popularity that it is considered bound to win the general election in two years' time, provided, of course, that a free election should be made possible. There appears to be little doubt that abuses, serious abuses, have occurred from time to time within the administrative bodies of the State, but abolition would obviously not provide the remedy. The solution would appear to be 'purification' by the exercise of vigorous action against the black market operators at the top rather than at the bottom or mid--way up the vicious ladder. It still remains to be seen whether this will be attempted and accomplished or whether ardent supporters of the present régime are to escape the net. There are so many 'stories' being recounted of grave abuses in fairly high places in connection with isolated 'deals', that one is tempted to enquire whether the energetic drive against black-market operations is being conducted against the root as well as the branches of the disease and, what is important, whether the effort of the authorities proposed from now onwards, as stated in the communication of the Ministry of National Economy, to reduce prices and to make available greater supplies of certain commodities, especially those produced in Portugal and its colonies, will succeed […]

Patrick J. O'Byrne

104
Ofício, Encarregado de Negócios *ad interim* irlandês em Lisboa ao Secretário-Geral do DEA: Lisboa, 15 de Outubro de 1946[123]

I have the honour to refer to my report (ref 6/3) of 14th inst., which I am sending you in the present consignment of mail, on the economic position in Portugal and to state that the Government have published a decree authorising further increases in the emoluments of civil and military servants to alleviate some of their distress. I shall send you a translation of the decree as soon as possible.

I have been informed, reliably and confidentially, that there were noisy scenes and very plain talking in the course of the cabinet meeting held to consider the drafting of the decree in question. The Minister for War in particular had been insisting on the grant of much greater increases to the Army than the Minister for Finance was willing to accept. The Minister for War had received from the Military Governments a document demanding very substantial increases to the armed forces and insisting that such increases should be accorded if the loyalty of the forces was to be assured. I am aware that a copy of the document in question came into the possession of at least one Military Attaché here shortly after it was presented to the Minister of of War.

I shall send you a minute shortly in the subject of a small military revolt that took place at Oporto about a week ago.

Patrick J. O'Byrne

105
Ofício, Encarregado de Negócios *ad interim* irlandês em Lisboa ao Secretário-Geral do DEA: Lisboa, 24 de Outubro de 1946[124]

I have the honour to state that on 5th September the Government issued a semi-official communication to the press in relation to the application made for

---
[123] NAI, DEA, Embassy Lisbon, 6/3 Economic and social conditions in Portugal, 1943-1946.
[124] NAI, DEA, 313/11A Confidential reports from Lisbon Legation, 1946-1951.

Portugal to be admitted to the organisation of the United Nations. The following is a translation of the note issued from the office of the Presidency of the Council of Ministers.

[…][125]

It is doubtful whether the Movimento de União Democrática has strengthened its position by its attacks on the régime for the apparent failure in relation to the application for Portugal to be admitted to membership of the United Nations Organisation. The obvious result, foreseen and desired by the Government, and expressed to me (vide my cabled report of 24th July, N.º 53), is that Russian policy in the matter of the proposed new world order has been brought clearly into the limelight, a contribution not only to the enlightenment of the outside world but also to the understanding of visionaries and sceptics in Portugal itself, a matter of great domestic importance. This does not by any means imply that the Movimento de União Democrática has seriously undermined the position it has attained. The internal problems of the present time, mostly in the economic domain, which have, so far, been handled with such little intelligence by the present régime, offer it full scope for the eventual successful appeal to the electorate.

I should add, in the present connection, that two of the persons who signed the manifestos of the MUD, Professors Marco de Azevedo Gomes and Bento de Jesus Caraça, have been removed from their respective chairs in the university. A note on the subject has been issued in the Press by the Ministry of National Education and I shall let you have the text in the next consignment of mail.

Patrick J. O'Byrne

---

[125] Texto da nota, incluído com o ofício.

106
Ofício, Encarregado de Negócios *ad interim* irlandês em Lisboa ao Secretário-Geral do DEA: Lisboa, 14 de Novembro de 1946[126]

[...]

There are three significant points about this occurrence:[127]
1. A mere handful of armed men succeeded in leaving the garrison town of Oporto in military motorised vehicles without any interference.
2. They had travelled a distance of over 100 kms before they were intercepted at Mealhada [...]
3. The place where they were intercepted is only about 30 kms from Santa Comba Dão where Dr. Salazar was then staying in his country home; and the insurgents were proceeding in that direction.

It is noteworthy that the substantial garrison at Oporto is not mentioned in the part of the Government communication which commends the spirit and the energy of other garrison forces.

A month after the event, the affair is still wrapped in mystery; but there appear to be few people in Portugal, whether nationals or foreigners who regard this as having been a mere isolated attempt by a handful of madmen to bring about the downfall of the Government. It is believed by very many foreign representatives that there was a carefully prepared military plot to seize the Head of the Government as the preliminary move, and then to notify the garrisons throughout the country of the successful coup. The setting up of a provisional military Government would have been the third and final step with – or without – the consent of General Carmona who, it is recalled, himself played a prominent part in the military revolt in the North of Portugal in 1926, which resulted in the placing of the present régime in power [...]

Patrick J. O'Byrne

---

[126] NAI, DEA, 313/11A Confidential Reports Lisbon, 1946-1951.

[127] Revolta do Porto, 10 de Outubro de 1946, sobre a qual o Governo publicou uma nota traduzida e enviada junto a este ofício.

Parte II
(1947-1955)

A segunda parte desta colecção é, de certa forma, a menos movimentada, pois a agitação da guerra tinha já passado e a questão colonial não tinha ainda surgido. Patrick J. O'Byrne, pela segunda vez Encarregado de Negócios, encontrou-se com o Ministro dos Negócios Estrangeiros, Caeiro da Matta, um evento que ele próprio qualificou como sendo de pouco interesse (Documento N.º 108), e acompanhou o Bispo de Galway e Kilmacduagh, Doutor Michael Browne, numa visita a Salazar. Sendo Browne, Professor de Teologia em Maynooth, um dos principais defensores do «vocacionalismo», o corporativismo português foi o principal tópico de discussão. Há depois um longo intervalo até à chegada, em Agosto de 1948, do Conde Gerald O'Kelly de Gallagh, figura dominante desta colecção em virtude dos longos anos passados em Lisboa, e que, à chegada à capital portuguesa, travou conhecimento com Salazar, visto o Ministro dos Negócios Estrangeiros, Caeiro da Matta, estar ausente do país.[1] Até finais de 1955 dedicou-se O'Kelly de Gallagh a comentar a política portuguesa sem grandes pressas e sem o intuito de através dela aprender algo; longe já estavam os dias em que o Estado Novo era tido como um modelo. Outra preocupação do novo Encarregado de Negócios irlandês foi documentar a excelente relação oficial entre Portugal e Espanha.

O'Kelly de Gallagh, seguindo a linha dos seus antecessores, manifestou sempre uma hostilidade clara à oposição portuguesa, especialmente ao General Norton de Matos, candidato presidencial em 1949 (Documentos N.º 117, 118). Embora noticiando as irregularidades dessa mesma eleição (Documento N.º 120),

---

[1] O Conde Gerald Edward O'Kelly de Gallagh et Tycooly nasceu no condado de Galway em 1890, sendo o seu título hereditário atribuído a um antepassado pelo Sacro Império Romano. Ferido na Primeira Guerra Mundial, iniciou a sua actividade diplomática (numa capacidade não-oficial) junto da recém-criada Sociedade das Nações, ainda antes da independência irlandesa, cuja propaganda fez. A partir de 1921 foi representante da Irlanda em Bruxelas, transitando para Paris, como Ministro Plenipotenciário, em 1929, ficando nessa posição até Julho de 1935, quando se reformou, criando um negócio de importação de vinhos – embora tenha retido o título de «conselheiro especial» junto da Legação até 1948. Voltou ao serviço diplomático esse ano como Encarregado de Negócios em Lisboa, cidade onde residiu até sua morte em 1968. Foi Encarregado de Negócios em Lisboa de 1948 até 1955, quando se reformou pela segunda vez, e de 1962 até 1967, tendo sido convidado a voltar ao serviço diplomático pela terceira vez.

defendeu O´Kelly de Gallagh a ideia de que essas mesmas irregularidades tinham sido desnecessárias, dada a maior popularidade do Marechal Carmona, por quem O´Kelly viria a manifestar uma grande simpatia, especialmente depois da sua morte. Este acontecimento finalmente forçou, após anos de alguma inércia, O'Kelly de Gallagh a escrever um ofício (Documento N.º 127) sobre as opções políticas de Salazar, embora pouco tenha dito sobre o processo de escolha de Craveiro Lopes como candidato oficial à Presidência. As eleições presidenciais levaram O'Kelly de Gallagh a escrever um longuíssimo ofício (Documento N.º 128) no qual a sua simpatia pela situação e por Salazar é evidente, linha essa que se manteve intacta durante toda a sua estadia em Portugal (ver, por exemplo, o Documento N.º 149, sobre as eleições de 1953). A sua descrição inicial de Henrique Galvão (Documento N.º 130) – 'a hypocritical humbug completely discredited' – é disso mais uma prova clara.

Em 1952 deu-se um incidente desagradável entre os dois países que veio a afectar seriamente a opinião irlandesa de Portugal. Navios da Marinha de Guerra portuguesa visitaram a escola de guerra anti-submarina em Londonderry (Derry, para os irlandeses), na Irlanda do Norte. O Governo irlandês da altura, de novo liderado (após a derrota eleitoral de 1948) por de Valera, tinha por política pedir a governos dos países da NATO que não autorizassem visitas das suas forças militares a bases britânicas na Irlanda do Norte, já que tal acção implicava o reconhecimento da soberania britânica sobre os seis condados do Ulster. A resposta do Governo português (Documento N.º 134) foi intransigente, já que a visita não era um evento protocolar, mas uma obrigação derivada dos compromissos portugueses para com a NATO. Este acontecimento teria como consequência uma maior relutância irlandesa, num futuro próximo, em aceitar o ponto de vista português em relação a Goa, Damão e Diu. O caso aparece mesmo como o maior defeito do regime de Salazar numa breve apreciação do mesmo elaborada no ano seguinte (Documento N.º 137). Embora não esperassem necessariamente que o Governo português mantivesse os seus navios afastados de Londonderry, queriam os irlandeses pelo menos um sinal de que Portugal faria ver a Londres a necessidade de mudar a localização de uma base essencial para a NATO – mas não receberam esse sinal (como o tinham recebido, por exemplo, do Governo holandês), e sentir-se-iam ofendidos por longos anos.

1953 foi marcado pelo encontro entre Salazar e de Valera, catorze anos após o primeiro convite feito pelo ditador português. Acompanhado pelo filho (Doutor Éamon de Valera), pela nora e por uma figura religiosa, o padre O'Doherty, o *Taoiseach* passou quatro dias em Portugal, tendo chegado na tarde de 11 de Setembro e partido na noite de 14. Os detalhes da visita (Documento N.º 147) demonstram o carácter religioso desta. Infelizmente não foi possível encontrar um relato da conversa com Salazar, em São Bento, às dez da manhã de Sábado, 12 de Setembro. O encontro entre os dois homens demorou uma hora, com O'Kelly de Gallagh a servir de intérprete e de única testemunha; os arquivos pessoais de Salazar e de de Valera nada têm a acrescentar ao relato de O´Kelly de Gallagh.

1954 foi o ano em que, pelo menos nesta correspondência, a questão do Estado Português da Índia começou a tornar-se aguda, e desde logo, para os irlandeses, a resposta às dificuldades do Governo português foi condicionada pelo problema da Irlanda do Norte (e por isso, em parte, pela reacção portuguesa ao pedido de 1952). A excepção a esta atitude foi O'Kelly de Gallagh, que desde logo, embora entendesse qual o desfecho provável da crise, manifestou a sua simpatia pela posição portuguesa, sendo a sua análise baseada na visão do Estado Português da Índia apresentada pela propaganda portuguesa. É também importante notar a atenção com que Dublin seguiu a política da Santa Sé em relação a Goa, marcada pela necessidade de proteger os interesses da Igreja Católica na União Indiana (Documentos N.º 163, 181, 183). No ano seguinte, 1955, nota-se um maior intervencionismo do Governo português junto da opinião internacional, com o Encarregado de Negócios em Dublin, Amílcar Lino Franco, a informar o DEA do que se passava na Índia Portuguesa e das resoluções do Governo de Salazar – embora as suas *démarches* fossem acolhidas com a maior reserva – e com outros diplomatas irlandeses a relatar conversas com colegas portugueses em que estes abordaram deliberadamente a questão de Goa.

1947

107
Carta manuscrita do Encarregado de Negócios *ad interim* irlandês em Lisboa ao Secretário-Geral do DEA: Lisboa, 24 de Fevereiro de 1947[2]

CONFIDENTIAL[3]

[Opinião do Embaixador britânico, Sir Owen O'Malley]

Religion and communism were gradually lining up against each other, in Europe; Christian-Democrat parties were being formed in strength; Russia was making every effort throughout the continent; 'the cards are being laid on the table and the big show-down is coming'. Salazar is perfectly aware of this. He is watching the new trends of democracy and is anxious, above all, to keep Portugal tranquil and to pursue his programme (which can only be done by an enforced internal peace) so that a strong, civilised and prosperous Portuguese State may one day crown his efforts. With this end in view he desires to avoid any overt action, which may be avoided, that would strengthen the hands of his enemies within the country. Above all, he desires to keep clear of religious controversies and criticisms of others so as to obviate counter-propaganda; and therefore, public action at the present time to collaborate in the sense of the Dail resolution might be considered as embarrassing.

[Opinião do Núncio Apostólico, Monsenhor Mazzoni]

[...] was more direct [...]. He said: 'He (Salazar) will do nothing at all, he will be perfectly sympathetic but nothing more'. The time was inopportune. Freemasonry was very strong in the country and other anti-clerical elements were very strong. The State was being assailed from outside, the Communists

---

[2] NAI, DEA, 313/11A Confidential reports from Lisbon Legation, 1946-1951.

[3] Este ofício está relacionado com a presumível atitude portuguesa a uma resolução do parlamento irlandês sobre a repressão da Igreja na Europa de Leste. O'Byrne discutiu o assunto com uma série de personalidades.

were concentrating on Spain, if they succeeded Portugal would soon follow. In this regard I should say that Sir Owen O'Malley has [...] reminded me that 'the answer to nearly every Portuguese problem is to be found in Madrid. You cannot solve Portuguese questions here.'

[...]

Sir Owen O'Malley thinks that this (Russian designs on Spain) will go near to succeeding. The opposition plan in Spain is to create a federal republic of the formerly independent states; should the plan succeed Portugal would be forced into the federation and the bolshevisation of the Peninsula would be a 'fait accompli'. Again, Salazar is aware of this; it is religion versus the Russian conception of life. He is doing his best to consolidate Portugal as a Christian State and in the prosecution of this programme he wants to be left alone – not to be drawn into controversy with Yugoslavia or other countries on matters of persecution. 'The moment is not opportune' [...]

Patrick J. O'Byrne

108

Ofício, Encarregado de Negócios *ad interim* irlandês em Lisboa ao Secretário-Geral do DEA: Lisboa, 8 de Abril de 1947[4]

I have the honour to state that in response to a request I had made the Minister for Foreign Affairs received me at the Ministry on 21st March. My reason for requesting a special interview as that I was suffering from an attack of influenza on 10th February and was unable to be present on that date at a reception of the Heads of Missions by the newly appointed Minister.

Of my interview there is nothing of much interest to report. The Minister was extremely friendly and referred to our previous meetings – at Geneva in 1935 when he presided over a League Committee, and last year when I sat beside him at the Irish-Portuguese football match [...]

---

[4] NAI, DEA, 313/11A Confidential reports from Lisbon Legation, 1946-1951.

Early in the conversation I referred to the interview I had had with Dr. Salazar on the subject of the Dail resolution concerning persecution, and told him of the extremely good impression that the interview made on my mind notwithstanding that his predecessor had not been able to give any promise for a definite line of cooperation with the Irish Government on the matter. Dr. Caeiro da Matta, as I expected, 'jumped the question', and went into generalities about the breakdown of international law, the suspension of a jurisprudence (as is evidenced at Nurenberg, for example), and the necessity to re-educate the world. I drew this last mentioned statement by asking him whether he found the Ministry for Foreign Affairs restful after his 'arduous duties' at the Ministry of Education. He said that his work at the latter Ministry was certainly very difficult; the education question was no longer a purely national one – it had become a important international one. All countries would now have to await an indication of the 'new jurisprudence' and the new learning which confronted nations in this new world.

Before completing a hurried conversation, compressed into about twenty minutes of time, I commented on the 'evident progress' that was being made in Portugal in the spheres of economic and social welfare – the importation of foodstuffs from abroad, the opening of new schools and hospitals, the training and increasing numbers of teachers and nurses, etc, and I remarked that the general atmosphere in the country was now so optimistic compared with the despondency which was such a feature during the summer and autumn of last year. He repeated that certainly a certain amount of progress had been achieved but the 'internal situation was still bad.' I have little doubt in my mind but that he was thinking of the political opposition which is now definitely a force to be reckoned with.

Patrick J. O'Byrne

109
Ofício, Encarregado de Negócios *ad interim* irlandês em Lisboa ao Secretário-Geral do DEA: Lisboa, 9 de Abril de 1947[5]

[...]

When considering this[6] or any other aspect of economic or social discontent which may occur in this country, it should be borne in mind that the Portuguese people, as a whole, are most industrious and, if not exactly thrifty, are at least conscious of their domestic responsibilities and rights. As workers, both men and women are second to none; it is edifying to observe the enthusiasm with which these people put their back into their work; this is particularly noticeable in the case of the dock and other manual labourers. Considering the paucity of their nourishment restricted, as it is, by the present price level, it is remarkable how much energy they can bring to bear in the performance of their daily labour.

Patrick J. O'Byrne

110
Ofício, Secretário-Geral do DEA ao Encarregado de Negócios *ad interim* irlandês em Lisboa: Dublin, 16 de Abril de 1947[7]

With reference to the last paragraph of you minute of the 8th April (6/9) concerning your interview with the newly appointed Minister for Foreign Affairs, we should be glad to know whether the recent changes in the Portuguese Ministry are interpreted locally as indicating an intention on the part of Dr. Salazar to proceed gradually to a more liberal system of Government. We should

---

[5] NAI, DEA, 313/11A Confidential reports from Lisbon Legation, 1946-1951.

[6] Segundo este ofício, trabalhadores da construção naval protestaram contra uma proposta de introdução de duas horas extraordinárias, das quais apenas uma seria paga como tal. Esta onda de protestos, segundo O'Byrne, parecia estar a alastrar a outros sectores da economia, incluindo as companhias do gás e da electricidade e a Carris.

[7] NAI, DEA, 313/11A Confidential reports from Lisbon Legation, 1946-1951.

particularly appreciate hearing of the reactions to the departure of Colonel Boethel Moniez [sic] from the Ministry of the Interior.

F. H. Boland

111
Ofício, Encarregado de Negócios *ad interim* irlandês em Lisboa ao Secretário-Geral do DEA: Lisboa, 5 de Maio de 1947[8]

I have the honour to enclose two copies of the official publication "Portugal" (December 1946 issue) and to invite your special attention to the leading article entitled "The Indian Portuguese demonstrate their fidelity to Portugal". The article has been particularly inspired by a speech made in the National Assembly at Lisbon by the Deputy for Portuguese India, Dr. Froilano de Mello who – to repeat a sentence from the article – "proclaimed the complete divergence of interests between the Portuguese Indians and India (formerly known as British India), and the spiritual fidelity and mutual interests that are maintained between Portuguese India and Portugal".

Goa, in the words of King Charles I, "the gem of the Portuguese Crown", has been ruled, developed and christianised by Portugal during four centuries; and to-day its population which consists mainly of Hindus, with a sprinkling of Muslims, is Catholic and shares the Western civilisation of the governing country. The people not only share this culture but they regard themselves as being Portuguese citizens and have no desire to sever the connection. A succession of enlightened colonial administrations, supported by Portuguese traditional missionary activities, seem to have brought this colony well within the ambit of Western civilisation and, to a corresponding degree, to have alienated it from sentiments which racially should unite it to India. The natives, I am well informed, regard the aspirations of their brethren, Hindus and Moslems alike, in British India with sympathy and understanding, but have no desire at the present time, at

---

[8] NAI, DEA, 305/271 Goa and other Portuguese enclaves in India, 1947-1954.

least, to become incorporated in the political system of the present India with all the hazards [sic] they foresee in the fortune in the light of the experience of the apparent irreconcibility [sic] of race and caste interests which are being demonstrated in such barbarous fashion by the warring elements in India itself. The people of Goa, as a whole, are not influenced by the ideology of Ghandi, Nehru etc which has for its purpose their re-union with countless millions of compatriots with whom they consider to have reached a state of civilisation as yet much inferior to their own level.

The importance of this tiny Portuguese colony, numbering approximately one half of a million people, in the external relations of Portugal, cannot be overlooked. The least cause of perturbation for Portugal in the immediate future, is the bad relations that are bound to be established directly between this little country and mighty India – as from next year when England is due, of her own volition, to surrender her rule to an independent Indian administration. What is likely to happen? The gauntlet of the Indian National leaders has been taken up by the Portuguese Government; this has been made evident by the resolutions on the subject that have been passed by the National Assembly at Lisbon a few months ago:

1) It (the National Assembly) affirms its confidence in the principles of justice and the right of the nations to see that integrity and inviolability of that territory is respected.
2) It greets the State of India which for over four centuries has formed part of the Portuguese Nation.
3) It reaffirms the sentiments of fraternity which link Portuguese throughout the world to their Indo-Portuguese brethren [sic] who, both within and outside the fatherland, have exalted the name of Portugal by their culture and mutual understanding of the greatness of the Nation.
4) It guarantees the Government and Governor General of India every support in action taken in defence of the superior national interests.

It is worthy of note that Deputy Froilano de Mello in the course of his speech recalled that the British and the Americans "on the occasion of the temporary loan of our bases in the Azores" contracted "moral and international obligations with the Portuguese Government for the guarantee and integrity of territories under our sovereignty".

It will be interesting to observe in due course how Great Britain and the United States of America will be able to reconcile the wartime guarantees referred to above with the exigencies which are bound to arise, in the interests of enduring peace, when India formulates her claim to the United Nations Organisation for decision – or will she, on the other hand, taking her cue from Moscow, solve the problem by marching into Goa with overwhelming force, justifying herself with the plea that she is only taking possession of what really belongs to her?

Patrick J. O'Byrne

112

Ofício, Encarregado de Negócios *ad interim* irlandês em Lisboa ao Secretário-Geral do DEA: Lisboa, 3 de Setembro de 1947[9]

CONFIDENTIAL

Re. WIRELESS SERVICE

[...]

It is not, I feel sure, necessary for me to accentuate the importance for Portugal of a sound atmosphere in Brazil! There are Communist columns (whether of the 5th or 6th degree makes little difference) in all of the S.A. countries; and they are directed towards the bringing down of the régimes of Franco and Salazar. Should Moscow succeed in creating 'hell' in the Iberian Peninsula, then the Moscow programme, insofar as this end of Europe is concerned, is achieved. And with France in its present, deplorable condition – as unfortunately it is – anything might happen [...]

Patrick J. O'Byrne

---

[9] NAI, DEA, 313/11A Confidential reports from Lisbon Legation, 1946-1951.

113
Ofício, Encarregado de Negócios *ad interim* irlandês em Lisboa ao Secretário-Geral do DEA: Lisboa, 14 de Novembro de 1947[10]

I have the honour to state for your information that the Most Reverend Dr. Browne, Bishop of Galway, arrived here from Spain on 6th instant and left yesterday be air for London. On arrival he was met by the Very Reverend Father Enda McVeigh O.P. and myself […]

His Lordship stayed at the Dominican House at Corpo Santo. He spent two days at Fatima and on Wednesday 13th, was received by Dr. Salazar – an interview which, I am happy to say, I was able to have arranged at Dr. Browne's special request.

I accompanied His Lordship to Dr. Salazar's residence with the intention of waiting to conduct him back to Corpo Santo. Dr. Salazar, however, came through the ante-room where I was seated, greeted me most warmly and brought me in to be present at the interview.

Dr. Salazar had been made aware of the Bishop's interest and knowledge of the development of the various vocational organisations in Portugal and the conversation flowed easily on the subject for about forty minutes. Dr. Salazar answered questions put to him by Dr. Browne on the Grémios and other matters and in turn made enquiries about vocational organisations in Ireland. The Minister enquired particularly about our fishermen and expressed surprise at the difficulties standing in the way of organising them in Ireland. The organisation of the fishing community is one of the outstanding successes in Portugal. The conversation then drifted on to an explanation by the Bishop of the relationship between the Church and State in Ireland, the system of education of clerical students and the functions of Maynooth College. The Minister was deeply interested in the matters and gave an outline of the system obtaining in Portugal.

Dr. Browne has expressed himself as greatly impressed by the warmth of his welcome by Dr. Salazar, the modesty he displayed when replying to questions

---

[10] NAI, DEA, 313/11A Confidential reports from Lisbon Legation, 1946-1951.

about his own country and his sincere interest in Ireland. Before the interview terminated Dr. Salazar enquired about the Taoiseach and requested the Bishop to convey to him his 'most respectful greetings'.

On leaving Dr. Salazar helped Dr. Browne to put on his coat and accompanied him to the hall. Calling me aside he asked if he could provide us with a car to bring us home (we had one waiting in the roadway). On shaking hands he thanked me for having arranged the interview and said he was delighted with the opportunity of meeting His Lordship.[11]

Patrick J. O'Byrne

1948

114
Memorando para o Governo: Dublin, 7 de Agosto de 1948[12]

APPOINTMENT OF A CHARGÉ D'AFFAIRES *EN TITRE* IN LISBON

1. Owing to stringency in the staffing position in the Department of External Affairs, it has not been possible to assign an officer of suitable rank as Chargé d'Affaires to the Irish Legation in Lisbon since 1945, when the last Chargé d'Affaires en titre vacated the post. In the meantime the duties of the post have been discharged by an officer of the rank of second secretary.
2. The Portuguese Government have enquired several times when we proposed to fill the vacancy and they have recently made formal approaches requesting the early accreditation of a Chargé d'Affaires en titre.
3. Additional work falling on the Department in connection with the European Recovery Programme has made it increasingly difficult to fill the Lisbon vacancy from the ranks of the existing service. In the circumstances, the

---

[11] Sobre a viagem do Bispo de Galway, Dr Michael Browne, ver *The Standard*, Dezembro 1947/Janeiro 1948.

[12] NAI, DEA, 317/40 Appointment of a Chargé d'Affaires at Lisbon, 1941-1948.

Minister for External Affairs proposes to recall Count Gerald O'Kelly, formerly Minister Plenipotentiary in Paris to full-time duty and to appoint him Chargé d'Affaires en titre in Lisbon.

4. Count O'Kelly was born on the 11th March, 1890. He was retired from the service in 1935 but, in the same year, was appointed special counsellor to the Legation in Paris. The post of special counsellor in Paris will be suppressed from the date on which Count O'Kelly takes up duty in Lisbon and the pension payable to him in respect of his previous service as Minister Plenipotentiary will be withheld for the period of his re-employment [...]

115
Ofício, Encarregado de Negócios irlandês em Lisboa ao Secretário-Geral do DEA: Lisboa, 20 de Agosto de 1948[13]

I presented my letter of credence yesterday at 6 o'clock to Dr. Salazar, acting Foreign Minister. There was no ceremonial attached to the act [...]

I arrived at 5.55 and was at once ushered into Dr. Salazar's waiting room whence, after two or three minutes delay, I was brought by a member of the President's cabinet into the President's room. The latter received me very cordially. He took the letter which I handed him but did not even open it, saying that he would hand it to Dr. da Matta on the latter's return from Vettel. He then questioned me about Ireland at considerable length, two points seeming to retain his special interest – A) the Ulster problem and B) our relations with the Commonwealth. He seemed certainly well informed concerning recent parliamentary debates on those subjects, though obviously more than a little puzzled concerning the facts and the historical background. I explained the position as fully as I could. Our conversations lasted from 20 to 25 minutes. On leaving I was introduced in the ante-room to the Spanish Ambassador, who as you know is General Franco's brother. Indeed he is exceedingly like him physically.

---

[13] NAI, DEA, 317/40 Appointment of a Chargé d'Affaires at Lisbon, 1941-1948.

With reference to the elections which are due here next year I noted a certain unease in the Foreign Office circles that I have met concerning their outcome. I gathered that everything in the garden was not so lovely and that the dissatisfaction caused by the high cost of living might react unfavourably, in which case 'on courrait à l'aventure'. On the other hand I had a conversation the day before yesterday with Dr. Augusto Vasconcelos, former Prime Minister and Minister for Foreign Affairs, who represented Portugal at the League of Nations the year we were elected to the Council. He is an old man now, though exceedingly alert, and very much the elder statesman. I have heard it said that he was one of the very few Portuguese statesmen who was sincerely republican. I have known him on and off for nearly 25 years. Questioned concerning the outcome of the elections he expressed confidence in the Government's victory, adding that the elections would be like all dictatorship elections. He said this with evident satisfaction, not compatible, perhaps, with the purest republican doctrinaire, but probably a fair statement of an old man's desire for stability and of his opinion that any change from the Salazar régime would be a change for the worse.

O'Kelly de Gallagh

116
Ofício, Encarregado de Negócios irlandês em Madrid ao Secretário-Geral do DEA: Madrid, 22 de Setembro de 1948[14]

The morning and evening papers of the 21st instant all gave the place of honour on the front page to the renewal on the 20th idem of the Iberian Pact between Spain and Portugal. The Treaty of Friendship and Non-Aggression was originally signed for 10 years on the 17th March 1939, and an additional protocol on the 29th July, 1940. Although article five of the original treaty said that it should be considered as tacitly prolonged unless either party gave six months'

---

[14] NAI, DEA, 314/44 The Iberian Pact. Treaty of Friendship and Non-Aggression between Spain and Portugal, 1948-1952.

notice of denunciation, it was apparently considered desirable, partly perhaps as a gesture, to prolong it for another ten years by way of formal agreement six months before it was due to expire.

"Arriba", the Falangist organ, extolled the Iberian Bloc as having been the inevitable expression of the determination of the Iberian Peninsula to defend its neutrality during the world conflagration; for the future it guarantees and secures the peninsula for Christian civilisation.

"Ya" says that the Peninsula constitutes for Europe a reserve and an example of order, peace and Christian values.

On the following day both papers again carried articles extolling the benefits past and future of the Treaty. "A.B.C." had an editorial recalling in the warmest terns the glories of Portuguese history and the community of outlook which in spite of occasional differences has always existed between the two countries.

G. Ógalliobair

117
Ofício, Encarregado de Negócios irlandês em Lisboa ao Secretário-Geral do DEA: Lisboa, 29 de Dezembro de 1948[15]

With reference to the forthcoming Portuguese Presidential elections, you are doubtless aware that General Norton de Matos has entered the lists as a candidate against Marshal Carmona.

General Norton de Matos is 83 years of age and some 20 years ago was High Commissioner in Angola. He has come out strongly as the champion of democracy, freedom of the press etc. He has not the slightest chance of being elected but may, possibly, obtain a certain number of votes from the malcontents of the present régime.

A measure of his sense of practical realities is his solemn statement published last week that the atomic bomb does not exist and is a myth.

---

[15] NAI, DEA, 313/11A Confidential reports from Lisbon Legation, 1946-1951.

The general view about Marshal Carmona is that he is the 'Grand Old Man' of the country and that as long as he stands for President he will be elected. At the same time it is felt that he is failing mentally – at interviews and in speeches he loses the thread of his thoughts and repeats himself somewhat incoherently – and it would be better that he retire [...]

O'Kelly de Gallagh

1949

118
Ofício, Encarregado de Negócios irlandês em Lisboa ao Secretário-Geral do DEA: Lisboa, 24 de Janeiro de 1949[16]

[...]

The article[17] was a blunder so colossal as to be explained only by a sectarianism exacerbated to the Nth degree. Even the excuse of senility – he is 84 – cannot explain the blunder because his advisers are not all old men. [...]

As Salazar put it very well in his speech in Oporto last week, this election is not merely a choice between two presidential candidates, but between two régimes.

[...]

(I understand that the resurrection of the body is likely to be demonstrated in a big way and that numerous are the dead who will vote one way.)

[...]

O'Kelly de Gallagh

---

[16] NAI, DEA, 313/11A Confidential reports from Lisbon Legation, 1946-1951.

[17] Artigo de Norton de Matos no jornal *República*, atacando a Igreja Católica e o culto de Nossa Senhora de Fátima.

119

Ofício, Encarregado de Negócios irlandês em Lisboa ao Secretário-Geral do DEA: Lisboa, 28 de Janeiro de 1949[18]

I note uneasiness among Government supporters concerning the forthcoming Presidential elections. The possibility of a Left victory is being canvassed, in which case, I am informed, the attitude of the Army would be to say to the victors: 'All right, you have won at the polls and we accept you, but on condition that the Ministries of the fighting services – army and navy – stay in our hands. We are prepared to give you a run for your money, but if after three months you don't deliver the goods, we will turn you out'.

I still think the Government will weather the storm, but there is a tremendous amount of propaganda in full blast among them. Russian wireless floods the country every night in perfect Portuguese, and though I have not yet seen one, I am told that you now frequently find coins with hammer and sickle stamped thereon.

The dissatisfaction in the country is indefinite. A great number who have no special grievance against the régime, apart from the discipline it imposes on profiteers and others, are inclined to vote against it because they are tired of hearing Salazar called a just man. He is himself, perhaps, too much of a recluse, and too little of a tribune, to move the masses. They just want change. I do not think that the majority of them who might vote for a change, quite realize its implications. For should Portugal go Left, it would probably be a prelude to a Spanish revolution. The success of such a swing in the Peninsula would mean that the Atlantic islands – Azores, Canaries, etc – would fall under Left control and that would hardly be viewed with equanimity in Washington.

[…]

A few days ago the Military Governor of Lisbon, General Pereira Coutinho, gathered together 500 officers whom he got to make a declaration of loyalty to

---

[18] NAI, DEA, 313/11A Confidential reports from Lisbon Legation, 1946-1951.

Carmona. It was a most ill-considered gesture and I believe very embarrassing to the Government [...]

O'Kelly de Gallagh

120
Ofício, Encarregado de Negócios irlandês em Lisboa ao Secretário-Geral do DEA: Lisboa, 24 de Fevereiro de 1949[19]

As you are aware the Presidential elections here were held on February the 13th and resulted in a virtual walkover for President Carmona, General Norton de Matos having withdrawn his candidature four days before the poll. He, General Norton de Matos, justified his withdrawal on the plea that he had not received sufficient guarantees that the poll would be free. The Government denied this, stating that the opposition were granted facilities to check the polling, but that, through not complying with the legal formalities prescribed, many of their nominees were disqualified from so doing. While I believe that this statement is correct I think it quite probable, from information received, that the Government discounted this failure to comply with the regulations and did not greatly regret it. Whatever the contributing factors the result was an overwhelming paper victory for Marshal Carmona – which means for the Salazar régime.

[...]

An eyewitness at one of the booths assured me that he saw one of the commissioners slipping a bundle of voting papers into his breast pocket – to prevent the catastrophe of the number of votes counted being in excess of the number on the register [...] so much for the technical methods employed which, apparently, are traditional and date from the time of the monarchy. The control of these technical methods undoubtedly added to the Government majority obtained. The question that remains is, 'would the Government have obtained this majority without this control?' I think the answer is undoubtedly in the affirmative. That they

---

[19] NAI, DEA, 313/11A Confidential reports from Lisbon Legation 1946-1951.

would not have obtained such an overwhelming majority is certain, but it is equally certain that free elections or faked elections, they would in any event have obtained a majority – which experts put at 70%. There was complete freedom of campaigning.[20]

O'Kelly de Gallagh

121
Ofício, Encarregado de Negócios irlandês em Lisboa ao Secretário-Geral do DEA: Lisboa, 1 de Setembro de 1949[21]

I have the honour to enclose herewith a short note on the forthcoming parliamentary elections due to be held next November.

O'Kelly de Gallagh

Ref. 6/9

PARLIAMENTARY ELECTIONS IN PORTUGAL – NOVEMBER 1949

Next November – that is to say nine months after the Presidential election which renewed Marshal Carmona's term of office for another seven years – Portugal will be in the throes of a general parliamentary election. This election is held in accordance with the normal operation of the constitution which limits the life of parliament to four years. The last elections were at the end of 1945.

An entirely new, though not entirely unexpected, feature will, however, characterise the assembly to issue from the November election and that is the fact that it will be endowed with "constituent" powers. An exceedingly important announcement to this effect was made this week by the Minister of the Interior, Mr. Cancela de Abreu, almost incidentally, in the course of a ceremony inaugurating the new Civil Governor of Viana do Castelo in the province of Minho. There has

---

[20] No entanto, O'Kelly de Gallagh admitiu, neste ofício, haver uma dificuldade básica com o registo eleitoral, compilado quando não havia eleições no horizonte e por isso razão para os críticos do Estado Novo se recensearem.

[21] NAI, DEA, 313/11A Confidential reports from Lisbon Legation, 1946-1951.

been no official comment, nor, so far as I know, any press comment on the very casual statement of the Minister. Normally one would have expected a decision of this importance to have formed the subject of a Government communiqué, and, so far as I am concerned, I find it difficult to understand why this particular method of publication was not chosen. However the man in the street and, indeed, diplomatic opinion also interpret the announcement as a perfectly logical sequence to certain more or less veiled hints thrown out by various political leaders at the conclusion of the Presidential elections. Those criptic [sic] utterances were chiefly concerned with the urgency of the need to find a more substantial constitutional basis for the exercise of the executive power and stressed the desirability of guaranteeing that power a greater degree of stability. Thus Salazar himself, in the course of a post-election speech which was the subject of a good deal of speculative comment at the time, stated that the election in question was the last opportunity which the adversary – the opposition – would have got of achieving a legal coup d'état. This somewhat sibylline pronouncement was stressed and even elaborated by the Minister of the Interior and various other speakers who unanimously deplored the necessity of having to hold frequently recurrent elections for the choice of the chief magistrate of the state, on the basis of universal suffrage. The ordinary Portuguese citizen, they claimed, was too immature politically and consequently too vulnerable to be allowed a voice in the choosing of the chief magistrate, on whom, in the last analysis, depends the whole political orientation of the country.

It seems, therefore, more than probable that the chief business of the new Assembly next winter will the [sic] recasting of the existing electoral laws. And it is almost certain that, prominent among the reforms to be effected will be that concerning the election of the President. Instead of being elected by universal suffrage for a period of seven years as at present, he would be elected by a limited electoral college and for a much longer period. In the existing circumstances the choice of the members of the electoral college would not present much difficulty. They would presumably be chosen from among such members of the Corporative Chamber, the National Assembly and the communal authorities as enjoy the full confidence of the Government party – the National Union. It is hoped in this manner to obviate in the future a repetition of the (from the Government point of view) alarming and even paradoxical situation of last winter, when the passing popularity of the opposition candidate – General Norton de Matos – had seriously threatened the popularity of the outgoing President, whose re-election was the indispensable sine qua non of the survival of the régime.

As for the elections themselves such persons as manifest any interest are still wondering whether the opposition, at present apparently slumbering, will, as in the case of the Presidential election, decide to take up the government challenge or whether it will simply revert to the 1945 tactics and withdraw beneath its tents.

The Government's own attitude is equally an unknown quantity. Will it allow freedoms of assembly and freedom of the press during the elections or will the temptation to revert to the old-time practice of overtly or covertly suppressing both, prove too strong for it? There are not wanting plenty of prophets to foretell either of those attitudes, but personally I feel that liberal counsels are more likely to prevail.

My reason for holding this opinion is that there seems to be a tendency among various leaders of the National Union to welcome the candidature of certain more or less independent moderate elements, provided they are not suspect of being communistic fellow-travellers or of having a sectarian anti-christian bias. Such elements, it is fondly hoped in government circles, might eventually come to constitute a sort of "His Magesty's [sic] Opposition" – which it is the pipe dream of all authoritative régimes to possess.

O'Kelly de Gallagh

122
Ofício, Encarregado de Negócios irlandês em Lisboa ao Secretário-Geral do DEA: Lisboa, 28 de Outubro de 1949[22]

I have the honour to inform you that General Franco, who was on a few days' official visit to Portugal, left by plane yesterday morning for Madrid. While he was

---

[22] NAI, DEA, 313/11A Confidential reports from Lisbon Legation, 1946-1951.

here he was lavishly entertained by the Portuguese authorities. He was lodged in the palace of Queluz, a Royal Palace in the environs of Lisbon. The official programme, so far as the public was concerned, included a review of the garrison troops in Lisbon, a banquet in the Palace of Ajuda offered by President Carmona, a lunch followed by a further review at Mafra, a bullfight in Lisbon, a lunch at Coimbra when an honorary degree was conferred upon him, a Gala at the Opera and finally a banquet followed by an enormous and completely chaotic reception at the Spanish Embassy. During the course of his visit he was made a Major General in the Portuguese Army. During his presence in Portugal the British, French and American Ambassadors were absent on leave. The British Ambassador is expected back tomorrow. The Chargés d'Affaires were present at all functions. At the Spanish Embassy reception, confined, en principe, so far as the Diplomatic Corps was concerned, to heads of missions and the military and naval and air personnel, it was noticeable that the American Embassy was represented not only by the Chargé d'Affaires and the fighting services, but by numerous other secretaries and attachés.

There has been a lot of talk of a secret meeting between Franco and Don Juan, but I do not think one took place. I understand that there was a certain reticence on the latter's part. In view of the stressing of the military character of the visit it is possible that existing military accords were strengthened, but so far as I have not been able to obtain information on that subject.

A body calling itself a group of Portuguese anti-fascists took the opportunity to circulate through the post a poorly produced leaflet, translation of which is enclosed.[23]

I also enclose the invitation cards etc. concerning the various functions, in case they should be of interest to the Protocol Section.

O'Kelly de Gallagh

---

[23] Original e tradução incluídos com o ofício.

1950

123
Ofício, Encarregado de Negócios irlandês em Lisboa ao Secretário-Geral do DEA: Lisboa, 9 de Agosto de 1950[24]

CONFIDENTIAL

I have the honour to inform you that I called officially on Professor Cunha, the new Minister of Foreign Affairs, the day before yesterday. The manner of it was as follows. A couple of days previously I had received a typed circular informing me that the New Minister, desirous of meeting the Heads of Missions, would receive me at 17:40 hours on Monday the 7th. I thereupon telephoned the Chef du Protocol and asked what was to be the "tenue". He replied that some of my colleagues had expressed a willingness to come in morning dress, "et que évidemment cela serait gentil". That left me in no doubt as to the official view of the proper dress for the occasion and I appeared at the Foreign Office on the dot of 17:40 in morning coat and tall hat complete. There I found some twenty of my colleagues, less than half of them "en jacquette", and each of whom had been convoqué for a given hour. As for the Chef du Protocol himself and his colleague they were both in lounge suit. It appears that the individual appointments were made at ten-minute intervals. Some Heads of Mission spent over half an hour, others less, but nearly all exceeded the ten minutes. The result was a décalage of more than an hour and a half by the time I was ushered in at precisely 19.20 hours.

The Minister received me very affably, but in view of the lateness of the hour and of the fact that there were eight or ten more candidates I did not think that this was the time to discuss business with him. His head must have been in a whirl already so I merely congratulated him on his appointment and expressed my pleasure at having to deal with him, saying that when the time came I would not hesitate to use the good offices which he so cordially put at my disposal, but that

---

[24] NAI, DEA, 313/11A Confidential reports from Lisbon Legation, 1946-1951.

I did not wish to abuse of his time now when so many others were waiting. We parted on a very cordial note, but the interview had only the significance of a prise de contact.

Next day I was received by the Count de Tovar, the new General Secretary of the Department. I think Mr. Cremin knew him well in Berlin. He is a very different type from his Minister. Very able and certainly inclined to be friendly, but I should judge, inclined to be "difficile" in his ordinary relationships. I told him of our difficulties over trade matters and of the almost impossibility of getting definite replies to requests for import licenses from the Conselho Técnico. He appeared aware of the situation and said he intended going into the matter. I fancy that if he once gets his teeth into anything he will achieve results. I hope to cultivate him when I return from leave and to get on the same terms with him as I was on with Dr. de Faria.

O'Kelly de Gallagh

124
Ofício, Encarregado de Negócios irlandês em Lisboa ao Secretário-Geral do DEA: Lisboa, 6 de Outubro de 1950[25]

You will have seen in the press last week the reports of Salazar's meetings with Franco both in Ferrol and in Oporto. These meetings gave rise to a great deal of comment – some of it, I think, a bit wild. Official circles were discretion itself and were almost aggressive in proclaiming that the meetings were just routine meetings arising from the treaty relations between Portugal and Spain, and vigorously denied that there was any ulterior meaning of any sort to be read into them. One newspaper editor, however, whom I met at lunch at the Belgian Legation, was equally positive in stating that the meetings were the result of an American suggestion to Salazar to discuss once more with Franco the means of bringing Spain into the Atlantic Pact. I find it hard to marshal positive reasons for

---

[25] NAI, DEA, 313/11A Confidential reports from Lisbon Legation, 1946-1951.

accepting one thesis rather than the other, beyond the fact that, in any event, the official attitude of negation would be quite normal, whereas it is hard to see what purpose the newspaper editor in question would expect to achieve in giving me in private conversation the information he did give me if it should prove to be false. The human tendency to sensation mongering is hardly a sufficient motive.

Be that as it may, the manifestations of Iberian cooperation succeed each other. This week we have had, with a tremendous flourish of trumpets, the tour through Portugal of the relics of St. John of God, (a Portuguese-born saint, though most of his missionary life was spent in Granada where the relics usually dwell). The huge silver-gilt châsse containing the relics was lent by the Spanish ecclesiastical authorities (read the Spanish Government) to pay a visit of friendship to Portugal. It was accompanied from Granada to the Portuguese frontier with full honour including the Archbishop of Granada and many other dignitaries. At the frontier it was met by the Cardinal Patriarch of Lisbon, appointed ad hoc papal legate, and escorted by dignified étapes to Lisbon […]

[…] I would sum up by expressing the opinion that, while the very real spiritual side of the manifestations was duly stressed, it would be perhaps a little naïf to imagine that the spiritual was the only side of it. It was a great manifestation of the Militant Christian Unity of purpose of the two Iberian peoples.

O'Kelly de Gallagh

1951

125
Ofício, Encarregado de Negócios irlandês em Lisboa ao Secretário-Geral do DEA: Lisboa, 19 de Fevereiro de 1951[26]

I have the honour to inform you that the local press announces that the U.S. Senate has sent a bill to the White House for Presidential signature whereby

---

[26] NAI, DEA, 313/11A Confidential reports from Lisbon Legation, 1946-1951.

Portugal will be indemnified to the extent of U.S. $20,255,952 for damages caused by the accidental air bombardment of Macau during the last war.

O'Kelly de Gallagh

126
Ofício, Encarregado de Negócios irlandês em Lisboa ao Secretário-Geral do DEA: Lisboa, 9 de Março de 1951[27]

I have the honour to enclose translation[28] of the interview Dr. Salazar gave to the United Press as published in the *Diário de Notícias* of March the 4th.

The interview aroused a great deal of interest though it contained nothing sensational. It was felt that the very request for the interview was a tribute to Dr. Salazar [sic] personal prestige in the international field.

The most interesting statement in the document from our point of view is that contained in the third paragraph of page 2 which I have marked and which runs as follows:

"From the foregoing, I draw two inferences: first, the duty we have to examine dispassionately all national aspirations and conflicts of interests, if these are represented as the source of international malaise; secondly, the precautionary organisation of a force capable of reducing or annulling the possibility of another force overcoming it."

How far the sentiments expressed therein can be appealed to in our case is problematical, though their wording seems to fit like a glove to the PARTITION problem. I will try to sound the authorities on the subject if I can do so discretely, and will let you know the result.

O'Kelly de Gallagh

---

[27] NAI, DEA, 313/11A Confidential reports from Lisbon Legation, 1946-1951.
[28] Incluído com o ofício.

127
Ofício, Encarregado de Negócios irlandês em Lisboa ao Secretário-Geral do DEA: Lisboa, 23 de Junho de 1951[29]

I have the honour to enclose herewith translation of Dr. Salazar's speech of the 5th inst. dealing with the political problems raised by Marshal Carmona's death.[30] Since then the candidature of General Craveiro Lopes for the Presidency of the Republic has been announced officially in the Government organ, the *Diário da Manhã*, in the 20th inst.

I would like to make the following general commentary which will, I hope, make it easier to understand the speech, the circumstances in which it was delivered, and the choice of Carmona's successor.

With the death of Marshal Carmona a very difficult problem faced Dr. Salazar – the choice of a successor. The survival of the régime being the "supreme lex", considerations of procedure and even of constitutionality had to be relegated to the background when they imperilled the régime.

Carmona had been a man of the revolution of 1926 and had always worked more or less in accord with Salazar. During the past ten years his functions had become more and more of a ceremonial nature, and it was Salazar who governed. Carmona, however, was the man of the Army and as such, could not be dispensed with. When in 1947 there was an abortive plot led by some Army elements to overthrow Salazar, Carmona (inertia, political convictions or advanced age?) did not support it, but, owing to his influence the plotters after being tried and convicted, were set free after about a year's imprisonment.

On Carmona's death, Salazar didn't want to become President because he could find nobody whom he could trust as Prime Minister to carry out his policy: he didn't want to be President and Prime Minister on the American model because of the extra work and responsibility involved and also because he rightly feared the reaction such a manifestation of dictatorship, as it would have been

---

[29] NAI, DEA, 313/11A Confidential reports from Lisbon Legation, 1946-1951.
[30] Incluído com o ofício.

dubbed, would have on the Western democracies; he didn't want a President of the Republic on whom he could not count – (the Constitution gave the President complete power to dismiss the Government at any time). He would be glad enough to have a military chief who would swing the Army to him, but he feared a soldier who might take the Army's side against him – remembering Carmona's sympathy, ineffectual though it proved, with the rebel leaders in 1947 – and finally he didn't want a civilian President with too powerful business or family connections – and without such connections none was likely to be a good standard bearer. It is clear that Salazar's problem was no easy one.

The new Constitution of the Republic discussed in March and April has an important clause governing the Presidential Elections. The incoming President must be approved by the Council of State (a Government-nominated body), and having been approved, must swear allegiance to the "Estado Novo" – Salazar's Corporative State – a state incidentally without functioning corporations. This clause automatically eliminates any Presidential candidate not approved by Salazar. It is a very effective solution – on paper, in any event, of Salazar's problem and the opinion is that he came brilliantly out of an apparent impasse.

Now as regards the candidature of General Craveiro Lopes there appears to be little doubt that this has been decided on secretly by Salazar long ago – long before the question was being canvassed in public.

Marcelo Caetano, the acknowledged theorist of the "Estado Novo", a possible candidate for the Presidency and a prominent candidate for the premiership, has been gracefully eliminated and compensated with a lucrative billet as director of the Bank of Angola.

Unity in the party has been substantially achieved around the name of General Craveiro Lopes. Though he has no tremendous personal prestige, the Army elements are gratified to have a military President, while the powerful União Nacional, grouping more or less harmoniously the monarchists, the corporativists and, generally speaking, all the elements of the right who might have preferred a civilian, are satisfied because the General (at present Governor of Tomar) has been for the past six years Commander-in-Chief of the Legião Portuguesa (the Portuguese equivalent, tempered to the gentler Portuguese concept, of the Fascist militia) and because there is no doubt about his devotion to the Estado Novo.

I enclose herewith a short curriculum vitae of General Craveiro Lopes as it appeared in the Diario da Manhã of the 20th inst.[31]

The Presidential Election is fixed for the 22nd of July. That there may be one or two pace-making candidates in the field is not only possible but probable. The Communist underground party – the party, as such, has no legal existence – is pretty certain to put up a candidate "pour la forme", simply to embarrass the Government, but they will obtain but negligeable support.

I find the opinion here that, unless something quite unforeseen arises, the elections should be almost of a routine nature with the classic overwhelming "ayes" for General Lopes. If the elections were free the picture would doubtless be different – and I think, pretty chaotic.

O'Kelly de Gallagh

128
Ofício, Encarregado de Negócios irlandês em Lisboa ao Secretário-Geral do DEA: Lisboa, 3 de Agosto de 1951[32]

As has already been reported in the press the Portuguese Presidential elections went off on Sunday July 22nd without incident and, as far as I could judge from wandering through Lisbon on the afternoon in question, in an atmosphere of serenity bordering on indifference. The National Union candidate – General Craveiro Lopes – was, of course, elected. The circumstances of the election are worth recalling. Dr. Salazar, who has exercised the effective power either as Minister or as President of the Council for the past 25 years, declined to assume the presidency, though strongly urged to do so, invoking reasons of "age", "health", "fatigue". At one time it was thought, in certain circles, dominated doubtless by wishful thinking, that his refusal might leave the way open to a

---
[31] Incluído com o ofício.
[32] NAI, DEA, 313/11A Confidential reports from Lisbon Legation, 1946-1951.

restoration of the Monarchic form of Government presided over by Dr. Salazar as Regent during the minority of Don [sic] Duarte's eldest son. Colonel Santos Costa, the Minister for Defence, is credited with being in favour of this solution, but to its realisation, there were so many obstacles, both internal and external, that it ceased to be practical politics.

In the circumstances the only other solution was to find a candidate to succeed Marshal Carmona who would conform to the definition of an acceptable candidate given by Salazar in the speech in which he declined the Presidency for himself. The new president must be a "parfait honnête homme" in the 18th century interpretation of the term – that is to say a man of proved integrity – and in the circumstances of the case, an absolutely sure man from the point of view of loyalty to the régime. Implicit in all this was the sine qua non that he must be prepared to work with Salazar as did Carmona, and, in the last analysis, follow his line.

After casting around in many directions the National Union party – that is to say, the Government party – picked on General Craveiro Lopes as their candidate.

But in the meantime the opposition elements – republicans, monarchists, liberals, democrats and communists – began to stir, as they have done whenever they had an opportunity since the end of the War.

Deprived of party organisation, without a press, closely watched by the political police, the opposition has been more or less muzzled for last [sic] quarter of a century but, since the end of the War, has none the less always profited of every electoral occasion to stir up public opinion. On this occasion it took the field in dispersed formation, under two leaders – one leading the extreme leftist elements and the other the moderates. The Head of the extremists, Dr. Rui Luís Gomes, is a professor of mathematics of national repute. He was the standard bearer of the National Democratic Movements, which has no enemies to the left however far you go. The leader of the Moderates was Admiral Quintão Meirelles.

Constitutional practice makes it necessary for candidatures to the Presidency to be examined and accepted by the High Court and the Council of State. Acceptance of a candidature is conditional on the candidates undertaking to respect the existing fundamental constitutional principles – in other words he must guarantee that he will not attempt to overthrow the social, political or economic order established by the New State. This was the rock on which Dr. Luís Gomes foundered, for it was self-evident from his published program – adherence to the Communist mystique in social matters and to the Stockholm Peace Congress in international matters – that the New State would not survive his advent to power by twenty-four hours. The High Court and the Council of State threw out Dr. Luís Gomes' candidature.

The case of Admiral Quintão Meirelles was different. The Admiral was one of the men of the revolution that brought Carmona to power and was even once a Government colleague of Salazar, having been for a short while Minister of Foreign Affairs once in the early years. He is, I believe, 75 years of age. He is alleged to be anti-clerical and a mason, and it is certain that the list of those who signed his political proclamation included many extreme elements, including the freemason mayor of the village of Ourém who brow-beat and persecuted the Fátima children at the time of the Apparitions of 1907 [sic]. But he paid lip service to the New State and accepted "en principe" the continuance of the Salazar régime. There was consequently no valid reason to throw out his candidature and it was accepted. His supporters clamoured for a "modification" – as distinct from the destruction – of the existing régime on the basis of "a general reconciliation of the whole Portuguese family" which, they said, was the object the military leaders had in view 25 years ago when they established it.

The Meirellists have vigorously denounced the political monopoly exercised by the "União Nacional" – Dr. Salazar's single party – the many cases of traffic of influence and of corruption in the handling of State funds, the political persecutions and the press censorship.

During the fortnight preceding the election they succeeded – often with most inadequate means – in rousing public opinion throughout the country and I think there is no doubt that they scored a considerable success in Oporto and the North.

But like Dr. Luís Gomes, the Admiral insisted as a condition precedent to waging his campaign, that there would be guarantees as to the honesty of the polling – say a continuous check on the voting papers from the time they were placed in the urns until the final counting. This guarantee was denied him in the strength of the existing electoral law which provides but a sketchy check on the polling operations. In the circumstances Meirelles withdrew his candidature a few days before the poll.

As a result General Craveiro Lopes, the Government Candidate, remained alone on the field and it was stated semi-officially that at least 70% of the electors on the register gave him their vote.

The whole electoral campaigns [sic], the elimination of one opposition candidate and the withdrawal of the other, is strictly according to pattern and I do not think it would be an unfair comment to say that the holding of the elections at all was in intention more of a conventional gesture in deference to established usage than an appeal to the arbitrament [sic] of the ballot. Indeed, Dr. Salazar, in the course of one of his electoral speeches made no bones about his views on the subject. In substance he said that while the régime did not exclude, a priori, appeals to the ballot in certain cases, it did not consider the ballot the best solution of political problems. "There are other methods of effective Government that appeals to the electorate" was his reply to the opposition thesis that a return to the electoral system, in vogue in most civilized countries, was the only method of reuniting the politically sundered Portuguese people.

While Admiral Quintão Meirelles urged the return to civic freedom and fusing of all the people in one grand patriotic sweep forward, Salazar insisted on the inherent superiority of a régime which wasted as little time as possible on politics and concentrated all its energies on the solution of the great administrative and economic problems which confronted all Governments nowadays.

Naturally enough, this was sheer blasphemy to the opposition parties whose ranks include many of the old time doctrinaires [sic] democrats as well as retired Army and Navy officers, many of whom paradoxically enough, were on the active list when their then chiefs wielded the "pronunciamento" as a means to promotion and utopia. But besides these elements the opposition has undoubtedly captured the sympathies of many in the administration itself and in the bourgeoisie, some of them with axes to grind, but the majority simply imbued with the old liberal democratic tradition, of which, after a quarter of a century, they forget the practical shortcomings in a country like Portugal, and remember only the "principes immortelles". "Que la République était belle sous l'Empire"! Whatever the relative importance of the elements of which the opposition is composed, I think it certain that it will more and more have to be reckoned with and that the régime will have many a headache in handling it.

From the moment that a hard core of the opposition definitely rejects Salazar's conception of what the evolution of the régime should be – that is to say the National Union thrown open to all men of good will in the Country – the crucial question so far unsolved remains – what form will this evolution take? This is the question that dominates all others, the more so as I believe there is no doubt that Salazar is anxious to retire from the scene as soon as he judges that he can do so. And that decision will depend entirely on how the new Craveiro Lopes – Salazar team pulls together.

In the meantime the Monarchists are not idle and continue to work for the restoration of a Monarchy of the "autoritaire" brand. So far they have supported Salazar in the obvious hope of themselves filling the vacuum his retirement would inevitably create.

What, in that event, would be the attitude of the New President? Constitutionally the Head of the Portuguese State is all-powerful. He can dismiss and name Governments at will. Hence the importance of the Presidential personality. General Craveiro Lopes, a practicing Catholic is credited with being a fervent supporter of Salazar and of the régime, and if he accepted the Presidency it is because the Army wished him to do, and the Army, in the last analysis, is master of the régime. A disciplinarian and himself "subject to authority" he is 57 years of age and has hitherto confined his activities entirely to things military. So far has had little or no political experience. Scion of a line of soldiers, of austere lives and irreprochable integrity, the new President is true to his family traditions. He is himself austere by temperament, essentially a family man, has several children and six grandchildren. His favourite relaxations are riding and flying. At the moment of his election he commanded the 3rd Military district with headquarters at Tomar and was professor in the École des Hautes Études Militaires.

This is the man in whose hands may lie the destinies of his Country within the next few years – or months. Politically he is as yet quite unproven.

The official proclamation of the President's election will take place by the Supreme Court on the 3rd inst. The normal procedure is for the scrutinising body appointed to check the poll to meet at latest on the fourth Sunday after the elections (22.7.1951). This lapse was provided to allow for the overseas results to come in. In this election, however, the overseas results are being sent telegraphically and will be submitted to the Supreme Court on the 3rd. I have secured an advance copy of the Affaires Etrangères Circular which will be issued to the Diplomatic Corps on the 5th announcing that the President would assume his functions on the 9th and inviting us to attend the ceremony at the National Assembly Palace.

The Circular adds that on the following morning the President will receive the Diplomatic Corps at the Palace of Belém.

O'Kelly de Gallagh

129
Ofício, Encarregado de Negócios irlandês em Lisboa ao Secretário-Geral do DEA: Lisboa, 7 de Dezembro de 1951[33]

I have the honour to enclose herewith a short report on the Congress of the National Union held at Coimbra on November 22nd and the following days.[34] The most dramatic feature of the Congress was the deferring sine die of the question of a Monarchical restauration. Yet on the 29th of November the funeral of the late Queen Amélia was celebrated in the Church of St. Vincent, in Lisbon, with all the pomp and circumstance which could possibly have been accorded had Queen Amélia been on the Portuguese throne at the time of her death.

The ceremony was magnificent. The coffin, as has been reported in the press, was brought to Lisbon from France in a Portuguese warship sent to Brest for the

---

[33] NAI, DEA, 313/11A Confidential reports from Lisbon Legation, 1946-1951.
[34] Incluído com o ofício.

purpose by the Salazar Government. It was met at the quay-side in Lisbon with full honours and conducted processionally through troop-lined streets, to the Church of St. Vincent which holds the coffins of the Portuguese Royal Family.

The streets were packed with a very orderly population, attracted doubtless in part by the grandiose spectacle, in glorious sunshine, but also, I believe, by a sincere sentiment of veneration for the memory of the late Queen.

The "ordonnance" of the religious ceremony within the Church was very impressive. To begin with the funeral drapings were lavish and admirably done, displaying a wealth of material for the purpose that was staggering. Richly embroidered purple hangings over fifty feet long hung from the roof at either side of the chancel, while the roof itself, throughout its whole length, was festooned in black draperies with white borders.

In the Sanctuary itself were two thrones on the Gospel side. One, near the altar, was occupied by the Cardinal Patriarch. Next to it, and slightly lower, was the throne occupied by the President of the Republic, while between it and the Sanctuary railings were the chairs occupied by the members of the Government, Salazar at the head of them. Two enormous tribunes, draped in gold embroidered black, flanked each side of the nave immediately outside the Sanctuary. The tribune on the Gospel side was occupied by the President's wife and a great number of Official and semi-official notabilities. The tribune on the Epistle side was for the Diplomatic Corps in uniform. In the centre between the two stood the catafalque, flood-lit from above and flanked be eight enormous candles and bearing the coffin, covered by a sumptuous gold embroidered pall. On top of the pall was stretched the Portuguese Royal standard. It was a faded old flag and I learned afterwards that it had been the flag flown on the Royal yacht before the revolution. It was rather touching.

Beneath the Diplomatic tribune and, consequently, between it and the catafalque was a narrow one-row tribune containing the principal mourners in the following order: The Princess of Thur and Taxis (sister of the Duke of Braganza, pretender to the Throne, who had tactfully gone to conduct a similar ceremony in Switzerland), the Count and Countess of Paris (he is a nephew), the Count and Countess of Barcelona (I know not what relationship), the Archduke and

Archduchess Joseph of Hapsburg and the Princess Therese of Orleans-Bragança (sister-in-law of the Count of Paris).

[...]

Needless to say all this ceremonial for the widowed and dethroned Queen, whose husband has been assassinated forty-three years ago and whose dynasty has been exiled a few years later caused a certain flottement and many puzzled comments among the strangers present. Were we "en république" or "en monarchie"? Was this a Royalist manifestation? How could one square it with the Union National speeches at Coimbra the previous week? What exactly was the meaning of the attitude of the crowds? I discussed the matter with various people (including the Conde De Tovar) and the conclusion to which I have come is that this was the contrepoids of his Coimbra speech quite deliberately organised by Dr. Salazar to console the Royalists and bring about as great a measure of unity as possible in the Nation. Dr. Salazar, politics apart, had a great and lasting friendship for the late Queen and, I am told, himself supervised all the arrangements for the funeral, both in the Church and out of it. The ceremony had nothing of a Royalist political manifestation and it can be taken that not one per cent of those who crowded the streets to pay their homage to Queen Amélia had any political arrière pensée. If it manifested anything it manifested the kindly tolerance of the Portuguese people and their debonair attitude to their former princes. They are not iconoclasts.

There is no doubt, I think, but that the Queen was not terribly popular in Lisbon during her reign, largely owing, so I gather, to her support for the Jesuit order. I am inclined to think, however, that her unpopularity was not so much spontaneous as organised by the anti-clerical and masonic elements at the time. Now a new generation have grown up who remember little of that far--off period and who, having entirely forgotten its animosities, have found it in their nature to give rein to very human feelings of compassion for an old Queen dying in exile and around whom a certain legend has grown with the passing years.

O'Kelly de Gallagh

[Documento incluído com o ofício]

The Congress of the Portuguese "National Union", held recently in the buildings of Coimbra University was of particular importance inasmuch as it was called upon to deal with the future of the régime itself.

Two dominating factors contributed to give the Congress a character of quite unusual importance:

A) The possibility widely canvassed in the coulisses that Dr. Salazar was seriously contemplating retiring to private life after his 20-odd years at the tiller.

B) The attitude of the opposition, which in the recent presidential elections developed two distinct tendencies – to right and to left respectively. This lack of cohesion allowed the Government to discount a longer period of internal political truce than would otherwise have been the case.

It fell to Dr. Salazar himself, as President of the National Union, to inaugurate this, the third Congress held by the Union in the course of its twenty years of life. Fourteen hundred delegates attended.

The Prime Minister at once recalled that 20 years ago he had left the University of Coimbra, where he held the chair of Finance – a curious chair which has not its counterpart, I believe, in most universities – in order to become Minister of Finance. After this long absence he was returning to the University. "For" he stressed "I am in fact returning to the University". This statement was interpreted by many – if, indeed, it needed any interpretation – as indicating that he had already made up his mind about his retirement. The "when" and "how" seem to be all that is left to speculation.

Salazar then proceded [sic] to trace a picture of world developments during these twenty years – a picture which could hardly fail to be sombre, and with which he contrasted the forward march of Portugal over the same period. Thus, while Europe and the world at large went from upheaval to upheaval, Portugal not only succeeded in staging a come-back but was able to labour in an atmosphere of calm and to achieve a relative prosperity.

Dr. Salazar attributed this happy result to two factors, firstly the geographical situation of Portugal – far removed from what he termed the "ideological frontier", and from frontiers offering a temptation to "ambition"; secondly, the virtues of its political régime. On the subject of the advantages of the régime he extended himself, going into much detail. He had praise for the methods followed, which, he said, consisted essentially in reverting to "the soundest traditions of the country" and "delving deep into the heart of the People". Indeed, when he referred in passing to the present world situation in general his suggested remedy was for every nation to seek for a solution in consulting its own national genius and in being true to its traditions" [sic] – that being the best contribution each country can bring to the formation of that "integrated" Europe so much on the tapis at the present time. Dr. Salazar stressed that the apparent inability of Europe "to find its own solutions" and "to live its own ideas" exposed her to the danger of "moral colonisation", be it from the USA or the URSS [sic].

Having called attention to the originality of the Portuguese régime, Dr. Salazar proceded [sic] to praise the continuity of action of his Government. "Recent history has demonstrated", he said "sometimes with tragic force, the superiority of 'political stability' over the constant changes of 'political action.'" "But", he added, "it is obvious that a 'political plan'" – a term by which he defines the "ensemble" of the Government and the Administration – presupposes the support of the nation. This support, as well as the comprehension of the nation is indispensable. It is necessary to obtain a "living acceptance" of the principles on which the Government is based – a delicate and fragile point.

The very clear impression emerges from Dr. Salazar's words that the régime known as the National Revolution has but to stick to the principles and methods which time has tested, but must also constantly seek the support and adhesion of the Nation. Anything tending to divide the Nation should be shunned. In this spirit, when faced by certain suggestions in the Congress in favour of adopting Monarchical institutions as the best guarantee of that stability of Government (and of the future of the régime) which is the base of everything, Dr. Salazar took up a "via média" position. While implicitly agreeing that the Monarchy has the merit of assuring continuity at the head of state, he does not consider it a question calling for immediate settlement. And this for two reasons – One must avoid the "fétichisme of formulae" and one must also distinguish between "institutions" and "régimes". Thus, he declared, "the Monarchical Institution would not, per se, be a guarantee of the continuity of the régime".

While not closing the door to an eventual restoration he is careful to advise that all division on the question be rigorously avoided. "Let us by all means discuss everything, but let us not be divided by anything."

In conclusion, while insisting on the character of a "ressemblement [sic] national" which he attributes to the Union Nationale, Dr. Salazar declared once again that the Union remained open to all sincerely desirous of serving. "Without asking you all to adhere to the Union Nationale, we ask all of you to serve your country".

Mr. Marcello Caetano, Professor at the University, President of the Corporative Chamber, who is the leading theoretician of the régime and is usually considered the heir apparent of Salazar, also spoke of the future of the régime. He went quite straight to the point, declaring that "Salazar is not immortal" and declaring that the moment was not yet ripe for a Monarchist restoration. According to him other social and economic problems are of greater urgency than the problem of a restoration which even if achieved, would not, per se, be a solution. He argued that the régime had proved itself and could carry on its own steam. It had an independent existence.

While the question was fully debated by the delegates in their meetings, the Congress as such, in its final conclusions – (drafted, incidentally, by Mr. Marcello Caetano himself) – followed the lines indicated by both Salazar and Caetano. – The question of a Monarchic restoration is not of present interest. Naturally enough this conclusion will not have pleased the extreme right wing of the Royalists belonging to the National Union. On the other hand it will have satisfied Republican sentiment in the Union. And there is no doubt but that it will have pleased the rank and file whose whole political education has been made under the auspices of the régime.

Among the opposition the problem of a restoration and all the discussions about it, meet with a good deal of indifference. They consider the question unreal. They think that any importance it may have is illusory and the result of a kink of Salazar's mind and of the minds of a few "rightist" members in the party. They just don't take it seriously.

On the other hand the Congress did express a positive wish that the Corporative Régime be definitely installed – in accordance with the Constitution. This may be considered a personal triumph for Marcello Caetano who, in season and out of season, has constantly proclaimed that Corporativism is the ideal solution for the Portuguese problem. He also dealt with the political formation of the youth of the country, more particularly the working class youth, as well as with the desirability of giving more elasticity to the internal organisation of the National Union so as to strengthen the bonds between this virtually "single party" organisation and the Government and to develop its propaganda at all social levels.

O'Kelly de Gallagh

1952

130
Ofício, Encarregado de Negócios irlandês em Lisboa ao Secretário-Geral do DEA: Lisboa, 17 de Janeiro de 1952[35]

You will have seen in the press reports of a political plot discovered and scotched last week by the Portuguese Police.

The first reports in the local (censored) press were bald and unconvincing and many people just shrugged their shoulders. Owing to the hush-hush attitude of the authorities it was very difficult to obtain anything like satisfactory information on the subject. I have, however, now been able to obtain from what I consider a reliable source, the following information:

The plot very definitely existed and was on the point of being executed when the Political Police swooped and arrested the leaders. The arrested leaders are as follows:

---

[35] NAI, DEA, 313/11B Confidential reports from Lisbon Legation, 1952-1954.

1) <u>Brigadier António de Sousa Maia</u>. A retired Army officer, generally disgruntled. In opposition under the label of Royalist. Actually cuts no ice in Royalist circles.
2) <u>Colonel Luís Gonzaga Tadeu (retired)</u>. An old Republican of the traditional "romantique" type. Generally respected among his circles, but in no ways an outstanding figure.
3) <u>Major Daniel Alexandre Sarsfield Rodrigues (retired)</u>. Constitutionally a "frondeur", but considered a "sérieux" republican.
4) <u>Captain Henrique Galvão (retired)</u>. Playright. Former deputy. Has been mixed-up in money scandals which did not prevent him making highly moral homilies from his place in the chamber. A hypocritical humbug completely discredited.
5) <u>Reserve Captain Joaquim Pereira de Macedo</u>.
6) <u>Naval Commander (retired) José Moreira de Campos</u>. A veteran of the 1914 war. Left-wing socialist. Considered a communist fellow-traveller.
7) <u>Pires Guerreiro</u>. A business man, director of an import concern called "Pro-America". He is a former journalist and is (or was) a persona-grata with the American Embassy here. An unpleasant type, I gather.

These gentlemen, it has transpired, had in spite of the Royalist label of Brigadier Sousa Maia, considerable ramifications among the leftist non-commissioned ranks in the Army, quite a number of whom they had suborned. The programme which miscarried was based on the cooperation of the two "sous-chefs" of the Political Police who had been won over. Their role was to commandeer a certain number of tanks and armoured cars to which they had access and with some 500 men on whom they felt they could count on, surround the Headquarters of the Political Police and imprison the heads thereof. After that operation they were to proceed immediately to Salazar's house and arrest him "for his own protection" and then call on President Lopes to hold free elections for both Parliament and Presidency. While this was being done all the military Chiefs throughout the Country were to be forcibly seized and, if not won over, suitably disposed of. The lists of these Chiefs, together with the names of the persons assigned to deal with them were discovered. As you will judge, this romantic programme follows the classic pattern in such matters. The plot was divulged by one of the two sous-chefs who, having aroused the suspicion of his superiors, was arrested and confessed everything.

He and his colleague, also in the plot, seem to have been actuated by nothing graver than dissatisfaction with recent increases in pay, which, while nominally 10% really figured out at about half that. An outstanding fact revealed by the episode is that the police as a whole have been perfectly loyal to the régime. The same may be said of all the senior ranks in the Army. How far the non--commissioned ranks were implicated, I cannot tell, but a priori, the seditious elements must have been relatively unimportant or there would have been disturbances, arrests or no arrests.

Another point to bear in mind is that, taken altogether, the arrested conspirators cannot be said to have had any real following in the country. As you will see from the comments after their names they included honest visionaries, frankly undesirable and tainted political adventurers and disgruntled retired colonels. At the same time there is no doubt in my mind from conversation in many circles that opposition to the régime is very prevalent among the professional classes and the intellectuals.

In all Latin countries there are, by definition almost, the unruly and undisciplined elements who cannot be expected to take kindly to a régime which prefers stability to fireworks. But they do constitute a political safety valve and I doubt if it is practical politics to sit on that valve indefinitely.

O'Kelly de Gallagh

131
Extrato de um "Political Survey on Portugal", enviado pelo Encarregado de Negócios irlandês em Lisboa a 18 de Março de 1952[36]

[…]

During the year Portugal seems to have loyally played her part as a member of the Atlantic Pact, though with what mental misgivings it is hard to guess. She

---

[36] NAI, DEA, 313/11B Confidential reports from Lisbon Legation, 1952-1954.

certainly had far less misgivings in boosting the Spanish Alliance and in working for the admission of Spain into the Community of Atlantic Nations. Her approach to the question would be by way of a tri-partite pact – USA, Spain and Portugal – which formula seems to her to give her greater guarantees for her independence. The old British lion appearing to be jaded, Portugal flirts with the idea that perhaps the American Eagle might well be tempted to take under its powerful pinions a country like Portugal – whose interest for America lies perhaps chiefly in the fact that she has a grown-up "son" – Brazil – on the American Continent and that this grown-up "son" not only manifests increasing affection for its parent, but is the mainstay of American influence in South America where it effectively counter-balances Argentinian hostility to the USA. For what role Brazil will eventually be cast in the Atlantic Community remains to be seen, but she certainly seems to have caught the producer's attention and Portugal will do her best to bring her to stardom in due course.

132
Ofício, Encarregado de Negócios irlandês em Lisboa ao Secretário-Geral do DEA: Lisboa, 17 de Abril de 1952[37]

I have the honour to enclose herewith translation of a Portuguese Foreign Office Communiqué which appeared in this morning's press.

I take this meeting to be largely routine and intended to stress once more Salazar's well-known opinion about Iberian strategic unity.

I have not yet had time to hear any comments on the meeting, but if I should learn anything I will report immediately.

O'Kelly de Gallagh

Generalissimo Franco and the head of the Portuguese Government, Dr. Oliveira Salazar, met in Ciudad Rodrigo on the 14th and 15th inst. for the purpose of examining together the current problems affecting the Iberian Peninsula.

---

[37] NAI, DEA, 314/44 The Iberian Pact. Treaty of Friendship and Non-Aggression between Spain and Portugal, 1948-1952.

In these meetings, characterised, as usual, by the closest comprehension and cordiality, the dominating factor was the common position long ago taken up by both peoples and Governments in the forming of a united solid front against the dangers which threaten Christian civilisation.

The Generalissimo and the President of the Portuguese Council, carrying on from previous conversations, were able to declare their complete agreement on the question of the strategic unity of the Peninsula – a unity deriving logically from existing commitments, and indeed, the necessary and inevitable consequence of the adoption of adequate measures for common defensive action within the general framework of Western defence.

Generalissimo Franco was accompanied by his acting Foreign Minister and by Lt. General Vigón, Chief of the Spanish General Staff, while on the Portuguese side, Dr. Salazar was accompanied by his Ministers of Foreign Affairs and of Defence. The Portuguese Ambassador to Madrid and the Spanish Ambassador to Lisbon were also present.

133
Apontamento de conversa entre o Secretário-Geral do DEA e o Encarregado de Negócios português em Dublin:
Dublin, 14 de Agosto de 1952[38]

I asked the Portuguese Chargé d'Affaires[39] to come to see me this morning. He arrived at 12:45 p.m.

I told him that we had learned that Portuguese frigates and a submarine of the Portuguese navy were going to visit the Derry Anti-Submarine School and remain there from the 29th August to the 12th September.

I gave him copies of he following documents:

Mr de Valera's statement regarding a similar visit by the Dutch Navy in January 1951;

---

[38] NAI, DEA, Embassy Lisbon, 6/29B, Secret and confidential matters, 1952.

[39] Eduardo Brazão.

Bulletins dated 15th and 22nd January 1951, containing Mr de Valera's statement and the statement by the former Minister for External Affairs. These bulletins also contained extracts from Irish and Dutch papers on the subject;

Telegram to the Dutch representatives at the Council of Europe signed by Messrs de Valera, MacAntee, and Aiken;

Pamphlets issued by the Mansion House Committee;

Pamphlet in French by Donal O'Donnell.

The Chargé d'Affaires said that he had not heard of the proposed visit. I told him that I was sure that the invitation had been sent by the British Government and that the Portuguese Government were not aware of the significance that would be attached here to its acceptance by the Portuguese Government. I pointed out that the Irish people bitterly resented Partition and that acceptance by the Portuguese Government of a British invitation to use Derry would give the impression to our people that the Portuguese Government was coming down on the British side.

The Chargé d'Affaires said that the Portuguese Government were most friendly to Ireland but perhaps it was their commitments under the Naval Treaty which forced them to take part in the exercises based on Derry.

I pointed out that the British had many other ports which to base exercises of this kind and that basing them on Derry was deliberately offensive to us.

The Chargé d'Affaires told me that he would immediately get in touch with his Government on the matter and get all the information he could about it.

Séan Nunan

134
Apontamento de conversa entre o Secretário-Geral do DEA e o Encarregado de Negócios português em Dublin:
Dublin, 19 de Agosto de 1952[40]

The Portuguese Chargé d'Affaires came to see me this afternoon at 4 o'clock. He read me a telegram he had received from Lisbon which was to the effect

---

[40] NAI, DEA, Embassy Lisbon, 6/29B, Secret and confidential matters, 1952.

that the Portuguese naval visit to Derry was not a courtesy call but arose out of their commitments under the NATO agreement. They could not refuse to take part in these exercises, and they were informed that the port upon which they would be based was Derry. The telegram went on to express the warm feelings that the Portuguese Government had for Ireland but stated that the matter of partition was a question for settlement between Ireland and Great Britain.

I said I was disappointed at his statement by I recognised that he had done his utmost. I urged him however to communicate with Dr. Salazar and recall to him the statement he made early in 1941 when it was proposed that the British or the Americans should take over the Azores without being invited to do so by the Portuguese Government.

I said that our people had exactly the same feelings about the Six Counties, and about the use of them by the British and other Governments, as Dr. Salazar so well expressed in that statement which I read in the *New York Times*.

I asked him to write again to Lisbon urging his Government to endeavour to get the British to change the port for these exercises and pointing out that the British had quite a number of ports available which would suit.

I pointed out that while I recognised that the actual negotiations for the settlement of Partition would have to take place between the British and ourselves, it was an interest of all European Governments that Partition should be settled. I told him that a very prominent European statesman had agreed with me that it was a European interest. I hoped that the Portuguese would do their utmost to point this out to the British Government.

The Chargé d'Affaires promised to send me the gist of the telegram in the form of a Note and write to Lisbon along the lines I suggested.

Séan Nunan

135
Ofício, Encarregado de Negócios irlandês em Lisboa ao Secretário-Geral do DEA: Lisboa, 11 de Dezembro de 1952[41]

I have the honour to inform you, a propos of the death of Charles Maurras, that the *Diário da Manhã* – the Government organ – of today carries a paragraph from its Paris correspondent stating that the current issue of the weekly *Aspects de France* prints on the first page, across three columns, the text of the telegram sent to Jacques Maurras by President Salazar, as well as the full text of the speech made in the National Assembly here by Deputy João do Amaral. Personally I have seen neither text, but call your attention to the incident as a pointer of the Salazarist political philosophy in case you wish to refer to the *Aspects de France* issue in question.

O'Kelly de Gallagh

1953

136
Ofício, Encarregado de Negócios irlandês em Lisboa ao Secretário-Geral do DEA: Lisboa, 8 de Janeiro de 1953[42]

I have the honour to enclose herewith a report in duplicate of the recent conspiracy trial which concluded on the 17th December.

O'Kelly de Gallagh

On the 17th of December 1952, the Lisbon Military Court condemned two reserve officers and acquitted six other persons charged with plotting against the safety of the State.

---

[41] NAI, DEA, 313/11B Confidential reports from Lisbon Legation, 1952-1954.
[42] NAI, DEA, 313/11B Confidential reports from Lisbon Legation, 1952-1954.

The accused men were charged, in the first instance with sedition, the preparation of terrorist acts and association for criminal purposes, but, when the actual trial came on, the latter two charges were dropped and only the charge of sedition or plotting against the safety of the State was maintained. In January last, when the "plot" was originally discovered, the police had arrested a great many number of suspects – over 100 it is said – but finally proceedings were instituted against only ten – six officers and four civilians – as follows:

Officers: Generals Sousa Maia.
              Major Gonzaga Tadeu.
              Capt. Galvão.
              Comdr. Moreira Campos (retired naval).
              Major Mário Pessoa
              Lt.Col. Reis
              (Major Mário Pessoa and Comdr. Moreira de Campos were dismissed from the proceedings at an early stage of the investigations).

Civilians: Former Chief of Police Fernandes.
              Sr. Ilidio and Sr. Sousa Machado (barristers).
              Sr. Tendeiro (merchant).

All these individuals came from the Nationalist Ranks, having all either actually played a part – however minor – in bringing the present régime to power, or else having actively supported it once it got there.

Little by little, for reasons which in most cases – not I believe in Galvão's – I think to have been influenced by personal considerations at least as much as by those of the public weal – the accused drifted rather than moved deliberately into the opposition. The principal accused is certainly Captain Galvão. He had at one time been a pillar of the régime which had on various occasions entrusted him with important missions – the direction of the National Broadcasting, the Inspection-General of the Colonies etc. A curious figure this Captain Galvão. Undoubtedly one of the ablest of the younger Portuguese Colonial Administrators, at the same time a talented playwright, the Captain would assuredly have been called upon to play an important role in the present régime had he not fallen foul of it a couple of years ago as the result of a stormy intervention he made in the National Assembly in a discussion of Colonial Administration.

In the course of a tour of inspection in the Portuguese African Colonies he had laid bare certain scandals in which his reports involved, more or less gravely, some forty-three different individuals. Finding that his charges were not being investigated with all the zeal he could have wished, and being definitely of opinion that both the Minister for the Colonies and the Ministry he directed were equally incompetent, the Captain, who was then also a deputy, took the bull by the horns and made a speech in the National Assembly which was a violent and merciless criticism of the Ministry of which he was an official (N.B. – Under this régime there is no incompatibility between the Legislative and the Administrative functions).

In the course of the presidential election of 1951 he passed over to the opposition. This opposition, rallying around the defeated presidential candidate, Admiral Quintão Meireles, comprised two distinct wings:- A) The National "dissidents" largely recruited from the Army, and B) the traditional left-wing liberals and democrats. While there was nothing like a permanent fusion of these two currents, they did unite in support of that clause in the Meireles programme calling for the abolition of the "organic dictatorship". The two wings of the coalition were very unequal in strength. The left wing was numerically weak and included but few names known to the public, whereas the right wing, vastly more numerous, lined up an impressive team of well-known retired senior officers – Admirals, Generals and Colonels galore – and in that wing, Captain Galvão was cast by circumstances and by his own personality to play a leading role. He held two trumps. First of all, having been so long in politics he possessed a solid political background, and secondly – and this was perhaps the greater asset – he was the only one really familiar with the workings of the Government and with what might be called its secrets – "Nourri dans le sérail il en connait les détours".

In the event as has been seen, the opposition never went to the polls in the last Presidential election, but this time they did not throw up the sponge. They decided to form a Civic Organisation, the chief object of which was to maintain a permanent liasion between the diverse elements of the Opposition. The dispersal of the Opposition after each electoral campaign had hitherto been a great source of weakness. Captain Galvão decided to overcome this weakness by the creation of this Civic Organisation as a future rallying point for all adversaries of the régime. He was further the inspirer of a real mud-slinging campaign during the election, which had proved very effective – so effective indeed that he seems to have thought the moment ripe for the preparation of a manoeuvre intended to bring the régime crashing. There can be no certainty on this point, but one fact is certain, and that is that in January 1952 the police raided the H.Q. of the Civic Organisation, and closed it, arresting everybody found on the premises as well as a number of suspects who were simultaneously arrested in their houses.

Eleven months later the case came for trial before the Lisbon Military Tribunal, presided over by General Lionel Vieira. The trial took place in an atmosphere of marked leniency, devoid of any severity. The "terrorist acts" charge had already been dropped by the State. Most of the accused had only to face a charge of "having held meetings in view of a possible plot" – a charge terribly difficult to sustain, and, I would think, unknown to any law. Galvão and Tadeu were, however, more deeply involved. In their houses the Police had found, not only the plans of carious barracks but, in Galvão's house, the plan for a revolutionary movement. This certainly called for an explanation and the two officers concerned put up a very poor defence. The situation of the other accused was much less grave, and, encouraged one might almost say, by the obvious good will of the court, they had little difficulty in satisfying everybody that the incriminated meetings were either simply concerned with the affairs of the Civic Organisation – which was perfectly legitimate, there being no law against friends meeting to discuss – discreetly – the Res Publica; or, alternatively that they were simply private gatherings of no political import whatever. Some of the accused were even able to "prove" that they had not been where the police had seen them, or, again alternatively, that if, in fact, they had been there, then it was by pure accident.

The principal witness for the prosecution, a notorious morphine addict, and almost certainly an "agent provocateur", who had actually belonged to the Civic Organisation and had supplied the Police with the basis of many of their charges, collapsed in the witness box like a pricked toy balloon. He tied himself up in knots, withdrew most of his accusations, and finally – and this was the high-spot of the trial – was himself committed and jailed for perjury.

Still, in spite of everything, it was evident that seditious plans did exist, and their existence could not be laughed off. These plans might, perhaps, never have been put into execution and the law is not concerned with vague intentions but their very existence could legally be considered that beginning of seditious actions necessary to set the forces of the law in motion.

The trial lasted about a week. Only Galvão and Tadeu were convicted and they were condemned to three years' and two years' penal detention respectively. This sentence does not entail hard labour of any sort, but the conviction does entail loss of pension, forfeiture of all honours and loss of State employment.

The condemned men have appealed to the General Court Martial of the Army, as has also the State prosecutor, but the latter's appeal is purely formal. This appellate jurisdiction consists of the same judges as the Lisbon Military Tribunal strengthened by the addition of two more General officers. Informed opinion here considers it likely that even the lenient sentences passed on the two convicted officers will be reduced on appeal. That they played their fire and deserved to have their fingers burned nobody denies but the feeling is general that that operation has now been completed.

Perhaps the best way of summing up the case is to repeat the question heard put by many during the past fortnight – "Has there ever really been a 'plot' or was the whole thing just a political manoeuvre?" I am inclined to opt for the political manoeuvre.

There would seem to have been no real conspirators in the ordinary acceptance of the term, but I think there was a very definite intention on the part of certain of the more active members of the Opposition to create an atmosphere of suspicion and discontent intended to give pause to the leaders of the régime and bring them to a more accommodating frame of mind. They wanted more particularly to impress Salazar and his immediate civilian entourage. The impression is that they used rather childish and romantic methods to achieve this end – meetings in theatres, written plans etc. – and that they failed completely […].

137
Apreciação do DEA sobre o Estado Novo (para consulta interna), 31 de Março de 1953[43]

<u>NOTES</u>
<u>Salazar régime in Portugal</u>

CREDIT

1. Has attempted to translate Catholic social teaching into practice, in such matters as a living wage, family as unit.
2. The Corporative system appears to be an honest attempt to reconcile the conflicting interests of capital and labour; but the practice seems to have fallen short of the theory.
3. Restored order.
4. Balanced budget, restored financial stability.
5. Anti-Communist.
6. Has been humane and beneficent coloniser.
7. Neutrality in World War II.
8. Old links through education of Irish students in penal times; Irish Dominicans.

DEBT

1. Portuguese war vessels in Derry, 1952.
2. An authoritarian régime, described as a dictatorship.
3. Freedom of speech and assembly curtailed.
4. No opposition in parliamentary democracy sense. Freedom of elections doubtful. (Count O'Kelly's report 24.2.49).
5. Régime does not appear to have been successful in raising standard of living, still very low, in country areas at least.
6. Similar failure as regards literacy.

---

[43] NAI, DEA, 313/11B, Confidential reports from Lisbon Legation, 1952-1954. Numa margem, escrita à mão, uma lista dos processos em que este documentos se deve incluir: 313/11B; 335/327 (não identificado); 341/92/4: Proposed visit by Portuguese war vessels to Six Counties – August/September 1952 (1951-1958).

138
Ofício, Encarregado de Negócios irlandês em Lisboa ao Secretário-Geral do DEA: Lisboa, 14 de Maio de 1953[44]

The much heralded visit to Madrid of the President of the Portuguese Republic begins this evening when General Craveiro Lopes boards the Madrid train at the suburban station of Santa Apolónia at 21.50 hours. The Lisbon press has been writing up the visit for the past fortnight.

[…]

Defence and Foreign Policy will be the subjects discussed. It is not anticipated that anything very startingly new will emerge therefrom.

O'Kelly de Gallagh

139
Ofício, Encarregado de Negócios irlandês em Lisboa ao Secretário-Geral do DEA: Lisboa, 26 de Maio de 1953[45]

The world press will have given you about all there is to know about President Craveiro Lopes' visit to Madrid last week. The visit was tremendously played up in the Portuguese press, but in all the reams of writing about it, including the Foreign Minister's published statement at its conclusion, I could not make out anything of real interest. There are no points of dispute between Spain and Portugal at the moment, and their outlook on matters of defence and foreign policy are practically identical. The feeling among certain of my colleagues here – and I share it from personal observation – is that the visit to Madrid fell into the cadre of a general build-up of the President by the Portuguese Government. When the President returned last week the Heads of Mission and the whole population of Lisbon were mobilised to welcome him back. The day was

---

[44] NAI, DEA, 313/11B Confidential reports from Lisbon Legation, 1952-1954.
[45] NAI, DEA, 313/11B Confidential reports from Lisbon Legation, 1952-1954.

proclaimed a half holiday and everything was shut during the afternoon [...] He drove to the Palace at Belém – some ten kilometres – standing up in an open car through streets lined with most of the Lisbon garrison. The public stood behind the troops, but were mostly just courteous in their applause and no more. It was an organised official welcome – not a popular one. The contrast with a Carmona parade was painful.

O'Kelly de Gallagh

140
Ofício, Encarregado de Negócios irlandês em Lisboa ao Secretário-Geral do DEA: Lisboa, 26 de Maio de 1953[46]

I have the honour to enclose herewith translation of an item in the *República* of the 13th inst. which is self-explanatory. It consists of a) an open letter to the President of the Republic by General Norton de Matos, unsuccessful candidate at the last Presidential elections, and nearly seventy sympathisers (I will append a note giving the background of some of the signatories) and b) the Government's reply. The letter to the President is of interest as indicating the ferment, the extent of which it is very difficult to gauge, simmering beneath the surface of Portuguese politics.

Government sympathisers are naturally inclined to play the whole thing down, but my own feeling is that the unrest is real among the intellectuals and the liberal professions who feel that they might have been robbed of their prescriptive right to govern (or misgovern) the country for their own benefit. The Masonic tradition dies hard. Only the prestige of Salazar, supported with varying degrees of conviction by the great majority of a population politically immature and largely illiterate keeps them under. If and when Salazar quits the helm, what may happen is anybody's guess. If the present President is still in office and is fortunate in the choice of Salazar's successor the régime may weather the storm.

---

[46] NAI, DEA, 313/11B Confidential reports from Lisbon Legation, 1952-1954.

But I feel that in all probability the President and his collaborators will have to be firm to the point of ruthlessness if they are to survive. Is the President the man for that? I do not know. Nobody knows. He is being constantly built up by Salazar and, given time, may achieve the necessary prestige. From the manifestation organised on his return from Madrid last week, I should judge that he has still a long way to go to gain the popular confidence and affection in anything like the degree that Marshal Carmona had then. In this he is certainly handicapped by his presence, which is insignificant, whereas the old Marshal was an imposing figure of a man, built on much the lines of Pétain, and was a popular idol. I am assured by those who should know that Craveiro Lopes' standing is growing and I am prepared to believe it, but it is a slow process. Though good, I believe, from any point of view, conscientious and patriotic, he lacks the "fluid" and the personality which captures the popular imagination. This may not be a drawback if he is given time, because it would mean that if he comes to be really loved and respected it would be for his sterling qualities and not for any meretricious charm. But should Salazar disappear before he has had time to be properly appreciated it might leave the state rudderless at the critical moment. And that would be the moment for Norton de Matos and Company to come into their own.

O'Kelly de Gallagh

141
Resumo da situação política em Portugal em 1952[47]

Portugal 1952

Political Survey

Extract from Annual Report 1952 from Lisbon on file 359/4

1. In a world of wars and rumours of war – of cold wars and less cold wars – Portugal, during the year 1952 has kept the noiseless tenor of her war, serene

---

[47] NAI, DEA, 313/11B Confidential reports from Lisbon Legation, 1952-1954.

and unruffled. If that nation be happy that has no history then Portugal can be accounted happy in 1952. Indeed, so little in her internal life constituted what is commonly called "news" that most of the great international News Agency branches in Lisbon found that this year they had telegraphed to their Head Offices less than half the number of words they had sent in 1951.

2. Perhaps the most canvassed question in the country during the year has been the possible retirement of Dr. Salazar. It is a question which I have heard discussed from time to time ever since I arrived here in 1948, but this year the rumours seemed more persistent, though not necessarily carrying more conviction. It is possible that this year's flock of them may be traced back to a remark attributed to Salazar himself in Madame Christine Garnier's book "VACANCES AVEC SALAZAR" which appeared last Spring and in which Salazar is said to have remarked casually in the course of conversation that he would deem himself unfortunate were he to finish his days as President of the Council. Whatever may be behind it the question was discussed in the National Assembly itself. It is interesting to note that the particular form of retirement canvassed was not a 100% retirement but rather a relinquishing of the more arduous duties of office while keeping close contact with affairs and a considerable "elder statesman" influence. According to this conception Salazar would remain President of the National Union, but would hand over the reins of actual Government to the more faithful and trusted of his lieutenants. As a corollary the Head of the State, General Craveiro Lopes, would then assume in fact the full responsibilities which are his by constitutional right but which, in practice, have hitherto been discharged by the President of the Council.

3. So much is common rumour. While it would be easy to exaggerate its importance from the point of view of actuality, it certainly should not be dismissed without consideration.

Salazar is in his 64th year, and, in the ordinary course of nature cannot be expected to carry on very much longer. He has shouldered a tremendous load of responsibility for the past twenty odd years. He has never considered himself a politician, but rather the "educator" of his people. Fundamentally he is still the University Professor at heart – his approach to every problem is that of the

Professor – and it would appear natural and in the order of things that he should himself envisage the Academic calm of the University as the predestined calm of his declining years.

[…]

5. <u>Armed Forces</u>. The year was marked by a complete reorganisation of the Air Force. Training equipment on a considerable scale has been supplied by the U.S.A. and this entailed a radical change in the organisation. Hitherto service in the Portuguese Air Forces had been voluntary but henceforth it is to be compulsory as in the ground forces.

At the same time the status of Civil Aviation has been strengthened and is now much more independent of state interference. The TAP company (Transportes Aéreos Portugueses) has become a commercial concern, with the commercial aspect strongly stressed and will dispose of a fleet of fast modern aircraft, destined to intensify her services with the Portuguese Colonies and to inaugurate a service to Brazil.

6. <u>Education</u>. An all-out campaign against illiteracy marked the second half of the year. I reported upon it at the time. This campaign, which in a certain degree, is coupled with the six-year plan of which more hereafter, aims at abolishing illiteracy within a space of ten years. This, however, is thought by many to be an optimistic estimate. It is claimed, with a great deal of truth, that the whole question of illiteracy is closely bound up with the economic conditions of the people. In the Portuguese countryside life is hard, and as most of the families on the soil can ill spare the labour supplied by the children, it is highly probable that regular school attendance will be very difficult to enforce.

7. <u>Colonial Policy</u>. A new organic law has been enacted, replacing the old "Colonial Act". The Colonies, henceforth to be known as "Overseas Territories", do appear to receive a certain very limited measure of local administrative autonomy. It is possible, even probable, that the Government has aimed at introducing, in however modest a scale, a new element of elasticity into the relations between the Colonies and the Mother Country. But the truth is that the Corporative Chamber so amended the project, that, save for a few minor details, things remain much the same as in the days of the Colonial Act. Indeed, the only

alteration worth noting is that, for the future, the members of the Administrative Councils advising the Colonial Governors will be more numerous – which probably means more jobs to be distributed.

8. The foregoing comments refer to the African Colonies. In Goa there would appear to be a real advance in the according of administrative autonomy. This is claimed to be in recognition of the superiority of the Indian over the Negro culture and civilisation, but one cannot help feeling that Indian military power combined with Indian proximity and the desire to placate the pro-Indian elements within the gates, were not factors that were completely ignored by the Portuguese authorities [...].

142
Ofício, Encarregado de Negócios irlandês em Lisboa ao Secretário-Geral do DEA: Lisboa, 6 de Julho de 1953[48]

I have the honour to inform you that the Indian Legation here closed on the 10th ult. The Chargé d'Affaires has been recalled having first been assigned a Mission in Geneva which is not expected to last more than a few weeks.

Mr. Kewal Singh, the Chargé d'Affaires, told me privately that his Government had originally opened a Legation here (Nov. 1949) solely for the purpose of negotiating the return to India of the Portuguese territories in India – Goa, Damão and Diu. The three and half years which have elapsed since then absolutely no progress has been made [sic], no answers having been vouchsafed to the various Indian notes on the subject. In these circumstances the Indian Government has come to the conclusion that the continued existence of the Legation is not justified and that "other methods" must be tried. What those "other methods" may be he did not say but it is obvious that even without resorting to actual force, the Indian Government has ample means at its disposal to exert pressure which in time must prove irresistible. A glance at the map suffices to see how hopeless

---

[48] NAI, DEA, 313/11B Confidential reports from Lisbon Legation, 1952-1954.

would become the Portuguese position should India really decide that the time for action had arrived.

Here the press has been heel-tapping the juridical and other claims of Portugal to the territories in question. From the point of view of international law the Portuguese position is evidently unassailable, but in the last analysis international law – should such a thing really exist – has little to do with this question. Some Portuguese authorities are perfectly alive to this fact, but the Government as a while seems to me "untraitable". They have over a long period so loudly proclaimed the union between the Fatherland and the Indian Colonies, that they have become prisoners of their own propaganda and it would take all of Salazar's immense prestige backed by a sustained full-scale publicity campaign to sell to the country the unpalatable fact that the Indian Possessions must sooner or later go. I feel that if they were realistic the Portuguese Government should strain every nerve to come to an agreement with their enemy while they are in the way of it. If they were to do so even now Nehru would by quite prepared to give them a face-saving compensation – favourable trade treaty, special recognition of their spiritual influence, etc. etc. – whereas if they maintain their opposition they will lose their Colonies anyhow and get nothing but humiliation in return.

O'Kelly de Gallagh

143
Ofício, Embaixador irlandês junto da Santa Sé ao Secretário-Geral do DEA: Roma, 3 de Agosto de 1953[49]

SECRET

I read Count Kelly's report (copy received in the bag this morning) of his talk with Kewal Singh, concerning Goa.

You will have read the speech made by Salazar on the 10th July, a mixture of lament and an audacious piece of imperialism, as bad as any British example: "We

---

[49] NAI, DEA, 313/11B Confidential reports from Lisbon Legation, 1952-1954.

cannot, whether with or without a plebiscite, negotiate the cession or transfer of a fraction of Portuguese territory"!

Alas! the Holy See has had a finger in the pie, and the Holy Father, on the 28th June, with a solemn letter, conferred the Golden Rose on the See and Basilica of Goa.

The Portuguese Government, no doubt, kept on pressing for some honour for the Portuguese Archbishop of Goa, their disgraceful attempts to have him made Cardinal, instead of Gracias, having failed.

The real purpose of the move was to consolidate the Portuguese hold on this portion of Indian territory. It is, indeed, most regrettable that the Holy See has once more allowed itself to be used for ulterior political purposes. St. Francis Xavier had waited quite a long time for this Rose without perfume, and, no doubt, he could have well done without it.

Of course, this action of the Holy See does Catholicism much harm in India, where the Church could easily run the risk of being considered an adjunct of imperialism.

J. P. Walshe

144
Ofício, Encarregado de Negócios irlandês em Lisboa ao Secretário-Geral do DEA: Lisboa, 10 de Agosto de 1953[50]

Further to my previous reports concerning the "building up" of General Craveiro Lopes, the President of the Portuguese Republic, I have the honour to inform you that quite an event has been made of the second anniversary of his assumption of office, two years ago, yesterday, Sunday the 9th. The papers contain column-long lists of the personalities who called to pay their respects to the President. There was no reception properly so called. Only very few Chefs de Mission are mentioned as having called, and I presume that the reason of their being so few was that they knew nothing about it. That was certainly the case with me.

---

[50] NAI, DEA, 313/11B Confidential reports from Lisbon Legation, 1952-1954.

The occasion was marked by the solemn conferring on the President of the collar of the Order of the Holy Sepulchre, by the Cardinal Patriarch of Lisbon acting on behalf of the Grand Master of the Order, Cardinal Nicolas Canali. The Cardinal Patriarch, accompanied by the Chef de Protocol, with a motorised escort of the Guarda Nacional Republicana, drove from the Patriarchate Palace to the Palace of Belém where the ceremony took place.

O'Kelly de Gallagh

145
Apontamento, Embaixador irlandês em Londres ao Secretário-Geral do DEA: Londres, 4 de Setembro de 1953[51]

I see a report dated the 7th August from the Legation at Lisbon about a new Portuguese Ambassador (Pereira) who has been appointed here.

Is this by any chance the nice fellow whom you knew rather well when you were in Washington and whom I met when I was there in 1947?

Yours sincerely,
F. H. Boland

146
Apontamento, Secretário-Geral do DEA ao Embaixador irlandês em Londres: Dublin, 7 de Setembro de 1953[52]

I have your note of 4th September about the new Portuguese Ambassador in London. Yes, Pereira is the man whom you met in Washington. As I recollect, he was "tall, dark, and handsome"!

Sincerely yours,
Séan Nunan

---

[51] NAI, DEA, 313/11B Confidential reports from Lisbon Legation, 1952-1954.
[52] NAI, DEA, 313/11B Confidential reports from Lisbon Legation, 1952-1954.

147
Ofício manuscrito, Encarregado de Negócios irlandês em Lisboa ao Secretário-Geral do DEA: Lisboa, 15 de Setembro de 1953[53]

[...]

The Authorities here, from Dr. Salazar down, did everything in their power to make the visit pleasant, Dr. Salazar actually postponing is annual holiday at Santa Comba in order to be able to receive the Taoiseach in Lisbon, and the Foreign Minister, who was himself absent, putting his car at the Taoiseach's disposal during the whole of his stay.

Having finally come to agreement in all the arrangements I left Lisbon by car on the morning of Thursday the 10th to arrange for dinner at Tomar on the 12th and to check the lodging arrangements at Fatima for that same night. From Fatima I drove on to Coimbra to call on the Archbishop with a view to obtaining for the Taoiseach an audience next day with sister Lucia, the last survivor of the Fatima children. The Archbishop was absent, but his secretary promised to see him last night an to let me know early next morning what his decision might be. From Coimbra I drove on to Bussaco, quite close to Luso Station, where it had been arranged that the Taoiseach and his party would leave the train and proceed to Lisbon by road via Coimbra. Next morning early I phoned Coimbra and learned that the Archbishop had consented.

The Sud Express was late at Luso at 14:16 hours on Friday the 11th. It was half an hour late. At the station was the Foreign Minister's car with the chauffeur, inspector of police in mufti, and a traffic policeman on a motor cycle. Immediately the train arrived the party alighted and within five minutes we were off for Coimbra. The Taoiseach was in excellent form. Arriving in Coimbra we drove straight to the Carmelite convent where we were introduced into the parlour. In due course Sister Lucia (who speaks only Portuguese) accompanied by the Reverend Mother (who speaks English) appeared behind the grill. After a short exchange of

---

[53] NAI, DEA, 313/11B Confidential reports from Lisbon Legation, 1952-1954. Cópia deste ofício encontra-se entre o espólio de Eamon de Valera, no Arquivo do University College Dublin, entre outros ofícios e cartas relacionadas com a viagem de de Valera.

salutations, all the company retired with the exception of the Taoiseach, who remained with Sister Lucia privately, the Reverend Mother acting as interpreter.

I should add that in the Archbishop's absence we were received by his secretary who handed us two letters from the Archbishop – one for the Taoiseach, which I passed on to him, and one for myself – excusing himself for not being present in person.

After the Taoiseach's interview with Sister Lucia – approximately 15 minutes – we got into the car again and headed for Lisbon, stopping twice en route – once to visit Batalha, and again to have tea at a wayside inn near Alcobaça.

We reached Lisbon about 8.45. There the press and the photographers were in force and the Taoiseach had to face many cameras and answer many questions. I would stress straight away that the press coverage was excellent and that the reception given to the Taoiseach in the papers was all that could be desired, though some of the photographs taken in Fatima were in more than doubtful taste. I enclose herewith such press cuttings as I have received to date.

On Saturday the 12th, at 10 o'clock we called on Dr. Salazar at his official residence adjoining the National Assembly building. The interview lasted about an hour. On arriving, the Taoiseach's party was presented to Dr. Salazar who put them in the hands of an English-speaking official of the Portuguese F.O. – Sr. Vasco Pinto – who showed them round the garden while he – Dr. Salazar – conversed with the Taoiseach in one of the ground floor reception rooms. I acted as interpreter.

After the interview the Taoiseach's party again shook hands with Dr. Salazar, photographs were taken and we drove off to call on the President of the Republic at Belém. After signing the book we next visited the Irish Dominican convent at Bom Sucesso where the nuns, and, incidentally, all the Fathers of Corpo Santo received the Taoiseach with great enthusiasm. The visit lasted about half an hour. It was followed by a visit to the famous Lisbon coach museum and by a call to the Chancery of the Legation, where the existing staff – Mr Mascarenhas – was presented. (Madame Martins, as I have informed you in a previous letter, is in hospital, for an operation in the course of which they removed some 230 stones from various internal organs. And that is reason why I am sending you this letter in manuscript).

From the Chancery we drove to the Legation for lunch, followed by numerous press interviews.

About 5 o'clock we left for Fatima by car, dining en route at Tomar. We reached Fatima about 10 o'clock, and after taking up the quarters I had prepared at the two Dominican establishments there joined the procession that was just about to start around the esplanade in front of the basilica which concluded with benediction from the dais at the head of the basilica steps. We got to bed about 2 o'clock. On Sunday morning the 13th we heard Mass and received Holy Communion at the Shrine. Mass was celebrated by Fr. O'Doherty at 8:20, this being the only time I had been able to book when making the advance arrangements. After Mass breakfast at the Dominican nuns' hostel, followed at 10:30 by procession around the esplanade. Then Missa Cantata by the Bishop of Evora on the dais in front of the Basilica. We were placed in the porch of the Basilica, with our backs to the Church – consequently behind the open air altar – with the Bishop of Leiria, who is 82 years old and infirm, in a bath [?] chair in the front row, facing outward. There was a sermon of which I did not understand much. At the end of Mass, there was Benediction of the Blessed Sacrament, the monstrance used being that presented by Ireland some three years ago. At the end the Blessed Sacrament was borne solemnly round among the numerous sick and infirm lined up at the foot of the steps of the Basilica. Doctor de Valera carried the white and gold umbrella used in lieu of a canopy. The Taoiseach was invited to come in front of the altar and the sign of the cross was made over him with the monstrance. Afterwards the Bishop of Leiria, still in his chair, addressed the Congregation – estimated at about 100,000 – spoke about the Taoiseach in moving terms and concluded by offering up three Hail Marys for Ireland.

The procession carrying the statue of Our Lady – which had opened the ceremonial – reformed – and finally reached the Shrine where the statue was replaced on its pedestal. The Taoiseach and his party followed immediately after the Bishop of Leiria. After a few moments of silent prayer the ceremony closed and the Congregation dispersed. Our party walked across to the hostel at the left of the esplanade (facing the Basilica) where the Bishop of Leiria entertained us to lunch. I should add that His Lordship manifested very great good-will in being present at all in Fatima – his residence in Leiria is some 24 kilometres away – and his action is to be considered a very real tribute to the Taoiseach.

Immediately after lunch we went to visit the parents of the Fatima children. They live quite close by. I had already met them at a previous visit to Fatima. After that we headed for home, where we arrived, after a short break for tea, at about 7 o'clock. Waiting for the Taoiseach at the Legation was King Humberto [sic] of Italy, the American Ambassador and Mrs Juggwhine, and Mr. Pulido Garcia, head of the Lisbon Municipal Gardens. King Humberto and the American Ambassador had both expressed a desire to meet the Taoiseach and Mr. Garcia was invited so as to make arrangements for visiting parts of Lisbon the next day. Dinner at the Legation.

Monday 14th

The morning was spent visiting the Estufa Fria and the Castelo San Jorge under the guidance of Mr. Garcia. We all lunched at the Legation together with the Corpo Santo Fathers. After lunch the Taoiseach received a delegation of the Holy Ghost Fathers, while I took Dr. and Mrs de Valera Junior downtown to do some shopping. The rest of the afternoon was spent quietly until we left for the airport about 7.30 where we were met by a representative of Dr. Salazar and a representative of the Minister for Foreign Affairs. There were further press interviews, photographs and a farewell message by the Taoiseach on the National Radio. Also telegrams were sent by the Taoiseach to Dr. Salazar and to the Foreign Minister thanking them all for all the kindness shown.[54] The Taoiseach and his party finally boarded the plane at 8.45 and it immediately took off.

---

[54] Telegrama, De Valera para Salazar.

10103 Lisboa Aeroporto 160 14/9/1953 20:26

BEFORE LEAVING PORTUGAL I WANT TO EXPRESS TO YOUR EXCELLENCY OUR VERY DEEP APPRECIATION OF YOUR COURTESY IN RECEIVING US AND OF YOUR KINDNESS IN POSTPONING YOUR HOLIDAY TO DO SO. WE HAVE ENJOYED OUR VISIT VERY MUCH AND OUR ONE REGRET IS THAT IT HAS BEEN SO SHORT. YOU KNOW THAT WE WISH WELL TO THE PORTUGUESE NATION AND OUR PRAYER IS THAT IT MAY CONTINUE TO ADVANCE AND PROSPER AND THAT YOU MAY LONG BE SPARED TO GUIDE ITS DESTINY

EAMON DE VALERA

Next morning I wrote letters of appreciation and thanks to the Archbishop of Coimbra, the Bishop of Leiria and to the Very Reverend Father Sylvari, Vicar--General of the Dominicans in Portugal, who was a veritable tower of strength to the party in Fatima.

I must apologise for sending you this letter in manuscript, but, owing to the sickness of Madame Martins, I have nobody to type it for me. The present position in the Chancery is chaotic and I fear it will be long before it ceases to be so.

O'Kelly de Gallagh

148
Ofício, Encarregado de Negócios irlandês em Lisboa ao Secretário-Geral do DEA: Lisboa, 10 de Novembro de 1953[55]

I have the honour to inform you that the Government's interest in sport is manifested by the announcement that it will pay for the training and other expenses of the swimmer Baptista Pereira who next summer will attempt to swim the English Channel. He has recently broken the record for the Straits of Gibraltar. This looks like prestige-hunting gone crazy. Imponderables, by definition, cannot be weighed, but I feel the money could be better expended.

O'Kelly de Gallagh

149
Ofício, Encarregado de Negócios irlandês em Lisboa ao Secretário-Geral do DEA: Lisboa, 21 de Novembro de 1953[56]

I have the honour to enclose herewith, in duplicate, a report on the general elections held in Portugal on the 8th of November.

O'Kelly de Gallagh

---

[55] NAI, DEA, 313/11B Confidential reports from Lisbon Legation, 1952-1954.
[56] NAI, DEA, 313/11B Confidential reports from Lisbon Legation, 1952-1954.

Report dated 21 November, 1953 from Legation at Lisbon
Portuguese Elections, November 1953

The most striking feature of the elections of November 8th is undoubtedly the fact that for the first time the União Nacional and the opposition met face to face at the polling booths.

In point of fact, though the opposition, which previously to 1945, had been systematically excluded from all political life, had since then regularly manifested itself in each electoral campaign, this is the first time that it actually went to the polls. Prior to that date all the opposition candidates, either at the general elections or at the Presidential elections, had invariable withdrawn their candidature at the last minute – declaring, with some show of truth, it must be conceded, that the cards were stacked against them.

In any attempt to analyse the political activity of the opposition parties in Portugal there are three points which must be kept in view:

1) The existence of political parties is not authorised under the Constitution;
2) No political activity of any kind is permitted without the sanction of the authorities; and
3) The supporters of the régime are all enrolled in the União Nacional which, having Dr. Salazar at its head, is to all interests and purposes a "parti unique".

From the foregoing it is clear that the opposition remains more or less outlawed and can only manifest itself during electoral campaigns. Lacking effective organisation, lacking a general staff, virtually without a press of its own – the "REPÚBLICA" is about the only daily at its disposal – lacking, so it claims, real freedom of speech, exercising not the smallest influence on the course of public affairs, it is obvious that when an election comes it faces certain defeat.

The result of this election as of all previous elections was a foregone conclusion and if, in the circumstances, the opposition this time decided to go to the polls, it was purely for strategic reasons.

A) They felt that they should not continue to discourage their supporters who were beginning to show signs of growing weary of the repeated last minute withdrawals of their candidates.

B) The technique of abstention being associated in the public mind with leftist, more particularly communist elements, it was felt desirable to disassociate the moderate opposition from this contamination.
C) They hoped to sap the position of the União Nacional by forcing it to exhibit in public the dissensions inevitable in any organisation grouping as numerous divergent elements as it groups.
D) They hoped to assert themselves by manifesting the existence of an opposition supported by an appreciable body of public opinion.

[…]

The leaders who directed the strategy of the opposition – that is to say of that section which went to the polls – were really men of standing. First may be mentioned Mr. Cunha Leal, former Prime Minister, and a veteran politician. Next António Sérgio, high-priest of cooperativism and ardent protagonist of democratic principles both in the political and economic fields; and finally the retired General Norton de Matos. His personality is well known, particularly since his candidature at the last Presidential Elections. He is the typical continental democrat, anti--clerical – indeed anti-Christian might be the more suitable epithet – and associated with everything that was most nefarious in the discredited Republican régime of thirty years ago. He is or was an able administrator and seems to have been a success as High Commissioner in Angola many years ago. He is in favour of what he styles the "legal coup d'état" and wants the proclamation of a "third" Republic. He is 81 years old.

A star of a slightly lesser magnitude in the opposition galaxy is Mr. Rolão Preto. A curious recruit this one-time fervent supporter of Salazar and chief of the "blue-shirts" – an almost nazi movement. He has travelled a long way back the political road since then and now proclaims his belief in what he terms the "reconquest of political liberty".

In themselves the political aspirations expressed by these paladins during the electioneering campaign are of little consequence. They certainly contain nothing new. What is of significance is that they were all united in clamouring for a change in the constitution – or at least for its interpretation "in a democratic sense." Indeed it is the leit-motif of all the opposition parties that the régime must change its political methods and adopt a democratic formula – the acceptance of opposition parties.

On this issue the classic "non possumus" of the Government was proclaimed by every Government speaker during the elections. Mr. Marcello Caetano, the Father of the Constitution, and now considered by many as the heir apparent of the régime, was quite definite on the subject. The Constitution is intangible. It must be accepted as it stands and not be made an issue at every election.

(How far the idea of the intangibility of a written Constitution of very recent origin can be impressed on the minds of an electorate more than half illiterate and still in a terribly retarded state of political evolution is another point. But it would appear to be a fundamental point (as far as the durability of the régime is concerned).)

[…]

Another perhaps not insignificant feature of the recent electoral campaign as compared with previous campaigns, is the place given in it to the question of Foreign Affairs. In previous elections the accent was almost altogether on questions of internal politics. This time, however, the opposition found it expedient to raise the issue of Foreign Affairs and to wonder how a Government "fundamentally anti-democratic" could find it in its heart to sign the Atlantic Pact – "a union of free and democratic states pledged by treaty to defend liberty and democracy" – "two ideologies basically indissoluble". The point is obviously a good debating point, but I cannot conceive that it would have much popular appeal in a country where very few outside the liberal professions know or care tuppence about foreign affairs.

[…]

The figures for the three districts in which the opposition took part are as follows:

	Registered Voters	União Nacional	Opposition
Lisbon	211,675	105,852	21,204
Oporto	134,445	70,989	15,831
Aveiro	77,341	41,450	6,738

[…]

Editorials in all the Portuguese Press, including the opposition evening paper REPÚBLICA, are full of praise as to how citizens performed their duties in such an orderly quiet manner, that so many persons turned up to vote, that there was an opposition, and they come to the conclusion that the real winner of the day was: The Country.

[…]

On the whole the opposition is pleased with the results. Their leaders are supposed to be requesting that their organisations be allowed to exist on a permanent basis. The Government's reply may take some time to come, but the opposition express little hope that their request be granted.

[…]

It is noteworthy that the principle elements of the opposition are recruited from the intelligentsia – the liberal professions – doctors, lawyers, journalists etc. Those are the very elements who in days gone by in Portugal profited by the advantage given to them by reason of their education over the amorphous mass of their illiterate compatriots, whom they shamefully exploited in every manner possible, with not the slightest thought of the public weal when it conflicted with their own financial interests. That among these elements there may be some single-minded and honest men is more possible that probable, but the bulk of them appear to be blood brothers of the French politicians of the fourth French Republic.

That is not to say that their accusations against the present régime of corruption in administration and of electoral sharp practice are devoid of all foundation. There has been corruption and there has been sharp practice, but the incidence of both has been so scandalously exaggerated by the opposition as to render their accusations false and one cannot escape the conclusion that it is not righteous wrath that inspires their strictures so much as a feeling of chronic frustration that their educational pre-eminence in a land of analphabetism is no longer a justification for robbing the national hen roost. When one compares their record and the record of their kith wherever they have had a free hand in any country in Europe, with the record of the Salazar régime here, their complete ineptitude is manifest for all to see.

Was there any real election rigging? Undoubtedly there was – though it was certainly not on a big scale. And my personal conviction is that it was both stupid and unnecessary, because if the elections had been as free as air the ultimate result – even as regards figures – would have been much the same.

O'Kelly de Gallagh

150
Ofício, Encarregado de Negócios irlandês em Lisboa ao Secretário-Geral do DEA: Lisboa, 25 de Novembro de 1953[57]

I have the honour to inform you that following an announcement made in the press that a sum of £325,000 had been earmarked for the construction of cooperative cellars in various parts of the country for the purpose of testing and improving the quality of Portuguese wines. The Minister for the Economy has issued a statement on the 19th inst. to the effect that an initial sum of £12,500 is to be spent on studying those wines which are considered suitable for the international market. The idea is to constitute reserves of Portuguese wines for selling abroad – wines that will be uniform in quality and produced by the most careful and sanitary methods. It is stated that the first wines to be so studied will be those of the Dão region.

While such an initiative is clearly all to the good I personally doubt the success of the venture which depends for its success on a meticulousness on the handling both of the grape and of the wine itself which I believe to be quite foreign to the Portuguese temperament. The raw materials are there, but the 'know-how' is lacking and this lack is not recognised by the producers themselves or by the local authorities.

O'Kelly de Gallagh

---

[57] NAI, DEA, Embassy Lisbon, 6/11, Portugal: Foreign Trade, 1945-1953.

151
Ofício, Encarregado de Negócios irlandês em Lisboa ao Secretário-Geral do DEA: Lisboa, 22 de Dezembro de 1953[58]

I have the honour to inform you that on Monday the 14th, the mortal remains of Sidónio Pais, a former President of the Portuguese Republic, were taken from the crypt of the Jerónimos Monastery to be finally buried within the Chapel of this same Monastery. President Sidónio Pais was assassinated 35 years ago at the Rossio Railway Station while about to depart on an official voyage to Oporto. He outlined, in the year that he was in power, a system of Government which can in a way be compared to what happened when Dr. Salazar came to power, by which Governments were not always at risk of falling by decisions of Parliament. At the ceremony which I attended, the President of the Republic and the whole Government were present as well as most of the Diplomatic Corps.

Sidónio Pais is generally considered a precursor of the present régime and his glorification is in line with the general policy of broadening the base of that régime. Though notoriously a freemason, I have heard him described by a priest as "a good freemason".

O'Kelly de Gallagh

1954

152
Ofício, Encarregado de Negócios irlandês em Lisboa ao Secretário-Geral do DEA: Lisboa, 6 de Janeiro de 1954[59]

I have the honour to inform you that it is reported from the Vatican that for the Marian Year of 1954, Sister Lucia dos Santos will make a pilgrimage to Rome.

---

[58] NAI, DEA, 313/11B Confidential reports from Lisbon Legation, 1952-1954.
[59] NAI, DEA, 313/11B Confidential reports from Lisbon Legation, 1952-1954.

(Note: Sister Lucia dos Santos is the only survivor of the three children that saw the Apparitions of Our Lady of Fatima in 1917. She is in the Franciscan Convent of Coimbra, where the Taoiseach visited her last September.)

O'Kelly de Gallagh

153
Ofício, Encarregado de Negócios irlandês em Lisboa ao Secretário-Geral do DEA: Lisboa, 20 de Março de 1954[60]

I have the honour to inform you that documents were signed to-day in the Ministry of Economy authorising work to start on the erection of the largest thermal (coal) electric power generating station ever built here. The new power station will be situated along the Douro river near Oporto, and will have a capacity of 250 million kilowatts; it will cost £2,245,000. It is to be a private enterprise with Government participation and is part of the Six-Year Development Plan alluded to in many of my previous reports. The Empresa Termo-Eléctrica Portuguesa, as the company is called, has been created principally to provide electric power when power fails from the various hydro-electric installations after long periods of drought. Coal mines exist very near to where the new plant will be built. The Minister of Economy, Dr. Ulisses Cortês, said the power problem for Portugal is now solved and that two other problems will next be tackled, that of the Iron and Steel Industry and that of the complementary industries of electro-chemistry.

O'Kelly de Gallagh

154
Ofício, Encarregado de Negócios irlandês em Lisboa ao Secretário-Geral do DEA: Lisboa, 5 de Abril de 1954[61]

I have the honour to inform you that Engineer José Frederico Ulrich, former Minister of Public Works, and the other members of the recently created Nuclear Energy Board, were formally installed by Dr. Oliveira Salazar.

---

[60] NAI, DEA, 313/11B Confidential reports from Lisbon Legation, 1952-1954.
[61] NAI, DEA, 313/11B Confidential reports from Lisbon Legation, 1952-1954.

The Prime Minister made a short speech, but what he said was of no international importance and had no political significance. Dr. Salazar said that Portugal was late, compared to other countries, in setting up an organisation for the study of nuclear questions, but that present and future Portuguese investigators would now be able to follow the movement of research that is proceeding in the World concerning these questions with the help of the modest resources at their disposal. The Premier mentioned that Portugal's main interest was for when nuclear energy could be used as a source of power, once the spirit of fear had diminished and peoples could live peacefully together. He said that Portugal had another interest in it, which was perhaps an act of Providence; "this country which is so poor in the known sources of energy such as coal, mineral oils, and even water-power, must mobilise the potential sources that we seem to possess here and in the overseas territories".

A British-owned mining company at Urgeiriça produced uranium. According to an article published some time ago in the US Magazine "NUCLEONICS", the Urgeiriça mines are one of the seven major uranium deposits in the World today. It is also very probable from surveys already made that uranium will be found in Angola near the Belgian Congo.

O'Kelly de Gallagh

155
Ofício, Encarregado de Negócios irlandês em Lisboa ao Secretário-Geral do DEA, Lisboa, 9 de Abril de 1954[62]

I have the honour to enclose herewith text of a Note[63] circularised by the Political Section of the Portuguese Foreign Office on the recent incidents in India.

It is an objective statement which I believe to be strictly factual. Juridically the Portuguese case is a cast-iron case, but it appears to me that in taking her stand purely on juridical grounds Portugal is lacking in realism. Nehru's attitude is that of

---
[62] NAI, DEA, 313/11B Confidential reports from Lisbon Legation, 1952-1954.
[63] Incluído com o ofício.

a bully and his methods are strangely reminiscent of the fable of the Wolf and the Lamb, but, whatever the ethics of the case, the facts are that India wants Goa; that she can put up a plausible case for its integration in the Indian Union; and that she has overwhelming force at her command should she care to use it.

Talking over the matter with Dr. Paulo Cunha – the Foreign Minister – yesterday I found that his attitude was that, though they knew that they could not hope to prevail in a show-down, they were prepared for it. "If Nehru attacks us then the mask will be off and he will appear for what he is – a bullying imperialist. The fear of this result may deter him for a while, but if and when he does attack, though we cannot hope to defeat him, we will give a good account of ourselves."

At this juncture I alluded to the Wolf and the Lamb fable and Dr. Cunha liked the comparison and nodded emphatic approval. I felt tempted to point out that the end of the story was the demise of the lamb who, had he moved away in time instead of arguing the point, might have lived longer. But I refrained from doing so, firstly because it was not my business to do so, and secondly because one cannot help sympathising with the gallantry of the Portuguese attitude, though the needless and ultimately useless loss of life which that attitude will eventually involve is tragic in the extreme. Its [sic] all very well to be able to say that "tout est perdu – hors l'honneur" but that is poor consolation for the maimed survivors and for the widows and orphans left behind.

O'Kelly de Gallagh

156
Ofício, Encarregado de Negócios irlandês em Lisboa ao Secretário-Geral do DEA: Lisboa, 15 de Abril de 1954[64]

I have the honour to inform you that Dr. Salazar made a 3,700-word speech on Monday the 12th entitled "GOA AND THE INDIAN UNION".[65]

---

[64] NAI, DEA, 313/11B Confidential reports from Lisbon Legation, 1952-1954.

[65] Ofício inclui texto do discurso.

The speech was broadcast by all the Portuguese radio stations, and sent out by short-wave to all Portuguese overseas territories. The speech is rather long, it took Dr. Salazar thirty-five minutes to read it [...]

The text that I am hereby enclosing is the Official English text handed to the Press by the Secretariado Nacional de Informação, and translated in the Ministry of Foreign Affairs.

I am informed that the British Government, and possibly the American Government, had advanced notice of the contents of the speech. In any event it is interesting to note that Teotónio Pereira, the Portuguese Ambassador in London, visited Lisbon a few days ago before the speech and saw Eden in London immediately on his return there before the broadcast was delivered.

O'Kelly de Gallagh

157
Ofício, Encarregado de Negócios irlandês em Lisboa ao Secretário-Geral do DEA: Lisboa, 9 de Maio de 1954[66]

I have the honour to inform you that various ceremonies took place at the Shrine of Our Lady of Fatima under the Presidency of the Cardinal Patriarch of Lisbon. Already pilgrims are on the roads to Fatima for the first big pilgrimage of the year on May 13th.

As a guest of the Defence Minister, Colonel Santos Costa and Mrs Costa, the Spanish Minister for War, General Muñoz Grandes and his wife will arrive by plane on May 12th, to take part in the pilgrimage of the 13th. General Grandes will return to Madrid the following day.

O'Kelly de Gallagh

---

[66] NAI, DEA, 313/11B Confidential reports from Lisbon Legation, 1952-1954.

158
Ofício, Encarregado de Negócios irlandês em Lisboa ao Secretário-Geral do DEA: Lisboa, 10 de Maio de 1954[67]

I have the honour to inform you that it is announced that a "Palácio do Ultramar" (Palace of the Overseas Territories) is to be erected at Belém, near the Monastery of the Jerónimos. Construction will start next year on the "L" shaped building which will cover 4 hectares and have a tower 77-metres high. Lifts will take visitors to promenades 42 and 64-metres-high over-looking the Tagus and the western parts of Lisbon. The building will contain everything to demonstrate the importance, extent and richness of the Portuguese overseas provinces.

O'Kelly de Gallagh

159
Ofício, Encarregado de Negócios irlandês em Lisboa ao Secretário-Geral do DEA: Lisboa, 20 de Maio de 1954[68]

I have the honour to inform you that Professor Marcello Caetano, president of the Corporative Chamber, flew to Madrid to preside over the Portuguese delegation at the II Congress of the "Latin Union" which is taking place there.

Note: A few years ago Prof. Caetano was generally tipped as the logical successor to Dr. Salazar, but later this idea seems to have lost ground; no other names have been put forward.

O'Kelly de Gallagh

---

[67] NAI, DEA, 313/11B Confidential reports from Lisbon Legation, 1952-1954.
[68] NAI, DEA, 313/11B Confidential reports from Lisbon Legation, 1952-1954.

160
Ofício, Encarregado de Negócios irlandês em Lisboa ao Secretário-Geral do DEA: Lisboa, 25 de Outubro de 1954[69]

I have the honour to send you by the same bag two copies of the review "PORTUGAL" for July and August issued by the National Secretariat for Information.

As might be expected, this issue is chiefly concerned with the Goa question, indeed the whole space from page 12 to page 66 being exclusively devoted to it. It concludes on a quotation from Ghandi which certainly is very telling.

Since my return I have avoided discussing the matter with any official personalities and I am glad to say that so far I have seen no sign of resentment concerning our attitude in the matter. I'm sure the authorities here understand our position, better perhaps, than Dr. Brazão did.

O'Kelly de Gallagh

161
Ponto da situação sobre a questão da Índia Portuguesa, para consulta interna do DEA, 29 de Outubro de 1954[70]

Cover No. 18   29 October 1954

Portuguese Possessions in India
[...]

Official démarches by Portuguese Chargé d'Affaires in Dublin

The then Portuguese Chargé d'Affaires, Dr. Brazão, made a number of démarches in July-August 1954 with the object of obtaining a message of support or sympathy from the Government on the subject of Portugal's occupation of Goa and other Indian territories. No message was in fact given, however, and

---

[69] NAI, DEA, 313/11B Confidential reports from Lisbon Legation, 1952-1954.
[70] NAI, DEA, 313/11B Confidential reports from Lisbon Legation, 1952-1954.

the Chargé d'Affaires was reminded in this connection of the state of public opinion in Ireland with regard to foreign occupations.

It should be mentioned in this connection that in 1952 when we took exception to the visits of Portuguese naval craft to Derry, the Portuguese Foreign Minister, Dr. Paulo Cunha, told the Chargé d'Affaires at Lisbon that Portugal was in a singularly weak position to question officially Britain's claim to sovereignty over the Six Counties as long as Portugal had British support over Goa and the other Portuguese territories in India – these territories being to India in virtually the same relationship as the Six Counties are to Ireland. This Portuguese reaction was borne in mind in the Department on the occasion of the recent Portuguese démarches but was not explicitly referred to as a reason for the decision taken.

Press Comment in Ireland

The IRISH TIMES in an editorial on 9th August said that admittedly the position of Goa was anomalous, perhaps even ridiculous, but her very loneliness coupled with her long tradition as a centre of Christianity in Asia made a unique appeal. Sooner or later in the nature of things, the paper added, Goa was bound to submerged into the great mass of sub-continent investing her.

The IRISH PRESS in an editorial of 6th August 1954, stated that the Indian claim to sovereignty over Goa was a fair one. The editor suggested that peaceful negotiation was the only appropriate method for settling the dispute.

The IRISH INDEPENDENT in an editorial on 16th August said that there was room for sympathy with both sides in the dispute and that it could only be hoped that the scandal of an open clash between two pacific nations could somehow be averted.

In a statement to the press published on 14th August 1954, Dr. Eduardo Brazão stated that the Indian Government was completely misrepresenting the facts in its news bulletins on the state of affairs in Portuguese India. The Chargé d'Affaires traced the history of the territories, stating that Goa, Damão and Diu were conquered from the Moors, then the traditional enemies, and not the Indians. He outlined the role of the Jesuit and other missionaries in Goa which became the centre of Christianisation, conducted by the Portuguese in the immense lands given by Pope Alexander VI to be conquered for God. Inter-

-marriage, a common language and a common religion had integrated Portuguese-Indian territories in Portugal.

[…]

Comment by Political Section

(i) <u>SEATO</u>

It seems likely that the increase in tension regarding Goa is related to the South East Asia Treaty. This Treaty has been under negotiation since May of this year and was signed in Manila in September by eight countries: United States, Britain, France, Australia, New Zealand, Pakistan, the Philipinnes and Thailand. The Portuguese Prime Minister, Dr. Salazar, in April last offered to give precise undertakings to the effect that Goa would never be used as a base for hostile operations against India. But India is opposed to SEATO and no dout feels that as long as a European power, like Portugal, holds territory in the sub-continent of India, there is some risk that the enclave will be used militarily for the implementation of Far Eastern policies which India does not endorse and which in her opinion may jeopardise peace in the Far East. The natural harbour of Mormugão in Goa could be used as a supply and trooping point in the event of a crisis even though India herself might well be neutral in the particular issue involved. A comparable example is the French use of Pondicherry and the Pakistan airfields during the war in Indochina.

(ii) <u>War</u>

Does the present tension in Goa represent an armed threat to world peace? While international deputies involving armed conflict anywhere may be said to threaten peace everywhere, nevertheless Goa does not appear to represent an immediate threat. As long as the Kashmir dispute with Pakistan is before the United Nations, India will hardly wish to take over Goa by force. The shooting has been in a very small scale. True, such Portuguese forces as are in Goa cold put up a dramatic, though ineffectual, resistance to invasion. Moreover, the various Goan action groups – e.g. the Free Goan Congress, the (Communist-led) Goan People's Party, the Pna Ja Socialists, the Goan National Congress and the United Front of Goans – are in a sense competing for attention among the Goans and Indians, and the more active they are the more publicity and popularity they may attain. Nevertheless, the Indian Government, convinced of eventual success and pledged to non-violence as a principle, may be expected to keep anti-Portuguese action within strict limits (as on 15th August) so that the risk of large-scale bloodshed is not an immediate one.

(iii) The Future

India is reported at an earlier stage to have offered Goa the status of an autonomous State within the Indian Union, maintaining strong links both with India and Portugal. The arrangement might include a customs union with India but the sovereignty of the self-governing enclave would remain. Whatever chance there might have been earlier of arriving at a solution on these general lines, both sides now seem committed to rejecting such a compromise.

The future of Goa seems to rest with India. The vernacular language, Konkani, has close affinities with Sanskrit and Marathi and is spoken by the neighbours of Goa on the Konkan coast in the State of Bombay. The majority of the inhabitants are Hindu, and India provides employment openings for the middle class of Goa and the fine natural port of Mormugão can best be developed by India, which occupies the hinterland. Goa's prospering iron and manganese mines are normally worked by Indian labour.

But, although the march of events in Asia seems to favour the eventual disappearance of the tiny enclaves, the time and manner of their incorporation in India continues to give concern, and to strain relations between important members of the non-Communist world.

162
Ofício, Encarregado de Negócios irlandês em Lisboa ao Secretário-Geral do DEA: Lisboa, 25 de Outubro de 1954[71]

I have the honour to enclose herewith translation of an interview given by His Eminence, Don Teodósio de Gouveia, Cardinal Archbishop of Lourenço Marques, to the Portuguese News Agency, on the 23rd inst.

---

[71] NAI, DEA, 305/271A Goa and other Portuguese enclaves in India, 1954-1956.

Cardinal de Gouveia, who is the only Cardinal in Africa, South of the Sahara, claimed that religious education of the Natives should precede other types of teaching. "Britain's experience in Kenya shows what happens when you try to put the cart before the horse". Likening the work of the Missionaires [sic] in Africa to the functions of an Army in time of war, the Cardinal continued:-

"Just as the military occupy a territory and are followed by an administrator to organize and develop the newly conquered land, so the White Missionary is the pioneer who occupies territory upon which he plants the Cross. But once he has marked the position occupied in the territory on behalf of Christ, before he can really reach the Native masses, he must be followed by Native Clergy".

[…]

These opinions expressed by Cardinal Gouveia have a special weight inasmuch as the Portuguese seem to be the only colonising power in Africa who have no "native" problem to face. From all I can learn from all sources the African natives in Portuguese Africa have no complaint against the occupying power. Theirs is certainly a unique case.

O'Kelly de Gallagh

163
Ofício, Embaixador irlandês junto da Santa Sé ao Secretário-Geral do DEA: Roma, 18 de Novembro de 1954[72]

With reference to form P.61 of 30th October concerning the Portuguese possessions in India, I might say that I understand from the Portuguese Ambassador that his Government is dissatisfied with the attitude of the Vatican in the matter of Goa.

He has apparently been endeavouring to enlist positive Vatican support for the Portuguese stand on this issue, but has not had much success. The view taken by the Vatican is characterized by what he calls "political realism" and it is not

---

[72] NAI, DEA, 305/271A Goa and other Portuguese enclaves in India, 1954-1956.

prepared to adopt a position which might militate against the interests of the Church in India or elsewhere. Generally speaking, he says, the Vatican line (Propaganda Fide is the determining Congregation) favours the Church in non--Christian countries like India being run by nationals and taking account of nationalist sentiment. It is thus not prepared to compromise the position of the Church in India by backing the Portuguese in Goa.

In the general context of the attitude of the Vatican towards non-Christian countries, my Portuguese Colleague called my attention to a curious reticence on the part of the "Osservatore Romano" in relation to he newly-accredited Chinese Minister. As you know it is usual when an Ambassador or Minister presents his Letters of Credence, for the "Osservatore Romano" to carry quite a lot of publicity about the event; it is generally reported very prominently on the front page, and there is generally too a photograph with a biographical note about the new representative on an inside page. The "Osservatore Romano" of 30th October carried a seven line item on the front page […]

C. C. Cremin

1955

164
Ofício, Encarregado de Negócios irlandês em Lisboa ao Secretário-Geral do DEA: Lisboa, 5 de Janeiro de 1955[73]

CONFIDENTIAL[74]

I have the honour to enclose herewith copies of the Speeches made by the Papal Nuncio and by the President of the Republic on the occasion of the New Year's Reception of the Diplomatic Corps at the Belém Palace.

---

[73] NAI, DEA, 313/11C Confidential reports from Lisbon Legation, 1955.

[74] Na margem, alguém no DEA escreveu, 'Has this word ceased to have any significance in such reports?'

The speeches are of interest when read against the background of Dr. Salazar's recent outburst against the Propaganda Fide concerning which I have already written to you. As I reported at the time, the Nuncio was in Madeira on an official tour when Salazar's speech was made and this is virtually his first public appearance since. His is a usually very affable and almost exuberant personality, but on New Year's day he seemed very piano. In his speech he went out of his way to throw bouquets at the President and the Foreign Minister for their recent voyages to South Africa and to Brazil – voyages which in themselves did not seem to call for mention in such a speech. His reference to "order and liberty" did not seem to have much point. It was not to be expected that he would refer to Goa and the Padroado, and naturally he did not do so, making only the most veiled allusion to the "ups and downs" that are the lot of Nations. It would seem, therefore, that the Holy See proposes to let Salazar's challenge drown in a bath of silence, and, indeed, an article published in the "Osservatore Romano" yesterday "The Fervour of Catholic Action in Portugal", and quoted in extense in the Government Organ of this morning, would seem to confirm this view. The article smothers Portugal in praises of its Catholic activity, going out of its way to name Salazar, as, next to Fátima, responsible therefore. Like the Nuncio's speech, this article likewise observe [sic] silence about Goa and I read the two combined as an indication that while the Holy See appreciates the Catholicism of Portugal in Portugal, it will not deviate from the line it has followed in India – and the Nuncio's speech and the Osservatore article are merely what the French call "eau bênite de cour".

The President's speech strikes in some ways a rather pathetic note. He speaks of trials ahead and moral comfort but very noticeably refrains from echoing the war-cries of Salazar's speech. It must not be forgotten that he has served in Goa as a soldier and consequently is likely to have a more realistic view of the situation there and of the futility of a last-ditch policy.

O'Kelly de Gallagh

165
Ofício, Encarregado de Negócios irlandês em Lisboa ao Secretário-Geral do DEA: Lisboa, 11 de Janeiro de 1955[75]

I have the honour to inform you that the Corporative Chamber held a special session to commemorate the 20th anniversary of its founding.

Various members spoke about the merits of the Corporative System, then the President, Professor Dr. Marcello Caetano, said that twenty years had shown the solid basis and utility of this institution. Institutions are not made for a day, but with the experience and the authority gained, and with personal interests put aside, they work for continuity with an outlook on the future. To consolidate and give more prestige to such an Institution should be the aim of statesmen who desire the continuity of that in which they believe and who wish a spirit of fertility to endure for more than the fragile duration of a human life.

The Corporative Chamber was constituted as a trial of new methods in political representation based on a study of the realities of man, of society and of the State. Those who were here in the beginning were filled with great anxieties but also with great hopes. The anxieties arising from the novelty of the conception; the hopes based upon the principles that inspired it. The passing of twenty years has dispelled our anxieties and has not killed our hopes. We know today what a Corporative Chamber should be and how to perfect it. We can define better the job it has to do. "We continue to hope that the Corporative Chamber, organised on the basis of corporations, will be called upon to exercise an ever larger and more important part in the functioning of a Corporative State."

O'Kelly de Gallagh

---

[75] NAI, DEA, 313/11C Confidential reports from Lisbon Legation, 1955.

166
Ofício, Encarregado de Negócios irlandês em Lisboa ao Secretário-Geral do DEA: Lisboa, 16 de Janeiro de 1955[76]

I have the honour to inform you that the following communiqué appeared in the DIÁRIO DA MANHÃ (the official organ) on the 14th inst. as emanating from the Minister of the Overseas Territories:-

1) "Recent legislation published in Portugal and applicable to all Portuguese territory has defined in new term the penal responsibility incurred by participation in any collective action intended to stir up public opinion or by any other activity (individual or collective) supporting claims of foreigners to separate from the Mother Country or to hand over to another country all or part of the national territory. The prison penalties attaching to such action are applicable to Portuguese and to foreigners guilty of such action on Portuguese soil, but in the case of foreigners the sentences will be less save where it is established that they came in to Portuguese territory in contravention of existing legislation.

The sentence may be served in provinces other than that in which the crime was committed. Foreigners convicted may also be expelled from the country should circumstances render such a course desirable. There is here a question of the efficient repression of crimes against the safety of the State normally considered of the utmost gravity by the national tribunals. And the measures herewith published shall not stop the Portuguese authorities from taking any measures deemed necessary to prevent the violation of its frontiers, the responsibility for the consequences of such measures laying obviously with the frontier violators.

2) It has been established that on frequent occasions recently persons have illicitly entered the territory of Portuguese India and have there committed the above mentioned acts. As there have been among such persons nationals of the Indian Union and as there are definite signs that more such acts will be committed

---

[76] NAI, DEA, 313/11C Confidential reports from Lisbon Legation, 1955.

(as a result of the deplorable propaganda and the campaigns of incitement in the Indian Union) the Portuguese Government considers it its duty to notify the New Delhi Government of the foregoing. For that purpose, the Portuguese Legation in New Delhi delivered to the Indian Ministry of External Affairs. On the 5th of January a note in which:-

A) it warned of the degree of penal responsibility incurred by Indian nationals who would henceforth persist in illicitly entering Portuguese territory and therein indulging in any or all of the above mentioned criminal activities.

B) it asked the Government of the Indian Union, in the interest of its own nationals, to make public the gravity of this penal responsibility, and, by every means in its power, to seek to prevent new movements of the so-called "Satiagrahis", or any similar movements attempting to cross the Portuguese frontier, disturbing the peace and tranquillity existing in the state of Portuguese India and exposing those guilty of these activities to severe legal sanction.

C) it informed the Indian Government, in reference to cases which have occurred before the delivery of this note (and in accordance with the legal provisions of the legislation in question) that the Portuguese Government has decided to return to the Indian frontier, without further penalty, such Indian nationals as had been previously arrested for the commission of acts mentioned in N.º 1 of the present Note."

Further the DIÁRIO DA MANHÃ announces the re-establishment of postal communications between Goa, Damão and Diu per the s/s Luabo.

A final paragraph states that UN. Debbar, who will lead the Congress Party for the next two years when he succeeds Nehru as leader next week, has declared his continuing support of the Alvarez "liberation" movement in Goa. Alvarez is the renegade Goan leader whom the Portuguese consider a traitor.

O'Kelly de Gallagh

167
Ofício, Encarregado de Negócios irlandês em Lisboa ao Secretário-Geral do DEA: 28 de Janeiro de 1955[77]

CONFIDENTIAL

I have the honour to enclose herewith the English text, in quadruplicate, of a Statement issued by the Portuguese Ministry of Foreign Affairs on the 11th inst. dealing with the notes exchanged on the Goa dispute. The appearances are that a show-down will not now be long delayed. I would be surprised were Goa in Portuguese possession at the end of the present year.

O'Kelly de Gallagh

STATEMENT FROM THE PORTUGUESE MINISTRY OF FOREIGN AFFAIRS

On January 11 last the Government of India replied to the Note whereby the Legation of Portugal in New Delhi had informed them of the legislation recently enacted in Portugal regarding the penal responsibility that so-called "Satyagrahis" incur.

In their Note of reply, which they released, the Government of India renewed their well-known and unfounded claims to the Portuguese State of India and stated that a peaceful settlement could only be reached if Portugal appreciated historical developments and the urge of the people to throw off "colonial rule". In the view of the Government of India, if Portugal refused to recognise these developments and attempted to take shelter behind legal arguments, it could only lead to a further deterioration of the situation existing in the Portuguese State of India. The Government of India, furthermore, formally refused to grant that the Portuguese Government had a right to consider as criminals, falling exclusively under the jurisdiction of the Portuguese authorities, Indians including Goans who dared to oppose Portuguese colonialism, as conditions in the Portuguese State of India are described by the Indian Government. The Indian reply ended by once again warning the Portuguese Government that if any

---

[77] NAI, DEA, 313/11C Confidential reports from Lisbon Legation, 1955.

Indians, including Goans, were sentenced to harsh terms of imprisonment or deported outside India there would be serious repercussions in the Indian Union.

In answer to this unacceptable standpoint the Legation of Portugal in New Delhi handed in a further note on January 20, worded as follows:

"The Portuguese Government saw fit to advise the Indian Government of the legal provisions henceforth applicable in Portuguese territory to so-called satyagrahis in view of the fact that those who have entered or engaged in any demonstration in the Portuguese State of India have all either been Indian nationals or proceeded from the Indian Union; and there – as is openly known – an intensive and systematic propaganda is being carried on, with the acquiescence and support of numerous responsible authorities, in order to incite Goans and Indians to break the peace and disturb law and order in the neighbouring Portuguese territories. The Portuguese Government's communication therefore was on the one hand an act of courtesy, and on the other an act of humanity inasmuch as the Government of India were being requested to let it be known, for the benefit of potential satyagrahis, what a serious responsibility the latter would incur.

It is a matter of regret to the Portuguese Government that this mere communication, made with the best of intentions, should simply have afforded the Government of India a pretext for once more publicising their reprehensible and unjustified designs of annexing the territories of a neighbour State. It must once more be stressed that the matter of these claims is one that the Portuguese Government cannot even consider […]

In formally rejecting therefore such comments and threats, the Portuguese Government cannot but bring out, yet again, the irrefutable truth that there is no colonialism in the Portuguese State of India. Nobody knows it better than the Government of India. But rather than acknowledge this truth they unfortunately seem to prefer repeating unfounded generalisations that have not the slightest relevance to the case of the Portuguese State of India, but more effectively serve the purposes of kindling and misleading Indian public opinion, purposes liable to lead to a repetition of the deplorable and unjustified acts of aggression which have already inflicted injury on Portuguese soil more than once and continue to oppress Portuguese territories [...]"

168
Ofício, Encarregado de Negócios irlandês em Lisboa ao Secretário-Geral do DEA: Lisboa, 1 de Fevereiro de 1955[78]

I have the honour to inform you that the Under-Secretary of State for Education, Dr. Veiga de Macedo, has declared that nearly 440,000 Portuguese had profited during the first two years of the Plan for Popular Education. The efforts to get more children to attend the schools have put 134,761 more of them into class-rooms and, in the two years, 304,083 adults had passed their examinations as being now able to read, write and do simple arithmetic problems.

The 1950 census of the population gave illiteracy at over 45% of the 8 ½ million inhabitants – that is to sat approximately 3,825,000. There has consequently been a drop in illiteracy of a little over 11% in these two years – a very encouraging result.

O'Kelly de Gallagh

169
Ofício, Encarregado de Negócios irlandês em Lisboa ao Secretário-Geral do DEA: Lisboa, 9 de Fevereiro de 1955[79]

I have the honour to inform you that yesterday a deputy, Dr. Augusto Cerqueira Gomes, severely criticised in the National Assembly the recent note signed by Vice-Admiral Mendes Cabeçadas and Dr. Armando Adão e Silva and handed to the President of the Republic, asking that a "Republican Movement" be allowed to exist on the same terms as does the "Monarchist Movement." He said

---

[78] NAI, DEA, 313/11C Confidential reports from Lisbon Legation, 1955.
[79] NAI, DEA, 313/11C Confidential reports from Lisbon Legation, 1955.

that the initiative does not seem to have caused a great awakening in the Country or evoked any ardent enthusiasm [...]

O'Kelly de Gallagh

170
Ofício, Encarregado de Negócios irlandês em Lisboa ao Secretário-Geral do DEA: Lisboa, 29 de Fevereiro de 1955[80]

I have the honour to inform you that Engineer José Frederico Ulrich, president of the Nuclear Energy Board, has made a statement concerning the achievements in other countries in the field of nuclear power and said that when the time comes for this new kind of power to be used in Portugal they will be prepared. It will not be in the immediate future. (The following day, Engineer Rogério Cavaca was installed as Director of the Prospection Services of the Board. He said that there were good reasons to expect that sufficient reserves of uranium would be found in Portugal for the requirements of the country).

Note:- The British-owned mine at Urgeiriça is one of the seven major uranium deposits in the World according to a past issue of "Engineer & Mining Jounal".

O'Kelly de Gallagh

171
Ofício, Encarregado de Negócios irlandês em Lisboa ao Secretário-Geral do DEA: Lisboa, 8 de Março de 1955[81]

I have the honour to inform you that under the headline "On the side of Portugal" the Madrid newspaper INFORMACIONES declares that nothing that is Portuguese can be of indifference to Spain, just as nothing Spanish can be indifferent to Portugal.

---

[80] NAI, DEA, 313/11C Confidential reports from Lisbon Legation, 1955.
[81] NAI, DEA, 313/11C Confidential reports from Lisbon Legation, 1955.

Referring to the "disrespect" that New Delhi shows for Portuguese rights in India, the paper adds that "we are more than neighbours, we are of the same family, and Spain will always be on Portugal's side in this matter." Whatever the sincerity of the sentiments expressed, I doubt that their value can ever be more than purely platonic.

O'Kelly de Gallagh

172
Ofício, Encarregado de Negócios irlandês em Lisboa ao Secretário-Geral do DEA: Lisboa, 31 de Março de 1955[82]

I have the honour to inform you that following up in the debate that was opened last week in the National Assembly on a motion for the promotion and protection of family life, a Deputy, Dr. Gastão Ferreira, declared that, as 94% of the population was Catholic, he was in favour of a pure and simple abolition of divorce; however he added that there were certain aspects of the question which would make it necessary for modifications in the divorce laws before complete abolition could be considered.

O'Kelly de Gallagh

173
Ofício, Encarregado de Negócios irlandês em Lisboa ao Secretário-Geral do DEA: Lisboa, 6 de Abril de 1955[83]

You will have seen in the press the announcement of the incitation issued by Queen Elizabeth of England to the President of the Portuguese Republic to pay a State visit to her next October. Here the visit has been headline news in all the papers and, so far as the public is concerned, was completely unexpected.

---

[82] NAI, DEA, 313/11C Confidential reports from Lisbon Legation, 1955.
[83] NAI, DEA, 313/11C Confidential reports from Lisbon Legation, 1955.

A comment I have heard, which seems credible, is that the invitation is the British counter-move to a recent visit of the Portuguese Minister for Economy to Germany – and is intended to primarily to boost [sic] trade and to bring Portugal within the orbit from which she appeared inclined to stray. There is already talk of a Presidential visit to the States and to France.

What gives verisimilitude to the diagnosis of the purpose of the British in issuing the invitation is the fact that in a contract just signed by the Portuguese National Railways for the partial electrification of their system, and the supply of rolling stock, electrical installation and equipment, the cake has been divided up among the following French, Swiss, and German firms. No British firm is mentioned:-

SOREFAME (Portuguese)
Alsthom (French)
Forges et Ateliers de Constructions Electriques de Jeumont (French)
[…]

You will also note that the automobile import figures given you in my minute 6/11 of the 23rd ult. show Germany first with Britain a very poor second.

[escrito à mão] It has just been reported that the Moçamedes Railway (Angola) has placed an order with a German firm for eight locomotives value £250,000.

O'Kelly de Gallagh

174
Ofício, Encarregado de Negócios irlandês em Lisboa ao Secretário-Geral do DEA: Lisboa, 4 de Junho de 1955[84]

I have the honour to inform you that President Craveiro Lopes returned to Lisbon this morning from his tour of the Portuguese West African Territories and of Madeira. He returned by sea on the cruiser "Bartolomeu Dias" and was received

---

[84] NAI, DEA, 313/11C Confidential reports from Lisbon Legation, 1955.

at the Belém landing stage almost directly opposite the Presidential palace. The Heads of all the Diplomatic Missions as well as the leading political and official personalities of the realm saluted him on his arrival. He came ashore at 10 o'clock, shook hands all round and then got into his car for the few hundred yards that separated him from the palace. A salute was fired by the ship's guns and a certain number of jet planes roared overhead.

The presidential car drove off through massed flags, chiefly, as far as I could observe, of civic bodies and girl guides with a certain amount of perfunctory clapping. There was no spontaneous popular manifestation such as would certainly have marked the occasion had it been Marshal Carmona that was returning. The building up of the present President is a slow process and the public, so far, have shown no signs if taking him to its bosom.

O'Kelly de Gallagh

175
Carta do Encarregado de Negócios português em Dublin ao Ministro dos Negócios Estrangeiros irlandês (Liam Cosgrave): Dublin, 15 de Junho de 1955[85]

Excellency,

The differendum between the Indian Union and Portugal about the so-called "Case of Goa" has reached a point so serious that I believe it requires a great deal of the attention of those who are entrusted with the guidance of international affairs in their respective countries.

Your Excellency and the Department of External Affairs are certainly aware of the declared attitude and actions of both mentioned countries. Nevertheless, there are facts, that, though grave as they are, have not been appearing in the press non obstant being potentially laden with enormous danger for humanity at large. For this reason, I have the honour to enclose herewith a resumé of some

---

[85] NAI, DEA, 305/271A Goa and other Portuguese enclaves in India, 1954-1956.

of these facts, showing the change of policy by the Government of the Indian Union which may cause grave complications.

The Portuguese Government has, since the beginning and on many occasions, asserted the firm decision of Portugal to resist aggression. And, at this moment, I feel it is my duty to inform Your Excellency that my country will most certainly resist the new form of aggression put into practice by the Indian Government, which I think can only be efficaciously avoided as far as a moderating action can be exercised in time by other countries and international public opinion.

I believe I should also let Your Excellency know that the Minister for Foreign Affairs of the Portuguese Government has already informed the Government of the Indian Union of the firm decision of Portugal to defend and maintain her rights, having declared that all consequences arising from the attacks mentioned in the enclosed resume and similar actions of aggression are the responsibility of the Indian Government.

I avail myself of this opportunity to renew to Your Excellency the assurance of my highest consideration.[86]

Amílcar Lino Franco

176
Carta do Subsecretário-Geral do DEA ao Encarregado de Negócios português em Dublin (Amílcar Lino Franco): Dublin, 24 de Junho de 1955[87]

I have the honour to acknowledge receipt of your letter of the 15th June and of the enclose thereto concerning the present position in Goa, the contents of which have been duly noted.

I avail of this occasion to express to you, Sir, the renewed assurance of my high consideration.

John A. Belton
For the Minister for External Affairs.

---

[86] Carta inclui um relatório de cinco páginas sobre a situação em Goa.
[87] NAI, DEA, 305/271A Goa and other Portuguese enclaves in India, 1954-1956.

177
Ofício, Embaixador irlandês em Madrid ao Secretário-Geral do DEA: Madrid, 1 de Julho de 1955[88]

[...]

The return-call of the Portuguese Ambassador started by following the usual routing of diplomatic conversations in Madrid at this time of the year, by relating mainly to our respective plans for the Ministerio de Jornado, or summer season, at San Sebastian. Unfortunately, Mr Nosolini at one point remarked that he and all his Portuguese diplomatic colleagues throughout the world had suffered an appalling summer last year and they expected a repetition of this in the present summer. When I asked why, the reply was "Goa" and I had to listen to a long disquisition on the subject of Nehru's perfidy lasting over an hour. I explained to the Ambassador how embarrassing a subject Goa was for us in Ireland. I said we had felt a good deal of sympathy with his then colleague Mr. Brazão when he sought our support in 1954, just after the present Irish Government took office. In the absence of my Minister and my Secretary, I had made a personal study of the Goa problem and our Taoiseach had been good enough to hear me out on the matter. He too had been sympathetic especially with the Portuguese argument that Goa was a stronghold of Christianity and the scene of one of St. Francis Xavier's principal missionary triumphs. Nevertheless, it was only too apparent to Mr. Costello and his colleagues, as, indeed, it was to myself, that so far as Irish public opinion was concerned, Goa stood for the "Six Counties of India". Accordingly, it was reluctantly decided to adopt a neutral attitude or, at any rate, to remain silent in the matter, declaring ourselves for neither side.

At this point in my monologue, the Ambassador (speaking in French) exclaimed that the partition of Ireland was quite unrelated to the situation of Goa. Our position, with which he had every sympathy, was just like that of Spain's in regard to Gibraltar (with which he also sympathised and which, incidentally, is being worked up again in the Madrid papers, with maps and photographs). The

---

[88] NAI, DEA, 305/271A Goa and other Portuguese enclaves in India, 1954-1956.

Ambassador asked me to try to distinguish between the case where a Great Power walked into an old civilised united country and occupied part of its territory by force and the case of peaceful penetration by a civilised State, hundreds of years ago, into a disunited continent like India. If America invaded Mexico now, he would be scandalised, but, on the other hand, he saw no reason why the Americans should at this stage get out of the United States in order to leave it to the Red Indians. For the sake of politeness I agreed with Mr. Nosolini that there did indeed seem to be a distinction and even a real difference between the Six Counties and the Goa situations, but I added that in my own view the Six Counties was unique and a crime unparalleled anywhere else in the world. Nevertheless, I had to explain that Irish public opinion, led by a very free Press, was simply not educated to these nuances and I saw little prospect of any Irish Government coming out 100% on the side of Portugal in this affair if it were to be revived again. The Irish people had strong feelings of friendship for Portugal which they regarded as one of the various countries of refuge in which their ancestors had found asylum in previous centuries. They also, in perhaps a vaguer way, recognised certain similarities of religion, constitutional theory and even geography between the two countries; but it must be remembered that India, like Ireland, is only just emerging from a long struggle for is freedom from Britain and that fact, rightly or wrongly, inclines the average Irishman to favour Nehru's national aim to unify as much of his Republic as he can. The fact that Nehru promised last year to preserve the right of the Goanese missioners to carry on their good work naturally appealed to the ordinary Irish observer. The Ambassador laughed at the Irish people's good faith in Mr. Nehru and he gave me a long description of the Pandit's double dealings in relation to the Goa question [...] I intervened to say that [...] so long as Goa remained a useful naval base for the Western Powers (SEATO) I supposed Portugal should keep on being intransigent. This undiplomatic remark obviously pained Mr. Nosoloni, but I thought of how the Portuguese President and Government had refused to even hear Count O'Kelly a couple of years ago when we instructed him to enter a protest about the visits of Portuguese ships to Derry for NATO exercises. Possibly we were wrong to expect any hearing and even mistaken in our policy at the time, but no other

NATO power had treated us so ruthlessly as Portugal in regard to a démarche involving Partition.

The conversation terminated at long last by the Ambassador begging me to ask our Government to endeavour to perceive the underlying legal principles involved and to ignore the superficial appearances, because one can fight the Communist bloc only by sticking to legal principles and never "appeasing" the enemy by surrendering principles to the threat of force for the sake of expediency. I agreed that this kind of argument might appeal more to an Irish Government that the mere "religious" one put to them last year; yet, at the same time, there would always be great difficulty in persuading the Irish electorate that anything which looked like Partition or Colonialism could possibly merit their positive support.

[...]

Michael Rynne

178
Ofício, Encarregado de Negócios irlandês em Lisboa ao Secretário-Geral do DEA: Lisboa, 12 de Julho de 1955[89]

I have the honour to inform you that as from July 2nd rumours started circulating wildly around Lisbon about the imminence of a re-shuffling of the Portuguese Government. By evening, each café knew who was taking whose place. The rumours grew during the next two days until finally on Wednesday evening the Press was given a list of changes to be published next day.

It was common knowledge that certain Ministers who have served the Government for many years wished to return to private life; the Minister for Overseas, Commander Sarmento Rodrigues, wishing to return to the Navy for promotion purposes, the gossip had it he could not be changed as the moment was unadvisable and his retirement might be interpreted as a reflection on his handling of the Goa question.

---

[89] NAI, DEA, 313/11C Confidential reports from Lisbon Legation, 1955.

The changes are as follows:

New Minister		Outgoing Minister
Presidency	Prof. Marcello Caetano	Prof. João Costa Leite (Lumbrales)
Finances	Prof. António M. Pinto Basto	Dr. Águedo de Oliveira
Overseas Territories	Prof. Raul J. Rodrigues Ventura	Cmd. Sarmento Rodrigues
Education	Prof. Paulo Leite Pinto	Prof. Pires de Lima
Corporations	Dr. Henrique Veiga de Macedo	Dr. Soares da Fonseca.

New Under-Secretaries of State		Former Ones
For Aeronautics	Major Kaúlza de Arriaga	There was none
Overseas Territories	Eng. Carlos K. Abecassis	Prof. Rodrigues Ventura

The appointment of Prof. Marcello Caetano is considered important as he becomes more closely associated with Dr. Salazar and it has often been rumoured that he would be his legal successor if the Prime Minister was to give up the reins of Government. People say that as President of the Corporative Chamber, Caetano held a position at least as important as Minister of the Presidency, as the Ministry is in a way something like that of an Under-Secretariat to Dr. Salazar. It is known how unselfish Caetano is where the affairs of the Portuguese "Estado Novo" are concerned. By his accepting this new appointment he also abandons his vast interests as a consultant-advising lawyer to various important commercial concerns here.

Under-Secretaries of the Budget, of the Treasury and of National Education are yet to be nominated.

O'Kelly de Gallagh

[Escrito à mão] P.S. In point of fact all the above changes are more of gossip interest that anything else. None of them seems to signify the smallest political change.

179
Ofício, Encarregado de Negócios irlandês em Lisboa ao Secretário-Geral do DEA: Lisboa, 25 de Julho de 1955[90]

I have the honour to enclose herewith text of a talk given last week at the American Men's Luncheon Group, by Commander Albano Rodrigues Oliveira, at one time Governor of Macau.[91]

The talk was very much a plea quo domo for the Portuguese thesis on the Goan question, but factually it is of interest.

It is all the more interesting as this morning's press carries the announcement of the closing of the Portuguese Legation in New Delhi at Mr. Nehru's request. In view of the latter gentleman's repeated declarations that he wished to solve his dispute with Portugal by peaceful means this seems hardly the way to start about it.

O'Kelly de Gallagh

180
Ofício, Embaixador irlandês junto da Santa Sé ao Secretário-Geral, DEA: Roma, 15 de Julho de 1955[92]

CONFIDENTIAL

Visit of Mr. Nehru to Vatican

As you know the Indian Prime Minister Mr. Nehru was received in private audience by the Holy Father on Friday last 8th July [...]

4. In the course of a press conference which he gave after his visit to the Vatican, Mr. Nehru answered questions bearing on a number of subjects – principally his impression of Russia, Goa, coexistence. In his remarks on Goa he saw fit to refer to his audience with the Holy Father in the following terms: "In

---

[90] NAI, DEA, 313/11C Confidential reports from Lisbon Legation, 1955.
[91] Incluido com o ofício.
[92] NAI, DEA, 305/271A Goa and other Portuguese enclaves in India, 1954-1956.

talking with His Holiness and on the problem of Goa I stated clearly that it is a political and not a religious problem and His Holiness was entirely in agreement with me on this point."

[…]

C. C. Cremin

181

Ofício, Embaixador irlandês junto à Santa Sé ao Secretário-Geral do DEA: Roma, 19 de Julho de 1955[93]

<u>India and Goa</u>

You are aware of the efforts of Portugal to enlist the support of the Holy See for its stand on Goa and of the failure of those efforts (see e.g. my report of 19th November 1954). I mentioned in my report 14/92 of 15th July, 1955, that Mr. Nehru, the Indian Prime Minister, had told the German Ambassador in New Delhi that he proposed to come to Rome to see the Holy Father for the purpose of talking about Goa. This information I received from the German Chargé d'Affaires and I saw something similar in an English Catholic newspaper quoting New Delhi sources. Presumably Mr. Nehru's aim was to remove any possible risk of the Vatican taking sides in the issue in favour of Portugal – something which in any event seems a priori very improbable having regard to the present and above all to the potential stake of the Church in India, and leaving aside altogether the long term improbability of Portugal being able to maintain her position in Goa.

2. During his press conference on 8th July, Mr. Nehru made some statements about Goa – in accents according to the papers of "absolute intransigence". Asked if the matter had been raised he said that "it was mentioned briefly in the sense that we are dealing with a political question and not at all with a religious question as the Portuguese Government would like done". To a question of whether the continuance of this dispute would adversely affect relations between the Government of India and the Catholic Church in relation to missionary

---

[93] NAI, DEA, 305/271A Goa and other Portuguese enclaves in India, 1954-1956.

activity, he replied that "In India there are 7-8 million Catholics whereas in Goa out of a total population of 600,000 there are in all 200,000 Catholics [...]"

3. Is is rather unusual for a statesman to invoke an opinion expressed by the Holy Father in a private audience (as Mr. Nehru has done) in support of a given view-point in a controversial issue. I am sure that the Portuguese resent both his doing so and the opinion attributed to the Holy Father. However, as far as I can make out Mr. Nehru more or less correctly summarised the substance of his conversation with the Pope on this point, although if the Vatican were to report the conversation (which it never does) it would undoubtedly have put the matter in a different way. Mgr. Dell'Acqua made a slight allusion to this statement when I was with him last week. What he seemed to say was that the problem can certainly be described as political inasmuch as we are dealing with a territory, but it is not entirely political.

4. I might mention that at the recent La Pira convention on Peace and Christian Civilisation in Florence there was quite an altercation between the Indian Ambassador and the Portuguese Minister to Italy. The former in the course of his declaration referred in strong terms to the very necessity to have Goa returned to India. The latter made a very vigorous intervention in reply in which he reiterated the Portuguese policy of "no surrender". Mr. Ferro's intervention was treated light-heartedly and even frivolously by much of the press as being characterised by undue vigour.

C. C. Cremin

182
Carta, Subsecretário-Geral do DEA ao Embaixador irlandês em Madrid (Michael Rynne): Dublin, 21 de Julho de 1955[94]

With reference to your recent report which, inter alia, you [sic] told us of your conversation with the Portuguese Ambassador concerning the position of Goa

---

[94] NAI, DEA, 305/271A Goa and other Portuguese enclaves in India, 1954-1956.

you may like to know that last month we received from the Portuguese Minister here a formal letter in the subject together with a memorandum setting out in detail the rights of Portugal and the wrongs of India. The substance of our reply was to acknowledge receipt of the letter and enclosure and to state that the contents had been duly noted. About the same time last month Count O'Kelly received a very lengthy memorandum from the Portuguese Ministry of Foreign Affairs on the same question for transmission to us.

I might add that a few weeks before I left Germany the Portuguese Minister in Bonn on at least two occasions went out of his way to explain the Goa question to me and to assure me how certain he was that the full sympathy of the Irish Government and people would be behind Portugal in this matter. I generally took the same line with him as you did with the Portuguese Ambassador in Madrid.

Yours sincerely,

J. A. Belton

183
Ofício, Embaixador irlandês junto da Santa Sé ao Secretário-Geral do DEA: Roma, 27 de Julho de 1955[95]

CONFIDENTIAL

Portugal and Goa

Further to my report of 19th July, 1955, concerning Goa, the Portuguese Ambassador confirmed in conversation a few days ago that his Government is extremely annoyed that Mr. Nehru in his press conference on 8th July should have seen fit to quote the Holy Father to the effect that the problem of Goa is political and not religious. Mr. Calheiros would have liked to have some kind of démenti or gloss printed in the Osservatore but he is not optimistic about this especially as he regards it as certain that the Holy Father did agree with Mr. Nehru that the problem is primarily if not entirely political. He told me on the other hand that

---
[95] NAI, DEA, 305/271A Goa and other Portuguese enclaves in India, 1954-1956.

Portugal had asked the Vatican to have the Holy Father in the course of his conversation with Mr. Nehru appeal to the latter to refrain from any acts of violence in relation to Goa and this he believes the Holy Father did.

Generally I get the impression from my Portuguese Colleague that Lisbon is very worried about Mr. Nehru's reference to the Holy Father and also with the absence of any striking support in the press for Portugal's position in Goa. For this reason the Portuguese authorities were very appreciative of the leading article in the London "Times" of 18th July headed "Asking for trouble" and also of the comment on Mr. Nehru's "indiscretion" in the "Tablet" of 16th July (page 50).

C. C. Cremin

184
Carta, Encarregado de Negócios português em Dublin ao Ministro dos Negócios Estrangeiros irlandês (Liam Cosgrave):
Dublin, 27 de Julho de 1955[96]

Excellency,

I have the honour to enclose herewith the translation of a statement made by the Presidency of the Council of Ministers, Lisbon, issued on the 22nd instant, in reply to the declarations to the press made by the Prime Minister of the Indian Union on the 19th of this month, about the so-called "case of Goa".

As Your Excellency will certainly notice, the Portuguese Government, faced by critical circumstances, have, once more, kept an attitude of calmness and firmness in the defence of the undeniable rights of Portugal, declaring again their sincere wish and willingness to find a peaceful solution to all the problems existing between Portugal and the Indian Union, which do not relate to cession of sovereignty; and that the Portuguese Government hope that they can continue to count upon the comprehension and sense of justice of the Governments of friendly nations and public opinion, which have been such a valuable support

---

[96] NAI, DEA, 305/271A Goa and other Portuguese enclaves in India, 1954-1956.

in their resistance to the pressures exerted by the Government of the Indian Union.

I avail myself of this opportunity of renewing to Your Excellency the assurance of my highest consideration.

Amílcar Lino Franco

185
Carta, Encarregado de Negócios português em Dublin ao Ministro dos Negócios Estrangeiros irlandês (Liam Cosgrave): Dublin, 28 de Julho de 1955[97]

Excellency,

I have the honour to inform Your Excellency that the Portuguese Chargé d'Affaires in New Delhi, on the morning of the 25th instant, was called to the Ministry of External Affairs of the Indian Government, where the Secretary General handed him a note in which it was declared that the Government of the Indian Union was of the opinion that there was not any usefulness in allowing the Portuguese Legation in New Delhi to continue functioning and, so, asked for the said Legation to be closed before 8th August next. The Portuguese Chargé d'Affaires was told, verbally, that the Indian Government did not intend, by this action, to sever relations with Portugal.

This decision of the Indian Government was based on the opinion which, in May 1953, was used to explain their closing of the Indian Legation in Lisbon: lack of practical usefulness of the diplomatic mission in view of the Portuguese Government's refusal to discuss the delivery of the Portuguese territories and population in the Hindustanic Peninsula. This new action of the Indian Government shows once more that to the repeated Portuguese offer of negotiations for the solution – respecting the sovereignty of both parties – of all problems arising from the contiguity and neighbourliness (reiterated again as recently as the 22nd

---

[97] NAI, DEA, 305/271A Goa and other Portuguese enclaves in India, 1954-1956.

instant), the Indian Union answers once more with the suppression of the normal means of international understanding, which are the diplomatic missions, showing very clearly that she is interested only in the illegitimate absorption of alien territories.

[…]

Amílcar Lino Franco

186
Pequeno apontamento (Leatan Miontuarisce)[98]

Mr. Belton: Seen by Minister and Secretary: Secretary thinks a simple acknowledgement should issue to both letters. 29/7/55.

[Assinatura ilegível]

187
Carta, Encarregado de Negócios português em Dublin ao Ministro dos Negócios Estrangeiros irlandês (Liam Cosgrave):
Dublin, 17 de Agosto de 1955[99]

Excellency,

The Portuguese Consulate-General in Bombay and the Portuguese Consulate in Calcutta were assaulted by Indian rioters. The shield and flag of Portugal were disrespected, archives were destroyed and furniture burnt.

The Ministry for Foreign Affairs in Lisbon released a statement about the above-mentioned riots.

As usual, I wish to give Your Excellency full information about the statements of my Government on the so-called "Case of Goa". But as I have not received the full text, I have the honour to enclose a translation of the resumé of this latest

---

[98] NAI, DEA, 305/271A Goa and other Portuguese enclaves in India, 1954-1956.
[99] NAI, DEA, 305/271A Goa and other Portuguese enclaves in India, 1954-1956.

communiqué, this being the only official information I have up to now about this matter.

I avail myself of this opportunity of renewing to Your Excellency the assurance of my highest consideration.

Amílcar Lino Franco

188
Carta, Secretário-Geral do DEA ao Encarregado de Negócios português em Dublin (Amílcar Lino Franco): Dublin, 18 de Agosto de 1955[100]

Sir,

In the absence of the Minister, I have the honour to acknowledge receipt of your Note No. 54 enclosing a translation of a statement released by your Ministry of Foreign Affairs, which I will bring to the Minister's attention on his return from holidays.

I have the honour to be,
Sir,
Yours faithfully,
Séan Murphy, Secretary

---

[100] NAI, DEA, 305/271A Goa and other Portuguese enclaves in India, 1954-1956.

Parte III
(1956-1961)

A Parte II deste volume ilustrou um período de algum desinteresse nas relações entre Portugal e a Irlanda, já que, se por um lado, as condições que ditaram a abertura da Legação irlandesa em Lisboa tinham desaparecido após 1945, por outro ambos os países mostravam pouco interesse nas respectivas causas nacionais (o Ulster e o Estado Português da Índia). A partir da entrada de Portugal e da Irlanda na ONU, esse desinteresse começou a transformar-se em irritação. Foi a questão colonial que ditou esta evolução gradual, pois a Irlanda, neste período, ainda em parte em função da questão da Irlanda do Norte, começou a identificar-se não só como uma nação ocidental e cristã, mas também como uma ex-colónia, ainda afectada e desmembrada por uma potência imperial. Tal atitude foi ao mesmo tempo responsável e reforçada pela decisão de manter a neutralidade do tempo da guerra durante a paz. Uma vez nas Nações Unidas, e enquanto Portugal apelava à solidariedade entre ocidentais, buscava a Irlanda o apoio dos países não-alinhados, entre os quais a hostilidade ao colonialismo era um ponto de contacto essencial. Em tais circunstâncias, uma posição comum era impossível de encontrar e sustentar.

A Parte III abre com um novo representante irlandês em Lisboa, Thomas Commins, cujos meses iniciais não foram muito produtivos (Documento N.º 191). O primeiro ofício de sua autoria incluído nesta colecção, dedicado à possível colaboração entre o Estado português e uma ordem missionária irlandesa tem interesse próprio, mas mais notável foi a reacção a esse mesmo ofício por parte do Embaixador irlandês em Madrid, Michael Rynne, cujas palavras foram de extrema dureza para com Portugal e os seus aliados da NATO: 'The Portuguese are as well-off as they are because they have managed to cling to a few ill-gotten gains abroad with the moral support of England and the NATO powers.' Esta atitude, se bem que ainda velada, seria cada vez mais determinante na política do DEA, apesar dos esforços do MNE português (Documento N.º 197). Mas foi em Nova Iorque, graças à constante pressão exercida sobre Portugal para circular informações sobre as "Províncias Ultramarinas", vistas por muitos países como simples colónias e por isso territórios sem auto-determinação, que o desgaste foi maior. No início de 1957 F. H. Boland, o Representante Permanente da Irlanda junto das Nações Unidas, votou a favor de Portugal na Quarta Comissão, já que, se o argumento português de que as províncias ultramarinas eram parte integrante de Portugal era pouco convincente, mais ainda o eram os argumentos do bloco Afro-Asiático, violentos e irracionais (Documento N.º 201). Tal atitude levou a um agradecimento por parte do Embaixador Vasco Garin, o homólogo português de Boland (Documento N.º 202). Mas no Outono do mesmo ano as instruções de Dublin eram já de manter uma posição de neutralidade na Assembleia Geral. Tentava Portugal travar qualquer resolução na Quarta Comissão e, se isso não fosse possível, pedir que qualquer resolução da Assembleia Geral sobre o ultramar português fosse tomada com base numa maioria de dois terços, sendo assim mais fácil a defesa dos interesses coloniais portugueses. Mas a Irlanda absteve-se quer na Comissão, quer na Assembleia Geral, apesar das diligências efectuadas junto de diplomatas irlandeses em Lisboa, Dublin, Nova Iorque, e outras capitais. Segundo o Conselheiro da Representação Permanente irlandesa junto das Nações Unidas, E. L. Kennedy (Documento N.º 211), se, por um lado, a linguagem da resolução então apresentada na Quarta Comissão era mais moderada do que a anterior, por outro a paciência de muitas delegações para com Portugal estava a esgotar-se.

A batalha para demover a Irlanda da sua atitude em relação ao Portugal ultramarino continuou nos anos que se seguiram. De especial interesse são as conversações tidas por Commins em Lisboa com algumas das principais figuras do MNE, Caldeira Queiroz e Franco Nogueira, durante as quais, mais uma vez, o tópico de visitas da Marinha de Guerra portuguesa a Londonderry foi abordado, tendo outra visita ocorrido em 1958 (Documento N.º 219). Houve no meio diplomático irlandês em 1958 uma curta discussão sobre a posição constitucional das províncias ultramarinas portuguesas, tendo a informação prestada por Commins (Documento N.º 223) sendo de molde a agradar o Governo português – mas sem resultados práticos.

Quanto à política interna portuguesa, esta foi seguida com algum interesse por Commins, que noticiou a morte de Berta Craveiro Lopes (Documento N.º 215), a tomada de posse de Américo Tomás (Documento N.º 217), e a formação de um novo governo (Documento N.º 218), onde não tinham lugar nem Marcelo Caetano nem Santos Costa. Onde Commins pecou, porém, foi ao ignorar quase por completo a figura de Humberto Delgado, levando, no início de 1959, a uma dupla chamada de atenção do DEA (Documentos N.º 224 e 225), que agora tinha, como Secretário-Geral, Cornelius C. Cremin. Num longuíssimo ofício (Documento N.º 227) Commins tentou sintetizar o caso Delgado e o seu impacto nas relações entre Portugal e o Brasil; quatro dias depois enviou Commins outro ofício sobre as relações entre o Estado português e a Igreja Católica – assunto sempre de grande interesse para Dublin – na sequência da carta do Bispo do Porto a Salazar, de 13 de Julho de 1958. Mais uma vez, porém, Commins, tendo listado os pontos de fricção, demonstrou alguma simpatia pelo Estado Novo, acusando a imprensa estrangeira de exagerar os problemas de relacionamento entre o regime e a hierarquia Católica. Aqui acabou a acção de Thomas Commins, substituído esse ano por Frank Biggar.[1] Na sua primeira conversa com Marcello Mathias, na época Ministro dos Negócios Estrangeiros, recebeu Biggar uma visão pessimista sobre o futuro do continente africano, cuja descolonização tinha já começado (Documento N.º 231). O tom da conversa foi um de paternalismo, não só para os africanos, que não podiam senão falhar, mas também para os irlandeses, que por eles exprimiam simpatia e encorajamento.

Foi notável o esforço de Biggar em Lisboa, sendo 1960 um dos anos em que a vida política portuguesa foi tratada de forma mais completa. A questão da sucessão de Salazar (Documentos N.º 233 e 246), o estado do clero em Portugal (Documento N.º 236), a natureza do colonialismo português (Documentos N.º 239 e 245), e o papel da PIDE (Documento N.º 241) foram alguns dos tópicos que mereceram a atenção de Biggar. Infelizmente, porém, a sua estadia na capital portuguesa foi breve, pois que em Novembro de 1960 surge um ofício, detalhando o fim das comemorações do quinto centenário da morte do Infante Dom Henrique, assinado por O'Kelly de Gallagh.

---

[1] Francis (Frank) Biggar nasceu em Dublin em 1917. Entrou para a função pública em 1934, trabalhando nos Ministérios da Agricultura e da Defesa. Foi nomeado Terceiro-Secretário no DEA em 1941, tendo depois servido no Consulado em Nova Iorque, na Legação em Roma e na Embaixada em Londres (de onde transitou para Lisboa em 1959); foi Embaixador em Bruxelas e Berna. Morreu em 1974, enquanto Subsecretário-Geral do DEA.

Durante o período em que Biggar se manteve em Lisboa, são de salientar ainda as diferentes leituras feitas por portugueses e irlandeses dos acontecimentos no Congo belga (sendo este país palco da primeira intervenção militar irlandesa ao serviço da ONU), e a breve estadia do *Taoiseach* Séan Lemass, sucessor de De Valera à frente do maior partido irlandês, o *Fianna Fáil*, em Setembro de 1960. Tal como de Valera, Lemass foi a Fátima, e tal como de Valera encontrou-se com Salazar – mas desta vez sobrevive um relato da conversa com Salazar (Documento N.º 251), que decorreu no Palace Hotel do Buçaco, não longe, por isso, do Vimieiro, onde Salazar se encontrava de férias. Esta foi uma longa conversa (duas horas e meia) durante a qual foram abordados variadíssimos tópicos, desde a natureza da política americana ao processo de integração europeia, passando pelo fenómeno da emigração e, claro, África.

Após um breve intervalo com, como vimos, O'Kelly de Gallagh à frente da Legação irlandesa, chegou a Lisboa J. W. Lennon,[2] que, como Biggar, se esforçaria por fazer uma cobertura atenta da actualidade política portuguesa num ano – 1961 – que se viria a revelar de enorme importância para o Estado Novo, e que abriu com o desvio do navio *Santa Maria*, a que cedo se seguiu o início do conflito em Angola. A cobertura da vida política, colonial, e internacional é constante e relativamente bem fundamentada, visitando Lennon o MNE regularmente e informando Dublin do teor das conversas lá tidas. O ano terminou com a invasão do Estado Português da Índia. Lennon descreveu a reacção em Portugal, sublinhando sobretudo o silêncio de Salazar e os rumores que se lhe seguiram (Documento N.º 292). Entretanto, em Dublin, a notícia da acção militar indiana foi tratada com a já habitual impassibilidade irlandesa em relação a todo este assunto (Documento N.º 290). As diferenças entre os dois países eram já inultrapassáveis.

---

[2] James Wilfred Lennon nasceu em Dundalk em 1915. Entrou no DEA com Primeiro-Secretário em 1947, vindo do Ministério das Finanças. Antes da sua breve estadia em Portugal foi Conselheiro na Embaixada em Paris, e partiu de Lisboa rumo à Holanda, onde foi Embaixador. Posteriormente, foi Embaixador em Madrid, Representante Permanente junto das Nações Unidas em Genebra, e Embaixador em Buenos Aires.

1956

189
Carta, Encarregado de Negócios português em Dublin ao Ministro dos Negócios Estrangeiros irlandês (Liam Cosgrave):
Dublin, 7 de Janeiro de 1956[3]

Excellency,

I have the honour to let Your Excellency know that the Portuguese Government have repeatedly received information – which is considered reliable – that a great number, perhaps thousands, of Portuguese flags and also a great quantity of uniforms of the Portuguese Armed Forces are being clandestinely made in Bombay.

Such facts can only show that a knavish stratagem is being prepared, which directly or indirectly will try to interfere with the sovereignty of the Portuguese territories and is causing apprehension to the Portuguese Government.

For this reasons and following the same procedure as in other serious matters about the so-called "Case of Goa", I consider it my duty to inform Your Excellency about the above-mentioned facts that may have grave consequences.

I avail myself of this opportunity of renewing to Your Excellency the assurance of my highest consideration.

Amílcar Lino Franco

190
Pequeno apontamento[4]

Miss Murphy,

Mr Belton handed me the Portuguese note of 7th January yesterday and asked me if we had any other data on the allegations made therein. I have

---

[3] NAI, DEA, 305/271A Goa and other Portuguese enclaves in India, 1954-1956.
[4] NAI, DEA, 305/271A Goa and other Portuguese enclaves in India, 1954-1956.

checked the file and recent press clippings and have found no other information. Even, if true, the allegations are, so far as we are concerned, almost impossible to substantiate.

In accordance with our now established procedure with Mr. Franco's representations regarding Goa I have drafted a bare acknowledgment.

Assinatura ilegível, 10/1/56

[Escrito à mão]:

"Attached memo prepared in connection with Mr Nehru's visit to Ireland. 2 copies ? to Taoiseach and Minister [...]"

191
Carta, Subsecretário-Geral do DEA ao Encarregado de Negócios irlandês em Lisboa (Thomas Commins): Dublin, 14 de Maio de 1956[5]

CONFIDENTIAL

Dear Tom,

You are, of course, aware of the keen interest which not only our Minister but the Taoiseach takes in reports received from our Missions abroad. Although the Circular Instruction on the sending of reports at least once a week is no longer regarded as being in force, it is felt that there are always sufficient happenings, in the various countries of accreditation, both of national and international importance, to enable every mission abroad to send interesting and informative reports at more or less regular intervals. Apart from one's own appraisal of events, abundant material should always be available from a number of sources such as one's talks with (1) the Ministers and officials of the Foreign Office and other Ministries, (2) colleagues in the Diplomatic Corps, (3) newspapermen, (4) prelates of the Church, (5) University Professors, leading industrialists etc. The main objective should be to furnish to the Department information, appraisal and

---

[5] NAI, DEA, 313/11D Confidential reports from Lisbon Legation, 1956-1957.

comment which are not normally obtainable from ordinary sources such as the newspapers, which are read daily in the Department, and Radio Eireann and BBC reports which are regularly listened to.

As the Secretary is anxious to avoid any embarrassing question on the absence of reports from Lisbon, we would be glad if you look into the matter as soon as possible.[6]

Yours sincerely,
J. A. Belton

192
Ofício, Encarregado de Negócios irlandês em Lisboa ao Secretário-Geral do DEA: Lisboa, 29 de Maio de 1956[7]

Mother Mary Martin, Foundress of the Medical Missionaries of Mary ended a ten-day visit to Lisbon on the 14th inst., when she returned to Drogheda. She had come here on the invitation of the Portuguese Ministry of Overseas Territories who wished to explore with her the possibility of establishing a house of the Order in Lisbon for the recruiting of Portuguese Vocations for the Mozambique and Angolan Missions. She was accompanied by one of the Sisters of the Order, Sister Monica, who left on the 23rd instant for Angola under the sponsorship of the Portuguese Overseas Ministry.

2. The visit of Mother Martin was spearheaded by the arrival in Lisbon in the middle of April of Rev. Fr. Bernard Keane, a member of the Congregation of the Holy Ghost, who conducts a Mission in Chiule, Southern Angola. Fr. Keane, who

---

[6] Em carta de 25 de Maio endereçada a Belton, Thomas Commins explicou as dificuldades que estava a encontrar em Lisboa: O chanceler tinha 80 anos; a dactilógrafa trabalhava apenas meios dias; e ele próprio tinha sido obrigado a mudar a residência da Legação. Escreveu Commins, 'I should perhaps have done this before now, but, candidly, the lack of response to my predecessor's representations led me to doubt that any possibility existed of persuading the powers that be i.e. the D/Finance of the desirability of putting this Mission in a position to operate other than as a minor Vice-Consulate'. NAI, DEA, 313/11D Confidential reports from Lisbon Legation, 1956-1957.

[7] NAI, DEA, 313/11D Confidential reports from Lisbon Legation, 1956-1957.

is about 47 years of age has been in Angola for the best part of 20 years. He is well known to our Minister and his father, Mr. W. T. Cosgrave.

3. A few days after coming here Fr. Keane called at this Legation and among other things told me that upon his arrival he had found waiting for him a message from Dr. Braga Paixão, Under-Secretary of the Ministry of Overseas asking him to call on him. He had done so and Dr. Braga Paixão had asked him to delay his journey to Ireland and remain in Lisbon for such time as necessary to invite Mother Mary Martin here and interest her in laying the foundations of a Portuguese house of the Order for the supply of Medical Missionaries – doctors and nurses – of Portuguese nationals to serve in the development of health and medical services for the native – and the Portuguese – in Mozambique and Angola. In Fr. B. Keane's Mission in Chiule, there are and have been for a couple of years back two Sisters of the Medical Missionaries of Mary – one a doctor who spent a six-months preparatory stay in Lisbon before going out and the second a qualified nurse. It is evident from Fr. Keane's accounts of life in the Mission that the life is very hard and that an immense amount of work remains to be undertaken to provide medical and teaching services for the native population even on the most slender scale. The reputation of the Irish Order and their success not only in Chiule (in a small way) but in British Africa apparently impressed the Portuguese and it is for that reason that the Authorities here were anxious to explore with the foundress, Mother Mary Martin, the possibility of extending the activities of the Order in Portuguese Africa – but with Portuguese personnel.

4. In a previous report I have referred to the insistence of the Portuguese authorities in retaining a completely free hand on the development of their colonial possessions. Offers of aid on a co-operative international basis, with all the side strings of objective investigation by e.g. the UN or other international bodies which interest themselves in the development of the underdeveloped areas of the world have no appeal. Portuguese policy as regards their African possessions differs fundamentally from the policy of e.g. Britain in relation to British African possessions and even South Africa as regards the future of the natives there. It can, I think, be conceded that the British – to quote a recent

editorial comment in the TIMES – regard "manifestations of African nationalism as in keeping with the spirit of the times, and embarrassing only as they conflict with the orderly development of the territories concerned." The South African Government and its aparthied [sic] policy recognise the right of the native African to develop himself and be provided, at the expense of the whole community of the Union with health, educational, and other services approaching, if not equal, to those provided for the European population. True, they demand that having been so provided for, the natives keep to themselves in their own communities – which rather takes the gilt off the gingerbread just at the point of tasting.

5. The Portuguese Government on the other hand operates an outright imperialist colonial policy. The Colonial Act reaffirms Portugal's "historical function of colonising the Discovered Lands under its Sovereignty, to impart and propagate among its population the benefits of civilisation simultaneously with the moral influence deriving from the Patronage of the East". This is by no means an empty formula, as is evidenced by statements made from time to time on the subject by Dr. Salazar over some years past. He is on record over the period as publicly regretting "the present crisis in colonial thought which finds expression in the summary condemnation of the work of colonisation undertaken by several European nations," of deploring "the ingenious and presumptuous manner in which the administration of the so-called dependent territories is discussed in international gatherings" and of holding that "it would go all the better with the world were it justly to appreciate the historic process of colonisation which, by virtue of special circumstances, or marked vocation, forms an integral part of the life and mission of some nations."

6. This concept, which is alive today as ever, must therefore always be kept in mind in assessing Portuguese reactions to any question of colonial administration. For her, in relation to her own possessions it implies no interference by individuals or international organisations, however idealistic, in which she regards as entirely her own affair. In the course of a short conversation which I had recently with Dr. Vasco da Cunha, Secretary General of the Ministry of Foreign Affairs, he commented with great bitterness on the actions of the French in

forgoing their Indian possessions and in adopting what he termed a policy of "near despair" in North Africa. The action on the part of the French, Dr. da Cunha holds, has diminished almost to breaking point European's prestige [sic] in Asia and Africa and has made it all the more necessary for e.g. Portugal to stand fast by her overseas possessions, in the interest of western civilisation. This, he affirms, they are determined to do at any cost.

7. For reasons of prestige, therefore, the Portuguese Government has an unbending determination to cling to their Asian possessions e.g. Goa, Macau and Timor. None of these possessions benefit her economically – rather the contrary. To be forced out of them would, however, in the Portuguese view, be only the first step towards facing a similar situation as regards the African possessions – Mozambique and Angola, possessions which are of the most vital economic importance to Portugal. It would not be unduly straining the truth to day that without the economic benefits which flow to Metropolitan Portugal from these areas, Portugal would, with the passage of time, find it difficult to maintain her independence as an economic and political unit. It comes as somewhat of a shock to a new-comer to the Portuguese political scene to observe the concentrated pre-occupation of many highly placed Portuguese with what they regard as the ever present threat of Spain to their political independence. One example of this is interesting. Lunching recently with Dr. Brazão, former Chargé d'Affaires in Ireland and now Under-Secretary of Information, he developed this point in the context of explaining the fundamental importance to the Portuguese of the Luso-Britannic Alliance. As an indication of the reality of the Spanish threat to Portuguese independence he instanced a journey which had made to Madrid in the course of the war. It was at the time of the major British set-backs at the hands of Rommel in North Africa and the atmosphere in Madrid was (according to him) charged with an almost hysterical anti-British feeling. Throughout the city there was to be found, white-washed in walls and buildings the slogan "TO GIBRALTAR" and side by side almost in every case was the slogan "TO LISBON!"

8. With the admission of Portugal to UNO and the preoccupation of that body – as well as the American Government independently – with the development of the underdeveloped areas of the world as a cooperative effort,

the Portuguese Government are faced with the new problems as regards Mozambique and Angola. From the point of view of world opinion they must, if they are not to be manoeuvred into being reduced to a nominal administration of these areas with real influence passing to external financial investors, be able to show – on paper at least – an energetically progressive programme of development in these areas. They are addressing themselves to this and plans are being developed within the Overseas Ministry for the introduction to the areas in question of schemes for educational and health development to redress the existing chronic deficiency. One such scheme envisages the building of 20,000 schools[8] in Angola, but here again the difficulty is to get teachers, doctors and nurses. To what extent these schemes will develop into factual realities remains to be seen, but it is in the context of the general policy that the efforts are being made by the Ministry of Overseas Territories to develop a Portuguese Branch of the Medical Missionaries of Mary in Lisbon.

9. It only remains to be said that Mother Mary was received with the greatest consideration by both the ecclesiastical and civil authorities – including the Cardinal Patriarch. The idea at the moment is that the Portuguese Government will provide a hostel for these Sisters in the new Lisbon University and pending that, if necessary, will provide them with a small house in Lisbon, where they can recruit vocations. Unfortunately the financial aspects of these arrangements are not yet very clear, not is it fully apparent that the Sisters will in practice be given facilities here to do much more that run the University Hostel. I understand that it is the intention of Mother Mary to return to Lisbon in October, that is, if her ardour is not dampened by the failure, to date at least, of the Portuguese Government to redeem their stated intention of bearing the cost of her recent visit which she made on their invitation!

Thomas Commins

---

[8] Escrito na margem deste documento: ' 2000(?) [Pop. of Angola is c. 4 million]'

193

**Ofício, Embaixador irlandês em Madrid ao Secretário-Geral do DEA:
Madrid, 26 de Junho de 1956[9]**

CONFIDENTIAL

<u>SPAIN AND PORTUGAL</u>

I have the honour to acknowledge the receipt of extracts from a report dated 29th of May from the Chargé d'Affaires at Lisbon in which (p.3) it is stated that many highly placed Portuguese are greatly preoccupied with what they regard as "the ever-present threat of Spain to their political independence".

This point of view comes rather as a surprise to me although I must admit that, owing to the difficulty of extracting frank statements of policy out of anyone in authority here, I am unable to either endorse or discount it.

On the whole I am inclined to think that Mr. Brazão may be still under the influence of his personal experiences in Spain which date from about fifteen years ago.

[…]

If the Portuguese high-ups are sometimes uneasy in their minds about Spain, that may be one result of a bad conscience. The Portuguese are as well-off as they are because they have managed to cling to a few ill-gotten gains abroad with the moral support of England and the NATO powers. Spain, on the other hand, is surrendering her claims in North Africa, is opposed to the English in Gibraltar, Cyprus, the Arab world etc., and has not yet been admitted to NATO.

As Mr. Commins points out, her overseas possessions are vital to Portugal's survival. Small countries, without considerable internal resources, cannot continue to exist in the modern world without (1) outlets for their surplus populations (2) cheap sources of raw materials etc. abroad or (3) foreign "aid". Perhaps, this provides the best answer to those who would like to check all emigration from Ireland overnight and it certainly seems to justify the Portuguese Government's uncompromising defence of hated "colonialism".

---

[9] NAI, DEA, 313/11D Confidential reports from Lisbon Legation, 1956-1957.

But, so far as Spaniards are concerned, their main rivalry with Portugal in recent times has been witnessed on the football field: Our "aficionados" of Soccer unanimously praised the superior tactics of the victorious Portuguese team.

Michael Rynne

194
Ofício, Encarregado de Negócios irlandês em Lisboa ao Secretário-Geral do DEA: Lisboa, 10 de Novembro de 1956[10]

Events in Hungary and the Middle East

[…] The dramatic events in Hungary and the Middle East over the past twelve days have received the most detailed reportage in the Portuguese press. Editorial comment has, however, been almost exclusively confined to the Hungarian-Soviet conflict and direct Government pronouncements entirely to that conflict […]

6. In contrast with the almost frenzied editorial condemnation of the Russian intervention in Hungary (largely attributable, it must be said, to the cynicism of the Russian "putsch" and the barbarity of the treatment meted out to the insurgents) there has been no editorial criticism of the Anglo-French action against Egypt, and what comment there has been adds up to support of this action while recognising the hasards [sic] involved therein unless its objectives can be speedily and decisively attained. In an editorial on the 31st ult., the "A VOZ", influential Catholic paper, referred to the Franco-British action against Egypt as a necessary show of resolution, – taken a bit late in the day, – to restore the standing of Western Europe in Africa. "This action", the editorial concluded "holds great dangers for them (i.e. Britain and France) and for us, but to have refrained from taking action would have been to signify the total abdication of Europe".

[…]

8. […] It is also true that most people here believe that in the development of that attack there was collusion between Britain, France and Israel. The almost

---

[10] NAI, DEA, 313/11D Confidential reports from Lisbon Legation, 1956-1957.

precipitate acceptance by the latter of the Franco-British ultimatum contrasted vividly with Israel rejection [sic] two days before of President Eisenhower's appeal to arrest mobilization. But in the Portuguese view it had become a matter of paramount importance to call a halt to Col. Nasser, whom they regard as the evil genius behind all France and Britain's troubles in Algeria, Morocco, Cyprus etc.

9. This view was confirmed to me by Dr. Caldeira Queiroz in the course of my conversation with him to which I have referred earlier. He agreed that great dangers were inherent in the action taken by Britain and France but held that as the United Nations had shown itself ineffective in securing any lasting settlement of Arab-Israelian [sic] differences he, personally, he said, was glad that Britain and France had, despite the dangers involved, taken this action. He hoped it would have for its principle [sic] good effect the fall from power of Col. Nasser and his replacement by a more moderate and pro-European leader, such as Col. Neguib.

10. This attitude on the part of Portugal is not strange when seen against the background of Portuguese traditional policy towards Africa, which is a frankly colonial one. Portuguese opinion has invariably deplored what it considers to have been weak policies on the part of France towards her African and Asian possessions since the war, policies which, in the Portuguese view have operated to reduce almost to vanishing point West-European power and influence on those areas and opened the door to infiltration by the Communists, using as their tools adventuresome and, in large measure, fanatical and ignorant native leaders. It has at all times been a cardinal principle of Dr. Salazar's creed that Europe must hold Africa or perish. In a speech made some month's [sic] ago to the Congress of the "União Nacional", Dr. Salazar again referred to this subject in the following words:- "Africa is the natural complement of Europe, essential for her life, her defence and her subsistence. Without Africa Russia could at once dictate to the West the terms on which she would allow it to live. The independence of the North African countries is not a serious European problem only so long as it is possible to ensure their close co-operation with Europe. Europe could never consider herself safe, nor was she, except when the extensive African Mediterranean front could in some way be considered a friend or ally. Neither Greece, Italy, France, Spain nor even we, ourselves, can afford to have enemies there."

11. It is not surprising, therefore, that Portuguese opinion looks with distrust and abhorrence on the Pan-Islamic policies of Col. Nasser and the growth throughout North Africa, through what they are satisfied is primarily his influence, of bitter anti-European antagonism. It is unnecessary to add that the Arab side of the case has not been improved by the recent assassination in Morocco of two Portuguese citizens, in the course of the trouble which broke out there after the recent French arrest of the five Algerian leaders.

[…]

Tom Commins

195
Carta, Encarregado de Negócios português em Dublin ao Ministro dos Negócios Estrangeiros irlandês (Liam Cosgrave): Dublin, 25 de Junho de 1956[11]

Excellency,

Under instructions from my Government, I have the honour to inform Your Excellency that, according to the news agencies, the Prime Minister of the Government of the Indian Union, in a speech made at a political meeting on the 4th instant, asked the Western Powers to define precisely their attitude in relation to Goa. The Prime Minister declared that it is a case of colonialism of the worst type and that many of the western nations are being neutral clearly because they are also colonialist countries.

The Portuguese Government have repeatedly demonstrated that Portuguese India is not a Colony; it is an integral part of Portugal, its population, which has the same statute as those of all other parts of Portuguese territory, does not reveal any tendency to separate itself from the mother-country. The best proof of the integration of the Goanese in the Portuguese nationality is the attitude of those living in the Indian Union. These facts are universally known, and it should be emphasised that, in his above-mentioned speech, Mr. Nehru paid homage to

---

[11] NAI, DEA, 305/271B Goa and the other Portuguese enclaves in India 1956-1958.

the attitude of the Goanese when he said that they have done nothing "for the fight for liberty".

Under these circumstances, the Portuguese Government does not fail in forewarning the Governments of the countries where the Government of the Indian Union seems to intend to take steps in order to try and win acceptance of its point of view and obtain declarations detrimental to Portugal; and to express the hopes, and even the conviction, that the Irish Government will continue to maintain, as in the past, an attitude at the same time friendly and rigorously coherent with the historical and political truth of the problem. Any deviation from this truth would certainly be used by any other party to injure the legitimate interests of Portugal.

I avail myself of this opportunity of renewing to Your Excellency the assurance of my highest consideration.

Amílcar Lino Franco

196
Ponto da situação sobre a questão da Índia Portuguesa, para consulta interna do DEA (Julho de 1956)[12]

GOA

Indo-Portuguese Dispute

[...]

Attitude of Ireland

In 1954 informal efforts were made by the Portuguese Chargé d'Affaires to elicit a statement from the Government indicating some measure of sympathy for Portugal in the Goan dispute. No such statement was made, the Chargé d'Affaires being reminded of the state of public opinion in Ireland with regard to foreign occupations. In this connection it will be remembered that when in 1952 the then Minister for External Affairs protested against the visits of Portuguese

---

[12] NAI, DEA, 305/271B Goa and the other Portuguese enclaves in India 1956-1958.

naval craft to Derry under the auspices of NATO, the Portuguese Foreign Minister indicated that Portugal was in a singularly weak position to question Britain's claim to sovereignty over the Six Counties, that territory being in the same relationship to Britain as Goa to Portugal.

Attitude of the Holy See

During a visit to Rome last July, Mr. Nehru was received by the Pope. At a subsequent press conference he said that he had discussed the Goan problem with His Holiness who agreed with him that Goa was not a religious problem. The attitude of the Vatican was later confirmed by an article in the Osservatore Romano which, after referring to Portugal's "glorious missionary tradition" and to India's assurances of respect for the rights of Goan Catholics if they should come under her control, went on:

"Contrary to what has been asserted by some, the problem of Goa is not a religious question. There is, however, a political question, lively and acute.

Now, it is known that the Holy See does not intend to interfere in purely political questions or matters of this kind. It is, and wishes to remain, impartial and neutral."

This must be a bitter blow to Mr. Salazar who had spoken of Goa as "an indispensable base for the conservation and spread of Christianity in India", but no doubt the Vatican had in mind the continued well-being of the five million Catholics in India. Cardinal Gracias Archbishop of Bombay, has stated in relation to the Goan dispute that Catholics in Goa have nothing to fear from incorporation in India.

Attitude of the USA

A joint statement issued by Mr. Dulles and the Portuguese Foreign Minister last December, after the conclusion of formal talks in Washington, said that they had discussed various statements attributed to Soviet rulers visiting Asia including "allegations concerning the Portuguese provinces in the Far East" (while in India the Soviet leaders had expressed full support for India's claim to Goa). Questioned by the Press as to whether the USA considered Goa to be a Portuguese province, Mr. Dulles replied: - "As far as I know all the world regards it as a Portuguese province. It has been Portuguese for 400 years." This inept statement led to a storm of protest in India and to sharp comment in the USA. At a further press conference Mr. Dulles said that the USA was in no way a party to the dispute and that he had not sought to express any opinion on the merits of the case in the joint statement which was directed primarily against the Soviet declarations.

General attitude of neutrality

In effect neither party to the dispute has succeeded in eliciting open support from the Western Countries. Speaking to a group of Indian Goans on the 4th June last, Mr. Nehru called on the Western Powers to define precisely their attitude in relation to Goa. In a note dated 25th June the Portuguese Chargé d'Affaires drew the attention of the Minister to this statement and expressed the hope that the Irish Government would continue to maintain a friendly attitude.

There can be few, however, who believe that Portugal will be able to retain this foothold in the Asian Continent.

Political Section,
Dept. of External Affairs

197
Ofício, Encarregado de Negócios irlandês em Lisboa ao Secretário-Geral do DEA: Lisboa, 2 de Julho de 1956[13]

This afternoon at 4 p.m. Dr. Caldeira Queiroz, Director of Political Affairs in the Ministry of Foreign Affairs, asked me to call on him.

After the usual preliminary courtesy remarks he explained that the object of his request to see me was in connection with Mr. Nehru's speech in Bombay on the 4th June, prior to his tour to a number of world capitals. In that speech, inter alia, Mr. Nehru had expressed the conviction that third countries could not, as a matter of principle, continue to fail to express themselves positively on one side or the other in the Indian-Portuguese dispute over the Portuguese possessions in

---

[13] NAI, DEA, 305/271B Goa and the other Portuguese enclaves in India 1956-1958.

India. This, Dr. Queiroz stated, had caused the Portuguese authorities great concern since it clearly implied that Mr. Nehru in his visits to the various capitals was determined to seek public expression of sympathy with the Indian position from Government spokesmen. In these circumstances, the Portuguese authorities had instructed their diplomatic representatives in the countries which Mr. Nehru proposed to visit, to make a special démarche to the Governments concerned to emphasize the critical importance which the Portuguese Government attached to this matter and to request that the Governments concerned would, in the interests of continued friendly relations with Portugal take steps to guard against any official pronouncement on the Indian-Portuguese issue which might possibly be construed – and exploited by the Indians as such – as endorsement or even sympathy with the Indian position.

Dr. Queiroz went on to say that in the case of Ireland, thought they did not think at the time that a visit to Dublin was on Mr. Nehru's itinerary, they had, because of Madame Pandita's official position as Ambassador to Ireland, instructed the Chargé d'Affaires in Dublin to make a similar démarche to our Government. A note was, Dr. Queiroz continued, accordingly presented by the Chargé d'Affaires to your goodself [sic] on the 26th June. You had, he added, as always, received the Chargé d'Affaires in the most warm and friendly fashion and assured him that you would bring the Portuguese request to the immediate attention of our Minister and would underline the importance attached to it by the Portuguese Government.

In the meantime, Dr. Queiroz went on, there had been a further important development in the sense that they had since learned that Mr. Nehru, accompanied by his sister, would in fact make an official visit to Dublin on the 7th to 9th July. In the light of this, the Minister for Foreign Affairs, Dr. Paulo Cunha, had instructed him to see me and request me to emphasize to my authorities in Dublin the very great importance which the Portuguese authorities attach to the request presented by their Chargé d'Affaires on the 26th June. Both he personally, Dr. Queiroz continued, and his authorities were confident that our Government would not wilfully make any public pronouncement in the course of Mr. Nehru's visit which would hurt Portuguese interest but there was, they feared, always the danger that unless great care to prevent it was taken, it might happen that in the course of the naturally friendly greetings which understandably would be proffered to Mr. Nehru on his arrival or during his stay in Ireland, something might be said which the propaganda-minded pro-Indian side would be ready to pounce on and exploit – even out of its context – as an official expression of support for India in the Portuguese-Indian dispute. The Portuguese authorities, therefore, wanted to be absolutely certain that our Government had a crystal-clear awareness of the depth of the Portuguese concern on this matter and it was entirely for that reasons that they were requesting me to put the matter again to my authorities in Dublin, in reinforcement of the démarche made by their Chargé d'Affaires on the 26th June.

I told Dr. Queiroz that I would not fail to transmit this message to Dublin, where, I added, I was confident that it would be considered most sympathetically.

Thomas Commins

198
Carta, Subsecretário-Geral do DEA ao Encarregado de Negócios português em Dublin: Dublin, 10 de Julho de 1956[14]

Sir,

I have the honour to acknowledge receipt of your Note of the 25th June relating to the position in Goa, the contents of which have been duly noted.

I have the honour to be, Sir,

Yours faithfully,

J. A. Belton
For the Minister for External Affairs.

---

[14] NAI, DEA, 305/271B Goa and the other Portuguese enclaves in India 1956-1958.

1957

199
Ofício, Encarregado de Negócios irlandês em Lisboa ao Secretário-Geral do DEA: Lisboa, 25 de Janeiro de 1957[15]

STATE VISIT OF QUEEN ELIZABETH II TO PORTUGAL

[…]

I assume that it will be proper for me to accept the three invitations to which I referred above, in common with my other colleagues. I should be very grateful for early instructions should, however, the contrary be the case.

Thomas Commins

200
Telegrama, Estero à Representação Permanente da Irlanda junto das Nações Unidas (UNEIREANN): Dublin, 1 de Fevereiro de 1957[16]

UNEIREANN

(PERMANENT MISSION OF IRELAND TO THE UN BEAUX ARTS HOTEL 307 EAST 44TH ST RM 901-N) NEW YORK

23 MINISTER HAS RECEIVED REPRESENTATIONS FROM PORTUGUESE CHARGE D'AFFAIRES REGARDING UN INTENTION TO DISCUSS POSITION OF PORTUGUESE OVERSEAS TERRITORIES CHARGE D'AFFAIRES MADE CASE (1) THERE ARE NO NON-AUTONOMOUS PORTUGUESE OVERSEAS TERRITORIES THEY ARE IN PRECISELY THE SAME POSITION PORTUGAL ITSELF (2) IN THESE CASES WHOLE QUESTION IS DOMESTIC AND ANY DISCUSSION AN INFRINGEMENT OF PORTUGUESE SOVEREIGNTY (3) ASSEMBLY HAS NO RIGHT UNDER ARTICLE 73 OF THE CHARTER TO DEFINE TERRITORY STOP NO PROMISE WAS GIVEN TO CHARGE

---

[15] NAI, DEA, 313/11D Confidential reports from Lisbon Legation, 1956-1957.

[16] NAI, DEA, Permanent Mission to the United Nations, X17, Portugal, 1956-1963.

D'AFFAIRES STOP THE MINISTER LEAVES MATTER ENTIRELY TO YOUR DISCRETION MINISTER WOULD LIKE YOUR VIEWS SOONEST ON THE LINES TO BE TAKEN ON ALGERIA

ESTERO

201
Ofício, Representante Permanente da Irlanda junto das Nações Unidas ao Secretário-Geral do DEA: Nova Iorque, 7 de Fevereiro de 1957[17]

With reference to your cypher telegram No. 23 about the representations received by the Minister from the Portuguese Chargé d'Affaires regarding the difficulty experienced by the Portuguese delegation here in connection with the Portuguese overseas territories, I beg to state that I had already been approached on this question by the Portuguese Ambassador here before I received your telegram.

You will, no doubt, be familiar with the point involved. Portugal insists that her overseas territories are not colonies at all but provinces of Portugal on the same footing as the provinces of the Portuguese mainland. On that ground, Portugal, when she became a member of the United Nations, did not furnish any list of her overseas possessions, as members of the United Nations are required to do. This point was raised by the Indian and other Afro-Asian delegations in the Fourth Committee as part of their general drive against "colonialism".

We had very grave doubts about the wisdom and soundness of the Portuguese stand. Her position that Portugal is not a Colonial Power at all because her overseas possessions are really part of the mainland is, to say the least of it, naieve [sic]. On the other hand, the Afro-Asian drive against "colonialism" has become so irrational, immoderate and undiscriminating that, at the present stage, probably more harm than good is done by lending it encouragement on points of this kind. This is all the more so as the Afro-Asians themselves show no regard whatever for the principles on which they base their attacks on the Colonial Powers in cases in which their own interests happen to be involved.

---

[17] NAI, DEA, 305/271B Goa and the other Portuguese enclaves in India 1956-1958.

Examples of this are the Indian attitude on Kashmir and Indonesia's claim that West New Guinea should be a part of Indonesia simply because Indonesia and West New Guinea were comprised under the same Dutch Colonial administration. Balancing these conflicting considerations against one another, I felt that this was a case in which we could justifiably lend support to Portugal and we, accordingly, voted in her favour when the matter came up at the Fourth Committee. The vote went against Portugal by 35 to 33 but I gather from the Portuguese Ambassador that he has some hopes of being able to swing the vote in the other direction when the matter comes to the Plenary Assembly.

F. H. Boland

202
Carta, Representante Permanente de Portugal junto das Nações Unidas ao Representante Permanente da Irlanda junto das Nações Unidas: Nova Iorque, 7 de Fevereiro de 1957[18]

N.12

Your Excellency,

I have the honour to refer to the debate concluded on February 5th in the 4th Committee concerning the transmission of information under article 73 e) of the Charter of the United Nations.

It is my privilege to express to Your Excellency, on behalf of my delegation and of myself, our most sincere thanks for the vote cast by your delegation on the draft resolution submitted (document A/C.4/L.467).

My Government have been informed of the invaluable support which the Irish Delegation has given Portugal and they are conveying their appreciation directly to your Government.

I have the honour to present to Your Excellency the assurances of my highest consideration.

Vasco V. Garin

---
[18] NAI, DEA, Permanent Mission to the United Nations, X17, Portugal, 1956-1963.

203
Ofício, Encarregado de Negócios irlandês em Lisboa ao Secretário-Geral do DEA: Lisboa, 28 de Fevereiro de 1957[19]

<u>STATE VISIT OF QUEEN ELIZABETH II TO PORTUGAL</u>

I have the honour to report as follows:

The visit of Queen Elizabeth and the Duke of Edinburgh, which ended on the 21st inst. created the most intense enthusiasm here among all sections of the population and can unreservedly be said to have fulfilled the highest expectations.

2. From the Portuguese official point of view this outcome was doubly welcome. In the first place it has served as a "shot in the arm" to the centuries-old Portuguese-British alliance and present this alliance to the younger people as a real living force; in the second place it has served to dispel criticism of the enormous amount of money which was spent in preparation for the visit – criticism which was quite widespread before the visit took place. What the exact figure of expenditure was had not been divulged but a figure as high as Esc. 80 million (£1 million) is held to be not wide of the mark. Many people, however, put it at very much higher.

3. As far as one learns, the Royal visit was not made the occasion of discussion of any specific political question. The Queen was, of course, accompanied by the Foreign Minister, Selwyn Lloyd, and the latter had one private conversation with Dr. Paulo Cunha at the Ministry of Foreign Affairs. Dr. Salazar also called on the Queen at Queluz and spent about three quarters of an hour in private conversation with her.

4. The speeches made at the official banquet by President Craveiro Lopes, welcoming the Queen and by the Queen in reply contained nothing over and above recalling the traditional friendship between Portugal and England, unbroken since the Treaty of Alliance signed in 1373. This Treaty has remained in force ever since with only slight modifications under subsequent instrument,

---

[19] NAI, DEA, 313/11D Confidential reports from Lisbon Legation, 1956-1957.

mainly to meet new procedural requirements of changing times. It is interesting to note that under the Treaty, in the case of an attack by a third party on any part of the Portuguese territories Britain is automatically committed to come to the aid of Portugal, but in the converse situation, i.e. an attack on Britain, Portugal is not likewise committed. Britain must request Portuguese intervention if she wishes it. The major advantage of this situation to Portugal is that she does not require to maintain a Navy of the proportions which otherwise would be necessary to protect her overseas possessions. In case of need the British Navy is committed to her defence.

5. It is by virtue of this Treaty – though indirectly – that the US secured the use of the Azores during the last war. These facilities were not, however, granted at the direct request of the US. Portugal, in fact, refused such a request on the part of the US but suggested to them simultaneously that they get the British to request these facilities under the Alliance. This was done and the use of the Azores was granted to Britain within 24 hours of her démarche. The facilities so granted were straight away transferred by Britain to the US as her Allies. The US bases in the Azores are, of course, now held under the Portuguese-US. Mutual Defence Treaty of 1951 which expired on 1st September last and towards the renewal of which negotiations were begun at service level about six months ago. It was announced, however, on January 23rd that these negotiations were temporarily postponed owing to the illness of the Portuguese Foreign Minister but that pending their resumption the facilities conceded by the 1951 Accord would be carried on. I was told, however, by the US Naval Attaché very recently that the illness of Dr. Paulo Cunha was pleaded simply as a cover to hide the real situation, which was that the Portuguese authorities, dissatisfied with US policy in the handling of the British-French intervention in Egypt, culminating in the fall of Eden from power, and, secondly, anticipating the UN debate which has just ended (in the Trusteeship Committee and General Assembly) and which was aimed specifically at Portugal's administration of her overseas territories, abruptly interrupted the Treaty discussions where matters had reached the point of submission to Ministers, until the outcome of that debate – including in particular the line taken by the US therein – became known.

6. On the face of it this story appears plausible enough, since in the absence of some such special consideration, there was no apparent reason why the Treaty negotiations should not have been seen through by Dr. Marcello Caetano, Minister of the Presidency – and second only to Salazar in the Government hierarchy – who took over the Ministry of Foreign Affairs in Dr. Paulo Cunha's absence. All the more so as there have been (and continue to be) strong rumours that Dr. Paulo Cunha because of illness and for other reasons which I have dealt with in a separate report, is not likely to remain as Foreign Minister very much longer.

7. To revert to the Queen's visit, it was pleasing to note that in no instance, in the press of radio, was she referred to as Queen of Northern Ireland.

8. At the reception for the Diplomatic Corps held at the Palace of Queluz on the morning of the 19th inst., only Heads of Missions and their wives were present. The procedure was that each Head of Mission (and wife) was introduced in their turn to the Queen and Duke of Edinburgh and had a few seconds conversation with them. In my case, after the usual standard remarks in the sense of asking me how long I had been in Portugal, where I had served before, etc., the Duke of Edinburgh (who, of course, had been some four months out of England) asked after Mr. Fred Boland, former Ambassador in London. Before I could reply the Queen turned to him and said that Mr. Boland was now our representative at the United Nations. She then made some complimentary remarks about his Ambassadorship in London and wished him well in his new "and arduous" post.

9. Immediately afterwards I had a few minutes conversation with Selwyn Lloyd (to whom the members of the Corps were introduced by the British Ambassador after speaking to the Queen and Duke of Edinburgh). He expressed general interest in our elections and said that he had the pleasure of meeting our Minister in New York at the UN National [sic] assembly in November last. He referred especially to Mr. Cosgrave's address to the Assembly on the 30th November as "among the finest and most telling speeches ever made before this Assembly."

Tom Commins

204

Ofício, Encarregado de Negócios irlandês em Lisboa ao Secretário-Geral do DEA: Lisboa, 5 de Março de 1957[20]

RECENT INTERNATIONAL DEVELOPMENTS

I have the honour to report as follows:

The recently concluded debate in the UN Trusteeship Committee and General Assembly on the resolution proposed by Siria [sic], Lebanon, Mepal [sic], Ceylon and Greece regarding non-self-governing territories was followed with intense interest – and, indeed, a degree of indignation – in Portugal. The resolution being aimed entirely at Portugal, the eventual outcome resulting in its defeat in the General Assembly was received here with great acclaim and no little relief.

2. For, had the motion been carried, Portugal would have been faced with the choice of agreeing to subject all or some of her overseas territories to the investigation processes of the UN, or alternatively, of withdrawing from the Organisation. There is little doubt that she would have chosen the latter. Though such a threat was never specifically formulated, statements from various Ministers here during the course of the UN discussions made perfectly clear Portuguese intentions in the matter. For instance, the Minister of the Presidency, Prof. Marcello Caetano, referring on the 9th February to the outcome of the debate in the Trusteeship Committee stated that in no circumstances could Portugal "so degrade her political constitution as the [sic] change it for deliberations or decisions within the UN." He went on to express the hope that some States which had voted against Portugal in the Committee and "which we consider friendly and have acted in good faith" would change their viewpoint and come to accept the proper doctrine i.e. that under the charter the basic constitution of every member State must be accepted as inviolable and not open to question. Similar remarks were earlier made by the Minister for Overseas Territories, in Lisbon, in which he reaffirmed that Portugal did not have any territories that were not

---

[20] NAI, DEA, 313/11D Confidential reports from Lisbon Legation, 1956-1957.

autonomous, the Overseas Provinces being self-administered in the same way as Metropolitan Portugal.

Tom Commins

205
Carta, Subsecretário-Geral do DEA ao Representante Permanente da Irlanda junto das Nações Unidas: Dublin, 16 de Setembro de 1957[21]

CONFIDENTIAL

Just before leaving for New York, Conor O'Brien[22] happened to mention to Sheila Murphy that the Minister has decided that the delegation should not support Portugal at this Session on the "Goa" issue. As Sheila told Conor, we have, for some months past, been negotiating with the Portuguese about the abolition of discrimination against the Irish flag in Continental Portugal, a matter that is of considerable interest to Irish Shipping Ltd. You will see from the attached memo that agreement in principle has been reached with the Portuguese, but that it may be some little time before the necessary exchange of notes can be effected. Would you be good enough to bring the matter to the Minister's attention? We will, of course, keep you informed of developments at this end

Yours sincerely,
John. A. Belton

206
Telegrama, Estero a Uneireann: Dublin, 23 de Outubro de 1957[23]

118 ABSTAIN ON GOA VOTE WITHOUT EXPLAINING STOP TAOISEACH THINKS WE DO NOT KNOW ENOUGH AS TO ACTUAL SITUATION TO VOTE

ESTERO

---

[21] NAI, DEA, 305/271B Goa and the other Portuguese enclaves in India 1956-1958.

[22] Conor Cruise O'Brien. Nascido em 1917. Diplomata irlandês, serviu na Embaixada em Paris e depois na Representação Permanente junto das Nações Unidas. Mais tarde foi o Representante Especial do Secretário-Geral das Nações Unidas no Congo. Autor de *To Katanga and Back* (1962).

[23] NAI, DEA, Permanent Mission to the United Nations, X17, Portugal, 1956-1963.

207
Telegrama, Uneireann a Estero: Nova Iorque, 4 de Novembro de 1957[24]

132 OUR LAST 130 SHOULD BE NUMBERED 131 YOUR 118 FOR MINISTER OPERATIVE PART OF RESOLUTION JUST INTRODUCED IN FOURTH COMMITTEE AND SPONSORED BY FIFTEEN COUNTRIES AS FOLLOWS

QUOTE (1) INVITES THE SECRETARY GENERAL TO PREPARE A SUMMARY OF THE OPINIONS AS GIVEN IN REPLIES OF THE MEMBERS TO THE COMMUNICATIONS OF THE SECRETARY GENERAL ON THE SUBJECT OF THE TRANSMISSION OF INFORMATION COMMA IN THE STATEMENTS MADE BY THE MEMBERS DURING DISCUSSION IN THE COMMITTEES CONCERNED COMMA AND IN RELEVANT TREATISES ON THE INTERPRETATION OF THE CHARTER SEMI COLON

(2) DECIDES TO ESTABLISH A COMMITTEE OF SIX MEMBERS TO BE ELECTED BY THE FOURTH COMMITTEE ON BEHALF OF THE GENERAL ASSEMBLY IN ORDER TO STUDY THE SECRETARY GENERALS SUMMARY AND TO REPORT ON THE RESULTS OF ITS STUDY TO THE NEXT ORDINARY SESSION OF THE GENERAL ASSEMBLY UNQUOTE OUR 133 FOLLOWS

UNEIREANN

208
Telegrama, Uneireann a Estero: Nova Iorque, 4 de Novembro de 1957[25]

133 OUR 132 THIS RESOLUTION RESEMBLES THAT ADOPTED BY SMALL MAJORITY IN FOURTH COMMITTEE LAST ASSEMBLY BUT WHICH DID NOT OBTAIN NECESSARY TWO THIRDS MAJORITY IN GENERAL ASSEMBLY ITSELF STOP VOTE LIKELY WEDNESDAY STOP IN LIGHT YOUR 118 PRESUME WE SHOULD ABSTAIN

UNEIREANN

---

[24] NAI, DEA, Permanent Mission to the United Nations, X17, Portugal, 1956-1963.
[25] NAI, DEA, Permanent Mission to the United Nations, X17, Portugal, 1956-1963.

209
Ofício, Conselheiro da Representação Permanente da Irlanda junto das Nações Unidas ao Secretário-Geral do DEA:
Nova Iorque, 7 de Novembro de 1957[26]

I have to refer to your cable N.º 132 regarding the question of the transmission of information on non-self-governing territories under article 73e of the Charter (agenda item 35c) and to our cable N.º 139 in which we indicated the result of the vote in the Fourth Committee on the 5th November on the resolution, copy of which is enclosed herewith. It will be noted that Portugal is not mentioned on the text but the non-self-governing territories of Portugal were principally in the mind of the sponsors.

2. The debate on this item concluded in the Fourth Committee this morning and it is expected that the resolution will come before the General Assembly about the middle of next week.

3. It will be recalled that at the last General Assembly a resolution on similar lines to the enclosed was adopted by the Fourth Committee. When it came later before the General Assembly however, a vote was taken as to whether a decision on the resolution should be decided by a two-thirds majority in accordance with article 18.3 of the Charter. A majority of members in the Assembly (including Ireland) voted in favour of the two-thirds majority and the resolution itself failed, in the subsequent division to achieve this two-thirds majority. In these circumstances the resolution was not adopted.

4. [...]

5. [...]

6. [...]

7. The vote next week in the General Assembly will be of great importance because it is likely that there is not a two-thirds majority in favour of the attached draft resolution. We would propose, if you agree, to abstain on the vote as to whether a two-thirds majority is necessary in line with our previous abstentions

---

[26] NAI, DEA, Permanent Mission to the United Nations, X17, Portugal, 1956-1963.

in the Fourth Committee on votes to the question of Portuguese non-self-governing territories. If you would not agree with this proposal we feel the next best alternative would be to vote in favour of the two-thirds majority as we did in the last Assembly and adding an <u>explication de vote</u> in which we would say that we had decided to vote on the issue in the same way as we did in the last Assembly because we feel that this is an "important question" and because we do not wish to change our vote on the issue until the 6th Committee's considered views on the whole question are received.

8. In connection with our recommendations above we must bring to your attention the fact that the Permanent Representative of Portugal has made the most urgent and pressing representations to us in favour of Ireland voting for the proposal to decide the resolution by a two-thirds majority. He stressed the fact that the issues raised in the resolution are of the utmost importance to Portugal and that it is the clear sense of Article 18.2 that "important questions" should be decided by a two-thirds majority. He also referred to the fact that the whole vote in question is, as mentioned above, now before the 6th Committee and that, in these circumstances we might await its considered opinion before changing our vote in the last Assembly in favour of a two-thirds majority. Finally he stated categorically that if the resolution is adopted by the General Assembly it will strain Portugal's relations with the United Nations to the utmost and might even result in Portugal leaving the Organisation. He has mentioned the fact that, in line with the vote in the Fourth Committee, the other members of Western Europe will, in all probability, vote in favour of the two-thirds majority so that if Ireland does not do so she probably will stand alone in this respect among the countries of Western Europe who have such close bonds of friendship with Portugal.

9. We should be grateful for your cabled instructions before the middle of next week.

E.L Kennedy for Permanent Representative

210
Telegrama, Estero a Uneireann: Dublin, 11 de Novembro de 1957[27]

140 FROM MINISTER FOR AMBASSADOR CONTINUE TO ABSTAIN ON GOA QUESTION

ESTERO

211
Ofício, Conselheiro da Representação Permanente da Irlanda junto das Nações Unidas ao Secretário-Geral do DEA:
Nova Iorque, 13 de Novembro de 1957[28]

URGENT

I have to refer to your telegram N.º 140 and our minute J/16/1 of the 7th November regarding the question of the transmission of information on non-self-governing territories [...] The voting in this occasion in the Committee was 42 in favour, 27 against, and 8 abstentions. The voting last time was 35 in favour, 33 against with 4 abstentions.

2. [...]

3. It will be observed that the main trend of the voting in the Fourth Committee in this Assembly as compared with the last Assembly is away from opposition to the motion i.e. a weakening of support for the position taken up by Portugal. Five countries (including Ireland) which were against the motion in the Committee's vote at the last Assembly, abstained this time [...]

4. The main reasons given by Delegates both in the debate and in private conversation in explication of the trend away from the support of Portugal were:

(a) The resolution (A/C.4/L.504 Rev. 2) adopted this year is a milder and more reasonable text than that before the Committee last time. The latter was

---

[27] NAI, DEA, Permanent Mission to the United Nations, X17, Portugal, 1956-1963.
[28] NAI, DEA, Permanent Mission to the United Nations, X17, Portugal, 1956-1963.

directed specifically at new members and was particularly resented by Portugal; the present text does not refer to new members at all, and merely calls for a study by the Secretary General of the problem.

(b) There has also been a growing impatience with the continued unwillingmess of the Portuguese authorities to comply with the provisions of Article 73 (e) of the Charter. Delegations find it increasingly difficult to accept the fact that such territories as Damao, Diu and Goa in India, Macau in China, Portuguese Timor, the Cape Verde Islands and the Islands of San Tome and Principe, to say nothing of Angola and Mozambique, are self-governing territories and an integral part of Portugal.

(c) [...]

E. L. Kennedy for the Permanent Representative

212

Telegrama, Uneireann a Estero:
Nova Iorque, 26 de Novembro de 1957[29]

150 YOUR 140 GENERAL ASSEMBLY TODAY DECIDED THAT TWO THIRDS MAJORITY NECESSARY STOP VOTING WAS 38 FOR 36 AGAINST 7 ABSTAINING INCLUDING IRELAND STOP VOTING LATER ON RESOLUTION ITSELF WAS 41 FOR 30 AGAINST 10 ABSTAINING INCLUDING IRELAND STOP RESOLUTION THEREFORE REJECTED AS REQUIRED TWO THIRDS MAJORITY NOT OBTAINED

UNEIREANN

---

[29] NAI, DEA, Permanent Mission to the United Nations, X17, Portugal, 1956-1963.

213
Ofício, Embaixador irlandês em Madrid ao Secretário-Geral do DEA: Madrid, 9 de Dezembro de 1957[30]

CONFIDENTIAL

<u>Re Goa, the Portuguese Enclave in India</u>

The Portuguese Ambassador spoke to me at a recent function in the Spanish Diplomatic School on the subject of Ifni, which is, of course, exercising the minds of everyone here.

He commented on the new sympathy the Spaniards seem to have found for the French occupants of Algeria, saying that Spain is at last beginning to feel the pinch that other colonial Powers have already had to experience from Arabs and other native peoples.

I agreed that the Spaniards are certainly having a bad time but that, of course, one must realize that no State liked having an enclave, such as Ifni, penetrating into its national territory. We, in Ireland, understood the Moroccan point of view in the matter also.

Mr. Nosolini then suggested that the Irish people would surely be making a mistake if they identified their problem with that of every part of the world which white Europeans had colonised and civilised. Ireland was a white, European and fully civilised country throughout her long history and therefore the notion of "colonialism" should not be thought by the Irish people to have the least application to Ireland.

I replied that, in common with a lot of other twentieth-century people, we in Ireland just did not find it possible to sympathise with "colonialism" or, perhaps, to put it in another way, we believed in self-determination.

My friend asked me if I meant plebiscites for all, because our Moroccan colleague had made some such suggestion about Algeria (on which he said he had declined to express a view). The Portuguese Ambassador, thinking of the

---

[30] NAI, DEA, 305/271B Goa and the other Portuguese enclaves in India 1956-1958.

various foreign elements comprised in Morocco asked the Moroccan if his Government would like to run a series of plebiscites in their new State, just to ensure that everyone got exactly the régime they wanted!

After some further remarks of this kind, my Portuguese colleague mentioned to me that Ireland had taken the Indian side at UNO in regard to Goa. He felt we had made a mistake, especially if we had been basing our attitude on some imaginary similarity between the Goa situation and that of the Six Counties. Goa was an enclave, but Canada could be argued to be the same in that part of the American Continent which the USA (calling itself "America") might claim to be entitled to control in its entirety. Civilised Europeans had been establishing enclaves for centuries in various parts of the world, generally bettering the standard of life in those places and sometimes, as in the case of Goa, succeeding in creating a kind of new self-contained entity, which while "happily married" to the hinterland, had no desire for total absorption. "Colonialism", he added, was now a fashionable byword and everyone connected with developing the resources of undeveloped areas to the betterment of all concerned, was regarded as a "criminal".

I had not been specifically briefed by the Department in the latest Goa developments (when in charge of the Department's Political Section myself, I had favoured a neutral attitude to both Goa and Kashmir) so I was extremely glad to be saved by an interruption from continuing this rather embarrassing discussion with Mr. Nosolini.

Perhaps it would be possible, sometime, to supply our Embassies (ours in particular), with an outline of the present policy vis-à-vis India. There is, as yet, no Indian Mission at Madrid: Nehru's Government has scarcely a friend here, among either Spaniards or the foreign representatives accredited to Spain.

Michael Rynne

214
Carta, Secretário-Geral do DEA ao Embaixador irlandês em Madrid: Dublin, 19 de Dezembro de 1957[31]

With reference to your recent report PR7/57 of 9th December concerning Goa, I am to enclose for your information a brief summary of the position as supplied to the Chargé d'Affaires at Lisbon.[32] You should note that Ireland abstained on all the resolutions voted on during the recent UN session. India voted in favour of the resolution directed against Portugal in both the Fourth Committee and General Assembly. India also voted in favour of seeking the decision of the Sixth (Legal) Committee on the question of the majority required to adopt a resolution of the type proposed and voted against the General Assembly resolution making a two-thirds majority necessary.

Yours sincerely,
C. C. Cremin

1958

215
Ofício, Encarregado de Negócios irlandês em Lisboa ao Secretário-Geral do DEA: Lisboa, 7 de Julho de 1958[33]

Senhora D. Berta Craveiro Lopes, wife of the Portuguese President, died rather unexpectedly (that is, from the public's point of view) on Saturday evening last. Following what appears to have been a general nervous breakdown two weeks ago, her condition got increasingly worse and culminated in a brain haemorrhage on Friday. She was 59.

---

[31] NAI, DEA, Embassy Madrid, I.P. 4/51/1, Portugal 1941-1963.
[32] Incluído com o ofício.
[33] NAI, DEA, 313/11E Confidential reports from Lisbon Legation, 1958.

She was accorded what might be described as a semi-state funeral, in the sense that while no formal military or other honours were rendered, the President elect, Admiral Américo Thomaz and his wife together with the entire Government, headed by Salazar, all Heads of Diplomatic Missions led by the Nuncio, the Bishop of Mitilene representing the Cardinal Patriarch and all other civil and military dignataries attended a solemn Requiem Mass at 11 a.m. on Sunday last at the Church of Jerónimos […]

As a footnote to the above I have head a number of highly placed Portuguese express the opinion that Senhora Craveiro Lopes' swift decline in health was due in no little measure to the cavalier treatment shown to her husband in the context of the recent Presidential election. This is a matter which I am covering in a separate report which I am preparing on the elections and its [sic] significance. Suffice it to say here that the powers that be, having decided against Craveiro Lopes as their nomination for the next seven-years term, seemed to go out of their way to treat him with deliberate discourtesy. On the announcement of Almirante Thomaz as the candidate no reference of any nature was made to Craveiro Lopes either by way of explanation of his not standing again or of appreciation for his work during the last seven years and it remained for Dr. Salazar, at his last speech to the União Nacional, the day before the election to say the first and very few words of appreciation of Craveiro Lopes for his conduct of the Presidency during his period of office. All of this is said to have had a most deleterious effect in [sic] the health of the President's wife, who had truly gained the affection and respect of all classes and who did not spare herself in the discharge of her many and demanding duties. This may have a bearing on the fact that Dr. Salazar's personal participation in her obsequies was obviously very much more than the formal appearance which such an occasion would normally demand of him.

Thomas Commins

216
Ofício, Encarregado de Negócios irlandês em Lisboa ao Secretário-Geral do DEA: Lisboa, 6 de Agosto de 1958[34]

CONFIDENTIAL

Item 36 of provisional agenda of the Thirteenth regular session of the United Nations 16th September 1958
Portugal and Article 73 of the Charter

I have the honour to report that in the course of a general talk with I had yesterday on a number of matters with Dr. Caldeira Queiroz, Secretary General of the Ministry of Foreign Affairs, he brought up the above question and asked whether I thought we would maintain at this year's Assembly debate the same attitude as we took last year. I told him that I had no indications from Dublin on the matter and he went on to express the great disappointment caused here by our vote last year, when, with the exception of Greece (which voted against the Portuguese) we were the only Western country to indicate, by our abstention, lack of support for Portugal in this vital matter. Out attitude he said seemed to him to be out of harmony both with the traditional relations of friendship between Portugal and Ireland, and with a proper interpretation of the Charter.

2. Referring to the closeness of last year's voting, which muct certainly be expected to be repeated this year, he said he could not emphasize how far-reaching would be the consequence of an adverse vote this year. Under no circumstances whatever, he said, could or would Portugal permit the veracity of the Portuguese Constitution to be questioned in the United Nations, and that was what their acceptance of an obligation under par. 73, either voluntary or in deference to a UN vote would entail. The importance to them of the Irish vote in these circumstances was self-evident he said, but it meant even more in the sense that from the moral point of view it had a special importance in itself as the vote of Ireland.

---

[34] NAI, DEA, 313/11E Confidential reports from Lisbon Legation, 1958.

3. He could not doubt, himself, he said, that the Irish Government of which he had personal experience on the spot and which he respected unreservedly as responsible, objective and inspired by high ideals, must have had what to them appeared very good reason for the change of heart last year as compared with the year before but, frankly, he said, those reasons must lie either outside this specific problem or else in a misinterpretation of the Portuguese position viz-à--viz the provisions of the Charter. He hoped very much, he said, that we would find it possible to review our attitude on the matter before the next debate and was anxious to do everything possible towards that end to clarify the Portuguese position in order to dispel misunderstandings or misinterpretations which he felt might underly the position taken up by us last year.

4. He asked me if I would be willing to discuss the matter in this sense with the Dr. Franco Nogueira, Head of the United Nations Section, in the following day (i.e. today) and I said that I certainly would and would be very happy to convey his views and those of Dr. Nogueira to my Government in detail and immediately. He thereupon arranged for me to call on Dr. Nogueira this morning.

5. Dr. Nogueira, who will accompany the Portuguese Delegation to New York, was a member of last year's Delegation and spoke with appreciation of the friendly relations he had had with members of our Delegation whom he met last year. He restated the problem in the same terms as Dr. Queiroz and emphasized the strong preoccupation which his authorities had about the Irish position. On the facts of the case, he said, and by reference to the provisions of Chapters 10 and 12 of the Charter he could not find an explanation of our attitude. Apart from this it seemed to him that in abstaining from supporting the Portuguese position here, we were acting against our own traditional interests in Africa in the long term. This, apart altogether from our interests as a member of the Western Community. Ireland's particular interests in Africa as elsewhere were, he agreed, never territorial, they were interests directed towards Christianity and civilising. He was the first to agree that this interest was fully reconcilable with the absence of any desire to exercise a territorial sovereignty and he also saw that in the Irish mind it should be equally possible for other countries to exercise a civilizing and spiritually uplifting influence in Africa without cleaving to territorial conquests

there. But surely, he agreed, it was fundamentally important to the Irish interests that freedom of access of Missionaries to those areas be assured. And was it not more than conceivable that substitution there of the writ of present day Russian--inspired Afro-Asian suzerainty for that of the existing Christian Western powers would end Christian Missionary access to those area [sic] just as completely as the latter had been ended in Eastern Europe?

6. Or was our attitude dictated by our ingrained aversion for and well known opposition to "Colonialism"? If one thinks "colonialism" in terms of that of the 19th Century which for the most part involved race discrimination together with repression and exploitation of the native populations to the sole benefit of the European colonist, he, himself, would share freely our antagonism. But Portuguese colonisation of her Overseas possessions was, by the 19th Century, already some three centuries old and was from the beginning based squarely on absence of race discrimination and 19th Century-type exploitation. In no part of the Portuguese possessions is there or has there been at any time a movement of the native population for separation from Portugal. This is true of Goa, as it is of Angola and all the other possessions. There is, therefore, no question and never has been of Portuguese possessions been [sic] maintained by repression of native political aspirations towards independence.

7. As to the Charter, it is perfectly clear, he said, that the guiding principle laid down with the matter of the treatment of populations of non-self governing [sic] territories is the welfare of the populations. The Chapters devoted to this in the Charter are three, a reflection of the recognition given in the Charter to the existence of different constitutional régimes affecting these areas. Portugal and its Overseas Provinces represented together one unitary state and it was significant that in the whole course of the debates so far this was not challenged by any Delegation. Nor was any of the Portuguese Overseas possessions claimed by any other State; indeed, even India did not put forward any claim to Goa in her contribution to the debate. It was on the constitutional ground and the implication involved that Portugal refused and must continue to refuse to make a declaration under Article 73 of the Charter. This Article was specifically designed to cover native populations whose evolution towards political independence might be

expected in a matter of say ten to twelve years. It was open to no other interpretation. There was no such movement towards independence in any of the Portuguese territories. The native populations there regarded themselves as Portuguese in the fullest sense of Metropolitan citizenship.

8. This being so, it seemed to be evident that it was in the maintenance of the status quo that the overriding requirement of the Charter as affecting these populations i.e. their own welfare was best assured. Was it possible to believe that the Afro-Asian bloc was moved by disinterested concern for the welfare of those natives? It was the Portuguese unshakeable belief that the truth was entirely otherwise. Their interest was, not in the welfare of the natives, but in the substitution of their own sovereignty for that of the Portuguese and other Western Powers even against the will of the native populations, a development, which should it come about, would ensure the passage of control of these territories to the Communist bloc with the most far-reaching consequences for the West.

9. It had to be clearly understood that Portugal, in refusing to declare under Article 73, was not closing the door to information on her administration of these territories. Quite the contrary, they have and will continue to give all possible information required on economic, social and cultural and other policies and plans under article 55 of the Charter. The information so provided differs in no significant way from that which would be called for by a declaration under article 73; it is no the other hand open to more objective discussion and examination within the Organization than it would be if supplied under the latter Article. This reflects Portugal's unhesitating willingness to co-operate with those members of the UN whose interest in her overseas possessions is sincerely related to the welfare of the native populations.

10. In the light of these facts, Dr. Nogueira said it was inexplicable to them how the Irish Delegation could, on the merits of the case align themselves with the Afro-Asian bloc, and he and others had, therefore, cast around for some other explanation. The immediate one that suggested itself was related to the partition of Ireland and the very understandable fear of the Irish Government to take a stand which might conceivably recoil on them should they at some future date

that seemed propitious with to raise in the UN the question of the partition of Ireland or related questions such as the alleged violation of Human Rights and discrimination against the nationalist population in that area. But if that were so, said Dr. Nogueira, he would plead that there was no similarity between the two cases. In this one, that of N. Ireland, the territory is a disputed one between two United Nations members. The UK may hold it as constitutionally part of UK territory but equally the Irish Constitution (as I had earlier pointed out to Dr. Caldeira Queiroz in another context) claimed it formally as part of Irish territory. In the Portuguese case there is no such rivalry of claimants; the only concern of the UN under the Charter is with the welfare of the native populations, the appropriate machinery for dealing with which is contained in Article 55.

11. Dr. Nogueira then proceeded to refer to remarks of mine to Dr. Queiroz which, he said, Dr Queiroz had retailed [sic] to him about the participation of Portuguese naval vessels in NATO exercises off Northern Ireland. This I had represented to Dr. Queiroz as constituting at best an unfortunate indifference to Irish political sentiment. This is the subject of a separate report (Ref.7/14). He asked whether this might be a factor influencing the Irish Government's attitude. I told him that I had no information whatever to suggest that this had influenced or would in the future influence our Delegation's attitude towards Portugal in the UN debate. I had, I emphasized, mentioned the matter to Dr. Queiroz only because I was distressed to find that a further visit of Portuguese vessels to this area had taken place under British and NATO auspices early last month. I had not spoken under instructions nor had I been instructed to take any action in the matter. I had felt, however, that my Government would wish me to take the opportunity offered to me by my conversation with Dr. Queiroz to indicate that the protest which was made in this matter in 1952 had lost nothing of its force in the meantime and that the participation of third countries in such exercises in this area constituted an affront on their part to Irish national sentiment which was ill-designed to strengthen the friendly relations otherwise existing between them and Ireland. At his request, I gave Dr. Nogueira a fairly comprehensive description of the origin and development of the partition question, pointing out the serious problems which it has created for us not only in the economic but in

the internal political sphere. For us, I emphasized, it was a major problem, however inconsequential it might be regarded by other countries not affected by it, and we expected of those countries who professed friendly feelings for us to avoid actions liable to be interpreted as an endorsement by them of the existing situation. He listened to my exposition with the greatest interest and expressed himself as sincerely impressed by our point of view. Emphasizing that he spoke absolutely without authority on the subject, he asked, as a purely personal question, whether I thought that if his Government could go some way to meet us on this it would make any easier a new approach on our part to Portugal's problem in the UN. I repeated what I had earlier said about the status of my remarks on the subject repeating also that I had no indication at any time that the two matters were in any way related. This being said, I added, I was sure that he would agree that the elimination of a sources of irritation and friction between Governments must inevitably contribute greatly towards the creation of a more sympathetic outlook on the part of each towards the problems of the other.

12. Dr. Nogueira said that he could offer no authoritative comment on this issue, which he observed was not immediately within the scope of his responsibilities but remarked that speaking personally he would frankly say that our view was eminently reasonable and though he could see formidable difficulties in the way of the Portuguese Government meeting our wishes in this matter in the way we would like them to be met, he thought it a matter that might, with advantage, be further studied by them. He expressed the hope however that we for our part would re-examine sympathetically our position on the Portuguese problem in anticipation of the forthcoming Assembly test and he hoped that we could find it possible to support Portugal on this occasion which promised to be a crucial one. Even if we finally felt bound to maintain our abstention on the substantive question of the importance of the matter we might find it possible to vote affirmatively in favour of the Resolution requiring a two-thirds majority. So great was the importance that the Portuguese Government attached to this matter that they would most willingly send a Delegation to Dublin to discuss the matter with our Minister and Department if our Minister thought that such would contribute to a better understanding of the Portuguese case.

13. I would be grateful to have, in due course your reactions to this approach. I regret that this report is so long, but I feel it necessary to give you as full a picture as possible of the representations as put to me.

Thomas Commins

217
Ofício, Encarregado de Negócios irlandês em Lisboa ao Secretário-Geral do DEA: Lisboa, 25 de Agosto de 1958[35]

INAUGURATION OF THE NEW PORTUGUESE PRESIDENT

I have the honour to report that the new President of the Portuguese Republic, Admiral Américo Thomaz, was sworn in on the 9th inst. in the presence of the Cardinal Patriarch, Dr. Salazar and members of the Government, the Diplomatic Corps and Senior Officers and representatives of all the Services, in the course of a full dress ceremony at the Assembleia Nacional. He will hold office for a term of seven years.

2. The election of Admiral Thomaz followed a four-week election campaign of quite unprecedented vigour on the part of the Opposition, to such an extent indeed that the violence of the criticisms levelled against the régime including Dr. Salazar personally and the passion which they aroused in the large segment of the people who clearly showed that they shared those criticisms, led Dr. Salazar to announce after the campaign that this would be the last Presidential election held under direct suffrage and that the Government would take an early opportunity of having the 1933 Constitution amended so as to provide that future Presidents would be selected by the Chamber of Deputies and the Corporative Chamber jointly. In other words by the dedicated adherents of the régime, since the only nominees acceptable to the União Nacional have any possibility of securing seats in either of these bodies.

---

[35] NAI, DEA, 313/11E Confidential reports from Lisbon Legation, 1958.

3. There was evidence, on the day of the inauguration, that the powers that be, specifically the Ministry of the Interior and the União Nacional, had expended considerable effort to stir up a popular demonstration of enthusiasm. Bunting and other festive decorations were spread over large areas of the City and on the route Lisbon to Cascais (about 30 kms.) where Admiral Thomaz has his private house, to which he was due to return on completion of the Lisbon ceremonies. Miniature national flags were to be seen handed out all over the place to adults and children and householders in the Estrela and surrounding district of Lisbon as well as in the districts bordering on the Lisbon-Cascais route received in the preceding week circular letter from one or other or both of the two official bodies mentioned exhorting them to decorate their houses and join the side walk crowds to cheer the President on his way. Diplomatic households on these areas got these letters just as did the others.

In the event, there was no great display of popular enthusiasm. Crowds were thin and for the most part the people took advantage of the holiday declared to go to the beaches. On the other hand there were no counterdemonstrations as feared. In the immediately preceding weeks strong rumours were current that strikes were being organised in various parts of the country for that day. However, the day passed without incidents of this nature.

4. Having taken the oath of office the new President made a brief address in which he recalled that the oath he had taken imposed on him the obligation of upholding and fulfilling loyally and faithfully the Constitution, of complying with the law of the land, of promoting the general welfare of the country and of maintaining and defending the integrity and independence of the Portuguese nation. In a reference to the election campaign and the discontent it had brought to the surface, he went on to say:- "Except for one or two episodes we have managed to lead a tranquil political life for the past thirty years with manifest benefit to the country's progress and good name. Quite recently we went through one of these periods of unrest characterised by a sinister display of passion capable of poisoning the harmony of our existence. It is well, however, to be heedful of the sentiments and criticisms which seem to be justified. In all human achievements not everything is well done or carried out in accordance

with the best intentions. It would be improper to deny or minimise the great deal of good which has been accomplished, but we must put on record not only that which turns out well but also what is left undone or is not done well. It is the duty of the Administration to be aware of mistakes committed and shortcomings as they become evident since those who rule the country should be animated by a firm desire and constant pre-occupation of truly serving the cause which they represent."

5. Thus the new President foreshadowed the changes in the personnel of the Government implicit in some passages of Dr. Salazar's post-election address to the União Nacional, in which he affirmed that "the road for the future should be defined on the basis of our victory and not on recrimination", that this road should be "to complete, renew and continue as heretofore" and that in order "to pursue the renovation or vivification of the régime, changes of staff will be called for at various levels." Floods of complaints had, however, he said, been received about certain bodies, complaints deriving in some instances, perhaps, from a general lack of leadership or, in others, from the feeling that the corporative organisation was serving as a means of multiplying the number of intermediaries, suppressing competition and upholding again [sic] all comers and, to the general detriment, the positions acquired by the few. It had yet to be determined whether the discontent affected principles or their faulty application, but complaints had been made about the staff of many bodies which did not surprise him; he was however surprised that these complaints should have been repeated without steps being taken to rectify them.

6. On the 12th inst., far-reaching changes were announced in the composition of the Cabinet; these changes are the subject of a separate report.

7. In a reference to the international situation the President reiterated Dr. Salazar's unchanging appeal for a closing of the ranks of the West in defence of their material and moral interests. Observing that the differences between the two great blocs into which the World was divided had become accentuated, he went on to say: "One of these blocs is characterised by a policy which, though disconcerting, is always objective and dynamic, the other bloc by acts which are often incoherent, hesitating and contradictory. From these two differing policies

have resulted tangible gains for one side and losses – practically irrecoverable – for the other". In order to avoid greater evils it would, he concluded, seem indispensable that the Western World should define and follow a homogenous policy capable of ensuring not only peace but the integrity of the countries concerned.

8. On the 11th inst. the President received the Heads of Diplomatic Missions in the Palace of Belém, when the Nuncio made a short address of felicitation on behalf of the Corps, to which the President replied in suitable terms but without any pronouncement of political interest.

9. Messages of congratulations were received by the President from the Heads of all friendly States (none from the Communist bloc) and published in the Press. Our President's message was published on the front page of the three principal newspapers on the 14th inst. I enclose the cutting from the DIÁRIO DE NOTÍCIAS.

Thomas Commins

218
Ofício, Encarregado de Negócios irlandês em Lisboa ao Secretário-Geral do DEA: Lisboa, 30 de Agosto de 1958[36]

NEW PORTUGUESE GOVERNMENT

I have the honour to report that on the afternoon of his inauguration as President of the Portuguese Republic, the 9th inst., Admiral Américo Thomaz received the resignation of Dr. Salazar and the Cabinet, and immediately entrusted Dr. Salazar with the formation of a new Government.

2. The new Government was announced on the 12th inst. It contains a number of changes which were generally expected and which were implicitly foreshadowed in a speech Dr. Salazar made to the União Nacional on the 30th June last on the outcome of the elections. It also contained at least one major

---

[36] NAI, DEA, 313/11E Confidential reports from Lisbon Legation, 1958.

change which came as a surprise to the majority of the people here i.e. the release of Col. Santos Costa who was replaced by General Botelho Moniz as Minister of National Defence [...]

6. It is early yet to assess the full implications of these changes; the only thing that can safely be said at this time is that they have been received by the general public with an apathy amounting to indifference and seem to have engendered new enthusiasm neither within the ranks of the dedicated supporters of Dr. Salazar nor among those – and they are many – whom the Presidential election showed to be severely critical of the régime and its policies. In a word, the general verdict, seems to be "the mixture as before" in the sense that the changes are taken to represent solely changes of personalities as distinct from changes in the direction of policy which many people not excluding ardent supporters of Dr. Salazar feel to be called for in the light of the forthright criticism of the régime made during the Presidential election campaign and the large body of discontent throughout the country which that campaign made manifest. Growing discontent notably among the intellectuals and younger independent professional men with the monolithic structure of the State machine which they claim effectively denies any say in policy or administration to anybody who is not a member of or active supporter of the União Nacional, discontent with the activities of the Police, with the censorship of the Press, with low wages and a low standard of living and housing for the ordinary man in the street and in the economic sphere generally discontent with the maldistribution of wealth and the small degree in which the Portuguese average worker has shared in the increase in the gross national income of the country over the past ten or twelve years.

7. And the evidence does, indeed, go to show that Dr. Salazar in effecting these changes had not in mind any departure from his known political doctrines on which the present régime is based, but rather a re-energising of the régime through the introduction of fresh minds for the better translation of these doctrines into action. Speaking to the União Nacional in a post-election address on the 30th June, he said: "If the Nation behaves with common sense and does not pay excessive tribute to the abstraction of systems and personal ambitions, which is called for is not a of [sic] parliamentary disorder and weak Governments,

not to destroy the experiment which has gained credit thanks to its efficiency, but to renew it if necessary in persons and methods and to go on ahead."

8. It was rumoured for some months back that Dr. Marcello Caetano, Minister of the Presidency, was anxious to be relieved of his office and to resume his private activities. Rumour had it that he had diverged from Dr. Salazar in favour of a more liberal political régime and a less conservative financial and economic policy. This must be taken with reserve, certainly none of his public statements reflected any such attitude of mind. His departure, however, as well as the of Col. Santos Costa, Minister of National Defence – has exploded hitherto widely spread prognostications that he – or if not, Santos Costa – would assume the mantle of Dr. Salazar on the latter's departure from the political scene. Recent rumours in responsible circles suggest that he will shortly be appointed to the Presidency of the Bank of Portugal or that of the Fundo de Fomento Nacional (National Development Fund) which will have an important role to play in the Second Development Plan 1959-1964.

9. The appointment of Dr. Teotónio Pereira as Minister of the Presidency in place of Dr. Caetano was also not unexpected. He is a man of considerable stature both at home and abroad – particularly in Britain where he has been Ambassador for some years. He has also served in Madrid, Rio de Janeiro and Washington. He is considered here one of the big figures of the National Revolution and is credited as being the brains and architect of the Corporative organizations as sought to be applied to this country but which, so far, has not been successfully completed [sic]. This, perhaps, rather than his other qualifications, may have led to his selection by Dr. Salazar for the second top post in the Government, since the latter has emphasized the necessity to go full steam ahead towards the completion of the Corporative Organization. Many of the present difficulties he ascribes to the fact that the Corporative Organization has both been completed earlier and that the Corporative Chamber "does not stand forth as the direct emanation of corporatively organised economic cultural and spiritual interests." As soon as this comes about he proposes that the National Assembly will, for one thing, amend the Constitution so as to provide for the selection of the Head of the State by the Corporative Chamber instead of by direct suffrage. The Chamber will, he holds, constitute in its membership

the properly wide basis necessary for this purpose. In principle the satisfactory development of such a Chamber should render superfluous the National Assembly itself. But it would seem that Dr. Salazar considers that the National Assembly might be continued as a useful institution through which to go some way towards providing a forum for responsible independents to express their views and so meet to some extent the present criticism that independent political thought and expression is being stifled [...]

10. The displacement of Col. Santos Costa was almost totally unexpected. He had been in the Government for twenty-two years and was generally regarded as the "strong man" of the régime. He was not popular but universally respected as a distinguished Minister who had made an outstanding success at the job of organizing the Portuguese Armed Forces, which as late as 1940 were, comparatively speaking, primitive in their training and equipment, into what competent observers now regard as a highly efficient and well equipped machine. He is known to have had excellent relations with American and Military personnel, notably Gen. Montgomery as NATO commander. He was – and continues to be – a staunch supporter of Salazar and the régime. He is, however, also an ardent Monarchist and this led him in the course of his career to make important enemies, amongst whom was the last President of the Republic, General Craveiro Lopes. Towards the end of the latter's term these two men were not even on speaking terms. The differences between these two men steamed to a crisis when the question of the selection of the Government's candidate for the recent Presidential election arose. Up to the last minute it had been expected that Craveiro Lopes would be nominated for a second term, although there had been persistent reports of serious policy differences between Dr. Salazar and himself. Craveiro Lopes was pictured as favouring a gradual liberalisation of the régime towards the eventual development of a Republic on parliamentary or similar lines. To put it another way, he felt that emphasis should be on the full development of the Republican concept, rather than of the régime within the Estado Novo (New State). Nevertheless, Dr. Salazar is credited with favouring him for re--nomination, principally, it is said because of difficulties being experienced in getting another suitable candidate willing to undertake the task. But in his ideas,

Craveiro Lopes met the most violent opposition from Santos Costa and he is said to have made it a condition of his standing again that Santos Costa be dismissed. This Salazar bluntly refused to do and withdrew his support from him at the final meeting of the Council of the National Union held on the candidature question the day before the new candidate was to be announced. The view is generally held that Dr. Salazar's decision to release Santos Costa is directly related to this crisis in the sense that Dr. Salazar felt it incumbent in him to assure above all unity of loyalty within the armed forces, a unity that, given Craveiro Lopes' unquestioned prestige among his fellow Generals, would always be threatened while Santos Costa held the office of the Minster of National Defence. But it is not likely that Santos Costa will remain permanently outside the political scene. Various rumours of new appointments for him are current. One is Governor of Mozambique and another is the interesting one of Inspector General in due course of a new Colonial Army of some 25,000 men which is supposed to be given thought and towards the formation of which his undoubtedly great organizational talents would be particularly adopted [sic]. [...] As a matter of interest, the successor of Gen. Moniz is Gen. Luís Pina, whose wife is a daughter of the most prominent lady in the Irish Colony here, Mrs. Sarah Horgan, of the Horgan family in Cork. Both the General and his wife are well known to the Legation.

[...]

Thomas Commins

219
Ofício, Encarregado de Negócios irlandês em Lisboa ao Secretário-Geral do DEA: Lisboa, 6 de Setembro de 1958[37]

<u>PORTUGUESE NAVAL PARTICIPATION IN NATO EXERCISE OFF NORTHERN IRELAND</u>

I have the honour to report in a short discussion of the above which I had with Dr. Caldeira Queiroz on the 5th instant. It came up incidental to another

---
[37] NAI, DEA, 313/11E Confidential reports from Lisbon Legation, 1958.

discussion on our probable attitude to the Portuguese case in the projected debate at the next Regular Session of the United Nation on the question of Declarations under article 73 of the UN Charter. The latter is the subject of a separate report. (Ref. 6/22 – P.R. 9/58).

2. I think I should say at the onset that Dr. Caldeira Queiroz, who spent some years as Chargé d'Affaires in Dublin, has always shown himself well disposed towards us and never ceases to speak in warm and friendly terms of the great attachment he developed for Ireland and her people during his period of service there. To the extent, therefore, that he would feel it in his power to "go to bat" for us in a given situation, I feel he could be relied on to do so.

3. Referring to the attitude of abstention which our Delegation took in last year's UN debate on Declarations under Article 73, he expressed himself with considerable feeling that, other considerations apart, we should have acted in what he said he could not feel to be other than an unfriendly manner towards Portugal. He was at a loss to account for this given the traditionally friendly relations between the two countries and given that it was to him inconceivable that we should not be fully aware of the deep Portuguese resentment of the presumption to call into question within the United Nations the provisions of the Portuguese Constitution. In my report P.R. 9/58 I have dealt with this in detail. His thesis in effect was that any action which in any way implied lack of full recognition of the incontrovertible constitutionality of the Portuguese Unitary State, constituted an affront to Portugal.

4. I, of course, assured him that out attitude on that occasion did not reflect any criticism of Portugal but was attributable in the broad sense to our conviction that the United Nations constituted a proper forum for the open discussion of all matters constituting differences or divisions between member states. In such discussions, states such as Portugal with which Ireland had long and happy relations cold rely on our unbiased and sympathetic approach to their view-point by the Irish Delegation.

5. Having disposed of this matter as described in P.R. 9/58 we discussed a few other questions, notably our request for a provisional authorisation for Air [sic] Lingus to operate in Lisbon next year, which actually was my reason for

seeing Dr. Caldeira Queiroz in the first instance. Towards the end of the interview I asked after the new Foreign Minister, Dr. Mathias, and was told he was due to take up his post about the end of this month. Dr. Caldeira Queiroz then made some references to the last Minister Dr. Paulo Cunha which called for some complimentary remarks from me, which I qualified, however, by saying that it was a matter of regret to me that Dr. Paulo Cunha had shown singularly little understanding for us on the occasion of the formal approach made to him in 1951 [sic] about the participation of Portuguese naval vessels in NATO exercises operating from bases in Northern Ireland. (It will be recollected that Dr. Cunha at the time indicated that Portugal could not undertake to do anything about this, basing himself entirely on the accepted British character of the area by reference to existing international law and on Portuguese legal commitments within NATO) Incidentally, I said, I was sorry to learn from the press of a further visit of Portuguese vessels for the same purpose early last month.

6. Dr Caldeira Queiroz listened closely to my remarks, which I told him I was not making on instructions but rather because of my feeling that my authorities would wish me to take any suitable opportunity, such as the present, of making it known that our feelings on this had not changed. He then remarked that he thought we were being too touchy and perhaps a bit emotional on this subject. After all, what could the Portuguese do […]

7. […] I replied that when we has made our first formal protest on this matter in 1951 it was to the Netherlands in relation to an invitation issued to them by the British Admiralty to send a Naval Air Squadron for training to Derry. They had told us in reply that much as they regretted it they were unable, owing to the completion of arrangements to get out of participating in the projected exercises which were the subject of the protest. They expressed regret, however, at what they recognised as constituting an affront, – however unintended – to us and undertook to use such influence as they disposed of within NATO to secure that they would not have to send their Air or other forces to that area again. I confessed that I could not say for certain whether they had succeeded on keeping out of further exercises there; my impression was that they had, but even, in fact they had not they had gone a considerable distance to meet us and

had not dismissed our claims in the matter by reference to legal niceties. We would wish a similar reaction from the Portuguese [...]

8. This, Dr. Caldeira Queiroz said, he personally would like very much to do, but it would create immense difficulties for Portugal, by reference not only to her commitments in NATO and also by reference to Goa. He did not expand on this latter but Dr. Nogueira did so afterwards to the extent of expressing a personal view that any questioning by Portugal of the status quo in Northern Ireland in this context would face them with the danger that Britain might accept Indian pressure for a declaration that the Anglo-Portuguese Alliance does not extend to Goa.

9. We did not pursue the matter further but in view of the unexpectedly open-minded attitude subsequently shown by Dr. Nogueira, we may possibly hear something more on the subject.

Thomas Commins

220
Ofício, Secretário-Geral do DEA ao Representante Permanente da Irlanda junto das Nações Unidas: Dublin, 10 de Setembro de 1958[38]

1. In my note of yesterday, on the United Nations agenda, I suggested (under N.º 3) that the proper course for us would be to continue to abstain on the issue of Goa.

2. Since doing that note we have received a report from the Chargé d'Affaires in Lisbon of two conversations he had with officers of the Portuguese Foreign Ministry on the 5th and 6th September in the course of which it was put very strongly to him that we should endeavour this year to change our vote from one of abstention to one in favour of the Portuguese thesis or, at the least, do this when the matter comes up in the Assembly.

3. As the Minister is aware the immediate issue here is not whether Goa should go to India but whether Portugal should submit the reports called for

---

[38] NAI, DEA, Permanent Mission to the United Nations, X17, Portugal, 1956-1963.

under Article 73 (e) of the Charter in respect of Goa and the other Portuguese possessions as being "non-self-governing territories". Portugal contends that the areas in question are not "non-self-governing territories" in as much as under the existing Portuguese Constitution they form an integral part of Metropolitan Portugal.

4. On the assumption, which is reasonable, that the matter will follow the same road this year as at the Eleventh and Twelfth Sessions of the Assembly the following will be the course of events:

a) The Fourth Committee will adopt a resolution which will at least implicitly require Portugal to submit reports in respect of Goa and which Portugal will oppose;
b) When this Resolution comes before the Plenary Assembly a vote will be taken on the majority required for the adoption of the Resolution – on whether a simple or a two-thirds majority is required;
c) A vote as determined under b) will then be taken on the Resolution.

5. I think there is a good case for our abstaining on the vote in the Fourth Committee. The Portuguese contention is in many ways rather far-fetched. Indeed one might wonder whether the constitutional position on which the Portuguese take their stand was not thought of with an eye precisely to the situation that has arisen; it was only in December 1946 (i.e. after Portugal had applied for admission to the United Nations) that the status of Goa was changed from that of a colony to that of a province of Metropolitan Portugal. There is also, as far as we are concerned, the special consideration that although the two cases are not at all on all fours, for us to adhere to the Portuguese argument by reference to the ground on which Portugal takes its stand (that under the Constitution Goa is an integral part of Portugal) might make us appear to renounce the right to raise the Six Counties issue (for the reason that under British legislation the Six Counties are an integral part of the United Kingdom).

6. Portugal will, of course, endeavour to ensure that the Assembly will find that a two-thirds majority is required to pass the resolution emerging from the Fourth Committee. The discussion and vote on this particular point (i.e. 4(b)) could be very important at the forthcoming Session. Whereas at the Eleventh

Session the majority in favour of a two-thirds majority being required on the Resolution proper was 38 for to 34 against, last year the corresponding figures were 38 to 36. Every single vote on the point may therefore play a vital role on the next occasion.

7. If we abstain on the vote on the Resolution in the Fourth Committee it would be logical that we do likewise on the votes in the Assembly: it could appear somewhat anomalous that having, by abstention, shown ourselves more or less indifferent to the fate of the Resolution in the Fourth Committee we would act in the Assembly in such a manner as to make it more difficult for the Resolution to pass. As against this, however, one can advance a number of considerations.

8. Under the Charter (Article 18(2)) decisions of the Assembly "on important questions" require a two-thirds majority. Some such "important questions" are defined: these include "questions relating to the operation of the trusteeship system" but, although there is a prima-facie similarity between the trusteeship system questions and those concerning non-self-governing territories, the latter category is not included in this list. One might argue (as Portugal of course does) that the particular question with which we are concerned does rank as "important" and, therefore, is subject to a two-thirds majority on the ground that it involves questioning the validity of the Portuguese Constitution. There is also the point whether in cases of this kind the United Nations should go behind an attitude of the member concerned. The evidence I have seen on this point is somewhat conflicting; the Brazilian Delegate in an intervention at the Eleventh Session argued strongly and eloquently that it had become the practice of the United Nations to rely entirely on the Member country concerned by a resolution of 1949 [No.334 (IV)] seems to suggest otherwise, and of course if one draws a parallel between the Portuguese case and that of the "United Kingdom" we should be reluctant to hold that the "administering member" has the final say.

9. Another factor extraneous to the Charter but which cannot be ignored in favour of holding that the question is "important" is that such evidence as is available suggests that if the vote goes against Portugal in the Assembly she might seriously consider withdrawing from the United Nations. There may,

perhaps, be an element of bluff in the statement made to our Delegation last year by the Portuguese Delegate (and reported in paragraph 8 of Mr. Kennedy's minue of 7th November, 1957) but our Chargé d'Affaires in Portugal stated in his report of 5th March, 1957 that if Portugal were faced "with the choice of agreeing to subject all or some of her overseas territories to the investigation processes of the United Nations or alternatively to withdraw from the Organisation there is little doubt that she would have chosen the latter". This possible consequence of a vote in the Assembly unfavourable to Portugal must therefore be borne in mind.

10. It may be noted that, as the Portuguese officials did not fail to point out to Mr. Commins, all non-Communist European countries with the exception of Greece and at one point Turkey (which abstained with us in the vote in the Fourth Committee) voted against the Resolution in the Committee last year; in the vote in the Assembly we appear to have been the only such country to abstain.

11. The Portuguese officials also appealed to our Christian traditions as a reason for acting as they suggest. Other things being equal we would presumably respond to such an appeal. However I do not think that this particular argument is valid in the present context although this aspect of the matter could have some importance if by any chance Portugal withdrew from the United Nations after an unfavourable vote in the Assembly. On the special case of Goa, the Vatican has of course shown great prudence, refusing to commit itself to Portugal as against India.

12. I think that when we have made up our minds as to what to do on this issue and assuming that our attitude does not conform to that which Portugal has requested us to adopt we should allege, as the grounds for it, the Partition angle. The ground should all the more be appreciated in Lisbon as the former Portuguese Foreign Minister had the following to say to Count O'Kelly, our then Chargé d'Affaires in Lisbon when the latter spoke to him about the participation of Portuguese vessels in NATO exercises in Derry in 1952: (report from Lisbon of 1st October, 1952, file 341/92/4):

"After stating that, whatever might be the moral situation, in international law the Six Counties could only be considered as British territory, he added that

Portugal was in a singularly weak position to question officially Britain's claim to sovereignty over the Six Irish Counties while it, Portugal, was seeking and obtaining British support in its dispute with India over Goa and the other Portuguese enclaves in India – these territories being to India pretty nearly exactly what the Six Counties were to Ireland".

13. In the representations made to Mr. Commins it was intimated that the importance attached by the Portuguese Government to this matter is such that it would willingly send a delegation to Dublin to discuss the matter with the Minister and the Department if the Minister felt that this would "contribute to a better understanding of the Portuguese case". I do not think that there is any purpose in getting Lisbon to send a delegation here. Our knowledge of the problem is already substantial, the representations recently made to our Chargé d'Affaires were comprehensive, and the Portuguese Chargé d'Affaires in Dublin could provide any additional data we might require.

C. C. Cremin

221
Telegrama, Uneireann para Estero:
Nova Iorque, 16 de Setembro de 1958[39]

112 OUR 100 MINISTER PARTICULARLY ANXIOUS TO KNOW WHETHER ARTICLE 135 OF THE 1933 CONSTITUTION OF PORTUGAL HAS IN ANY WAY BEEN AMENDED SINCE THE END OF LAST WAR STOP HE BELIEVES THAT DEPARTMENTS FILES CONTAIN THE NECESSARY DETAILS

UNEIREANN

---

[39] NAI, DEA, Permanent Mission to the United Nations, X17, Portugal, 1956-1963.

222
Ofício, Encarregado de Negócios irlandês em Lisboa ao Secretário-Geral do DEA: Lisboa, sem data[40]

"THE ROAD FOR THE FUTURE" – DR. SALAZAR.

I have the honour to refer to my report of the 30th ult on the Portuguese Government, in which I referred in one or two places to Dr. Salazar's post-election address on the 30th June to the União Nacional.

I enclose herewith five copies of an English translation of this address which has been published in the meantime by the Secretariado Nacional da Informação. The speech is of particular importance as indicating the thinking of Dr. Salazar on the future direction of policy in Portuguese internal political affairs although it does not shed any further light on the big question of his plans if any for his personal successor or for the orderly transference of power from his own hands when (and this "when?" is an equally big related question) he decides to retire from the active conduct of affairs or in the event of his unforeseen departure from the scene. Many people believe that he must at this stage have well-conceived plans for his succession designed to ensure to the best of his belief and ability the continuance of the régime which he has established, but if so he is careful to avoid any such suggestion in his public pronouncements. This is a source of no little concern to the large body of supporters of the régime and to established business circles who fear, and, I think, with some justification, that if through an act of God he were suddenly removed from the scene at this juncture it would be difficult to prognosticate what direction events would take and the régime might be hard put to it to weather the internal political storms which would undoubtedly erupt.

Of special interest is Dr. Salazar's exposition of his ideas on the press censorship and his stated readiness to examine the possibility of having it modified to some extent. This is a major concession to public pressure. The press censorship – which might possibly be more accurately described as press direction

---
[40] NAI, DEA, 313/11E Confidential reports from Lisbon Legation, 1958.

– had been one of the major weapons availed of by Dr. Salazar towards the creation and development of a Portuguese political conscience in line with his own political doctrines. And it may well be conceded that in the early years of the régime its necessity could be readily defended. One might go further and say that even in later years a good case might be made in the particular circumstances of Portugal for its continuance in modified form. But with the passage of the years it has tended, according to those who must work closely with it, to become more and more autocratic, to the extent of rendering objective news reporting almost entirely out of the question [...]

Thomas Commins

223
Ofício, Encarregado de Negócios irlandês em Portugal ao Representante Permanente da Irlanda junto das Nações Unidas (F. H. Boland): Lisboa, 30 de Setembro de 1958[41]

I regret very much that your telegram of the 16th inst. regarding the Portuguese Constitution came while I was out of Lisbon on annual leave so that it is only on my return from leave yesterday that I was able to deal with it.

2. I send you herewith an English copy of the present constitution, the text of which is that approved by plebiscite in 1933 and subsequently amended by various laws since enacted. The text is annotated to show the latter amendments and the laws which brought them into effect.

[...]

3. The designation of the Overseas Territories as "provinces", contained in article 134 was brought into effect on 11th June 1951 by amending law N° 2048. In the Constitution as it stood prior to that date, these territories were designated as "Colonies". But the latter designation obtained not only during the immediately years back to 1920. In all Portuguese Constitutions prior to 1920, the Overseas

---

[41] NAI, DEA, 313/11E Confidential reports from Lisbon Legation, 1958.

Territories of Portugal were described as "Provinces". The change in the Constitutional designation of these territories from "Provinces" to "Colonies" in 1920 (by law 1005 of 7th August 1920) can be laid to the general post-war international atmosphere at the time which rather frowned upon too close integration of Overseas with Metropolitan territories. One might put it that "Colonies" were fashionable at the time and the Portuguese, as always, were anxious to be "up with the Joneses" – the Joneses in this case being the American, British and French.

[…]

8. The 1920 amendment was bitterly criticised at the time in many quarters and it is true to say that this criticism continued all through the '30s and indeed in greater or lesser degree up to the re-introduction of the description "Provinces" by the amendment of 1951 […]

9. It would seem to me to be a fair conclusion from the above that Portugal has traditionally looked upon her overseas territories as provinces; only for a period of thirty years (1920-1951) in over four centuries of rule has she designated these territories constitutionally as Colonies. It would also, in the circumstances, seem rather harsh to hold that the reversion to the description "Provinces" in 1951 was dictated solely or primarily by fear of UN intervention in her affairs. There can, of course, be little doubt that this was a factor, but the reversion was primarily a return to a traditional status.

[…]

Thomas Commins

1959

224
Carta, Secretário-Geral do DEA ao Encarregado de Negócios da Irlanda em Lisboa: Dublin, __?__ de Fevereiro de 1959[42]

CONFIDENTIAL

It has been alleged in the British and American press in January this year and in November last year that certain pressures were used against General Humberto Delgado, the defeated candidate in the Presidential elections held last June. It is reported that these pressures have led to his retirement from the army and caused him to seek asylum in the Brazilian Embassy as a political refugee. It would be appreciated if you could let us have a report on the political significance of these events.

C. C. Cremin

225
Carta, Subsecretário-Geral do DEA ao Encarregado de Negócios irlandês em Lisboa: Dublin, 25 de Março de 1959[43]

URGENT

Dear Tom,

The "New Statesman" of the 21st March in a report from their Lisbon correspondent headed "The Terror" states that Salazar's refusal to recognize the asylum granted by the Brazilian Embassy to General Delgado and to allow the Ambassador to take him out of Portugal is creating friction in the relations between Brazil and Portugal and that Salazar has been informed that unless a satisfactory solution is found to Delgado's case Brazil will withdraw support

---

[42] NAI, DEA, 313/11F Confidential reports from Lisbon Legation, 1959.
[43] NAI, DEA, 313/11F Confidential reports from Lisbon Legation, 1959.

for Portugal in the United Nations. Presumably this withdrawal of support would relate to the question of Goa. This article goes on to say that the Brazilian Ambassador has now given political asylum to Captain Galvão to which Salazar has replied by cordoning the Embassy with armed police. References are made to the strengthening of the oppressive machinery in Portugal by setting up new police stations and increasing the units of secret police. Later the article states that with Salazar's followers now divided and with the revolt of the Catholic Church spreading, officials foresee the end of the régime. The following are given as examples of the strained relations between the Church and State.

1) The Bishop of Oporto is now being followed by the police, and civil servants have been forbidden to attend religious ceremonies presided over by him
2) The speeches of Cardinal Cerejeira are now radically censored.
3) Government representatives no longer attend religious ceremonies.
4) The festival of Our Lady of the Immaculate Conception, the Patroness of Portugal, was not attended by members of the Government and became a day of silent manifestation of a church in revolt.

In your PR.3/59 of the 4th of February, you refer to the strained relations between Church and State in Portugal deriving from serious disagreements of principle between Dr. Salazar and certain of the Portuguese Bishops, notably the Bishop of Oporto. You added that you were preparing a separate report in the matter. We would be glad to have this report at your earliest convenience together with a report on the other matters referred to above notably the present relations between Portugal and Brazil.

Yours sincerely,

J. A. Belton

226

**Carta, Encarregado de Negócios irlandês em Lisboa ao Subsecretário-
-Geral do DEA (John Aloysius Belton): Lisboa, 7 de Abril de 1959**[44]

Dear John,

Your letter 313/11F of the 25th ult. I hope to let you have the reports in question issued before the end of this week.

Meanwhile I think I should say straightaway that the "New Statesman" article which you describe is like Mark Twain's death but even more so. This particularly as regards the relations between the Church and the régime. There have been and continue to be strained relations between the two in the sense areas of disagreement [sic] in e.g. education and social principles and in recent months this situation has been heightened by, specifically, the publication, subrosa, of a letter of 13th July last from the Bishop of Oporto to Dr. Salazar in which the Bishop took serious issue with him on many points. But it would be the height of exaggeration and misjudgement to suggest that on the broad plane the Church and the régime stand in fundamental disharmony or that the responsible leaders of the Church here would look with complacency on the downfall of the régime at the present time. There are indeed factors which suggest a very difficult time for the régime and indeed its ultimate survival is quite open to question, but it may be take as certain that the Church as a body will be the last to precipitate such a situation.

The examples given of strained relations between the Church and State are highly coloured and at least three of them are, as far as I know, not in any way based on fact. This view is shared unequivocally by the Papal Nunciature here, with the Chargé d'Affaires a.i. of which, Monsignor Birini, I have discussed these matters on more than one occasion.

[…]

Yours sincerely,

Thomas Commins

---

[44] NAI, DEA, 313/11F Confidential reports from Lisbon Legation, 1959.

227
Ofício, Encarregado de Negócios irlandês em Lisboa ao Secretário-Geral do DEA: Lisboa, 11 de Abril de 1959[45]

CONFIDENTIAL

<u>PORTUGUESE-BRAZILIAN RELATIONS</u>

I have the honour to report as follows:

For many years past, and markedly since the official visit of President Café Filho of Brazil to Portugal in 1955 a major objective of Portuguese foreign policy has been the development of the closest possible relations with Brazil in the political and economic fields. Portugal's interest in so doing is clearly apparent; Brazil is a former Portuguese Province, Portuguese-speaking, and, as such, the natural, of not indeed the only country of potentially large-scale emigration for the Metropolitan Portuguese. As the population of Metropolitan Portugal increases – as it is doing – (it is now in the region of 9 million) it is fairly clear that given the extremely limited natural resources of this country, an outlet for suitable emigration is desirable and indeed necessary if the already low standard of living here is not to be depressed further as the years go by. Brazil, with its tremendous economic potential still virtually unexplored represents, therefore, a natural target for Portuguese graduates in engineering and other professions – as well as skilled and semi-skilled labour – in the future. It represents also a future vehicle of international prestige for the Portuguese – a prestige which is of prime importance to the hope of Portugal's present day leaders to create, in the course of time, a new Portuguese Empire or Commonwealth.

2. And, as far as one can observe from this distance, this general outlook is shared by the present Brazilian Administration. In his pre-inauguration visit to Portugal in January 1956, President Kubitscheck declared that "Brazil's solidarity with Portugal on the Goa question will not only continue but will strengthen in the future. We shall also increase our other ties with Portugal including Portuguese emigration to Brazil".

---

[45] NAI, DEA, 313/11F Confidential reports from Lisbon Legation, 1959.

3. The last President of the Portuguese Republic, General Craveiro Lopes, accompanied by the then Foreign Minister, Dr. Paulo Cunha, and a suite of high ranking Portuguese personalities, paid a return State visit to Brazil in June 1957. This was the occasion for the signing by the two Presidents of a "Treaty of Friendship and Consultation" covering the broad field of Portuguese-Brazilian relations in political and economic matters and providing an ambience for the specific treatment of questions of extradition, dual nationality, visas, reciprocal suppression of identity cards, etc. The constant theme of public statements from both sides throughout the visit was the evolution of a live Luso-Brazilian community with the closest possible co-operation in economic and political fields. I recollect that Dr. Caldeira Queiroz (then Director of Political Affairs and subsequently Secretary General) who accompanied the Presidential party, told me on his return that the Portuguese party were not only immensely satisfied with Brazilian reaction to the visit but were astonished at the unexpected extent to which they found the Brazilians were anxious to promote concrete ties between the two countries in the direction of the evolution of a real Luso-Brazilian community.

4. The Treaty of Friendship and Consultation provided, above all, for mutual consultation on all aspects of foreign policy, and my information both from the Portuguese and Brazilian sides here is that in this respect the Treaty has been fully respected since, to the extent indeed that such consultation is now almost axiomatic. On the economic side the Treaty went far to iron out some of Portugal's irritations with Brazil e.g. importation of olives from Portugal instead of Italy and in the Brazilian interest to secure Portuguese support and co-operation in matters such as the rationalisation of Brazilian-African coffee production.

5. It is not, of course, to be assumed that as a result of all this harmony of ideas and outlook was established on all fronts with every section of the Brazilian people. Papers like the "CRUZEIRO" and "ÚLTIMA HORA" (the latter reputedly "pink" if not openly communist) and "O ESTADO DE S. PAULO" have continued critical of Salazar and his "repressive" policies, a criticism shared by a significant proportion, but by no means the majority, of the Portuguese colony in Brazil. Even the "DIÁRIOS ASSOCIADOS" owned by Assis Chateaubriand, the present

Brazilian Ambassador to Britain (of whom more anon) have from time to time been critical in their observations on the Portuguese scene. Also in many matters covered by the Treaty which both sides undertook to promote specific agreements, little or nothing of note has since emerged. These matters I have already mentioned as extradition, dual nationality, suppression of identity cards etc. But on the international political front it can be said that the ideal of increasingly close co--operation has been maintained between the two administrations. This co--operation is evidenced by the warmth of the support extended to Portugal by Brazil within the United Nations and, on the Portuguese side, by calls for the e.g. admission of Brazil in NATO, a call that was repeated only a week or so ago by Dr. Paulo Cunha who, though no longer a member of Dr. Salazar's cabinet is still very much a spokesman of the Government on foreign affairs.

6. There is no good reason to believe that recent developments in the Delgado case, have – so far in any event – diminished this mutual regard or prejudiced the position of either side vis à vis the other in the foreign relations field. Allegations, such as appeared in an article in the NEW STATESMAN on the 21st March that Dr. Salazar's refusal to recognise the asylum granted by the Brazilian Embassy to Delgado and to allow the Ambassador to take him out of Portugal has brought about a threat from the Brazilian Government to withdraw support for Portugal in the United Nations unless a satisfactory solution is found, are entirely without foundation. Certainly there is an element of friction between the two Governments on this point, but I have been assured by the Political Director of the Ministry of Foreign Affairs and a reliable spokesman of the Brazilian Embassy that no such threat has at any time been made by Brazil to the Portuguese nor does either side envisage that the Delgado incident could ever bring about such a situation. Given the special ties between the two countries the withdrawal of such support by Brazil would be almost tantamount to a breaking of diplomatic relations with Portugal and it is inconceivable that either side would invest the Delgado episode with such overriding importance.

7. In order better to understand the positions taken by both Governments on this question it may be well to recapitulate the incident. Following his defeat in the Presidential election – a defeat which in the circumstance of the electoral

machinery here was a foregone conclusion – General Delgado was relieved of his post as Director of Civil Aviation and presented himself to the Secretariat of the Army for duty. He was reassigned to active duty but continued to interest himself in political affairs and with a number of principal oppositionists e.g. António Sérgio de Sousa, Mário Azevedo Gomes, Jaime Cortesão (elected on November 10th President of the Portuguese Society of Writers), Francisco Vieira de Almeida etc. who formed the "National Independent Movement" with the declared objective of unseating the present régime. There can be no doubt that this Movement had the full support of the Communist party (sub-rosa, of course) and there followed in the months October, November and December, incipient strikes, silent demonstrations against the Government characterised by an almost universal wearing of black ties, illegal sub-rosa dissemination of pamphlets criticising and insulting the Government, Salazar and individual cabinet ministers, and an invitation to Mr. Aneurin Bevin to come to Portugal and give a series of public talks under the sponsership [sic] of this body etc etc. The result was that he was put under military arrest on November 25th for having signed his name "to subversive manifestos which were clandestinely distributed." At the same time the other personalities which I mentioned in this paragraph were arrested for the same reasons and released later that evening. An official announcement stated that they were being released pending the preparation of a process against them before a competent judicial tribunal. So far there have been no further developments in their case.

8. General Delgado was, however, on the 7th January subjected to disciplinary action by the Under-Secretary of Aviation. The official announcement stated that "independently of any liabilities of a criminal nature for which he may later be held responsible, General Delgado was <u>removed from service</u> in the terms of Article I of Decree N.º 32329 of October 19th 1942 and Art.14 of the Statute of Army Officers." It was explained later that "removed from service" does not mean dismissed or retired. It means separated from active service with loss of right to wear uniform, insignia or military medals. The General was allowed the maximum pay appropriate to his rank as if he were retiring, i.e. 75% of the pay he had been receiving.

9. On Monday, January 12th 1959, General Delgado presented himself at the Brazilian Embassy and requested asylum as a political refugee, saying that he considered himself in danger of imminent arrest. He was accorded asylum by the Ambassador who reported the matter immediately to the Portuguese Ministry of Foreign Affairs. The latter indicated that they had no objection to the General installing himself in the Embassy but went on to say that no warrant of arrest existed against the General nor was there any intention of arresting him for "subversive" acts committed up to the present. Consequently his pretext for seeking asylum was groundless. In an official statement made later the Ministry re-iterated the above and went on to say that it had been pointed out to the Brazilian Ambassador that if the Portuguese authorities had the intention of arresting General Delgado they would have applied a prison sentence to him instead of "benevolently" separating him from active service on three-quarters pay [...] In these circumstances, the statement concluded, the Portuguese authorities would not intervene in the matter in any way and would not be prepared to accede to the General the status of a true political refugee by issuing a safe conduct for him to leave the country.

10. It is at this point that matters still rest. On the face of it the Portuguese attitude seems quite logical but their position is one which, of course, has been taken by them post-factum. Looking at it from Delgado's side – and this must necessarily be the side which the Brazilian Ambassador had to consider when he acceded asylum – there was at least some reason for him to fear arrest and imprisonment. The official statement that his separation from active service was "independent of any liabilities of a criminal nature for which he may later be held responsible" at the very least implied a danger of arrest and trial by the civil authorities for "subversive acts". With the example of Capt. Galvão before him (sentenced in March 1958 to a further sixteen years imprisonment for issuing subversive pamphlets and letters insulting to the Government, while in jail), it is not difficult to appreciate Delgado's fear of like action being taken against him. It is also possible – and has been widely suggested though not shown – that Delgado was, personally or through his Movement, concerned with promoting the escape of Galvão from the Santa Maria Hospital on January 16th and that he

realized that if the escape were successful (as it was) he would undoubtedly be picked up by the Political Police.

11. Here then lies the problem between the Portuguese and Brazilian Governments. With both it is a matter of principle. Both accept the concept of political asylum. The Brazilian hold that asylum having been granted it can be terminated only by the issue of a safe-conduct to permit the refugee to be brought safely out of the country. The Portuguese on the other hand hold that political asylum should be granted only where it is evident that the authorities are unable to give normal protection to the refugee or are unwilling to accede him freedom of movement including freedom to leave the country as a normal citizen.

12. The satisfactory resolution of the matter has been made considerably more difficult by a press offensive initiated in the "DIÁRIOS ASSOCIADOS" of Brazil against the Brazilian Ambassador here. The owner of this group of papers is Assis Chateaubriand, Brazilian Ambassador in London. There is some evidence to suggest that he was encouraged in this by the Portuguese Administration and Dr. Salazar in particular when he paid a visit here shortly after Delgado had entered the Brazilian Embassy. In editorials in the "Jornal do Rio de Janeiro" and other papers in this group, all through late February and March he has roundly attacked his colleague here (Álvaro Lins, also a Journalist and formerly on the staff of the "DIÁRIOS ASSOCIADOS") for not accepting the word of the Portuguese Government and "turning the Lisbon Embassy into a centre of conspiracy against the Portuguese régime." A most curious phenomenon this, given his official position as Ambassador of Brazil to Britain and given that the Brazilian Government has made it perfectly clear that in their view Ambassador Lins acted quite properly and retains their confidence [...]

12A. Dr. Franco Nogueira, Assistant Director of Political Affairs, told me the other day that they are in constant consultation on the matter with the Brazilian Government but that their views against the issue of a "safe-conduct" to Delgado remain unchanged. He was hopeful, however, that a formula which would not involve "safe-conduct" but which would be acceptable to the Brazilians would be found. If not, he said, Delgado can remain where he is and neither the Brazilians nor themselves will worry unduly about it when with the passage of time it ceases to command public attention. He emphasized to me at the same time that this incident had not in any way caused a deterioration of their relations with Brazil. The conversations on the issue were being conducted in the most friendly fashion with the sincere desire on both sides to evolve a situation which would respect the points of principle held by each. He described as ridiculous the suggestion that Brazil had threatened withdrawal of support for Portugal in the United Nations.

13. Before concluding, perhaps I may once again refer to the NEW STATESMAN article of 21st March. The article goes on to state that the Brazilian Ambassador has since given political asylum to Captain Galvão to which Salazar responded by cordoning the Embassy with armed police.

Nothing could be further from the truth. As a matter of routine every Embassy and Legation has an armed guard stationed outside. After the escape of Capt. Galvão on the 16th January last, the guards on all the South American Embassies were doubled and I personally never saw more than two outside the Brazilian Embassy. When, on February 17th Galvão sought and was given asylum in the Argentine Embassy, the extra guards were taken off, to such a extent that the Venezuelan Ambassador told me, when on the night of March 19th a Cavalry Officer of the Portuguese Army, presented himself at the Venezuelan Embassy and requested asylum on the ground that he was in danger of "immediate arrest and torture by the PIDE", there were no guards on duty! This request was granted.

14. The Brazilian, Argentine and Venezuelan Ambassadors are working in close collaboration with a view to arriving at a solution with the Portuguese authorities which would permit them to see their uninvited guests safely off their premises. In all three cases "safe-conducts" have been requested but refused. I have explained why, in the case of Delgado. In Galvão's case the Portuguese refuse collaboration on the grounds that he is not a political refugee but a Portuguese citizen convicted by due process of law who has illegally evaded his sentence. They are not prepared to permit him to leave the country. In Calafate's case, the Portuguese authorities have told the Ambassador that they have

nothing against him and that he is perfectly free to leave. They have represented that he is mentally unbalanced and suffering from an imaginary persecution complex. The Ambassador has told me, however, that he is unable to accept this judgement and is convinced from his talks with Calafate, that he was in some danger of arrest when he came to the Embassy. Calafate was, it appears, one of the leaders in an alleged plot within the Army – uncovered in its entirety later – to assassinate a number of political figures including Dr. Salazar and force the Army to take over control with a view to the institution of a new régime which would, specifically 1) release all political prisoners, 2) abolish censorship of the press, and 3) abolish the PIDE (International Police for the Defence of the State (political)). No publicity of any kind has so far been given to this and it is difficult to find out whether it was of serious proportions or not. My impression is that it did not represent a movement of any consequence within the army against the present régime.

Thomas Commins

228
Ofício, Encarregado de Negócios irlandês em Lisboa ao Secretário-Geral do DEA: Lisboa, 15 de Abril de 1959[46]

CONFIDENTIAL

PORTUGAL AND NATO

I have the honour to report as follows:

On the 10th inst., Prof. Paulo Cunha, former foreign minister and, though no longer in the Cabinet, still and authoritative spokesman for the régime on foreign affairs, spoke in the Lisbon Law Faculty on the subject of NATO and Portuguese External policies. He expressed the view that only the existence of NATO has prevented Russian domination of Europe and Africa and repeated the Portuguese concern that the NATO nations should strive towards acting as a cohesive unit in

---

[46] NAI, DEA, 313/11F Confidential reports from Lisbon Legation, 1959.

matter political as well as military. NATO, he went on to say, is for Europeans and for the safeguarding of European civilization a much more realistic concept than the UN. A serious matter for Europe – and for Portugal in particular – was, however, the absence of Spain from NATO and he urged the other signatory countries to bury their prejudices and repair this omission.

2. Portuguese material contribution to NATO was, he agreed, small so far as military forces were concerned, but he went on, Portuguese participation in and her contribution to this defensive system was vital because of the facilities afforded it in the Azores and because of the firm control maintained by the Portuguese in their Overseas Territories. It was of vital importance to Portugal that NATO should combine and develop in strength and should assure the maintenance of the status quo in the African territories not only of the Portuguese but of the other signatory countries. (This is a theme which Portugal has been pushing consistently within the NATO council).

3. Having criticised countries which foster "premature nationalism" the Professor concluded by saying "It is necessary to open our eyes fully and combine our joint efforts for the maintenance of the European stake in Africa, leaving aside anti-colonialist concepts, since it is neither a moral nor philosophical idea which is at stake but the survival of Europe."

Thomas Commins

229
Ofício, Encarregado de Negócios irlandês em Lisboa ao Secretário-Geral do DEA: Lisboa, 15 de Abril de 1959[47]

CONFIDENTIAL

PORTUGUESE CHURCH-STATE RELATIONS.

I have the honour to report as follows:

The question of the relations between the Portuguese Church and State authorities has assumed increasing proportions here and in press circles abroad

---
[47] NAI, DEA, 313/11F Confidential reports from Lisbon Legation, 1959.

since the Presidential election of July 1958. Press comment abroad in so far as it appears to seek to interpret certain divergences of view between e.g. individual Portuguese Bishops and the State authorities on particular questions as foreshadowing a revolt of the Portuguese Church against the present political régime, should be treated with extreme reserve. The true position is that allowing the undoubted existence of serious divergences of view between individual Church Representatives and the State authorities on specific issues, harmonious relations still exist between the Church and the State on a broad plane.

2. The Church in Portugal, represented by a Hierarchy led by the Cardinal Patriarch of Lisbon, D. Manuel Cerejeira, does not forget the half-century of repression which it suffered under the pre-Salazar administrations and in particular the Law of Separation of 1911 which officially denied recognition to the Church, ignored its constitution and organization and worked as if it did not exist. And it is equally mindful of the fact that it was the Salazar régime which, with the conclusion of the Concordat with the Holy See in 1940, set the seal on the work of restoration of the place and rights of the Church which was begun by the Government of Sidónio Pais in 1917. The Concordat provided fundamentally for 1) recognition and sanction by the Church and by the State of their respective autonomies and liberties and 2) co-operation between Church and State for the common good of the Portuguese in the sphere in which both meet, such as public education and the constitution of the family.

3. In an address which he gave in November 1956 dealing with the Concordat, Cardinal Cerejeira expounded the Hierarchy's attitude to the Salazar Régime in the following terms:

"The Hierarchy in Portugal have never pronounced officially on the political régime such as it is. It neither approves nor condemns it. It is a problem that does not pertain to her in so far as the State does not touch Catholic morals and doctrine. It leaves it, as befitting, to the conscience of the citizens. Faithful to her own mission, the Church is above and outside the political field of régimes, parties and organisations.

But, through fidelity to herself, she honours the present régime. She sees incarnated in it, although for a different reason, the divine authority. An integral part of her teaching is the duty of conscience to obey the constituted power and to honour those who represent it. And the Church makes no apology for testifying to her gratitude for the work of peace and religious liberty undertaken by the régime and for its acceptance of Christian principles." Concluding his address he remarked "the Church in Portugal lies in peace with the State and the Nation."

4. Though a certain amount of water has passed under the bridge since, and though certain deficiencies in the full implementation of the spirit of the Concordat in e.g. the realm of public education which the Cardinal duly noted in the address above referred to, have, perhaps, become aggravated rather than resolved with the passage of time, there is reason to believe that if the Cardinal, speaking for the Hierarchy, were to express himself again at this stage on the subject of the régime, he would do so in not dissimilar terms. It may certainly be taken for granted that it is far from the policy of the Portuguese Church to favour or promote the downfall of the present régime in favour of a more liberal dispensation. Liberalism in Portugal has always been associated with anti--clericalism and there is no reason for the Church to expect better treatment from any foreseeable substitute of the Salazar régime than it has got and continues to get from the latter.

5. This being said, it remains to deal with the points of dissension between the Church as a body and the State, the most important of which is the matter of public education. The Concordat envisages close co-operation between the two in this field, a co-operation which in the eyes of the Church authorities has fallen far short of the spirit of the Concordat. To such an extent indeed that in July 1954 at a meeting of the Hierarchy in, I think, Fátima, presided over by the Cardinal and attended by the then Papal Nuncio (now Cardinal Cento) the Hierarchy passed a resolution "condemning unanimously the educational policies of the Portuguese Government." No reference to this ever appeared in the Portuguese Press, but the report was published in a Barcelona paper "Christiandad".

The problem is this: The State gives no help of any kind to Catholic as distinct from State Schools while at the same time subjecting them to the full rigour of the State educational programme, inspections, etc. All the State Schools are undenominational and are deprived of all religious complexion. The State programme provides for <u>a maximum</u> of two hours per week for the teaching of "morale", which may be interpreted at will to represent either religious instruction, physical training or Portuguese history. The State does not insist or provide that teachers in the State schools should have or teach religion, but does permit the Church authorities to send priests to the schools to teach religion in the time allotted. The trouble is that there are so few priests that this demand cannot even begin to be met, with the result that for the most part the younger generation of Portuguese are growing up without any well grounded religious knowledge. The effect of this is to be seen in the very small numbers of religious vocations obtained, a factor which is the most serious concern to the future of the Church in Portugal. Statistics (1956) from the Vatican showed that Portugal had one priest for every 1630 Catholics as against, for instance, one for every 440 in Switzerland, 490 in Holland, 530 in Belgium and England, 560 in Ireland, 620 in France, 690 in Italy, 940 in Austria and 970 in Spain. The same statistics showed one seminarist on Portugal per 6640 Catholics, as against 1130 in Ireland, 3400 in Spain, 3640 in England, 4400 in France, 4870 in Italy, 4990 in Belgium and 5330 in Holland. More recent statistics would be likely to show Portugal in a worse rather than better comparative position.

6. A second point of difficulty is the supply of religious assistance to the armed forces. According to the Cardinal Patriarch, Portugal is the only country in Europe which has not this matter properly organised i.e. in the sense that the Portuguese Army has no organised Corps of Chaplains integrated into the forces in the same way as is done by other NATO countries. "I do not maintain", he has stated, "that the provision of religious assistance outside wartime is an express obligation of the Concordat, its absence foes not run contrary to the written law, but is surely contrary to the spirit."

7. These are but two or the more important of a number of issues arising between the Church and State in the matter of the implementation of the Concordat. Procrastination on the part of the State on these matters has, in the eyes of the Church leaders, prevented the Concordat from developing into a live instrument towards the evolution of modern Portugal as a fully Christian as distinct from basically laic State.

8. A third, and equally serious point of irritation for the Church is the tendency of spokesmen of the present political régime – particularly at election time – to use the Church as a vehicle of political support. There is widespread tendency for such spokesmen to present the régime as the "defender of the Church" with the subtle implication that should this régime not be supported politically the Church would be the major sufferer. This indeed it was that created the situation which culminated in the now famous letter of 13th July 1958 to Dr. Salazar from the Bishop of Oporto in which he took issue with Salazar on almost all aspects of the latter's social and political principles. He castigated the propagandists of the União Nacional in the Braga and Oporto districts in the course of the Presidential campaign who, he said, "asked that as the one method of salvation we should close our ranks behind the Estado Novo." "We must, and do, at all times", he said, "pray God to give us strength to face up to incomprehension and even martyrdom on the cause of truth and justice. But, can we here state this straightaway in terms of the Estado Novo? Or, to put it another way, shall we shelter within the Pax Augusta of the Estado Novo irrespective of what it has in common with truth and Justice?" He then went on to criticise the social principles of the régime adumbrated by Salazar in his speech of 30th May. Principal among them was Salazar's reply in that speech to the opposition (Delgado's) that the right to strike should be recognised. "Here we part ways", Dr. Salazar had stated, and went on to conclude "a strike is, among us, a crime. We do not accept the idea of incompatibility of interest between the employers and the worker, but of their permanent solidarity. If an incompatibility of the moment creates the risk of a clash between the two parties it is necessary that the defender of the common interest shall decide the matter in accordance with justice and the common good."

This the Bishop stated was a principle unacceptable within the scope of Catholic social teaching and he quoted the philosophical social principle laid down by Pius XI that "where injustice is committed such as seriously disturbs the social order, the inferior social group should be accorded those functions which they are in a position to exercise themselves".

[…Segue-se descrição do documento…]

9. It is not possible to give a detailed exposition of all the arguments and points made by the Bishop in his letter. In the first place it was not widely disseminated and then only semi-clandestinely. I succeeded in getting a copy on loan for some two hours. But in addition to taking Dr. Salazar to task on social principles and example of which I have given above, he also attacked the educational system and the Salazarian conception of the corporative State, which, he said in its present evolution had nothing in common with the bona-fide corporativism supported by the Church. What existed here was not corporativism, but collectivism and in monolithic form to which the extraordinary personality of Salazar had operated to give an extraordinary strength. In 1926 he went on, Portuguese syndicalism was moving precipitately towards bolshevism. At that point the Nation girded itself to a legitimate movement for its salvation. It was necessary to liberate the worker from Communist leadership and despotism and create for him the conditions in which he would make maximum human progress. To do this, many measures were called for, primarily that the new Administration should assume the responsibility and even the public dislike pertaining to the creation of peace and order leaving professional organisations the self-determination necessary to them and giving them the sympathetic consideration necessary to them in the infancy of the new régime.

Instead, the Bishop wrote, a beginning was made in the establishment of a collective life out of which power was drawn for the State. And thus, the professional organisations were deprived of any effective means of attaining new conditions or work or any other benefits. "We have to be frank" he concluded, "perhaps brutal: Portuguese corporativism was really a method of depriving the workers of their natural right of association, of which liberalism deprived them in 1891 and which they had recovered with suffering and bloodshed." [...]

10. The Bishop also attacked the policy of maintaining the "strong escudo" at the expense of the standard of living and recalled that President Kubitscheck of Brazil had recently confessed that when he visited Portugal in 1957, Salazar in a two-hour conversation with him tried to convince him that as the basis for modernising Brazil he should establish a strong currency (moeda sã). He

(Kubitscheck) resolved, however, not to follow his advice as it would inevitably bring discontent, distrust and possible revolution in its path. "I make no comparisons between persons or methods of work" said the Bishop "but when we see the present state of incipient revolution around us, can we fail to harken back to the reasoning of the President of Brazil?" […]

11. It is unnecessary to say that the revelation of this letter, which unquestionably exceeded in its demands anything that the Administration could possibly conceive as belonging to the exclusive domain of the Church, caused considerable and acrimonious discussions. No official reply was given, so far as is known but Dr. Salazar referred to it obliquely in a talk to the União Nacional on December 6th when he said that it appeared quite incongruous to him that Catholics should leave the National Front since by doing so they allied themselves with the Liberals and the Communists. The behaviour of some Catholics, he went on, was particularly painful to him since he had contributed in no little way to the freedom of the Catholic Church here and the position it enjoys today.

12. The principal result of the letter of the Bishop of Oporto was to create a tendency within the Catholic Action Organization to interest themselves specifically in the political scene. It was indeed a logical step for Catholic Actionists to take in the light of the Bishop's comments on the present régime. But, the Easter Pastoral of the Hierarchy, subscribed to unconditionally by the Bishop of Oporto, condemned any such departure and emphasized again the necessity for the Church to keep out of political affairs and to maintain its complete independence of any political party or régime. The official attitude of the Church was well summed up by the Catholic paper NOVIDADES when it said that the foremost duty of Catholics was to safeguard, at all costs the freedom of the Church to accomplish Her mission […]

13. Thus it may be taken that the general body of the Hierarchy, whatever their private views, did not openly support the Bishop of Oporto and he is generally regarded by them – I learn from the Nunciature – to have erred on the side of great imprudence in releasing his letter for limited public consumption. In the event, of course, his letter got a publicity far and away greater than he ever desired.

14. Which brings me to the article of the 21st March in the NEW STATESMAN in which a number of highly exaggerated observations were made on the present Church-State relations here.

1) There is no evidence to suggest the policing of the Bishop of Oporto and no foundation for the assertion that civil servants have been forbidden to attend religious services presided by him. This I have been assured of by the Nunciature as well as by highly placed officials whom I know personally in the Ministry of Foreign Affairs and the PIDE.

2) There is no foundation for the assertion that the Cardinal Patriarch's speeches are censored.

3) There is no foundation for the statement that Government representatives no longer attend religious services. The Minister of the Presidency and at least one other member of the Government were present at the Church of Jerónimos on last Sunday week for the blessing of the Cod-fleet. Dr. Salazar and members of the Government were at the Mass and ceremony, attended also be the Cardinal and Hierarchy (excluding the Bishop of Oporto), for the handing of the Cardinal's Biretta to Monseigneur Cento some two months ago. The President and the members of the Government have notified the Nunciature and the Cardinal of their intention to participate in the ceremony later this year for the consecration of the Statue of Christ the King newly erected on the banks of the Tagus. These are just a few examples.

4) It is not, as far as I know, the custom for members of the Government officially to be present at the religious services held in the festival of "Our Lady of Immaculate Conception, Patroness of Portugal". Certainly the Diplomatic Corps are never invited to these ceremonies and it would be most unusual for the Government to be there in a body without the Corps [...]

Thomas Commins

230
Ofício, Representante Permanente da Irlanda junto das Nações Unidas ao Secretário-Geral do DEA: Nova Iorque, 20 de Abril de 1959[48]

I enclose herewith, in case it has not already come under the Department's notice, an article by Richard Mowrer in the *Christian Science Monitor* of the 14th March dealing with Portugal's stand in regard to her African colonies.

As you know, Portugal has hitherto been able to maintain her position in this matter in the United Nations only by the narrowest of majorities. When four additional African countries, and perhaps Cyprus as well, become members of the United Nations in 1960, it may be impossible for Portugal to maintain her existing position any longer.

As you probably know, the tactics of African nationalism are now being coordinated fairly closely as a result of discussions at the last All-African Peoples Conference at Accra. For the moment, the Belgian Congo and the Central African Federation are the immediate targets. There is no doubt, however, but that the ferment of African nationalism will spread to Angola and Mozambique in due course and current rumours here of increasing unrest among the inhabitants of both territories suggest that that development may not be too long delayed.

F. H. Boland

231
Ofício, Ministro Plenipotenciário irlandês em Lisboa ao Secretário-Geral do DEA: Lisboa, 28 de Novembro de 1959[49]

I have the honour to report that I was received yesterday by the Portuguese Foreign Minister, Dr. Mathias. The immediate occasion of my visit was to give the Minister the copies d'usage of my Letters of Credence which I shall be presenting

---

[48] NAI, DEA, Permanent Mission to the United Nations, X17, Portugal, 1956-1963.
[49] NAI, DEA, 313/11F Confidential reports from Lisbon Legation, 1959.

on the 4th of December but our conversation lasted for over three quarters of an hour and was devoted almost entirely to the question of colonialism with particular reference to the situation in Africa where Portugal has of course very large interests. Although he made no mention of it, it seems not impossible that the Minister, in concentrating on this theme during our first meeting, had in mind the attitude towards colonialism which we have consistently adopted in New York. I must hasten to add, however, that there was no direct suggestion of this in the Minister's manner which was most cordial throughout the interview.

The gist of his remarks was that the nationalist and independence movements in black Africa were the height of folly. The new states, such as Ghana and Guinea which had already emerged or those which were in the process of doing so, lacked every qualification of genuine nations. They had neither ethnic, religious, cultural nor linguistic unity; their populations were largely illiterate and they were almost completely devoid of trained administrators, industry and capital resources. Their only "raison d'être" was the modern antipathy to colonialism and the emotional appeal of such slogans as democracy and independence. They might perhaps maintain some semblance of viability for a few years but their dependence on foreign assistance for both capital and technicians would eventually force them to return to the sort of tutelage from which they were seeking to escape. Colonialism would not disappear from Africa; it would simply have to acquire a new and more acceptable name.

In these circumstances, the vital question was who were to be the future colonial masters. The danger that they would in fact prove to be Russia and later China was obvious. The appeal of Communism in Africa was very great but it did not spring primarily from Marxist ideology; rather it was based on the immense prestige which Russia had won for herself by her achievement in advancing from the status of a technologically backward Power in 1917 to that of at least the second-strongest state in the world today. On the other hand the West had failed to capture the imagination of black Africa which saw in America only a capitalist country which tied strings to all the assistance which it offered and which, in any event, had failed to evolve a long-term and consistent plan of aid. The Russians on the other hand gave their assistance without ostensibly linking it to political conditions.

As for the extensive Portuguese possessions in Africa and elsewhere, the Portuguese people were determined "to fight for them foot by foot". In the Portuguese view these colonies were in quite a different category from those of other Powers, particularly Britain. Whereas the British had always sought to maintain the superiority of the colonist over the native, the Portuguese from the earliest stages had insisted both in law and in practice on the absolute equality of all the inhabitants of Portuguese territories whether metropolitan or overseas. The result had been the creation of a homogenous culture despite a great diversity of geography, blood and religion. This culture was now centuries old and possessed remarkable strength – so much so that there was little demand in Portuguese Overseas territories for independence or any form of secession from the Metropole. On the contrary, in one colony which had been penetrated recently by foreign agitators, the local population had spontaneously organised itself to deal with them – rather drastically, I gathered – even though no Portuguese forces had been stationed in the territory. Constitutionally, the Portuguese possessions overseas were integral apart [sic] of the Metropole and Portugal was determined that they should remain so.

As might be guessed from the foregoing account of our conversation, Dr. Mathias did most of the talking and I felt that, in my position as a newly arrived Minister meeting him for the first time, it would be impolitic to put our own attitude towards colonialism with any great force. I did however take the opportunity of suggesting that, whether the nationalist reaction against colonialism in Africa and elsewhere was likely to have good or evil consequences, it seemed an inevitable development in view of the immense power which nationalism had proved itself capable of generating; in these circumstances was it in fact possible to resist it? Dr. Mathias would not, however, agree. In his opinion, the theory of historical movements was nonsense; it was men who made events not the reverse.

After this rather length [sic] interview with the Minister, I had a quarter of an hour with the Secretary General, Dr. Norton, who has only recently been appointed as such after a long career abroad of which his last post was Ambassador to Turkey (incidentally he mentioned having known you when you were Chargé d'Affaires here). Our conversation was on a lighter plane but when I remarked with reference to his Minister's views on Africa that, shortly before leaving London, I had been speaking to the new British Ambassador to Dublin who had been Ambassador in Ghana for the last couple of years and felt that, all things considered, the Ghanians were not doing a bad job, Dr. Norton interjected rather bitterly that it was Ghana which had been leading the attack in New York on Portuguese colonialism.

I also asked Dr. Norton whether he expected any very interesting results from the forthcoming meeting of NATO Ministers in Paris which Dr. Mathias will be attending. The Secretary General thought there was unlikely to be anything sensational. He could see no likelihood of any substantial change in regard to Berlin or the German question generally, but he didn't feel that the absence of any striking news was necessarily a bad thing. I took the occasion to refer to the proposals which we have made at the United Nations for disengagement in Europe and for limiting the dissemination of nuclear weapons but time did not allow of any substantial discussion of these questions. I was also able to put in a few words on the subject of Partition.

Frank Biggar

232
Carta, Secretário-Geral do DEA ao Ministro Plenipotenciário irlandês em Lisboa: Dublin, 4 de Dezembro de 1959[50]

CONFIDENTIAL

We were very interested in your report (6/18) of 28th November concerning your conversation with the Portuguese Foreign Minister and the Secretary-General of the Ministry.

I doubt very much whether there is any real hope of persuading the Portuguese to modify their attitude in colonial questions. However outmoded

---

[50] NAI, DEA, 313/11F Confidential reports from Lisbon Legation, 1959.

their views on these subjects my be, they appear to hold them with great tenacity; and from my knowledge of Mathias (whom I knew in Lisbon in 1945-6 and later in Paris from 1950-54), he is certainly not a man to adopt an elastic line on such questions and I am afraid we are likely to have to live with the Goa issue in the United Nations for some considerable time.

Yours sincerely,
C. C. Cremin

1960

233
Ofício, Ministro Plenipotenciário irlandês em Lisboa ao Secretário-Geral do DEA: Lisboa, 5 de Janeiro de 1960[51]

CONFIDENTIAL

PORTUGAL – GENERAL POLITICAL SITUATION

1. It is generally believed here that a Governmental reshuffle is imminent, arising out of the expected resignation of the Minister of Education, Dr. Leite Pinto, on the grounds of advancing years. The results are not likely to be very startling. For years, the most important posts have been rotated among a limited group (almost invariably members of the União Nacional – the "non-party" organisation which supports Dr. Salazar) and there seems little reason to assume that there will be any departure from practice on this occasion. The main interest will, I gather, lie in the indication which the new allocation of portfolios may give as to whose star is rising and whose declining – and hence who may seem to be favoured for the eventual succession to the Prime Minister.

The question of Dr. Salazar's successor is indeed the crucial political problem here. That is not to suggest that it is an immediate one but it is one which seems to be in everybody's mind. Dr. Salazar has now held the supreme power (actual

---
[51] NAI, DEA, 313/11G Confidential reports from Lisbon Legation, 1960.

if not theoretical) in Portugal since 1927 – an unbroken span of 32 years – and while there appears to be no real threat to his position – nobody I have met here takes General Delgado seriously – he cannot, in the nature of things, be expected to go on for very much longer. He is now 70 and, although still working a long day (he is said to have virtually no interests outside his work), he is alleged to be no longer able to get through as much as he used to. On the other hand, his tendency to reserve all major (and many not so major) decisions to himself is reported to be growing more marked with a consequently slowing down of the machine of Government. It is widely believed that he contemplated retiring some years ago, but, to the regret of many who certainly could not be regarded as unsympathetic to his régime, eventually decided against it on the grounds that no suitable successor was available. It is still not clear whether Dr. Salazar considers that one has been found. Some people regard Dr. Theotónio Pereira, for many years an able Ambassador in London and now Minister of the Presidency, as a strong possibility but in these matters Dr. Salazar keeps his own counsel.

It is generally believed – or perhaps hoped – that, if there is difficulty about the succession when the Prime Minister goes, the Army will ensure that the problem will be resolved without disorder. Those who take this view do not necessarily envisage a military régime; they think that the Army will be content with ensuring the transfer of power to a civilian of their own choice.

Whether or not these hopes are unduly optimistic is something which I should not care to speculate upon after little more than a month here. What does seem clear, however, is that any effort on the part of the Army to achieve a peaceful transition of régime would have the support of the great majority of those old enough to remember the long years of chaos and bloodshed from which Portugal suffered before Salazar came to power. Elderly people still speak with horror of that period and the fear of its recurring seems to be the strongest single element in inducing them to back the present régime. But this must obviously be a declining force and one hears it said repeatedly that the younger people who have no personal experience of those years are concerned with "liberty" and "democracy" – words which here tend to be uttered in inverted commas.

There has, of course, been more to the Salazar régime than the restoration of order. Budgets have been balanced with remarkable – some would say fanatical – consistency and the escudo has long developed from one of the weakest to one of the hardest currencies in Europe. Much has been done to expand the economy, improve communications, provide better housing etc. etc. but agriculture is still backward technically; industrialisation is only beginning; capital is scarce (and an insistence on maintaining at least 51% national control is proving a serious obstacle to attracting the private foreign investor); illiteracy is about 50%, social and health services are rudimentary; wages are low even by Southern European standards and the cost of living is relatively high. The picture generally is one of wide-spread poverty with, by contrast, a handful of very rich. That this should be the situation after so long a period of personal rule is not necessarily unreasonable having regard to the position from which the country had to be rescued but it is equally not a condition of things likely to commend the régime to the younger generation.

Moreover, there can be no doubt that, under Salazar, Portugal has been and continues to be a dictatorship. It is true that it is a dictatorship very different from the fascist, nazi, communist or South American varieties. Salazar seems to have no personal ambitions and genuinely shuns publicity. One could live in Portugal for months and see no outward evidence of his presence. There are no pictures of him in public places, he never speaks on the radio and rarely grants interviews to the press. He is not sustained by mass organisations of fanatical supporters and I have seen no evidence of a fear to criticise the régime, at least in private. Nevertheless the press is censored, no genuine Opposition is permitted, Parliament is both hand-picked and powerless and political prisoners do exist – how many no-one knows but it is no secret that a large fortress on the road to Estoril is the jail for them and that most have been committed without trial.

If the dictatorship of Salazar is benevolent, it is none the less genuine and his failure, after so many years in power, to attempt even a partial liberalisation of the political side of the régime and thus provide some safety valve for popular economic discontent may – in the view of some well-qualified observers here – lead ultimately to its violent destruction.

F. Biggar

234
Ofício, Ministro Plenipotenciário irlandês em Lisboa ao Secretário-Geral do DEA: Lisboa, 18 de Janeiro de 1960[52]

CONFIDENTIAL

VISIT OF GERMAN MINISTER OF DEFENCE

As you will, not doubt, be aware from the press, Dr. Franz Strauss, the Federal German Minister of Defence, had been on an official visit to Lisbon. He has been received by the President and Dr. Salazar and has had conversations with his opposite number here and with the Foreign Minister. He has also toured defence installations and a number of armament factories. I understand that his visit, apart from its courtesy character as between NATO allies, was primarily in connection with the purchase of war material – cartridges, shells and hand grenades – of Portuguese manufacture for the Federal German Army. Dr. Strauss announced at a press conference on Friday that the Federal Republic was buying about £125 million of such material. These purchases will help to offset Portugal's consistently unfavourable balance of trade with Germany who is a major supplier of cars and other manufactures to this country.

[...]

F. Biggar

235
Ofício, Ministro Plenipotenciário irlandês em Lisboa ao Secretário-Geral do DEA: Lisboa, 28 de Janeiro de 1960[53]

CONFIDENTIAL

PORTUGUESE BUDGET – 1960

[...]

The 1960 budget has obviously been constructed with strict regard for financial orthodoxy. A conservative financial policy has, of course, been a funda-

---
[52] NAI, DEA, 313/11G Confidential reports from Lisbon Legation, 1960.
[53] NAI, DEA, 313/11G Confidential reports from Lisbon Legation, 1960.

mental principle of the Salazarian régime. It certainly succeeded in rescuing the finances of the country from the chaos into which they had fallen before Dr. Salazar came to power. Nevertheless many question whether Salazarian conservatism in financial matters has not been excessive, the suggestion here being that it may, in fact, have unnecessarily retarded the economic development which the country so badly needs. It is perhaps worth noting, in this context, that State expenditure in Ireland for a population of 3 million is at a significantly higher level than in Portugal with 9 million people in the Metropole alone and with vast but largely underdeveloped possessions overseas [...]

F. Biggar

236
Ofício, Ministro Plenipotenciário irlandês em Lisboa ao Secretário-Geral do DEA: Lisboa, 28 de Janeiro de 1960[54]

CONFIDENTIAL

THE CLERGY IN PORTUGAL

1. One of the most serious problems facing the Portuguese Church is the shortage of clergy. According to a recent Statement by Dr. Nunes Barata in the National Assembly, the total number of priests in Metropolitan Portugal is less than 5,500, that is, little more than in Ireland although the population to be served is three times as great. The Portuguese figure gives and average of one priest per 1,773 inhabitants, compared with a European average of one per 944 Catholics. In fact the proportion of priests to laity is the lowest in Europe.

2. The average figure for the whole country conceals the full gravity of the position in many areas since in some, mainly in the North where the people remain most closely attached to the Church, the number of priests is relatively high. In the Archdiocese of Braga, for example, there is one priest for 950

---

[54] NAI, DEA, 313/11G Confidential reports from Lisbon Legation, 1960.

inhabitants, which is not much worse that the European average (although still very low by Irish standards). In the Patriarchy (the Archdiocese of Lisbon), the proportion is 1 to 4,226 and in the Diocese of Beja, 1 to 7,500! As a result, many areas are without a parish church, primarily because there would be no clergy for it! The position in the rapidly expanding suburbs of Lisbon is particularly bad.

3. This shortage of clergy, in a country nominally so Catholic as Portugal, is no new thing and the reasons for it, historical and otherwise, are too complicated to discuss in this brief note. Lack of seminaries or seminarists does not appear to be a major cause. There are considerable numbers of clerical students; the trouble is that relatively few continue to ordination. According to Dr. Nunes Barata, no less than 80% of the seminarists fail to become priests. This compares with a figure of 30% in Spain, 40% in Ireland and 43% in Germany.

4. One reason for the high rate of defection from the Seminaries is the system of "child vocations" which prevails in Portugal. This is the system whereby boys are admitted to the Seminaries at a very early age and receive their entire education until ordination in them. With such a system, it would seem only natural that a higher proportion would ultimately decide that they had been mistaken in their vocation than in countries where clerical studies are not begun until a maturer age.

5. The system has another interesting effect. As the bulk of Seminarists come from peasant and lower middle class families and would normally, attend State schools (if indeed they received any schooling at all), the Church is, in effect, relieving the State of the cost of educating substantial numbers yearly, since the Seminaries receive no assistance from public funds.

F. Biggar

237
Ofício, Ministro Plenipotenciário irlandês em Lisboa ao Secretário-Geral do DEA: Lisboa, 15 de Fevereiro de 1960[55]

CONFIDENTIAL

I have the honour to refer to Mr. Molloy's circular minute of the 30th January regarding the meetings in Paris earlier that month on the subject of commercial policy, the future of the OEEC etc, and to report that I took the opportunity of a recent conversation with Dr. Ruy Teixeira Guerra, Director General of Economic Affairs at the Foreign Ministry, to discuss the matter generally with him. Dr. Guerra has attended the Paris meetings and indeed he tells me he is now working more with Dr. Correia de Oliveira, the Secretary of State for Commerce and Portugal's representative in EFTA and the OEEC, than with his own Ministry.

[…]

As to Portugal's finding itself in the EFTA rather than the EEC camp, Dr. Guerra said that it was quite true that Portugal's trade with the latter was greater than with the former. In his view, however, what the Portuguese economy needed was the sort of shaking up that could only come from free competition which in turn required the lowering of trade barriers. He is all in favour of letting in foreign capital and foreign technicians and encouraging foreign tourists. He thinks the alternative is the continuation of Portugal's position as a poor, underdeveloped nation with a standard of living already low relative to that of the industrialised countries and with the comparison steadily growing more unfavourable.

F. Biggar

---

[55] NAI, DEA, 313/11G Confidential reports from Lisbon Legation, 1960.

238
Ofício, Ministro Plenipotenciário irlandês em Lisboa ao Secretário-Geral do DEA: 24 de Fevereiro de 1960[56]

CONFIDENTIAL

OPPOSITION TO RÉGIME

The news has recently leaked out – nothing appeared in the press here at the time – that towards the end of January some republicans, opposed to the present régime, asked permission to hold a small ceremony at an Oporto cemetery on the 31st January, the anniversary of the first republican uprising against the monarchy which took place in 1891. It appears this was allowed but extremists managed to distribute enough clandestine propaganda to attract some 3,000 persons to what developed, in consequence, into a large scale demonstration. There was some clashes [sic] outside the cemetery with the police in which at least 10 people were injured. Amongst these was Dr. Arlindo Vicente, former candidate for the Presidency of the Republic who withdrew from the 1958 campaign in favour of General Delgado.

F. Biggar

239
Ofício, Ministro Plenipotenciário irlandês em Lisboa ao Secretário-Geral do DEA: 25 de Março de 1960[57]

CONFIDENTIAL

PORTUGUESE COLONIALISM

The fifth centenary of the death of the Infante Dom Henrique – more familiar to us, perhaps, as Prince Henry the Navigator – occurs this year and elaborate preparations are being made to celebrate it throughout Portugal and her Overseas Territories […] The centenary celebrations began officially on the 4th of March

---
[56] NAI, DEA, 313/11G Confidential reports from Lisbon Legation, 1960.
[57] NAI, DEA, 313/11G Confidential reports from Lisbon Legation, 1960.

with a TE DEUM in the Jerónimos Monastery at Belém (just outside Lisbon) which was the starting point of the expeditions and a Solemn Session of the National Assembly that same afternoon. The President, Dr. Salazar, the Cardinal Patriarch, the members of Government, the Diplomatic Corps and a large number of distinguished guests attended both ceremonies, Brazil being represented by a special Ambassador. The functions were most impressive, the TE DEUM in particular being a splendid occasion. Similar ceremonies were held on the same day throughout Portugal and the Overseas Territories.

The centenary celebrations will continue for most of the year, with exhibitions, congresses, special publications and the like. The climax will be reached in August with an international naval review off Sagres, the scene of Prince Henry's labours, and the unveiling of a monument to the Discoveries at Belém [...]

These prolonged celebrations can hardly fail to intensify the already strong Portuguese feeling about their colonies, past and present. The Discoveries and the benefits which the Portuguese thereby conferred on the world as well as on the homeland and the territories colonised, constitute one of the great Portuguese national myths – and, unlike some other historical myths, it has more than a fair basis in fact. Certainly the Portuguese have every reason to remember with pride the extraordinary achievements of Prince Henry's time and the immediately succeeding generations in discovering Brazil, exploring the African coast, pioneering the route to India and thence to the East Indies, China and Japan and – perhaps most remarkable of all – holding the sea sovereignty over all this vast area for more than a century. It is true that the immense effort involved overstrained Portugal's meagre economic and human resources – the population of the Metropole at the time can hardly have exceeded a million and nearly half the men and ships sent out never returned – and eventually exhausted the country, both physically and morally, but nevertheless the achievement was astonishing. Nor for the Portuguese people and especially for the early adventurers were the voyages ever a mere search for material gain. The fabulous wealth of the East was, of course, a primary object, great fortunes were made and there was much injustice and corruption but the Portuguese did genuinely seek to spread Christianity and the civilisation of Europe within their spheres of influence. Since these were, in fact, mostly confined to trading posts, forts and small settlements the ultimate result was tiny in relation to the huge areas and vast populations of the East but something did remain as witness Goa, Macao and above all, Brazil today. The hope of finding the lost Christian kingdom of Prester John was as valid, if not as dominating, a motive cf the Discoverers as that of locating the sources of the eastern spices; so equally was the desire to injure the Moslems, both by taking their Middle East empire in the rear and depriving them of their monopoly of the spice trade. Indeed the Discoveries were, in a very real sense, a crusade, the continuation of the centuries-old struggle against the Moor. He had at last been driven from the mainland of Portugal; he was now to be attacked in his own home. Prince Henry's first public appearance, as one might say, was his participation in the campaign which captured Ceuta in Morocco. It was also Portugal's first overseas effort.

All this glory has, of course, long since faded but the memory of it is still strong in the Portuguese mind and is an important factor in determining the Portuguese attitude to its present overseas territories. Under the Portuguese Constitution, these territories – Angola, Mozambique, Guinea, Goa, Macao and Timor – are not colonies, they are Overseas Provinces and as such an integral part of Portugal. This claims is by no means a recent one […] The Portugalidade, the "Portugueseness", of the Overseas Provinces is a constant theme of Government speakers, publicists and the press. In my short time in Lisbon, I have seen scores of articles on the subject and there is certainly going to be no falling off in this year of Prince Henry's fifth centenary.

How genuinely is the doctrine held? This is a difficult question for a foreigner to answer in a country where censorship and the secret police effectively prevent public discussion of Government policy. Perhaps the very fact that so much ink and oratory is devoted to the subject is in itself an indication of the Government's doubts as to the strength of the ordinary man's belief – the lady doth protest too much! Yet a certain case can be made in support of it. The Portuguese have been in their colonies for a very long time and, having little or no colour bar, they have had a better basis for developing them into integrated communities than in the case of colonies where white and coloured kept strictly apart. The Portugalidade of Goa, for example, seems real enough. Such Goans as I have met here – my doctor is one – appear to regard themselves as fully Portuguese and there is the "China Community", a group of mixed Portuguese and Chinese descent originally from Macao who frequent the Irish Dominican Church of Corpo Santo and who also seem to think of themselves as Portuguese even though most of them were born in Hong-Kong and speak English as their vernacular. Certainly neither Goa nor Macao appears in any hurry to cut the Portuguese connection and be absorbed by their giant neighbours or presumably they would have done so already.

As to Africa, a missionary (neither Portuguese nor Irish) who has worked for years in Angola told me recently that there is no evidence of any real desire on the part of the natives for independence. He attributed this primarily to their poverty and general backwardness, particularly the low level of education. He himself believed that the scarcity of schools in Angola was due, not to any deliberate policy on the part of the Portuguese Government to keep the native ineffectual, but simply to the fact that the Salazarian régime had, not unnaturally, given priority in educational matters to the Metropole which, of course, needed it badly – until recently the illiteracy rate in Continental Portugal was over 50. The result, however, had been to prevent the emerging of the sort of native intellectual elite which, in British and French colonies, provided the leaders of the nationalist movements. In addition, the white Portuguese, although not very numerous, tended to settle throughout the country rather than remain on the coastal fringe and each settlement was a centre of Portuguese influence. There was not much formal intermarriage but a great many less formal unions and a considerable half-caste population was developing. Apart from these, the Portuguese settlers themselves tended to remain rather than to return to Portugal after they had made their money. The ultimate result of these and other factors would, my informant thought, be the emergence in Angola of a separate nation, a sort of African Brazil, which would eventually demand its independence – but that time, he felt, was still a long way off. In the meantime, the natives were not too badly treated. It was true that all but the tiny minority who could meet the educational and other requirements for full citizenship were definitely second-class citizens, that there was a certain amount of forced labour and that the police were extremely powerful (they are in Portugal too!) but nevertheless the régime was not in general unduly harsh and the natives seemed reasonably content.

Much the same sort of views have been expressed to me by the Belgian Ambassador, who knows something of the Congo and has visited Angola. He places no credence – as, I think, does nobody here, in the claims which two representatives of an American group have been making in New York that, during the course of a recent "tourist" trip in Angola, they contacted a revolutionary movement well supplied with arms and that Angola would soon become a second Algeria if the Portuguese didn't get out quickly.

There may well be more substance in the TIME's report earlier this month to the effect that anti-Salazarian groups amongst the whites were endeavouring to stir up agitation in Angola with a view to embarrassing the Government here. However well-founded this may be – and its accuracy has been vigorously contested by the Metropolitan Angolese press – there seems to be no evidence as yet of a nationalist movement in any of the Portuguese African territories comparable to those which have occurred in other areas of Central and Southern Africa.

From the theory of the Portugalidade of the Overseas Provinces naturally follows the claim that these territories have no desire for an independent national existence. But it is clear that the nationalist movements in Asia and Africa – particularly Equatorial Africa where the Portuguese possessions are situated – is causing the Government here the greatest anxiety. The granting of independence to Ghana and French Guinea (which is believed to be casting eyes on Portuguese Guinea) and the forthcoming statehood of the Belgian Congo (many of whose inhabitants are of the same tribes as those across the border in Angola) and of Nigeria are all seen as threatening the Portuguese position in Africa despite the claims of Portugalidade. The standpoint of the Portuguese Government, however, is that these developments are not the result of indigenous movements but are of foreign inspiration, the consequence of Communist propaganda and agitaters [sic]. In a speech last year Dr. Salazar said "Africa is afire…let us not imagine it is due to internal combustion…Africa is burning because it is being set on fire from outside. (By "Africa" he means "Africa south of the Equator, whose sovereignty has been confided [sic] to European States"). He went on to analyse the African problem under three heads. First, "Africa is the complement of Europe, vital for its defence and a necessary support of its economy – (thus) Europe can be overthrown in Africa." Secondly, while a certain degree of progress had been achieved, the peoples of Black Africa did not possess the administrative, technical or economic resources to maintain a solvent or progressive economy. From this followed the third viewpoint, namely "in the absence of support from the former sovereign power, these peoples will have only two alternatives – regression or submission to new rulers" and he made it clear that the new rulers he foresaw were Russia or the Communist states of Asia. He concluded "the present and immediate need is to save Africa from the combined assault of the interests to which I have referred and to avoid its destruction by formulas that we know would be fatal to it." The Foreign Minister was blunter during my first conversation with him "We shall fight" he said "for the Overseas Provinces, foot by foot."

It can hardly be doubted that Dr. Salazar's analysis is unduly simpliste or that the Portuguese views generally regarding their Overseas Territories are anachronistic. It does not seem possible that the natives of Angola, Mozambique and Portuguese Guinea can be isolated indefinitely from the infection of nationalism that, with or without Communist support, is sweeping through the rest of Africa or that so small and poor a country as Portugal can hope to retain possession of vast areas there when the much stronger Powers, Britain, France and Belgium, have had to grant independence to the neighbouring peoples. Nevertheless there are two points which, I feel, are worth bearing in mind. First, while the fiction, no matter how hoary, of the Overseas Provinces being an integral part of Portugal can scarcely endure much longer, there does seem to be enough in the claim of their <u>Portugalidade</u> to suggest that these territories may eventually emerge as more homogenous and therefore viable communities that the highly artificial political groupings such as the Belgian Congo or some of the former British colonies which are now receiving statehood. Secondly, it does appear to be true that there is as yet little in the way of nationalist feeling or movements in Portugal's African territories and, while this position is unlikely to obtain indefinitely, it would seem unwise for the rest of the world to endeavour, in the name of nationalistic principles, to thrust independence upon peoples who are not yet seeking it are manifestly not yet ready for it. This is not, of course, to advocate the cessation of efforts to bring Portugal's Overseas Territories within the scope of Article 73 (e) of the United Nations Charter; obviously if these efforts prove successful they could well help to secure a much needed improvement in the social, political and economic lot of the natives and thus assist in creating conditions favourable to ultimate independence. It is merely to suggest the wisdom of hastening independence slowly in order to avoid, if possible, the repetition in these territories of the sort of problems now arising in connection with other African colonies who have assumed the responsibilities of freedom before being able to carry them, as described by the Permanent Representative to the United Nations in his reports of the 23rd and 24th February.

F. Biggar

240
Ofício, Ministro Plenipotenciário irlandês em Lisboa ao Secretário-Geral do DEA: Lisboa, 6 de Abril de 1960[58]

CONFIDENTIAL

INTERNATIONAL SITUATION – DR. SALAZAR'S VIEWS.

I have the honour to report that the Portuguese press has recently reproduced extracts from an interview accorded by Dr. Salazar to a representative of the Mexican paper "EXCELSIOR" in the course of which the Premier gave expression to views on the international situation. The following are some of the more important points he made:-

"The Western Allies cannot say that they won the war since they are unable to dictate the peace. It is an illusion to ask that Russia should accept a plebiscite for the re-unification of Germany. The Communists occupy territories which they

---

[58] NAI, DEA, 313/11G Confidential reports from Lisbon Legation, 1960.

are not willing to abandon under any pretext. As long as Communism is active and strong, either in the ideological or imperialist field, international conferences can momentarily relieve tension but cannot bring about really definite results."

Dr. Salazar also contested the American view that economic well-being is an adequate barrier against Communism. In his opinion, the spread of Communism is due not merely to poverty but to intellectual ideas and to bourgeois snobbery. In addition, Communism presents itself as a sort of doctrine or complete philosophy of man and makes converts independently of the individual's economic situation. "Only Catholicism can in part fight Communism. However, after a striking rise, Communism will gradually lose its power owing to internal contradictions which will cause its decline."

Speaking about democracy, Dr. Salazar said that, in our time, the parliamentary régime had exhausted its virtues and had become decadent in almost every country. It had certainly proved a failure in Portugal. The problem was to find a substitute. Portuguese Corporativism, which was one such attempt, had its defects but was being improved.

F. Biggar

241
Ofício, Ministro Plenipotenciário irlandês em Lisboa ao Secretário-Geral do DEA: Lisboa, 12 de Abril de 1960[59]

CONFIDENTIAL

THE POLITICAL POLICE

One of the professional hazards of the diplomatic life in Lisbon is the possibility of being asked for asylum by political fugitives. So far, only Latin American Missions have suffered in this respect – no doubt the fugitives felt that their appeals were more likely to be sympathetically received by such Missions having regard to the Latin American traditions of granting asylum to unsuccessful

---

[59] NAI, DEA, 313/11G Confidential reports from Lisbon Legation, 1960.

leaders in their periodic revolutions. However that may be, the Cuban and the Venezuelan Embassies has [sic] each been sheltering a political fugitive in its Chancery for some time. In the former is Manuel Serra, President of the Juventude Operária Católica, the Portuguese equivalent of the French JOC. Serra escaped to the Cuban Embassy from the hospital to which he had been admitted under guard as a result, it is said, of the maltreatment he received from the political police after his arrest on charges of subversive activities. The man in the Venezuelan Embassy, Horacio Gradim, a young architect, is a member of the Directory Council of the Youth Front. He sought asylum when he learned the police were looking for him.

[…]

These events are reflections of the darker side of Dr. Salazar's Government – the denial of political liberty, a stringent censorship and a powerful political police. Dr. Salazar has never, of course, pretended that his régime was democratic. Indeed he considers democracy, at least as generally preached today, to be a false doctrine with its origin in the Free-masonry and the liberalism of the French Revolution. It would not, I think, be unfair to summarise his view of individual liberty as the right to behave in conformity with the good of the State as interpreted by the Government. However one may regard this attitude, it is certainly true that the Portuguese experience of the working of parliamentary democracy in the century before Dr. Salazar came into power was not such as to endear it to the bulk of the Portuguese people – it was a long and painful story of political instability, financial ineptitude, economic backwardness and social decay culminating in national collapse. Dr. Salazar can with some justice claim to have rescued his country from the abyss and given it order, sound finances and a measure of social and economic progress (although many people here would deny it). But he did it as an autocrat – there may have been, probably was, no other way – and the inevitable corollaries of autocracy seem to be censorship and the political police. Certainly Portugal has both. And no attempt is made to deny the existence of either. Thus every newspaper bears the legend "seen by the Censorship Commission".

As for the political police, with which this report is primarily concerned, it is officially the Polícia Internacional e de Defesa do Estado, usually known as PIDE.

It is widespread, powerful and, in the general belief, ruthless. While it would be unfair to say that the Portuguese régime is one of police terror on the Nazi or Communist scale – it is very far from that – it is nevertheless true that people are arrested, tried for crimes against the State (which may, and frequently do, mean no more than possessing left-wing literature or inciting to strike) and sentenced to severe terms of imprisonment; even when these have been completed, the prisoners may be kept in goal [sic] indefinitely. Furthermore, it is widely believed that the political police freely use torture in their interrogations of suspects.

In this connection I have recently been shown a document which pains a grim picture of the situation. Although it is now over a year old, I do not think it has been brought to your attention before […] It is a copy of a letter addressed by some forty-five Portuguese Catholics to Dr. Salazar complaining about the constant rumours at home and reports abroad of the torture – even murder – of political suspects by the police and demanding a full and open investigation. Amongst the signatories are six priests and a nephew of the Minister of the Presidency. Another is Manuel Serra […] Copies certainly were sent to all members of the Government, to the Cardinal Patriarch and to the Nuncio. As it consists of ten foolscap pages of small type, I do not propose to translate it in extenso […]

The letter, which is dated the 1st March 1959, but was not despatched until the following 18th April, is couched in respectful but firm terms […]

[…] It quotes the Paris Revue "Presence Africain" edited by "the Negro Catholic intellectual" Alioune Diop, which, in its first issue, of April-July 1955 refers to the deaths of over a 1,000 people as a result of police action in the San Tomé Islands and says that in one night 20 to 45 prisoners died of asphyxiation […]

On the 23rd March 1957, the letter continues, 72 lawyers of Lisbon and Oporto asked the Government for an inquiry into the deaths of the two men in Oporto referred to by the Bulletin of the International Commission of Jurists and into other alleged irregularities. An inquiry was, in fact, opened and evidence of 26 cases of the ill-treatment of political prisoners was offered on the 23rd October but nothing has since been heard of the matter, except that one of the lawyers concerned was subsequently arrested but found not guilty in connection with incidents arising out of the inquiry. A demand for a similar inquiry was also made by 33 Coimbra lawyers, including the Deputy Civil Governor, but without result [...]

The most disquieting report which the writers have seen, however, is, they say, a book "Oppressed Portugal" by a Captain Queiroga, published in Rio de Janeiro in 1958. This book descrobes "dozens of murders...physical and mental tortures of every kind, gratuitous brutalities, inflictions of estatua to the limit of human endurance, whipping...the reduction of men to a more than animal subjection...the mass liquidation of men considered dangerous and collected in lorries to be shot by the Spanish during the civil war." (I, myself, have heard this last allegation several times) [...]

The presidential electoral campaign in the early summer of 1958 appears, continues the letter, to have led to increased police activities and, in the general belief, to the brutal ill-treatment of political suspects on a large scale [...]

The writers conclude by declaring that their action has been dictated by their conscience as Catholics and by appealing to the conscience of Dr. Salazar as a proclaimed Catholic for and "ample, total and final explanation" of the questions raised. They have certainly not received it. What effect the letter had and which action, if any, resulted is not the sort of information which can be come by easily under an authoritarian régime but the rumours of police brutality against political suspects still continue.

F. Biggar

242
Ofício, Ministro Plenipotenciário irlandês em Lisboa ao Secretário-Geral do DEA: Lisboa, 28 de Abril de 1960[60]

CONFIDENTIAL

HAGUE DECISION ON PORTUGUESE-INDIAN DISPUTE.

The decisions of the International Court of Justice at the Hague on the 12th April in the action which Portugal had brought against India over her right of

---

[60] NAI, DEA, 313/11G Confidential reports from Lisbon Legation, 1960.

access to the two enclaves of Dadrá and Nagar-Aveli from Damão on the North--West coast of India seem to have attracted little attention abroad but were treated in Portugal as a tremendous victory. For days after the decision was announced, the press here was almost entirely filled with messages of congratulations from everybody of any importance in Portuguese life and with articles lauding Dr. Salazar's stand against the Indian pretensions. The only message of congratulations from a purely foreign source which I noticed was that of the Spanish Ambassador here […]

F. Biggar

243
Ofício, Embaixador irlandês em Madrid ao Secretário-Geral do DEA: Madrid, 3 de Maio de 1960[61]

Seeing a reference in a report (P.R. 9/60 (Lisbon) of 25th March, 1960) of Mr. Biggar's to an earlier report on African matters (P.R. 3/60 (UNO) of 24th February, 1960) from Mr. Boland, I was reminded of the fact that page 2 of the latter report as circulated to us was missing.

[…]

I note, according to the report of the Minister at Lisbon, that he was informed by a missionary priest that in Angola the natives are "not being too badly treated" although there is "a certain amount of forced labour there".

As I told the Minister when at home last Christmas, a son of mine has just returned from Angola where he saw African dockers being threatened and hit with revolvers by police for not working fast enough. Coloured sailors on my son's ship took shoreleave everywhere down the West African coast but stayed on board at Angola. When the ship was ready to sail an Angolese [sic] stowaway was discovered but the master decided not to surrender him because of his belief that the death-penalty would be applied in Angola in such a case.

Michael Rynne

---

[61] NAI, DEA, Embassy Madrid, I.P. 4/51/1, Portugal 1941-1963.

244

Ofício, Ministro Plenipotenciário irlandês em Lisboa ao Secretário-Geral do DEA: Lisboa, 19 de Maio de 1960[62]

US PRESIDENT'S VISIT TO PORTUGAL

1. The sudden break-down of the Summit Conference caused President Eisenhower to advance his visit to Portugal from the 23rd May as originally intended to today. He arrived this morning and had a warm reception from the people of Lisbon. He lunched with Dr. Salazar and received the Heads of foreign Missions this afternoon. There will be a State banquet this evening and a reception afterwards. The President returns to Washington tomorrow.

2. As usual, the Heads of Mission were presented individually to the President, but, although he was extremely affable, there was no opportunity for more than a greeting [...]

F. Biggar

245

Ofício, Ministro Plenipotenciário irlandês em Lisboa ao Secretário-Geral do DEA: Lisboa, 30 de Junho de 1960[63]

CONFIDENTIAL

PORTUGUESE COLONIALISM

With reference to my P.R. 9/60 (Lisbon) of the 25th March concerning Portuguese colonialism, I have the honour to report that the Minister for Foreign Affairs reverted to the subject in the course of a conversation which I had with him on the 24th June. Dr. Marcello Mathias seemed to be particularly annoyed with two articles on the Portuguese Empire which had appeared in the London TIMES on the 21st and 22nd June and which severely criticised the Portuguese system of colonialism. Dr. Mathias described the articles as "stupid" and attributed

---

[62] NAI, DEA, 313/11G Confidential reports from Lisbon Legation, 1960.
[63] NAI, DEA, 313/11G Confidential reports from Lisbon Legation, 1960.

their motivation to jealousy at Portugal's success in retaining her Overseas possessions while Britain was being forced to abandon hers. He went on to claim – as is usual here – that the length of time the Portuguese have been in their colonies and their lack of any colour bar had produced integrated communities which were genuinely Portuguese in character and outlook [...]

I said that I was, of course, fully aware of the Portuguese Government's views on the subject but that I could not help asking myself whether Portugal's resources were such as to enable her to maintain possession of such vast areas in the face of the rising tide of nationalism both in Asia and Africa. No-one would wish Angola to become a second Algeria with Portugal subjected to the sort of strain on her resources that France had been and still was suffering. The Minister replied there was no possibility of Angola developing into an Algeria and that the Portuguese were fully aware of the limited nature of their resources. They had no illusions on that subject and they would offer no provocation to anybody but they were determined to use all their patience and tenacity to retain what they had. He instanced the case of Goa and the other Portuguese enclaves in India which Nehru, he said, had thought would be swept away by mere weight of numbers but it had not happened like that. The Portuguese had not attacked but they had given every warning that they would defend themselves if their territory was violated and when the Indians did try to overwhelm them with masses of agitators the Portuguese had in fact opened fire and killed a few. Nehru hadn't liked it, of course, but the Portuguese where still where they had been for centuries – long before there was any such thing as an Indian nation. They were still in Macau on the edge of China despite the fact that they continued to recognise the Government of Chang Kai Chek and the Indonesians had publicly announced that they had no claim to Timor. The Portuguese position was extremely difficult and they had, therefore, to tread very cautiously but they had no intention of surrendering a square foot of their territory. If they lost anything, it would be over the dead bodies of the defenders.

Dr. Mathias went on to condemn the policies of retreat in Africa before the native nationalist movements and argued – as Dr. Salazar and other Government speakers have also done – that Europe can be lost in Africa. The newly independent

Governments can deny access to essential resources and the likelihood of chaos plus communism is all too evident. It is to be remarked, nevertheless, that Portugal is sending a delegation for the Congolese declaration of independence – no doubt in persuance of her policy of patience and non-provocation.

Africa is, of course, of vital concern to Portugal and she has never sought to hide her concern at the course of events there. It is generally surmised that African questions were a principal subject of discussion at the recent meeting in Spain between Dr. Salazar and General Franco. Spain and South Africa are practically the only countries which share Portugal's views on colonialism and she is acutely aware of her isolated position but shows no sign of allowing it to affect her colonial policies. On the contrary she is trying, by encouraging emigration from Metropolitan Portugal, to expand the white population of her African territories and she has been seeking foreign, particularly German, aid to help her develop their resources. On the other hand, I have yet to meet any foreign representatives here (other perhaps than the Spanish and South Africans) who believe that Portugal can retain possession of her overseas territories for more than a very few years to come.

F. Biggar

246
Ofício, Ministro Plenipotenciário irlandês em Lisboa ao Secretário-Geral do DEA: Lisboa, 2 de Julho de 1960[64]

CONFIDENTIAL

FRANCO/SALAZAR MEETING

The meeting between General Franco and Dr. Salazar, which took place for two days last week in Merida, Spain, was the latest of a series which has been going on for a number of years at lengthy but diminishing intervals. There are, of course, much more frequent meetings between the Foreign Ministers of the two

---

[64] NAI, DEA, 313/11G Confidential reports from Lisbon Legation, 1960.

countries. On this occasion, the dictators were accompanied by their Foreign Ministers but the latter apparently took little part in the conversations, the more important of which seems, took place between General Franco and Dr. Salazar alone. The same secrecy has been maintained about the subject and nature of the discussions but the surmise in Lisbon is that the following were the major topics:

1) The inclusion of Spain in NATO
2) The restoration of both the Spanish and Portuguese monarchies
3) Anti-communist measures and
4) African questions.

As regards 1), Portugal has never of course made any secret of her views that Spain should be a member of the NATO alliance [...]

As regards the second supposed point of discussion, some people here take the view that, if and when the Spanish monarchy is restored, Dr. Salazar would like to see a simultaneous restoring of the Portuguese monarchy. General Franco has, of course, gone a long way to committing himself to the eventual return of D. Juan or D. Carlos and his meeting with the former some months ago gave rise to a fresh wave of speculations as to the likelihood of an early restoration but Dr. Salazar has, as far as I am aware, made no such commitment in regard to the Portuguese royal family. However, the problem of ensuring the continuation of the Salazarian system after the departure of Dr. Salazar himself is perhaps the central one of Portuguese politics and a restoration of the monarchy might help to solve it, particularly if the King's acceptance of the principles of the régime could be secured in advance. A period during which Dr. Salazar would continue as Prime Minister after the restoration could well be envisaged.

In support of this line of speculation is the fact that the royalist spirit is undoubtedly still strong in Portugal. D. Duarte, the Pretender, and his family live here quite freely and he was accorded a precedence immediately after the President at the Te Deum and the Jerónimos Monastry [sic] last March on the occasion of the opening of the Prince Henry quincentenary year. One of the leading Lisbon papers, A VOZ, makes no secret of its royalist views and one prominent official of the Foreign Office had no hesitation in telling me (as we were driving back from the Presidential Palace after presenting my Letters last December!) that Portugal wasn't really a Republic at all but a monarchy which only lacked a King to be complete. While that was undoubtedly an exaggeration, it does seem probable that the restoration of the monarchy would be within the range of possibilities, if Dr. Salazar really desires it.

Two further comments on this subject may be worth making. First I gather that there is some objection, even amongst the royalists, to the present Pretender D. Duarte on the grounds that his Portuguese is poor. He comes of a cadet branch of the Braganças which has lived in Vienna since before the end of the last century and it is said that German rather than Portuguese is his mother tongue. Secondly, many royalists would be opposed to the return of the king if it meant the perpetuation of the present régime.

As regards the question of coordinating anti-communist action in Spain and Portugal, there is no doubt that the security police of the two countries have long been cooperating closely in this regard. Whether the present meeting will result in closer cooperation and more intensive measures against communism will presumably be apparent from the further course of events.

As regards the fourth point, African questions, there is nothing I can usefully add to my P.R.19/60 of the 29th June.

F. Biggar

247
Ofício, Ministro Plenipotenciário irlandês em Lisboa ao Secretário-Geral do DEA: Lisboa, 15 de Julho de 1960[65]

CONFIDENTIAL

THE CONGO

The confused and tragic events in the former Belgian Congo are naturally being followed with a specially intense interest in Portugal on account of the

---

[65] NAI, DEA, 313/11G Confidential reports from Lisbon Legation, 1960.

proximity of Angola, whose frontier marches for hundreds of miles with that of the Congo, and of the presence there of a considerable Portuguese population, both white and black. Judging by the press, which has been devoting an immense amount of space to the Congo situation, many of the whites (and, it is said, some of the blacks) have fled to Angola which has also been a major reception centre for Belgian and other white refugees. Although earlier reports said that the Portuguese consulate at Matadi had been sacked, the Foreign Ministry tells me this is incorrect and there seem, on the whole, to have been relatively few casualties among the Portuguese. Indeed the claim is being made here that, especially in the towns, the Belgians were notably worst handled than the Portuguese. Some of the Portuguese refugees are already beginning to arrive in Lisbon.

I made an opportunity to discuss the situation yesterday with Dr. Lencastre da Veiga, Assistant Director of Political Affairs in the Foreign Ministry (the Director is in Dakar at the moment). My telegram N.º 31 of yesterday's date was based on this conversation. In general the authorities here do not appear to have much more information about the situation in the Congo than has appeared in the press. Their Embassy in Leopoldville has reported that the Belgian parachutists are in control of the capital – although their withdrawal to their bases has been demanded by Premier Lumumba – but the situation there and throughout the rest of the country remains tense and confused. The belief here is that the Congolese Government is not capable of restoring order by itself and that the intervention of a United Nations force will be essential [...]

I inquired whether there was any real evidence of Soviet influence behind the outbreaks. Although the Portuguese are constantly apprehensive of Communist machinations, particularly in Africa, Dr. Lencastre da Veiga said that the situation was too confused for certainty. There had been allegations of subversive action by the Czechoslovak Consul but one couldn't be sure. The artificial character of the new state, intertribal disputes, personal rivalries between the leaders, anti-Belgian and anti-white feeling and the general low level of education and administrative experience were obviously enough to explain the situation which had developed.

Dr. Lencastre da Veiga also thought that the secession movement in Katanga might have great significance. If the Congo was deprived of this, its wealthiest province, it was difficult to see how it could become viable. He agreed, however, that Congo would create great problems for Katanga, not the least of which would be the fact that it was entirely landlocked and would, therefore, have no direct access to the sea.

One of the question [sic] which is puzzling the Portuguese is why the Belgian [sic], even if reconciled to the necessity of granting independence at a relatively early date, should gave acted so precipitately. On this point, Dr. Teixeira Guerra, the Director General of Economic Affairs, remarked to me in an earlier conversation hat, when he was in Brussels towards the end of last year with his Minister, the Belgian Minister of the Colonies had told them that he was "an optimist" in regard to the Congo. By this he meant that, while many Belgians believed it would take ten years for the Congo to become independent, he was convinced that four years would see the end of Belgian rule. Nevertheless only a few months later the date had been advanced to the 1st July 1960. Neither Dr. Teixeira Guerra nor Dr. Lencastre da Veiga could offer any reason for this change of mind in Brussels except that possibly, as the latter said, the King had lost his head during his visit to the Congo during the winter.

While the present events there and the fate of the white population are, of course, deplored in Portugal, there is no concealing the existence of a certain "I told you so" attitude in regard to the Belgians and a decidedly pointed contrasting of the peace in Angola with the chaos next door. For Portugal, the developments in the Congo offer powerful evidence of the validity of Portuguese colonial theory. As you are aware, Portugal has all along opposed black nationalism in Africa and has watched with great concern the grant of independence to each former African colony. The smoothness of the transitions heretofore, while not causing her to alter her opinion in the slightest, has naturally, as she well understands, tended to weaken her case in the eyes of the rest of the world. Henceforth however Portugal will be able to cite the Congo in support of her views on Africa generally and her policy in her own African territories. With this in mind but of course without referring to it directly, I thought it well, when talking to Dr. Lencastre da Veiga, to point out that more than one country had been born in chaos and bloodshed – India being an outstanding example – and that, despite present appearances, the failure of the Congo experiment could it seemed to me, be by no means assumed.

F. Biggar

248
Ofício, Ministro Plenipotenciário irlandês em Lisboa ao Secretário-Geral do DEA: Lisboa, 25 de Agosto de 1960[66]

CONFIDENTIAL

DOM HENRIQUE CENTENARY

[…] the second week of August saw the climax of the celebrations in honour of the 5th centenary of the death of Prince Henry the Navigator. The principal items were a naval review off Sagres and the unveiling of a monument to the Discoverers at Belém near Lisbon. At the same time, President Kubitschek de Oliveira of Brasil (the "de Oliveira" is always emphasized here) paid a state visit to Portugal and was a leading figure at all the ceremonies […] Public enthusiasm on the whole seems to have been widespread and genuine although I have been told that the occasional comment could be heard amongst the spectators that, having regard to Portugal's poverty, the money might have been put to better use. It may also perhaps be significant that a documentary film of the events (done most effectively in colour) which I saw the other evening in one of Lisbon's leading cinemas evoked no applause whatever.

The naval review off Sagres was splendid and unique affair [sic] […] The procession of ships took perhaps an hour to pass the saluting point and at intervals squadrons of military planes, British, American and Portuguese, swept overhead. The spectacle, on a day of calm seas and brilliant sunshine, was superb.

---

[66] NAI, DEA, 313/11G Confidential reports from Lisbon Legation, 1960.

The Diplomatic Corps and hundreds of other guests witnessed the review from four vessels, including the liners "Vera Cruz" and "Angola", which had sailed from Lisbon on Saturday and returned the next day.

The dedication of the Monument to the Discoverers was a less spectacular ceremony but nevertheless carried out with pomp and pageantry. The Monument itself is a cut-stone structure designed to suggest in stylised form the prow and sails of a caravel; around the base are heroic figures of Prince Henry and captains and crews of his ships. The Monument stands at the water's edge in front of the Monastery of Jeronimos, the supreme masterpiece of manueline-gothic, near the spot where most of the voyages of discovery began.

The theme of the celebrations was naturally Portugal's "historic mission" in pioneering, colonising, and civilising so much of the world both east and west and her determination to continue to fulfil this mission by retaining and further developing her overseas provinces. The "daughter nation" Brazil was naturally accorded a central place in the celebrations as the greatest example of Portuguese colonisation; the closeness of the bonds which bind the two countries was a constant subject of oratory. The Brasilians [sic] certainly played up. Dr. Kubitschek's suite contained nearly 100 persons and there was in addition a Brasilian [sic] cruiser and several detachments of troops. Nevertheless, the Portuguese failed, although I gather they tried repeatedly, to get public support from Dr. Kubitschek for their present colonial policy. The occasion was also taken to sign a number of protocols to the Luso-Brasilian Treaty of Friendship and Consultation of 1953 [...]

F. Biggar

249

Ofício, Ministro Plenipotenciário irlandês em Lisboa ao Secretário-Geral do DEA: Lisboa, 7 de Setembro de 1960[67]

CONFIDENTIAL

[...]

I have discussed with the Protocol of the Foreign Office the question of what official call the Taoiseach should make whilst he is here and have been advised that the only person he need actually meet is Dr. Salazar. The Protocol will arrange for him to be received by Dr. Salazar on either Thursday 22 or Saturday the 24th and will let me know the precise arrangements later. I have suggested that the morning of the 22nd would be the most suitable time. I imagine you and I should accompany the Taoiseach on this occasion. Dr. Salazar, I understand, speaks fairly good French but very little English.

As far as the President of the Republic, it will be sufficient if the Taoiseach signs the book at his official residence, the Ajuda Palace at Belém [sic]. This could be managed quite conveniently when he is on his way to visit – as I imagine he will wish to do – the convent of Bom Sucesso [...] A call on the Cardinal Patriarch is not necessary [...]

As regards the trip to Fatima, this has been definitely fixed for Friday the 22nd.
[...][68]

---

[67] NAI, Department of the Taoiseach, S16892A, Nigeria: Independence, 6 August-7 October 1960.

[68] *Irish Independent* (Dublin), 24 de Setembro de 1960:
Lemass meets Salazar
Mr Lemass had a 45-minutes meeting with the Portuguese Prime Minister, Dr Antonio de Oliveira Salazar. Afterwards. Mr. Lemass and his wife had tea with Dr. Salazar.
Earlier, Mr Lemass and his wife attended Mass in Fatima, in the centre of Portugal. Then they visited the Convent of Alcobaça and the Monastery of Batalha [...]

250
Ofício, Ministro Plenipotenciário irlandês em Lisboa ao Secretário-Geral do DEA: Lisboa, 14 de Setembro de 1960[69]

CONFIDENTIAL

WORLD'S SITUATION – PORTUGUESE VIEW

I made an opportunity last week to call on Dr. Franco Nogueira, Director General of the Political Affairs at the Foreign Office. Although it was the eve of his departure for Mexico, where he will accompany the Portuguese delegation for the 150th anniversary of the declaration of Mexican independence, our talk lasted for well over an hour and ranged widely, with the main emphasis on the situation in the Congo and on Portuguese Colonial policy

[…]

Dr. Franco Nogueira replied that he thought it unwise to place too great hopes on the United Nations. Its original character had been greatly modified by the admission of the Afro-Asian states. At the moment, it suited these states to support it but in five or ten years' time they would be thinking more of their own interests that of the United Nations. I pointed out, in reply, that there existed a far great [sic] threat to the United Nations, namely the fundamental chasm between East and West which had bedevilled the organisation practically since the beginning but that, despite this, war had not yet broken out on a world scale and, as long as each side was afraid to fire the first shot, some such organisation as the United Nations was essential.

[…]

As regards the current position of the Congo, I said that I thought two opposing conclusions could be drawn. The first was that the negro was inherently incapable of governing himself; such a conclusion, however, was denied by the relative success of other African states, notable those of the French community and the British Commonwealth, which had recently attained independence.

---

[69] NAI, DEA, 313/11G Confidential reports from Lisbon Legation, 1960.

The other was that the negro was quite capable of self-government provided he had acquired sufficient experience and education and that it was the duty of the European power concerned to insure [sic] that he did so. It seemed clear that the Belgians had failed in this respect – hence the present tragedy in the Congo. Whilst we were anti-colonialists this did not mean that we believed that the doctrine must be applied automatically and without regard to the actual circumstances of each case. We had no intention of trying to prise Portugal out if its African territories but we greatly doubted that her present policies were the right ones. As I understood them they had as objectives the gradual evolution of integrated communities which would be Portuguese in culture and without any colour bar. Dr. Franco Nogueira agreed – Brasil [sic] was the classical example – and asked if there was anything wrong with these ideals? I said no – if they could be realised. But Portugal had already been in Africa for five hundred years and the proportion of assimilados (i.e. natives or those of mixed descent who have attained full Portuguese citizenship) was something like 0.3%. How long at that rate was it going to take them to realise their integrated communities and would the rest of Africa wait? Dr. Franco Nogueira claimed that the figure for assimilados was much higher but failed to quote it.

The conversation ended as so many of such talks in the Foreign Ministry with the assertion by Dr. Franco Nogueira that the Portuguese would stand firmly in their territories and that they felt themselves strong enough to do so successfully. He added incidentally that there were no more than 5,000 Portuguese troops in Angola (of which over half were native) and that the greater part of their overseas forces were stationed in India.

[…]

F. Biggar

251
Minutas da conversa entre o Primeiro Ministro (Taoiseach) irlandês, Séan Lemass, e António de Oliveira Salazar[70]

CONFIDENTIAL

Buçaco, 5.30-8 p.m., 23 de Setembro de 1960

The following is the substance of the conversation between the Taoiseach and Dr. Salazar which took place in the Palace Hotel at Bussaco from 5.30 p.m. to 8 p.m. on Friday, 23rd September, 1960, Mrs. Lemass, the Minister to Portugal and Mrs. Biggar, and Mr. Cremin, Secretary of the Department of External Affairs, being present.

2. The conversation opened with an enquiry by Dr. Salazar about President de Valera. He recalled that the President had, as Taoiseach, visited him in Lisbon in 1953. The Taoiseach told Dr. Salazar that the President is in very good form and that he wished the Taoiseach to convey his good wishes to Dr. Salazar.

3. The Taoiseach thanked Dr. Salazar for Portuguese support for Mr. Boland's election as President of the Fifteenth Session of the United Nations General Assembly. Dr. Salazar said that he was very glad that the Presidency is in the hands of such a capable person as Mr. Boland, but that he thinks that he will have quite a task, especially as the United Nations is in an awkward position. The Taoiseach remarked that we have a great trust in the United Nations and were glad to see it affront the task represented by events in the Congo. Dr. Salazar seemed rather sceptical about the prospects of securing any lasting outcome of value in the Congo. Generally speaking, he argued, and returned to this point frequently, that [sic] the situation in Africa is not being approached properly by the European States. He maintained that the African countries are neither nations nor states, but rest on a tribal social system. It is therefore a mistake, in his view, to apply western conceptions and ideas to the African scene.

---

[70] NAI, Department of the Taoiseach, S16892A, Nigeria: Independence, 6 August-7 October 1960.

4. In reply to a query from the Taoiseach about the prospects of an arrangement between the Six and the Seven, Dr. Salazar expressed his conviction that an arrangement will be found in time. He declared that the raison d'etre for the EFTA and the reason Portugal belongs to it is to facilitate an arrangement with the EEC. He regards a permanent breach between the two groups as "intolerable" and likewise improbable. The fact, for instance, that Germany sells more to EFTA than to the other members of the Six is, in his opinion, a decisive reason why such a breach cannot last. He feels that "immense efforts" will be made over the next year or two to bring the two groups together. It is, however, essential that Britain stand firmly with the other members of EFTA as, apart from Sweden, she is the only member of the group which is industrially strong.

5. To a query from the Taoiseach as to whether Portugal fears adverse effects for her economy from the lowering of the tariffs, Dr. Salazar replied that he hopes that such effects will not result and that the Portuguese industrial programme will not be compromised. He mentioned in this connection that Portugal has a long time in which to bring about the elimination of tariffs – 20 years.

6. On the question of foreign investment in Portugal, Dr. Salazar said that there is some evidence of a tendency on the part of members of both the Six and the Seven to look in that direction. For this purpose, Portugal offers certain advantages – relatively low taxation, low salaries and wages, and a social service system that is much less onerous than in some other countries, e.g. France.

7. On the subject of Africa generally, Dr. Salazar made a number of observations which may be summarised as follows:

8. He thinks that the idea of "Africanism", or Pan-Africanism, is dangerous as there is no fundamental common factor linking the various parts of the continent. In his view, the black peoples, in contra-distinction with the white races, have no urge or sense of obligation to work. The Portuguese find that the natives in their African colonies only work to a degree which enables them to secure the minimum sufficient for their requirements and that they spend without any sense of prudence. There is, Dr. Salazar mentioned, a certain current of emigration of workers from Mozambique to the South African mines. Having worked in the mines for a year or two, these will return home with all their earnings spent.

Unless some steps were taken to counter this tendency they would this return home empty-handed. For that reason Portugal had made an arrangement with the South African Government whereby a certain proportion of the wages earned by the Mozambique migrants is retained, paid over to the Portuguese authorities and made available by them to the worker (and his family).

9. The Taoiseach wondered whether Dr. Salazar was not a little severe on the capacity or willingness of the black African to work. He pointed out that it is a common experience that primary producers tend to aim at a fixed target in output and income and, once they have attained these, are disinclined to make further profit. Dr. Salazar conceded the validity of this point, but nevertheless insisted that their experience in Africa justifies the opinions he had expressed.

10. Dr. Salazar expressed himself as particularly uneasy about the trend of the American philosophy of life. He feels that it rests much too much on materialism – that the average American tends to think solely of, and in terms of, dollars. The Taoiseach conceded that there is a strong materialist element in the American philosophy, but he suggested that moral factors likewise play a significant role in the life of the nation as can be seen by the efforts made by candidates standing for election to demonstrate that their personal conduct conforms to a certain moral code.

11. Dr. Salazar expressed his anxiety about the "vacuum of power" which the American electoral system creates for a longuish period every four years: this vacuum exists for six months before and six months after the Presidential election and means in practice the USA has no real policy during that time. This is, in his view, especially dangerous for the West, of which the USA is the natural leader.

12. In an exchange of views on the subject of emigration, Dr. Salazar said that there is still a fair volume of regular emigration from Portugal. The bulk goes to Brazil (about 30,000 p.a.) and a much smaller proportion (3,000-5,000) to Angola and Mozambique. The Portuguese Government would like to give this surplus manpower employment at home, or alternatively to direct it to the African territories. In this connection he mentioned that large-scale enterprises give very little employment, which is to be found mainly in small transforming industries. He is often struck, he said, by misunderstandings on this point and

mentioned, in particular, the disappointment of Mr. Nehru about the employment-giving possibilities of his first Five-Year Plan. The Taoiseach agreed generally with Dr. Salazar's observations under this head and quoted as an illustration our experience in the 1955-56 recession. At that time production suffered more than employment, whereas in both 1959 and 1960 production has been growing faster than employment. He also mentioned in connection with Dr. Salazar's reference to Mr. Nehru the possibility of the Indian leader having made a not uncommon mistake and having tended to regard the achievement of independence as an end in itself, whereas it should be regarded by emerging states as primarily a means to a further end, viz. to give the people concerned the opportunity to work and develop their economy for their own benefit.

13. It was suggested in the course of the exchange of views under these points that one might, perhaps, overcome the tendency towards inertia of the peoples (African or other) by stimulating demand. Dr. Salazar, however, seemed to think that the artificial creation of demand is not a good thing as it generally rests on what is in the long-term an unsound basis.

14. Other points covered in the course of the conversation were our position in relation to the Commonwealth and the situation in regard to the Six Counties. Dr. Salazar enquired in some detail about the status of Irish citizens in Britain and their treatment as non-aliens. As regards the Six Counties he seemed to have a fairly good grasp of the subject. The Taoiseach gave him a brief account of the history of the problem and its evolution.

15. At the conclusion of the conversation, the Taoiseach expressed his thanks to Dr. Salazar for having come to Bussaco to meet him and for the hospitality shown to himself, Mrs. Lemass and his party. He also expressed his pleasure at having met Dr. Salazar and having had an opportunity of such a long conversation. Dr. Salazar, on his side, said that he was very happy to meet the Taoiseach and that he particularly appreciated the Taoiseach's readiness to come as far as Bussaco. He would, he intimated, have been quite ready to have gone to Fatima if the Taoiseach had chosen this (Fatima is somewhat over half-way between Lisbon and Bussaco).

15 October 1960

252
Carta do DEA ao Ministro Plenipotenciário irlandês em Lisboa:
Dublin, 27 de Setembro de 1960[71]

PERSONAL AND CONFIDENTIAL

Dear Frank,

We have your excellent report of 14th September, 1960, on your interview with Dr. Nogueira and feel that the exchange of views was most useful from our point of view.

The only matter to which I would like to refer is the figure you mentioned in your report of 0.3% as being the approximate proportion of assimilados in Portuguese African territories [...] there is some doubt here as to whether this figure is quite accurate and we are inclined to think that it my be much higher – possibly in the region of 3%. A member of the German Embassy here, who spent some years in Angola, thought that the figure must be higher and his opinion was that there was no colour bar of any kind in Portuguese territories.

I doubt if this point is of any great importance as far as we are concerned or that it would have any effect on policy but we should be interested in knowing whether the source of your information is accurate and, it it transpires that it is not, whether it would be possible for you to obtain any sort of reliable figure.

Yours sincerely,

(Assinatura ilegível,
mas apontamento na margem do texto feito por C. C. Cremin).

---

[71] NAI, DEA, 313/11G Confidential reports from Lisbon Legation, 1960.

253
Ofício, Encarregado de Negócios *ad interim* irlandês em Lisboa ao Secretário-Geral do DEA: Lisboa, 17 de Novembro de 1960[72]

CONFIDENTIAL

I have the honour to report that I attended, by invitation, the closing ceremonies of the Henry the Navigator fifth centenary celebrations, at Batalha on Sunday last, the 12th inst. These celebrations have occupied, as you are aware, a tremendous amount of the nation's time and energy over the past six months which have witnessed an unending succession of manifestations of all kinds in honour of Prince Henry, beginning with the inauguration in the spring of a very imposing monument to the "Descobridor" on the bank of the Tagus opposite the Monastery of Belém. Popular enthusiasm which, naturally, took the form of popular self-congratulation had been kept whipped up all through the summer. This is all perfectly in line with the unceasing policy of showing to the Portuguese the grandeur that was theirs with the implied corollary that that grandeur is theirs again so long as they stick to the present régime.

The closing ceremony at Batalha was very impressive. It consisted of Solemn High Mass in the Dominican Monastery there attended by the President of the Republic, the President of the Council, members of the Government, representatives of all the principal State Corps, the heads of all the diplomatic missions, and a very numerous congregation representing all that is prominent in Portuguese life. After the Mass Professor Caeiro da Matta, formerly Minister for Foreign Affairs, made an oration – unusually short for him – on Prince Henry's tomb in the special chapel containing the royal sarcophagi.

Afterwards a lunch was served in the Monastery of Alcobaça, twenty kilometres distant, and that concluded the day.

O'Kelly de Gallagh

---

[72] NAI, DEA, 313/11G Confidential reports from Lisbon Legation, 1960.

1961

254
Ofício, Ministro Plenipotenciário irlandês em Lisboa ao Secretário-Geral do DEA: Lisboa, 31 de Janeiro de 1961[73]

"SANTA MARIA" AFFAIR

The Portuguese press has printed almost everything of any importance on this matter. There have been a few items announced on foreign radio stations which have not appeared in the Press, however, as, for example, Mr. Gaitskill's reference in a question put in the House of Commons to the Salazar Government as a dictatorial régime.

One Lisbon newspaper, the "REPÚBLICA", regarded as in opposition to the régime, was suspended for three days on Tuesday 24th instant for its handling of the matter. This handling was negative, the newspaper sinning in not giving sufficient coverage to the seizure of the vessel – it disposed of the whole affair in about 12 lines and failed to publish the official communiqué issued to the Press by the authorities.

The apparent change in the attitude of the US Government towards Captain Galvão and his followers is causing dissatisfaction in official circles. Originally they were regarded by the US authorities as pirates, but as the week passed indications of dealings between the US and Capt. Galvão for the release of passengers, leaving the SANTA MARIA in the hands of the "rebels", caused some caustic comment in the newspapers, and have led to requests that the crew of the SANTA MARIA be released also.

At the week-end the newspapers claimed that Capt. Galvão was in fact only a front for the Spanish Communist opposition to General Franco and that not alone were the majority of his band Spanish communists, but that a part of the crew of 300 odd, taken aboard at Tenerife, were also Spanish and Communist. It

---

[73] NAI, DEA, 313/11H Confidential reports from Lisbon Legation, 1961.

was suggested at one stage that perhaps the SANTA MARIA would put in to a Cuban port, but this point did not receive any prominence.

The position of Brazil is the matter of interest. The newspapers have printed prominently all Brazilian statements which appear favourable to the Government, but have hinted over the week-end that the SANTA MARIA is marking time on the Equator until the new Brazilian President, Janio Quadros, takes over at the end of the month. President-Elect Quadros recently visited Portugal and left rather hurriedly with no reason given. A rumour is circulating that he had booked his passage on the SANTA MARIA, but actually travelled on a cargo boat as he had inside information on the plans for the SANTA MARIA. He is known to be a friend of Capt. Galvão.

I hesitate, in view of my brief experience here, expressing any opinion on the matter, but the impression I have obtained is that Capt. Galvão's action has, perhaps, strengthened the position of the régime rather than weakened it. I gather that he is not considered as a serious rival to Dr. Salazar – any more than is General Delgado, in whose name he is acting.

[…]

J. W. Lennon

255
Ofício, Ministro Plenipotenciário irlandês em Lisboa ao Secretário-Geral do DEA: Lisboa, 2 de Fevereiro de 1961[74]

Following a Plenary meeting of the Portuguese Episcopate on 15th ult. a Note was issued by the Bishops recalling the part played by Portugal in spreading Christianity in all parts of the world – America, Africa, Asia and Oceania – and presenting Brazil as an example. The Note went on to state that having introduced into so many countries this Christian civilization, which involved amongst other things respect of human dignity, establishment of authority, guarantee of liberty,

---

[74] NAI, DEA, 313/11H Confidential reports from Lisbon Legation, 1961.

promotion of economy and fraternisation of races, Portugal had acquired an heritage [sic], considered by all to have been confided in her by Providence, which must be guarded and conserved in the interests of civilisation and of the world. In this regard Portugal, although misunderstood by the Western world which seemed to have lost much of its moral values [sic], remains conscious of her mission of evangelisation and civilisation […]

This note has been played-up in the Press as representing Episcopal approval of the overseas policy of the present Government, although nowhere in the Note do the Bishops in fact express any such approval.

Another sidelight on the part played by the Church in political matters here is that the Cardinal primate of Portugal a few days ago addressed a letter to President Kennedy asking him to intercede in the "SANTA MARIA" affair to ensure that the crew of the ship should also be allowed to leave with the passengers if they so wished. It is rumoured, also, that the Government are trying to get the Vatican to intercede with the President in this connection.

J. W. Lennon

256
Ofício, Ministro Plenipotenciário irlandês em Lisboa ao Secretário-Geral do DEA: Lisboa, 9 de Fevereiro de 1961[75]

CONFIDENTIAL

"SANTA MARIA" AFFAIR

The ending of this affair has not been unsatisfactory from the viewpoint of the Portuguese Government. While Capt. Galvão's action undoubtedly resulted in the régime being brought to the forefront of international attention, the somewhat comic-opera aim of the seizure, heightened by the Captain's spectacular uniform and his apparently volatile temperament, has tended to reduce confidence in the opposition. Furthermore it now seems clear that only a small part of the band was of Portuguese nationality, the majority being Spaniards and South Americans.

---

[75] NAI, DEA, 313/11H Confidential reports from Lisbon Legation, 1961.

2. The reaction in Britain and the USA, which tended to admit that perhaps there were reasons to be dissatisfied with the régime and which failed to condemn Capt. Galvão as a pirate, caused some little comment in both the press and the National Assembly. One small English-language newspaper, produced by Portuguese nationals, the "Anglo-Portuguese News", likened Capt. Galvão's action to the seizure of the "QUEENS" by the IRA.

3. Brazil's decision to hand the ship back to the owners was well received, and it has been reported that consideration is being given by the new administration in Brazil to expelling Humberto Delgado, the so-called "President--Elect of Portugal", on the grounds that in engaging in political intrigue against a friendly régime he has forfeited the right of political asylum.

4. However, the sequel to the SANTA MARIA episode evidenced in the attacks on civil and military prisons in Angola, was not unexpected. Throughout the SANTA MARIA affair reference was made to Capt. Galvão's previous connections with Angola and the possibility of his landing there. The press has claimed that the mixed groups of Europeans and Africans carrying out the attacks in Angola have come from outside Portuguese territory and most speak French only. They were, of course, repulsed with losses heavier than those of the defending Portuguese troops. It is noteworthy that the seven Portuguese soldiers killed were all white.

5. In Metropolitan Portugal there have been other reactions to the SANTA MARIA case. Three persons who had been convicted in the trial last May-June of the twenty-three civilians and military alleged to have conspired against the régime and given short suspended sentences, requested, and were granted, asylum in the Brazilian Embassy. This was denied officially at a Press Conference on 1st February but has since been confirmed. On the 27th January a short letter was addressed to the President by thirty-seven leading members of the "Opposition" covering the following points:-

a) protesting against the suspension of the evening newspaper "REPÚBLICA";
b) recalling that a letter sent to him on 11th November last, which pointed out that real unity of the Portuguese people was more than ever necessary in view of attacks being made in UNO., had remained unanswered;

c) events since 11th November – notably the SANTA MARIA incident – show how the deplorable state of Portuguese political life is being accentuated;

d) if the political atmosphere, already threatening, becomes more involved, it will be impossible to think clearly on the problems which must be faced;

e) international opinion is more and more against the political methods of the Government party and

f) reaffirming that national peace and unity with a future in Europe, Africa and Asia and international respect of other states, particularly Brazil, can only be achieved under a democracy.

6. Three of the signatories of this letter was [sic], as reported in the foreign press, received by the President on the 6th instant, vide report in the LONDON TIMES of 7th instant. There has been no official communiqué in respect of this visit. The press of 8th instant carries an official release that the statement made by the persons concerned was without previous submission of the text to the Chief of the State and without his consent.

J. W. Lennon

257
Ofício, Conselheiro da Representação Permanente da Irlanda junto das Nações Unidas ao Secretário-Geral do DEA:
Nova Iorque, 3 de Março de 1961[76]

Portuguese Overseas Territories

On re-reading the interesting report which Mr. Biggar sent from Lisbon on the 14th September 1960 entitled "World's Situation – Portuguese View" (Ref. PR.24/69 – Lisbon 6/9 – 6/2A), we noticed on page 3 that Dr. Franco Nogueira, Director General of the Political Affairs at the Portuguese Foreign Office, said "he was sorry to see that Ireland was again taking a lead in the matter of the non-self--governing territories".

---

[76] NAI, DEA, Permanent Mission to the United Nations, X19, Portuguese overseas colonies, 1958-1965

By now you will have on file both our preliminary and final report on the debate in the Fourth Committee in the first half of the Fifteenth Session relating to the study of the principles which should guide members in determining whether or not an obligation exists to transmit the information called for in Article 73e of the Charter. As you will have seen from our reports it is quite inaccurate to say that Ireland took a lead in this matter. Ireland was one of 26 members which furnished its views to the Committee of Six which drew up the twelve principles later adopted by the General Assembly. We also cosponsored the resolution adopting these principles with Iraq, Nigeria, Venezuela and Bolivia. But, as our reports make clear, we were exceedingly careful to avoid any criticism either of Portugal or Spain and confined our interventions purely to the principles themselves. In these circumstances you might consider whether it would be desirable to furnish a copy of our final report on the item to the Minister at Lisbon so that, should this question arise again in conversations with the Portuguese Foreign Office it could be made quite clear that while we supported the question of principle we did not indulge in attacks on Portugal. It might also be useful to furnish the relevant documents, namely the report of the Special Committee of Six on the transmission of information (A/4526) and the Study of Principles which should guide members (A/4651)

E. L. Kennedy

258
Ofício, Ministro Plenipotenciário irlandês em Lisboa ao Secretário-Geral do DEA: Lisboa, 4 de Março de 1961[77]

CONFIDENTIAL

The two months which have elapsed since my arrival in Portugal have been noteworthy from the internal political point of view. The highlight was undoubtedly the "SANTA MARIA" incident, followed by trouble in Angola, but the

---

[77] NAI, DEA, 313/11H Confidential reports from Lisbon Legation, 1961.

less spectacular representations by the "Constitutional Opposition" may in the long run prove more effective.

2. In my opinion the average Portuguese while not entirely satisfied with the régime is prepared to tolerate it. Many remember the pre-Salazar chaos of 1910-1926 and all have been indoctrinated with the view that a change would mean a return to the conditions then prevailing. Improvements effected since Dr. Salazar came to power are obvious – good roads, new schools, stable currency, for example – and while much remains to be done the general attitude seems to be that prospects of having things done are better with Dr. Salazar than without him.

3. There is undoubtedly opposition to Salazar ranging from the extreme right to the extreme left, but it is very divided and has no effective leadership. It seems clear that Capt. Galvão or General Delgado are not of the calibre required and the so-called "democratic" leaders who have signed the letters addressed to the President, likewise appear to be lacking in the qualities required. It has been suggested that this opposition consists largely of the professional classes – doctors and lawyers mainly – who have been prevented by the régime from exploiting the people, hence their opposition.

4. The net effect of the "SANTA MARIA" episode would appear, at this stage, to have been an increase in Dr. Salazar's popularity. The return of the "SANTA MARIA" to Lisbon was the occasion of a popular demonstration – perhaps not quite as spontaneous as employers were "asked" to free employees to take part – and the funeral of the ship's officer killed by the rebels resulted in the largest public gathering seen in Lisbon for many years. This appeared to be genuinely spontaneous, but whether through sympathy with the régime or with the deceased officer, or for any other reason, is impossible to say.

5. Trouble in Angola following Capt. Galvão's action was not unexpected and the authorities appear to have been prepared. A newspaper correspondent to whom I spoke had rumours of massive re-inforcements of troops being sent to Angola and produced as evidence the fact that many TAP air services had been taken over by associated companies – e.g. BEA were handling all London flights. That the garrison in Angola was re-inforced is certain, but I was told by the US Ambassador that only 300 men had been sent there.

6. The coverage given in the newspapers here to the Angola incident was extensive, but had at all times the same tenor – communist risings inspired from outside the territory, in which the native Angolese [sic] had no part. Censorship within the territory seems to have been effective also and while all may now be quiet, it seems that the whites there ran amuck when the funeral of the white victims of the first attack took place and murdered many of the negroes.

7. Whatever the immediate future of the Portuguese territories in Africa may be, it seems to be accepted by the individual that to hold on to them, as at present, will be impossible. The borders between the different states are European conceptions, without local validity and cannot contain the nationalist movements blossoming all over the continent. The historical Congo – in the African sense – included Angola and all of the people – colleagues and Portuguese – to whom I have spoken in the matter, realise that in time Portugal must give way as did France and Belgium. Opinions differ as to how long the present attitude can be maintained, but five years was the maximum allowed by most.

8. Although the problem in Metropolitan Portugal is quite distinct from that in Angola, the policy of the Government is to associate them closely – "all Portuguese" etc. This may, in the long run, prove to be a mistake, as any considerable change in the position of the overseas territories could upset the régime in Metropolitan Portugal. Every effort will probably be made, therefore, to prevent any such change.

9. An important fact in the political situation here which must not be overlooked is that Dr. Salazar is now 72 years of age and reputed to be in ill health. There is no obvious successor, but my knowledge of the political scene does not extend to any appreciation of the position in this connection.

J. W. Lennon

259
Ofício, Ministro Plenipotenciário irlandês em Lisboa ao Secretário-Geral do DEA: Lisboa, 13 de Março de 1961[78]

CONFIDENTIAL

Just over a week ago a further letter was sent to the President by persons in opposition to the régime. This letter, which has not received any mention in the Press, was signed by amongst others Dr. Arlindo Vicente (who was a candidate in the 1958 Presidential elections but withdrew in favour of General Delgado), Sr. Vieira Almeida (a Monarchist) and Dona Isabela Aboim Inglês (very leftist). The signatories expressed themselves as being in complete agreement with the views expressed by the other opposition leaders in their interview with the President on 6th February and hoped that the objective of that visit, which they considered urgently required to safeguard national interests, would be achieved. Stating their intention to intervene on a nation-wide basis in the elections due later this year for the National Assembly they asked in the meantime for an amnesty for political prisoners and immediate abolition of censorship. In general remarks on restoration of fundamental rights to the people and retaining national units to ensure the salvation of the fatherland, they gave the impression that their line on colonial policy might not differ greatly from that at present pursued.

2. Another aspect of the Dictatorship v. Democracy controversy also appeared in the Press recently. The "DIÁRIO POPULAR" one of the larger newspapers ressurected an old bone of contention in connection with local Government. It said that Mayors of the different municipalities did not, in most cases, possess the proper qualifications, nor did they have necessary support of the proper type for performing their functions, as they were appointed by the Central Administration and not elected by the people in the towns in which they functioned.

3. During the 1958 Presidential campaign this point was frequently mentioned by the Opposition, and the "DIÁRIO POPULAR" claimed then that almost everyone agreed that certain concrete liberties should exist, one of which

---

[78] NAI, DEA, 313/11H Confidential reports from Lisbon Legation, 1961.

would be that townships should be allowed to conduct their own affairs, and called for the restoration in Portugal of municipal elections. The only result was a Decree-Law in March 1959 limiting the period of office of appointed mayors to an initial term of four years, with the possibility of re-appointment for a second four-year term.

J. W. Lennon

260
Ofício, Ministro Plenipotenciário irlandês em Lisboa ao Secretário-Geral do DEA: Lisboa, 20 de Março de 1961[79]

At a dinner party on the 11th instant I had an opportunity of discussing with the Foreign Minister and Dr. Archer, Director General of the Economic and Consular Division of the Foreign Office, the decision, publicised in the papers that morning, of the UN Security Council to include on its Agenda the Liberian motion on Angola. They were both very critical of the US failure to put the motion to a vote and claimed that, had this been done, at least five members (GB, France, Chile, Turkey and Equador) would have voted against, thereby eliminating the item. They said that if the matter were ultimately brought before the Assembly, Portugal might very well follow the precedents set by South Africa and France to boycott the debate. Moreover, the possibility of Portugal leaving the UN could not be excluded. However, no matter what resolutions were passed or decisions taken in the UN, Portugal had not the slightest intention of changing the status of her overseas provinces in which, incidentally (they claimed) there was no dissatisfaction with the Government, such agitation as had heretofore existed being Communist-sponsored and originated outside Portuguese territory. If it became necessary, Portugal would show that the spirit of five hundred years ago still lived and the people would fight to the end to maintain their position.

---

[79] NAI, DEA, 313/11H Confidential reports from Lisbon Legation, 1961.

2. The South African Ambassador, Dr. A. H. H. Mertsch, informs me that in the opinion of his authorities, the Portuguese claim that the trouble from Angola is sponsored by the Communist States, aided by misguided African nationalists, is well founded. In their opinion Portugal would go to the greatest extremes to retain their overseas territories. Whether they could succeed in doing so was another matter.

[...]

4. The local press since the preliminary debate in the Security Council has also been bitterly critical of the US failure to take a vote, and lays most of the responsibility at the feet of Mr. Stevenson. I have heard comment by non--official Portuguese that Portugal should recognise who are her friends and that to allow the US to continue to use the concessions allowed in the Azores would perhaps be unjustified in view of her attitude. In this connection it will be remembered that Portugal on the economic side some months ago opposed a Turkish application for credits simply because Turkey had been one of the NATO countries to take a line in the UN which was adjudged as hostile to Portugal.

J. W. Lennon

261
Ofício, Ministro Plenipotenciário irlandês em Lisboa ao Secretário-Geral do DEA: Lisboa, 23 de Março de 1961[80]

CONFIDENTIAL

Following the US vote on the Angola question in the Security Council, there has been a wave of anti-US feeling here, to the extent of a Portuguese citizen holder of a US decoration, sending the decoration to the US Ambassador, and demonstrations outside the US Embassy and the Consulates in Porto and the Azores. The demonstrators were largely students, and their principal slogan was

---

[80] NAI, DEA, 313/11H Confidential reports from Lisbon Legation, 1961.

"Quit the Azores". I understand that US opinion is divided on the necessity of the Azores as a base, but my informant said that the military are reluctant to let go while the diplomatic side recommends giving them up.

2. Mr. Stevenson continues to be the whipping block for the Press, but it is likely that President Kennedy will come in for his share before long. The Portuguese papers, I understand, were far from pro-Kennedy before last November's election. One newspaper has produced a heading to the effect that Kennedy, who makes common cause with the Russians in Africa, seems prepared to resist them in Laos.

3. The Press is also giving prominence to the possibility of Portugal quitting NATO and UN. Such vague threats have, I understand, been thrown out from time to time since November last, but opinion generally amongst colleagues here is that a protest is unlikely to go further than a temporary withdrawal from UN.

4. Next to indignation at the USA and the UN, the news highlight last week was the visit of the Spanish Foreign Minister, Don Fernando Maria Castella, who arrived in Lisbon on the 14th and stayed for five days. This visit, arranged at rather short notice, was in return to the visit to Madrid last year of the Portuguese Foreign Minister, Dr. Marcello Mathias. According to colleagues the reason for the short notice was threefold; firstly that the Capt. Galvão - Sta. Maria incident was directed at Spain as much as at Portugal; secondly, that Spanish possessions in Africa are also under fire, these two making it consultation and co-ordination of policy desirable; and thirdly that a reshuffle of Cabinet posts is pending which will result, inter alia, in the transfer to a post abroad of Dr. Mathias. Whatever the immediate reasons for the visit, the release to the Press claimed complete agreement on policy matters and that the relations between the two countries were closer than ever. Enclosed for information is a copy of the speech delivered by the Spanish Minister during his visit. It was announced just after the visit that the President of Portugal will visit General Franco in October next.

5. Referring back to the Cabinet changes [...] The present Minister to the Presidency, Dr. Teotonio Pereira, is rumoured as Foreign Minister, being replaced in turn by Dr. Marcello Caetano, a former holder of the post, who, I understand, from colleagues, is regarded as a possible successor to Dr. Salazar. Dr. Marcello Caetano is generally regarded as relatively liberal, and his removal from the

Ministry of the Presidency some years ago was due, it is said to his being too liberal for Dr. Salazar. His re-appointment would be interpreted as a concession by Dr. Salazar to the Opposition.

J. W. Lennon

262
Ofício, Ministro Plenipotenciário irlandês em Lisboa ao Secretário-Geral do DEA: Lisboa, 24 de Março de 1961[81]

CONFIDENTIAL

At the end of last week the local newspapers carried reports of "terrorist" activities in Angola, consisting of raids from neighbouring territories (obviously the ex-Belgian Congo) penetrating as far as 300 kms. into Portuguese territory. These raids seem to have been well planned and their objectives were centres of industry and commerce. The fact that penetration into Angola was so deep would seem to indicate that the Angolese [sic] did not try – apart from the Portuguese – to oppose the raiders.

According to my information, the position in Angola is more serious than the authorities reveal. All white women and children have been concentrated in Luanda or other large centres, while the men have been instructed to remain in the outlying farms and posts. The authorities I'm told are reluctant to arm these settlers effectively, as they don't know when the native population might try to seize the arms and turn them on the Portuguese troops. Relations between blacks and whites, formerly very good, have completely deteriorated, and this applies also to the "assimilados", who are joining the anti-Portuguese elements.

J. W. Lennon

---

[81] NAI, DEA, 313/11H Confidential reports from Lisbon Legation, 1961.

263
Ofício, Ministro Plenipotenciário irlandês em Lisboa ao Secretário-Geral do DEA: Lisboa, 30 de Março de 1961[82]

Anti-US feeling continued to manifest itself over the past week, culminating in a mass demonstration on the evening of 27th instant. The crowd, estimated variously at 20,000 to 100,000, consisted largely, as such crowds do, of a relatively small core of demonstrators, with a large body motivated principally by curiosity. The demonstrators carried banners calling on the US to leave the Azores, free Alaska and return the US to the Red Indians. Other banners asked was it the US intention to "Congolize" Angola, and why wasn't justice done to the negro in the US – the name Little Rock was in prominent display. The demonstrations culminated in a march on the US Embassy – at least 1½ miles from where it was held – where the windows of the US Information office, on the ground floor of the chancery, were broken and the front of the building marked with ink or paints thrown at the US flag. Demands on the Ambassador to appear naturally remained unanswered, but to my knowledge the reports of shots being fired – whatever of tear gas used to disperse the demonstrators – are not correct. Just what demonstrations of this sort are supposed to show is not clear – it is quite obvious that they could not take place without the connivance of the Government, and consequently must be regarded as an indication of Government tactics. It seems to me to be a rather dangerous weapon in the peculiar circumstances of the country. Signs that the mob could have got out of control were not lacking. I know of one case where a foreigner, actually English, was suspected of being American and narrowly escaped a beating-up. This seems to me to be quite contrary to the ordinary Portuguese attitude.

2. In my last report 8/61, I referred to a US decoration being returned to the Embassy by a Portuguese citizen. This act has been hailed by the Press as a "civic example" and it has been suggested that other Portuguese could appropriately follow it – persons occupying leading positions in US

---

[82] NAI, DEA, 313/11H Confidential reports from Lisbon Legation, 1961.

companies operating in Portugal could, it was suggested, find convenient ways to react.

3. In Angola a demonstration outside the US Consulate in Luanda on 22nd March developed into a near riot. The papers alleged that the US Consul had told the crowd to "go away this place belongs to the Negroes" and/or "The Portuguese must leave here". His car, parked outside, was wrecked and thrown into a bay. The Consul denied having spoken at all.

4. A new development in the matter has been the introduction of a religious angle. It has been alleged that Protestant Missionaries in Angola are fostering a spirit of revolt amongst the natives, and the papers of the 29th instant carried a headline that a foreign and Protestant missionary (stated in the article to be a Quaker) tried to incite the natives to an "operation of massacre". It is perhaps interesting to note that in Luanda, demonstrations have taken place outside the American Evangelist Mission.

5. Several foreign newspapers during the week carried articles emanating from Luanda saying that reforms are contemplated in the administration of Angola and Mozambique. The reforms are rumoured to be the appointment of Resident Ministers, with Cabinet rank, instead of Governors General; that the territories would have local autonomy in economic, fiscal and administrative matters, and that defence and foreign relations would remain in Lisbon. While these rumours are denied in Lisbon, they persist in coming up. In this connection I might add that the Minister for Overseas Territories has been in Angola since the 24th instant, and the DIÁRIO DO GOVERNO of 24th instant states that he disposed of "Legislative Competency" while there.

6. According to reports the Government is continuing to reinforce the troops in Angola, and I am informed that the Army reserve is being called up – at least in part.

7. So far as I can judge, the Government's attitude towards the "overseas provinces" has the support of the greater part of the people, including that of the "opposition". This support may not be 100% – there are undoubtedly those who might like more liberal régimes and greater degrees of home rule – but all seem to be determined that Portugal should retain her territories. The similarity between

the position here and that in France in 1956 is quite remarkable, and present indications are that Angola (and no doubt, in time, Mozambique) will develop in lines very like those which have come about in Algeria.

J. W. Lennon

264
Ofício, Ministro Plenipotenciário irlandês em Lisboa ao Secretário-Geral do DEA: Lisboa, 13 de Abril de 1961[83]

CONFIDENTIAL

[…][84]

While there may be criticism in metropolitan Portugal of Dr. Salazar's régime, there seems to be little doubt of the entire people's support for his overseas policy. The people seem to be quite determined to fight to retain the overseas territories, and appear to have no doubt of their ability to retain them. The most optimistic way of viewing the situation here is to point out that a federal solution of the Congo problem, with resultant stability, is in all probability in the offing. The southern border is already secure – South Africa can be relied upon – and it is expected that Sir Roy Welensky will shortly declare the Rhodesias independent and ally himself with South Africa. This, it is claimed, will make Angola secure.

There is no doubt that Portugal is preparing herself for a struggle in Angola, and I understand that financial circles are already taking fright. According to foreign press correspondents there has been a tendency for large scale transfers of escudos into foreign currencies since the SANTA MARIA incident and the Government may have to take straight measures in the near future to stop capital flow from Portugal.

J. W. Lennon

---

[83] NAI, DEA, 313/11H Confidential reports from Lisbon Legation, 1961.

[84] O início deste ofício está relacionado com a visita do Ministro do Ultramar, Almirante Vasco Lopes Alves, a Angola, e com um discurso de Salazar à Assembleia Nacional, no qual Salazar negou que quaisquer reformas administrativas estivessem para breve.

265
Ofício, Ministro Plenipotenciário irlandês em Lisboa ao Secretário-Geral do DEA: Lisboa, 14 de Abril de 1961[85]

CONFIDENTIAL

The news released yesterday afternoon, of the replacement of the Ministers for Defence, Overseas Territories and of the Army, and the assumption by Dr. Salazar of the functions of the Minister for Defence, came after two days of rumours ranging from the possible to the fantastic. The more reasonable rumours were that the Minister of Defence had had at least two stormy interviews with Dr. Salazar in which he had expressed the discontent of the Army and himself with matters generally and presented an ultimatum demanding reforms. The more fantastic rumours included a claim that a Military Junta had taken over, and that Dr. Salazar had gone into exile in Switzerland. Another more malicious rumour was that a very wealthy member of the Government had transferred his entire fortune to Switzerland.

A change in the Ministry for Overseas Territories is not surprising – Admiral Alves, the outgoing Minister, was very ill just over a year ago and has not since been quite well. On his recent trip to Angola he had two doctors in his entourage. According to my colleagues, however, the Minister for Defence was quite a strong man in a key position.

It might be inferred from the Cabinet changes that there must have been some reasons for the rumours circulating, but I think it must be equally be inferred, having regard to Dr. Salazar's assumption of the Ministry of Defence, that he is still in control and that perhaps more important still he retains the support of the Army.

The reason given by Dr. Salazar for the changes was "in one word – Angola". The position there, he went on, necessitated alone a position in which quick decisions could be taken and enable Portugal to defend Angola and with the Unity of the Nation [sic].

J. W. Lennon

---

[85] NAI, DEA, 313/11H Confidential reports from Lisbon Legation, 1961.

266
Ofício, Ministro Plenipotenciário irlandês em Lisboa ao Secretário-Geral do DEA: Lisboa, 2 de Maio de 1961[86]

It now seems certain that the dismissal of the former Ministers for Defence and Army and several high ranking Army officers were attributable to an unsuccessful attempt by the Ministers and Officers concerned to displace Dr. Salazar. Notwithstanding reports in some foreign newspapers that the Prime Minister was informed of the plot by a participating Army general, the truth would appear to be that little real effort was made at concealment, that the "plotters" approached the President, Admiral Thomaz, quite openly, and that he informed Dr. Salazar. It was then simply a question of which side retained Army support, and in this Dr. Salazar won.

2. For about two months past rumours of government changes have been prevalent, and expected from day to day […] According to reports, the reasons why the changes have not so far been announced is that the Prime Minister is having difficulty in obtaining agreement from prospective Ministers to serve in his cabinet – one such is reported to have said that he had no intention of committing political suicide by serving in Salazar's last Government. It now seems that, if and when a new cabinet is formed, many of the Ministers may be Civil Servants.

3. The Lay-Doyen of the Corps, the Turkish Ambassador, has just left Lisbon on re-assignment. He had an interview with Dr. Salazar before he left in which the latter said that "in Portugal the people were always looking for change, and he was prepared to leave the country if they (the people) wanted it".

4. On the surface everything here is calm. Dr. Salazar appears to be as strongly entrenched as ever. There exists a patriotic fervour and enthusiasm towards maintaining the overseas territories which reflects on Dr. Salazar. Nevertheless a feeling exists among colleagues that perhaps things are not quite as stable as they appear on the surface. From time to time the "opposition"

---

[86] NAI, DEA, 313/11H Confidential reports from Lisbon Legation, 1961.

requests concessions and more recently a new grouping, calling itself "young intellectuals", issued a political manifesto. I have been unable to see a copy of this manifesto or to obtain any information on this grouping except that they seem to be extreme-right – more so even than the régime.

5. Anti-US feeling, while somewhat less demonstrative, continues unabated and the reverse sustained in Cuba by the US has caused some satisfaction. Many well-informed and educated Portuguese have completely accepted the Government line and propaganda in the attitude towards the US, and really believe that the underlying reason for the US policy towards the Portuguese Overseas Territories is that the US wants them for itself and are determined to prevent this at any price, even I was told by a head of section in the Foreign Office who had let his enthusiasm run away with him, to the extent of an alliance with the USSR […]

6. As regards the Angola campaign – this continues and trouble spots are now spread all over the territory. Suitably edited reports of operations appear in the press and it is expected that now that the dry season is due to begin "pacification" of the troubled areas will be more effective and swift. It is of interest to note that in addition to the large re-inforcements of troups [sic] departing for Angola and other African overseas territories, first-time settlers are also leaving Portugal still – during the past week 300 left Lisbon for Angola. The religious aspect of the Angola situation continues to be evident – it will be recalled that by now both Protestant and Catholic clergy and missions have been accused. The Angolan Bishops recently said that while they hoped the clergy would refrain from participation in political matters, there were nevertheless many wrongs to be righted.

7. Signs that trouble is not unexpected in other areas apart from Angola are evident. Troop reinforcements have been sent to Cabinda and Guiné. The frontier guards in Mozambique have been strengthened. Attacks on frontier posts in Goa have resulted in some deaths. Taken all round the picture from the Portuguese aspect is a gloomy one, but there is no doubt of the determination of the Portuguese people to fight. It is perhaps of interest to finish this Note by referring to a statement made by Captain Galvão a few days ago, and reported in LE

MONDE, that while he was completely opposed to Dr. Salazar and all he stands for, he did not consider Angola ripe for self-determination.

J. W. Lennon

267
Ofício, Ministro Plenipotenciário irlandês em Lisboa ao Secretário-Geral do DEA: Lisboa, 4 de Maio de 1961[87]

CONFIDENTIAL

The long-expected Government changes were announced yesterday, 3rd instant. As expected, Dr. Alberto Franco Nogueira became Minister for Foreign Affairs. The new members of the Government (marked with X on enclosed list) may be described as technicians in the fields in which they have been appointed.

There is one unexpected change – Dr. Correia de Oliveira has been replaced in the post of Sub-secretary for Commerce, and the post upgraded to Secretary for Commerce. Dr. Oliveira will be remembered by our delegates to OEEC in recent years as the Portuguese representative at Ministerial level. I am informed that his removal is, however, only a preparation for greater things, as a new Ministry, charged with fostering foreign trade, is about to be established and Dr. Oliveira will be the new Minister.

J. W. Lennon

268
Ofício, Ministro Plenipotenciário irlandês em Lisboa ao Secretário-Geral do DEA: Lisboa, de Maio de 1961[88]

PORTUGAL AND THE UNITED NATIONS

In his speech to the National Assembly in November last, Dr. Salazar critized [sic] the UN on the grounds that it has tended to develop into an international

---

[87] NAI, DEA, 313/11H Confidential reports from Lisbon Legation, 1961.
[88] NAI, DEA, Embassy Madrid, I.P. 4/51/1, Portugal 1941-1963.

Parliament, without effective executive powers, in which all disputes, no matter how localised, tended to be internationalised, and in which all members had equal voices, notwithstanding ability to exercise judgment. He rejected UN interference in Portugal's affairs stating that "the General Assembly does not possess competence to declare territories of any power non-autonomous…if the interpretation of the texts had been other than this, we would definitely not have sought admission."

2. The topic has again become of interest with the appointment as Foreign Minister of Dr. Franco Nogueira, who has recently published a study entitled "AS NAÇÕES UNIDAS E PORTUGAL". In this study – a copy of which will be forwarded in the next bag – Dr. Nogueira presents, from the Portuguese viewpoint, the UN attitude towards colonialism, with particular reference to the Portuguese Overseas territories, and also presents the Portuguese defence, already familiar from the UN debates and statements.

3. When Dr. Nogueira was invested as Foreign Minister last week he made a statement on policy – in accordance with the custom here. The statement was in foreseeable terms and contained nothing new. So far as UN was concerned, he said "It would be a great mistake to measure the real national interests by trying to obtain a comfortable voting position in the General Assembly of the UN. The prestige and good name of the country are not affected by being in a minority there."

4. With the development in the UN of what is termed here the Anti--Portuguese campaign, references in the Press to the possibility of Portugal withdrawing from the Organisation have been frequent. While the possibility always exists that this could happen – the ultimate decision rests with one man – it seems to me that such a step is unlikely. It is true that there is strong resentment of the UN and of individual members also. Into the latter category fall fellow NATO members such as Norway, Denmark, Greece and Turkey, who have voted against Portugal. So far as I can judge the ill-feeling is not strong in our case – Dr. Nogueira said to me in conversation that he appreciated our theoretic attitude, but nevertheless thought that, as our official knowledge of Africa, and particularly of Portuguese Africa, must be relatively slight, we might

have abstained in the voting. However, he continued Portugal was not greatly concerned with the UN voting, as her mind was made up on the course she had to follow.

J. W. Lennon

269
Ofício, Ministro Plenipotenciário irlandês em Lisboa ao Secretário-Geral do DEA: Lisboa, 23 de Maio de 1961[89]

CONFIDENTIAL

On 22nd instant I called on Dr. Franco Nogueira, the new Minister for Foreign Affairs, for the first time in his new capacity. Our conversation was taken up almost exclusively by Angola and the Six-Seven relationship, and while he did not say anything new in either matter I think it well to report our conversation as presumably the views that he expressed are those of the Portuguese Government.

2. In regard to Angola he reiterated the firm intention of the Portuguese Government – and most of the people – to fight to the end in defence of their position in the overseas territories. His Government, and he personally, were firmly convinced that the trouble in Angola was sponsored by the Communist bloc as part of their anti-Western campaign, and Portugal was, in fact defending the Western cause. If Portugal lost out in Africa, then indeed would the Western cause suffer a considerable defeat – and not only in Africa, he added. In the light of the Portuguese approach to the problem in Angola, his Government could not admit any discussion of so-called "colonialism", and such discussion could be admitted only when the cold war had ended, and the Communists left the free world at liberty to develop peacefully and without outside interference. So far as the actual campaign in Angola was concerned, this was proceeding relatively satisfactorily from the Portuguese point of view and progressively more so. He hoped that the province would be pacified soon.

---

[89] NAI, DEA, 313/11H Confidential reports from Lisbon Legation, 1961.

3. So far as the Six-Seven relationship was concerned, Portugal was convinced of the absolute necessity of a solution to the two-blocs problem, but he thought that such a solution was far from imminent. Much negotiation would be required, and he would not preclude the possibility of a temporary arrangement between the two blocs pending the ultimate establishment of a larger Common Market to embrace all the Western European Countries. The OECD, he thought, would be an appropriate body in which to arrange such a temporary solution, but the importance of NATO in this connection was also great. He did not think that Britain would desert the other members of the Seven and enter the Common-Market, or make an arrangement with it, without them. So far as Portugal was concerned she had a special position in the Seven with concessions which took into account her particular problems, and she would expect similar treatment if she entered the Common Market.

J. W. Lennon

270
Ofício, Ministro Plenipotenciário irlandês em Lisboa ao Secretário-Geral do DEA: Lisboa, 30 de Maio de 1961[90]

CONFIDENTIAL

RECENT POLITICAL DEVELOPMENTS IN PORTUGAL

The highlight of political life in Lisbon in recent weeks was undoubtedly the visit of Lord Home [...] The exact purpose of the visit was not made clear, but it seems that the British are endeavouring to persuade the Portuguese to modify their attitude. In my view this is a hopeless proposition at the present stage.

2. The tempo of the war in Angola continues to mount. Large troop reinforcements leave for the overseas territories every week, not only for Angola, where a general offensive is being prepared, but also for Cabinda, where trouble has started, and Guiné, where it is to be expected. As I have already reported the

---
[90] NAI, DEA, 313/11H Confidential reports from Lisbon Legation, 1961.

Portuguese authorities are convinced that the trouble in their overseas territories is Communist-sponsored. A large Russian fishing fleet is off the Angolese [sic] coast, and it is claimed that Russian cigarettes have been found on captured "terrorists". The immediate Communist agents, however, are claimed to be the Ghanese. Not alone are the Ghanese training and inciting the terrorists, but they are also supplying them with arms similar to those in use amongst NATO forces.

3. An American friend of mine whom I had known in Paris and met quite by accident last week, and who is employed on a Public Relations basis by the Portuguese tourist body, told me that Seke Touré is known to have all the preparations made for invading Guiné, and is only awaiting an appropriate time.

[…]

J. W. Lennon

271
Ofício, Ministro Plenipotenciário irlandês em Lisboa ao Secretário-Geral do DEA: Lisboa, 14 de Junho de 1961[91]

CONFIDENTIAL

The impact of the Security Council decision on Angola was somewhat softened by its coming at the weekend which included Portugal's National Day and also the celebrations in commemoration of St. Anthony of Padua, who was born in Lisbon and is the city's patron saint. It was, therefore, a weekend of fiesta and pageantry from which, however, patriotic fervour, recalling Portugal's past greatness and modern military display, was not missing.

[…]

3. Press comment on the decision is remarkably wild – it is described as "shameful", "sorrowful", "scandalous", "a monstrosity", "inciting more atrocities" and juridically "absurd" and "scandalous", being an interference in the internal affairs of a member contrary to the charter of the UN. The complaint is made that the

---

[91] NAI, DEA, 313/11H Confidential reports from Lisbon Legation, 1961.

Portuguese authorities, endeavouring to restore order, are being condemned while the terrorists are condoned in their murder and pillage, which, of course, is Communist-inspired and has its origin outside Angola. Finally, the attitude is that the Security Council has presented requests which cannot be met.

[...]

5. It will be recalled that Dr. Salazar, in his interview given at the end of May to the NEW YORK TIMES, promised reforms in Angola "once order is established and peaceful activities resumed". The Press on 7th instant referred to a proposed Decree Law which would establish more municipal bodies in Overseas Territories and thus bring these territories into line with metropolitan Portugal. It is, to say the least, extremely unlikely that reforms of this type would satisfy Angolan Nationalists, but it is, of course, impossible for the régime to establish overseas a more liberal rule than exists in the metropole [...]

J. W. Lennon

272
Ofício, Ministro Plenipotenciário irlandês em Lisboa ao Secretário-Geral do DEA: Lisboa, 27 de Junho de 1961[92]

CONFIDENTIAL

The appointment of Dr. Teotónio Pereira, Minister of the Presidency, as Ambassador to the United States, and the announcement during the past week that this Ministry was to be abolished and its functions allocated to two Ministers of State, one of whom would be Dr. Correia de Oliveira, were expected.

Dr. Correia de Oliveira is specifically charged with supervision of External Economic Cooperation, of the execution of the Development Plan and of Statistical Services, and until a second Minister of State is appointed, will attend to all the functions falling to the former Ministry of the Presidency. He is young – middle 30s – and technically very competent and tends to support the impression

---

[92] NAI, DEA, 313/11H Confidential reports from Lisbon Legation, 1961.

already fairly definite that Dr. Salazar is surrounding himself with technicians rather than with politicians.

In accordance with local custom, Dr. Oliveira issued a statement on policy on taking up his new appointment. His principle [sic] task, he said, entrusted to him by the Prime Minister was co-ordination of the Ministries concerned with the economic welfare of Portugal to ensure the country's prosperity. To this end his first objective would be the amalgamation of the national markets to form one Portuguese national economy for all territories. His second objective is to ensure Portugal's participation in the new integration phase of European markets without, however, permitting such participation compromising the possibilities of national development. In this latter connection he said that Portugal would have enormous and difficult obstacles to overcome, as radical changes would be imposed on Portuguese productive activities in the new era of European trade. It should not be forgotten that, when the two European blocs have joined, the concessions obtained in Stockholm will not be enough "to save" Portugal, but he was convinced that international engagements – abolishing the stagnant and classical protection system – could be accepted without losing other more effective means of defending and stimulating private initiative.

Dr. Correia de Oliveira left for London on 24th inst. to represent Portugal at the EFTA meeting commencing on 27th idem.

J. W. Lennon

273
Ofício, Ministro Plenipotenciário irlandês em Lisboa ao Secretário-Geral do DEA: Lisboa, 28 de Junho de 1961[93]

CONFIDENTIAL

It was announced here on June 3rd that Air Force General Venâncio Augusto Deslandes, then Portuguese Ambassador in Madrid, was to be appointed Governor

---

[93] NAI, DEA, 313/11H Confidential reports from Lisbon Legation, 1961.

General of Angola and Commander-in-Chief of the armed forces there. It was stated at the time that his important appointment while testifying to the esteem in which the General's high qualities were held, also had in mind concentrating the military and civil power to enable a more efficient and rapid execution of the Angola policy both in the military and civil fields – a matter which was of vital importance at the present moment for that "most Portuguese" of the overseas provinces.

[…]

3. General Deslandes was sworn into his new post on 17th instant. The speeches made on the occasion by the Minister for Overseas Territories and by the General were long and significant. There were to be no half-way measures in Angola – said the Minister – the inhabitants will be either Portuguese or "wiped out by any means we can dispose of" […]

4. In his reply to the Minister the new Governor General was equally outspoken – and militant. He warned "the terrorist hordes which invade our homeland to expect from us a war without quarter. The only alternative we offer them is unconditional surrender or to be annihilated. They have made was on us: let them suffer the consequences".

[…]

7. The intransigent nature of these speeches tend to show that there is no softening of official policy towards Angola, and also that the Catholic Church is concerned with the position there just as much as the Protestant, but for some reason doesn't protest as much.

[…]

10. Here propaganda is increasing. The "stickers" on buses, taxis and in shop windows are more varied than previously, and while still avowing that Angola is Portugal, call for the defence of the Fatherland, now in danger, direct attention to the common enemy, plead for unity, etc. Knitting and sewing circles have been organised for the making of bandages, comforts for the troops, and the like. Nevertheless, I have the impression that discontent with the Government is becoming more widespread, but the possibility of a change is still, in my opinion, remote.

J. W. Lennon

274
Ofício, Ministro Plenipotenciário irlandês em Lisboa ao Secretário-Geral do DEA: Lisboa, 4 de Julho de 1961[94]

While the speech delivered by Dr. Salazar in the National Assembly on 30th ultimo contained little new, and might even be thought rather weak, it is outspoken in laying responsibility for Portugal's current problems where, in Portuguese opinion, it belongs. The main responsibility, of course, rests in the USSR and the Communist bloc, whose policy is to foster trouble amongst the Western nations however, and whenever, possible, using to this end such support as they can find, furnished by the Afro-Asian countries and unwillingly by the USA. The support by the USA of the Afro-Asian and Soviet groups in criticising in the UN Portuguese overseas administration is partly inspired by selfish motives – "with the avowed aim of collecting secure votes in deliberations concerning America versus Russia". This support encourages terrorism in Angola, thus furthering Russia's declared objective of using the subversion and disintegration of Africa as a means of overcoming Europe. The USA is, therefore, engaged in a course of action parallel with Russia and which is clearly irreconcilable with NATO objectives. While contradictions in thought may exist, contradictions in action between allies are inadmissible and if the US persists in her present course, it might easily happen that she, a prisoner of rigid ideological concepts, may eventually become a victim – the last victim – of such contradictions.

[…]

6. Naturally the speech was received with acclamation and without criticism, and the controlled press has reported only favourable comments – mainly in the overseas territories, Spain and Brazil – with one exception, that of the complaint by the US State Department of the references to the US, and even this is presented as the State Department "regrets that the Head of the Portuguese Government deplores the attitude which (the US) holds, unjustifiably, against our country".

---

[94] NAI, DEA, 313/11H Confidential reports from Lisbon Legation, 1961.

7. The press has received eagerly the news of the British action in Kuwait, which, they say, is the best possible comment in support of Salazar's statements that if Portugal gave independence to her smaller territories, neighbouring larger states would try to take over. The Kuwait situation has in today's (4th) press been given as the reason for the cancellation of the joint British-Portuguese manoeuvres which were to have taken place a week's time. The decision to cancel this exercise, however, was taken as long ago as last Friday, 30th June.

[…]

9. On the economic side the effects of the trouble in Angola are becoming more marked, and new heavy taxation was introduced on 30th June. I am submitting a separate report on this aspect.

J. W. Lennon,

275
Ofício, Ministro Plenipotenciário irlandês em Lisboa ao Secretário-Geral do DEA: Lisboa, 14 de Julho de 1961[95]

CONFIDENTIAL

INDONESIA AND TIMOR

My reports P.R. 10/61 and 19/61 referred to the position of Indonesia vis-à--vis Portugal. The news that Indonesian Cabinet Ministers have criticised Portuguese policy in Angola, Goa and Timor has been allowed to appear in the local press for the first time this morning, although the foreign press which circulates freely, has carried several references to it in recent weeks. Here the news is released as a news dispatch from all the Agencies, which finishes by saying that Indonesia is withdrawing her Ambassador from Lisbon. The late-news column of the papers include a further report from London that the Indonesian and Portuguese Embassies there deny any knowledge of a report by the Dutch Radio that Indonesia proposes breaking off relations with Portugal.

---

[95] NAI, DEA, 313/11H Confidential reports from Lisbon Legation, 1961.

2. The Government newspaper, DIÁRIO DA MANHÃ, carries a long leading article referring to the publication elsewhere in the paper of a "strange telegram from Djakarta" the substance of which cannot be reconciled with the facts as it is not true that Indonesia is withdrawing her Ambassador from Lisbon, and the other statements regarding Indonesian claims on Portuguese Timor are contrary to the information available […]

3. The denial of the departure of the Indonesian Ambassador is, I suppose, technically correct. He is a Minister – and leaves Lisbon tomorrow. The Legation is not being closed – yet – a new Second Secretary has just arrived in replacement of the former Secretary who left about a month ago, and will act as Chargé. My view, which I formed following a talk with the departing Minister, is that an Indonesian claim to all of Timor will certainly be forthcoming and the withdrawal of the Indonesian Legation is only postponed.

4. For the record, the island of Timor is about 12,900 sq. miles in area, and the Portuguese province, area about 7,600 sq. miles, consists of an enclave in Indonesian territory and the Eastern part of the island. The Portuguese have occupied the territory since early in the sixteenth century. The white population is small, and economically the territory has hitherto been of little value. However, it seems that oil has been discovered there within the past months, and this discovery may expedite both Indonesian claims and Portuguese resistance.

J. W. Lennon

276
Ofício, Ministro Plenipotenciário irlandês em Lisboa ao Secretário-Geral do DEA: Lisboa, 17 de Agosto de 1961[96]

CONFIDENTIAL

DEVELOPMENTS IN PORTUGAL AND PORTUGUESE TERRITORIES

The recapture by the Portuguese forces of Nambuancongo marks the end of the first stage in the Angola episode. This town had been in rebel hands since the

---

[96] NAI, DEA, 305/271B Part II Goa and other Portuguese enclaves in India, 1960-1968.

commencement of the anti-Portuguese campaign and was regarded as the head-quarters and capital of the movement. Its loss drives the rebels to operating solely from across the Congolese border and to stop such sporadic raids as will probably now develop, the Portuguese forces would perforce have to cross the border into the Congo. I would not exclude the possibility of such occurring.

2. Amongst my colleagues there seems to be a general impression that the Rebel campaign has resulted in the destruction of the year's coffee crop with the result that Portugal's main source of dollar earnings is ruined and that financially the economy is liable to collapse. My information is that the crop is not, in fact, destroyed, that destruction is about 12½ %, but as the crop is about 10% better than usual, the end result is that about 95% of the normal crop is still harvested […]

3. What the immediate future holds for Angola seems to be sporadic raids and outbursts of anti-Portuguese action, with a large army of occupation for the defence of the territory. With a view to ensuring the retention of the territory on a long-term basis, Ministers of the Government have been referring to the plantation in Angola of "soldier-colonists". It seems to me to be a case of "too late".

4. In other Portuguese territories there are indications of stirrings against Lisbon. The attacks on Portuguese Guinea from Senegal were unexpected in that they only came from Senegal and not from the former French Guinea or Ghana. The seizure of the enclave of S. João Baptista de Ajuda by Dahomey; the incorporation into India of two small "ex-Portugal" enclaves of Dadra and Nagar--Aveli, part of the Damão territory which were "liberated" into India in 1954; the request by the "Liberation Commission for Damão" to the Indian Government to take over Portuguese India by the end of this year; the invitation by the Portuguese Government to militia lieutenants of all branches of the forces, to serve as Captains in Timor; are all symptoms of the trouble affecting Portugal.

5. In metropolitan Portugal everything seems to continue as before. There is the odd arrest – seldom if ever reported in the local Press – of opponents of the régime. Cabinet Ministers make statements which are simply repetitions of what was said previously. Reports in the newspapers are what the Government wants published and the general tone of such reports is violently anti-Communist,

sympathetic to the France of the Generals, sympathetic to England, definitely pro-Spanish, and even yet somewhat anti-American (During the past week several editorials asked why was it that when bandits attempt to steal an aircraft they should be regarded as pirates, while only a few months ago when others captured a passenger liner, they were treated with respect by US officials).

6. On the question of the part played by religious groups in the Angola issue, it is of interest to note a statement made a week ago by the Foreign Minister, Dr. Franco Nogueira. Referring to the prominence given by many foreign newspapers to the detention of Protestant missionaries, he said that they ignored the fact that more Catholic than Protestant missionaries had been detained, as might be expected, there being more Catholic missionaries operating in Angola than Protestants.

7. There is no indication of any change in the policy of the régime either at home or abroad.

J. W. Lennon

277
Ofício, Ministro Plenipotenciário irlandês em Lisboa ao Secretário-Geral do DEA: Lisboa, 31 de Agosto de 1961[97]

CONFIDENTIAL

I have just made calls on the newly appointed Directors-General of the Political Divisions of the Foreign Office, respectively, Drs. Fragoso and Albano Nogueira. I discussed with them the present situation both as regards Portugal and generally and submit the following summary of the discussions:

<u>Political</u>. So far as Angola is concerned, the military campaign has almost finished, with success going to the Portuguese, as was to have been expected. It is thought that the Army will be able, without much difficulty, to maintain order. In regard to Mozambique, there is some slight apprehension that developments

---

[97] NAI, DEA, 313/11H Confidential reports from Lisbon Legation, 1961.

in neighbouring British territories may cause unrest, but no great difficulty is expected. The recent decree that all Africans are now full Portuguese citizens is regarded as a logical development of Portuguese policy over the many years of occupation, and not forced on an unwilling Government before an appropriate time. This should meet most of the African demands. There is, apparently, no intention of considering freedom independent of Portugal for the African, or any other territories, nor of educating the native populations towards such freedom. Policy for the future will be directed towards strengthening the Portuguese hold on the overseas territories by fostering settlement of whites from Metropolitan Portugal.

Portugal does not expect a war arising from the Berlin issue. In her opinion both sides are making propaganda and the matter will be settled in an appropriate time – after the German elections – by negotiation.

The Brazil issue, as might be expected, is of great interest to Portugal and the removal of Janio Quadros is regarded as a step in the right direction. He was generally thought of here as too much inclined to the left. Whether he will be succeeded by his Vice-President, or by a régime installed by the Army (which incidentally could turn out very like the system here) is anybody's guess.

Economical [sic] As might be expected our discussion centered largely on the position Portugal will adopt vis-à-vis the Common Market, now that Britain has applied for membership, and, in Portuguese opinion, is certain to join. Portugal is extremely reluctant to relinquish the concessions obtained under the Stockholm Treaty and her consideration of the line to be taken is very much coloured by her wish to retain these concessions, by the recently inaugurated drive towards a common market for Portuguese territories and also by a great reluctance to surrender any part of national sovereignty. Contrary to the belief expressed to me some months ago, Portugal now visualises association with ECE [sic] rather than membership, realising that the latter is incompatible with the concessions she will seek. In so far as the "Portuguese Common Market" is concerned, this means abolishing the tariffs which existed between the different territories. The establishment of this economic unity, I was assured, was always an aim of Portuguese policy, but it was, of course, necessary to wait until the time was ripe. Regarding the difficulty about surrendering part of sovereignty, the argument is that Portugal (including overseas) has a unitary Government and the Government would find it impossible to relinquish any part of its authority on Portuguese territory.

No decision has yet been taken, I was assured, on the question of Portuguese participation in ECE, but an application for membership is most unlikely, while an application for association is most likely.

J. W. Lennon

278
Ofício, Ministro Plenipotenciário irlandês em Lisboa ao Secretário--Geral do DEA: Lisboa, 6 de Setembro de 1961[98]

CONFIDENTIAL

NEW CHARTER FOR PORTUGUESE AFRICA

So much prominence is being given to the speech delivered in Porto on 28th ultimo by the Minister for Overseas Territories, and elaborated by him at a Press conference in Lisbon two days later, that a more detailed summary of the main points than that which appeared in the Press may be useful.

2. The Minister began by reiterating the view, frequently expressed by Dr. Salazar, of the dependence of African territories on Europe for technique, education, and capital, and that the needs of Africa in these connections could best be supplied by Europeans working for their country rather than on a mercenary basis. Thus the permanent settlement of European Portuguese overseas was a sound measure, the settler going to the overseas territory not to sell his services, but to live a normal life serving, together with the aborigines, the same and common interests. The Portuguese system showed less profits but involved more sacrifices and obligations, and those African peoples who chose an alternative path are now finding out by experience that they are heading towards

---

[98] NAI, DEA, 313/11H Confidential reports from Lisbon Legation, 1961.

a form of neo-colonialism or reverting to primitive conditions. In order, therefore, to further the Portuguese system in Africa, it is necessary to increase the number of European Portuguese settled there. This enormous and important task can no longer be left to individual initiative. Provincial Settlement Agencies will be set up in Mozambique and Angola to work in close contact with the emigration services of Metropolitan Portugal. In this way it was hoped to facilitate settlement of European Portuguese in Africa, including those now doing their military service there. There was no shortage of land for such settlement, in fact, due to the foresight of the administration there was a surplus of land. While the system of land tenure provided that all the land covered by a regional administration belonged to that administration, this did not prevent an individual from acquiring a concession for himself so long as the deed is approved by the administration councillors.

3. The Minister referred to the Statute of "Indigenato" which could now be repealed. Pointing out that this Statute applied to only Angola and Mozambique of the Portuguese Overseas territories, he said, that its abolition would make it clear that "the Portuguese people are subject to a political law which is the same for all, without distinction of race, religion or culture."

4. Referring to a decree promulgated in June regarding the re-establishment in Portuguese Africa of municipal institutions, the Minister stated that implementation of this decree would be effected by the election "in the traditional manner of the inhabitants" of rural administrations. To these administrations the regional militia would be linked to support law and order and maintain Portuguese sovereignty.

5. The Minister made it clear that Portuguese policy was to retain Angola and Mozambique, at whatever cost […] The only really new item was that of the abolition of the "Indigenato" system, and what this is expected to achieve in a country where most of the inhabitants cannot appreciate the difference is difficult to see. The parallel between this action and that of France in extending some years ago full citizenship rights to Algeria is marked, but I have not seen any comment on this.

J. W. Lennon

279

Ofício, Ministro Plenipotenciário irlandês em Lisboa ao Secretário-Geral do DEA: Lisboa, 29 de Setembro de 1961[99]

PORTUGAL AND KATANGA

As might be expected from a country with a major problem of its own constantly on its mind, the recent events in Katanga, while front page-news, took second place to events in Angola. The proximity of Angola to Katanga; the support by Leopoldville of the "terrorists" in Angola; the identification of President Thsombé's régime, which co-operates to some extent with the Portuguese and Rhodesia Governments in matters of rail transport, with a "moderate" African nationalism prepared to accept white guidance; all these coupled with a basic anti-UN attitude attributed towards "interference in Portuguese internal affairs", all tended towards Press support of President Tshombé's position versus the UN forces.

2. Throughout the whole action the Press reports were those showing the UN in the most unfavourable light, and the most exaggerated claims by the Tshombé Government were highlighted. So far as Irish participation was concerned, however, the press was not unsympathetic and succeeded in giving the impression that our troops had been involved in something against their will, even against the intention of our Government. The impression was conveyed that the Taoiseach had stated that Irish troops had gone to the Congo for police duties and that they should not be involved in military duties, and a member of the Irish contingent made prisoner by the Katanganese was alleged to have said that as a Catholic he objected to fighting for the Communist Government in Leopoldville. I did not see any attacks on Dr. O'Brien of the type indulged in by some of the British press. However, there continues deliberate misrepresentation of Katanganese news, the most recent example being in connection with the build-up, announced by Gen. MacKeown, of the UN air forces, which was presented as firstly, a statement by Tshombé that the UN was

---

[99] NAI, DEA, 313/11H Confidential reports from Lisbon Legation, 1961.

building up its forces for punitive action against Katanga, a denial by O'Brien, and the statement by MacKeown, with the comment "who is lying?". No reference was made in the report to the purpose of the build-up as announced by Gen. MacKeown.

3. [...]

4. The Portuguese attitude towards the late Mr. Hammarskjöld is interesting. The Katanganese exercise was labelled at its inception as "Mr. H's private war", and his death, with subsequent complications has not received as much prominence as one might expect. In all matters arising at the moment, however, it must be remembered that Portuguese thinking is naturally very much concerned with the question of the overseas territories, where, as regards Angola, the military situation is, perhaps, not as favourable as it might be, having regard to the proximity of the rainy season.

J. W. Lennon

280
Ofício, Ministro Plenipotenciário irlandês em Lisboa ao Secretário-Geral do DEA: Lisboa, 19 de Outubro de 1961[100]

CONFIDENTIAL

FORTHCOMING PORTUGUESE ELECTIONS

On 10th instant the Minister for State, Dr. Correia de Oliveira, in a broadcast statement on how the forthcoming elections may properly be conducted, revealed that yet another letter had been addressed at end September to Dr. Salazar by "Opposition" leaders in regard to these elections. This letter, together with Dr. Salazar's reply, were not published until 12th idem.

2. The "Opposition" requested free and honest elections, without interference by Government political or police organisations, to enable the large opposition masses to express their wishes. To this end they asked principally

---

[100] NAI, DEA, 313/11H Confidential reports from Lisbon Legation, 1961.

1) The release of "Opposition" members detained for political reasons.
2) Authority to publish the "Programme for the Democratisation of the Republic" submitted to Dr. Salazar in May last.
3) Permission to use national and foreign press, radio and television, public buildings etc. on equal terms with candidates of the Government party (the União Nacional).
4) Restricting Government employees, at any level, from interfering in the elections.
5) Prohibiting the press "which enjoys official favour" from using "condemnable measures" in referring to the campaign.
6) Establishment of a body with equal representation of all parties to check on and publish disputes about the campaign.

   3. Dr. Salazar's reply, dated October 9th, stated:

a) No "Opposition" members are under arrest for anything to do with the forthcoming elections, and the release of those detained for police investigations cannot be considered.
b) The "Programme for the Democratisation of the Republic" has been sufficiently divulged for it to be known. Publication now cannot be permitted. It cannot be allowed to serve as a basis for the Opposition campaign as it advocates alteration in the existing constitutional structure – a matter which cannot be discussed each time Deputies are being chosen for the National Assembly.
c) Official radio and television will be left out of the campaign. Public buildings can be used by all parties on an equal basis. National and foreign press being private enterprises, the Government has nothing to say about their use.
d) Government personnel will not intervene in the propaganda campaign, but the public must be enlightened at any time upon problems of interest to it.
e) The press must be relied upon to remain correct. The Government could interfere only by using censorship – a step which would be contrary to the principles of the Opposition.
f) Elections must be held in accordance with existing legislation, therefore, the establishment of an arbitration body of the type visualised would not appear possible.

   […]

J. W. Lennon

281
Ofício, Ministro Plenipotenciário irlandês em Lisboa ao Secretário-Geral do DEA: Lisboa, 26 de Outubro de 1961[101]

CONFIDENTIAL

Preparations for the forthcoming election to the National Assembly will consist of a Press campaign, and there is no indication yet of any enthusiasm or excitement. "Opposition" candidates are being weeded out on grounds of ineligibility for one reason or another (for example, imprisonment in the past for political reasons, connection with the civil service, intention to change the constitution, if possible, after election), some supporters have been arrested, and the general impression one gets is that an "opposition" deputy has no chance of being elected.

2. The curtailment of electioneering and the refusal to allow the "opposition" to push their "Programme for the Democratisation of the Republic", has restricted the "Opposition" scope, but they still continue to present utopian proposals to Dr. Salazar – the most recent being proposals for civil liberties in the overseas territories. Such proposals are obviously hopeless. How could the régime give to the overseas territories liberties denied in Metropolitan Portugal?

3. Rumours concerning Capt. Galvão persist. One day these rumours have him in the North – the next in the South. The most persistent is that he is in Morocco and expected to land in the South, and that to circumvent this, troops have been sent to the Southern province as coastguards. What Capt. Galvão could hope to achieve if he did land is obscure. Notwithstanding the troop commitments in Angola an other territories (a further 2,500 left on Saturday last), these are largely reserve forces, and the NATO-trained regular Army – which seems to be the real source of power – is still intact in the metropole.

4. The new Indonesian Chargé told me in a conversation a few days ago that Portugal has recently sent 2,000 troops to Timor, and that information available to him is that a policy of repression on the native population is being pursued.

---
[101] NAI, DEA, 313/11H Confidential reports from Lisbon Legation, 1961.

This looks like a build-up for anti-Portuguese action in Timor. I have long been of opinion that it is only a question of time before such action comes.

J. W. Lennon

282
Ofício, Ministro Plenipotenciário irlandês em Lisboa ao Secretário-Geral do DEA: Lisboa, 3 de Novembro de 1961[102]

CONFIDENTIAL

PORTUGUESE ELECTIONS

Enclosed for information is an article on the electoral system in Portugal.[103]

2. The campaign – if it can properly be so styled – proceeds in a manner entirely foreign to our conception of an election. So far there have been no public meetings of the type one accustomed to our system would expect, and election posters – the most noticeable of Northern European election features – are non existent. The newspapers carry election features, and these are entirely pro--National Union, the pro-régime "party".

3. [...]

4. Criticism of the régime comes from both Republican and Monarchist Oppositions. It covers economic, social and overseas policies. Over the past 35 years, it is claimed by the Monarchists, economic development has been inadequate, and the responsibility rests on the braking influence of the corporative system. The already traditional lack of initiative, courage and willingness to risk capital, all characteristic of Portugal, has been emphasized by State encouragement towards prudence and guarantee of profits. The enormous fortunes accumulated by a relative few, especially since the war, accentuate the injustices in income levels and do not help in advancing national income. Portuguese economic life has reached stagnation, and in recent years has just been carried by events. Only an energetic policy which will do away with

---

[102] NAI, DEA, 313/11H Confidential reports from Lisbon Legation, 1961.
[103] *Anglo-Portuguese News*, 28 de Outubro de 1961

unjustified monopolies and privileges, now consecrated by legislation or corporativism, and give freedom to private enterprise can result in a beginning of anything worthy of the name of economical [sic] development.

5. The Republican Opposition has included in its criticism a comparison of certain Portuguese statistics with other countries e.g. highest infant mortality rate in Western Europe, and in all Europe only Yugoslavia is worse: per capita consumption of electricity is only 15% of OEEC average; housing lagging behind; daily per capita consumption of calories only 2,470; six banks control 80% of the Portuguese banking system etc.

6. The propaganda of the pro-régime National Union "party" is on somewhat emotional lines – "Only a country with a mysticism like ours could fight like us in Angola"; "The Opposition does all it can to undermine the international prestige of the Government" and "is behaving itself in a most condemnable manner not worthy of men"; "Contrary to slanderous statements, our prestige has never been so high". A note issued by the Presidency of the Council in reply to criticism of overseas policy stated that this "criticism of the Government is the same as that by which the Afro-Asian and Communist blocs base their attacks on Portugal in the UN."

7. As the elections approach it seems likely that the opposition will withdraw. There is little point in their going forward, as their chances under the electoral system are nil.

8. Capt. Galvão's appearance in London and Stockholm must have been a relief to the authorities here. That they attached some credence to the reports of his landing in the South of the country is confirmed by the fact that cars coming to Lisbon from the South were stopped by military patrols for verification of identity, and yachts cruising in the Estuary of the Tagus here, on at least one day, have been inspected by a naval patrol vessel.

J. W. Lennon

283
Ofício, Ministro Plenipotenciário irlandês em Lisboa ao Secretário-Geral do DEA: Lisboa, 9 de Novembro de 1961[104]

CONFIDENTIAL

POLITICAL SITUATION IN PORTUGAL

As expected the "Opposition" has withdrawn from the elections to be held on 12th instant [...]

2. During the week just passed there were demonstrations by students, but these do not appear to be of any great significance. More important was the reaction to a request presented to the President that Dr. Salazar be dismissed from the Premiership. On the following day, the Army stated categorically that it would maintain the régime, and since then loyal addresses have been sent to Dr. Salazar from all parts of Portugal.

3. It is difficult to say how much discontent exists in Portugal against the régime. In this small country, roughly the size of Ireland, there is about 2½ times the population of Ireland. The far greater part of the population has a very low standard of living – barely subsistence in many parts – and is so depressed economically that it has no political consciousness. There is a relatively small, very wealthy, class which controls the economic life of the country, and as might be expected, these are the main supporters of the régime. The Army officer cadre is largely made up from these families, and while they continue to have Army support, any effort to assail their privileged position, or to upset the régime must fail. According to reports there is a large, underground, Communist party, but it must be very underground if it can continue to exist against the very efficient police forces.

4. It seems clear that some sort of demonstration against the régime was or is contemplated about the present time. The nervousness displayed by the Government on the rumours of Capt. Galvão landing in Portugal coupled with the latter's remarks about being in a free Lisbon by Christmas would tend to

---

[104] NAI, DEA, 313/11H Confidential reports from Lisbon Legation, 1961.

support this view. However, in my view, any action by Capt. Galvão, unless he can convince the Army to change its allegiance, must fail.

J. W. Lennon

284
Ofício, Ministro Plenipotenciário irlandês em Lisboa ao Secretário-Geral do DEA: Lisboa, 16 de Novembro de 1961[105]

CONFIDENTIAL

CURRENT CHURCH-STATE RELATIONS IN PORTUGAL

In ordinary times, the Church doesn't play a very prominent part in the life of the average Portuguese – the position, I understand, being much the same as in France, where, nominally, practically everyone is Catholic but only a small percentage are practising Catholics. However, when it appears necessary to any group to parade the Church as a champion of any particular cause, this is done, as in many other countries.

2. The "Opposition" set the ball rolling this time. In their "Programme for the Democratization of the Republic", they referred to the "objectives of the Portuguese Catholic sectors which wished to detach the Church from the methods of totalitarian government" as being identical with their own. This led the Episcopacy to issue on October 7th a statement recalling a solemn declaration made by them on 10th January 1959, that "The Church's mission cannot either be confused with a political mission under the tutelage of the State, or be subservient to the State", and continuing that the Church condemned political totalitarianism, whether Tsarist, communist, or demagogic, because it denied the mission and liberty of the Church and it sacrificed the rights of the individual on the altar of the State, of the classes, or of the people.

3. The issue of the Episcopal Note coincided with the Press conference held by the Opposition to announce their non-running in the elections, giving their reasons [...]

[105] NAI, DEA, 313/11H Confidential reports from Lisbon Legation, 1961.

4. Questions were posed on the position of the Church in Africa. It was stated that the Bishop of Beira in Mozambique, who always fought for justice for the natives, was forbidden to publish pastorals, and his newspaper was censored (!). However, in Angola, matters were worse. The Church's efforts to get close to the native was [sic], it was stated, contrary to official policy, and while, two years ago, fifteen negro or halfcaste priests were in the Luanda diocese, now only three remained, under constant supervision, the other twelve being either under arrest or in exile. The Vicar-General of Angola, arrested in Luanda in March and brought to Portugal, was mentioned specifically. He is now free, but must live in Portugal, and no denial or confirmation of the charges against him has been made public. When, it was stated, the Angola Bishops made a collective protest in June last against the "anti-Christian" affirmations of the new Governor General of Angola, General Deslandes, the protest was ignored.

5. The pro-Government National Union, when left with a clear field, in the newspapers referred to Church-State relations in such terms as the following: "In Portugal, no serious problems exist in relations between the Church and the State", "Catholics must live in a State [sic] of alert if they really wish that all can live, work and pray in peace". Photographs of the Cardinal-Patriarch of Lisbon casting his vote appeared. It appeared, of course, that he was voting for the Government, as they were the only candidates.

J. W. Lennon

285
Ofício, Ministro Plenipotenciário irlandês em Lisboa ao Secretário-Geral do DEA: Lisboa, 28 de Novembro de 1961[106]

CONFIDENTIAL

The principal event of the past week in the Portuguese political scene was the visit to Madrid of President Americo Thomaz, who was accompanied by the Minister for Foreign Affairs, Dr. Franco Nogueira, and various officials. The visit stressed the

---

[106] NAI, DEA, 313/11H Confidential reports from Lisbon Legation, 1961.

already obvious and well-known affinity between the two countries in matters of foreign and domestic policies, and from the propaganda point of view was a great success. From the actual policy point of view little can have been achieved because, although the Heads of State met, Admiral Thomaz has no real power [...]

2. [...]

3. In the Overseas Territories there appears to reign a period of relative calm. The Angola campaign still smouldering, however, might burst into flame at any moment. Signs of difficulty with India persist – only a few days ago the Department of National Defence announced an abortive attempt to land on Angediva Island from which, Mr. Nehru alleged in the Indian Parliament, shots were fired at a passing Indian ship. Troop reinforcements continue to leave regularly for the overseas territories.

4. To conclude, I should perhaps refer to the aftermath of the recent elections, which, as the Department will be aware, passed over with little incident. It is true that there were demonstrations in some parts of the country, and in Almada, just over the Tagus from Lisbon, a man was killed and one fatally wounded in an attack on a police station. However, now that the elections are over, it seem [sic] that the signatories of the "Programme for the Democratization of the Republic" no longer enjoy exemption from arrest, and are being interned. Also the number of dissidents seeking political asylum in Foreign missions here is on the increase. The new Assembly meets tomorrow, but no incidents are expected.

J. W. Lennon

286
Ofício, Ministro Plenipotenciário irlandês em Lisboa ao Secretário-Geral do DEA: Lisboa, 12 de Dezembro de 1961[107]

CONFIDENTIAL

PORTUGAL AND INDIA

The smouldering Portuguese-Indian dispute over Goa, which in recent months has shown more signs of flame than in recent years, has now reached a

---

[107] NAI, DEA, 313/11H Confidential reports from Lisbon Legation, 1961.

point where it is almost a conflagration. Nevertheless, notwithstanding newspaper reports, opinion here tends to the view that, once again, the fires will, in time, calm down.

2. The newspapers vilify Nehru – the "false pacifist" – and claim that action against Goa is imminent. All Indian claims and statements are denied, naturally, and counter-claims and counter-statements of a type appropriate to the situation are made.

3. Whether or not the Portuguese forces in Goa have been reinforced – and I am inclined to believe the Portuguese denial of this – it seems absurd that Portugal, with her commitments in Angola, could ever be a threat to India. The Indian case is, therefore, weakened by pleading this as a reason for troop concentrations on the frontier.

4. Indian exasperation at the Portuguese refusal to treat is understandable. While the present régime in Lisbon retains power – and it must be remembered that the régime is more than Dr. Salazar – this refusal will be maintained. The only way in which Goa could be united with India would be forceably [sic] – whether by annexation from without or by stirring up a union movement within the Portuguese territories, and this latter is what the authorities here fear the most.

5. Many here hold the opinion that the entire matter is an election stunt by Mr. Nehru, with appropriate counter-measures by Portugal to rally public opinion behind the Government. This could well be, but it assumes that Mr. Nehru will retain control of the situation in India and will be able to damp down the fires when he thinks fit. The real danger in the present situation, so far as Portugal is concerned, is that Mr. Nehru may lose control, even for a short time, and that Goa might be overrun with considerable losses on both sides.

J. W. Lennon

287
Nota, Legação portuguesa em Dublin ao DEA:
Dublin, 18 de Dezembro de 1961[108]

URGENT

The Legation of Portugal presents its compliments to the Department of External Affairs and has the honour to communicate, the following:

On December 17 at midnight (Goa local time), Indian troops crossed the northern frontier of Goa and occupied the post of Sinquervale. Later on powerful Indian forces launched their aggression against the whole territory, supported by strong land, naval and air forces. Portuguese armed forces entered into action in defence of the territory.

2. The Portuguese Government had repeatedly denounced the provocative attitude of the Indian Government and stressing its peaceful intentions, in order to avoid pretexts for an incident, precautions were taken to the point of withdrawing troops from some frontier posts. The Portuguese Government also declared that it was prepared to negotiate. On the other hand, the Governments of the United Kingdom, the United States of America, Brazil, Spain, amongst other friendly nations, had in the last few days made representations to the Indian Government against the use of force. In spite of all this, the Indian Government decided yesterday to go ahead with its premeditated aggression attacking the peaceful territory of the Portuguese State of India.

The Portuguese Legation avails itself of this opportunity to renew to the Department of External Affairs the assurance of its high consideration.

---

[108] NAI, DEA, 305/271B Part II Goa and other Portuguese enclaves in India, 1960-1968.

288
**Comunicado à imprensa da Legação portuguesa em Dublin:
Dublin, 19 de Dezembro de 1961**[109]

India has been spreading news that Portuguese troops have been surrendering, that Portuguese administration is on the verge of collapse and that the Governor and high officials had already abandoned Goa.

The Portuguese authorities categorically deny such news as totally untrue, and stress that Portuguese troops are opposing with all possible resistance the Indian army – by far superior in numbers and armament and having the support of aviation, which is not available to Portuguese troops in India.

The ruthless Indian attack is also aiming at non-military objectives with the clear intention of demoralising the population, thus assuming that they will revolt against the Portuguese authorities. However the civil population has been collaborating with the Portuguese forces.

In spite of increasing difficulties in the communications with Goa as a result of the bombing of the local radio station and airport, last reports received in Lisbon confirm that the Portuguese troops are tenaciously resisting the attack and that the morale of the population is high.

289
Ofício, Encarregado de Negócios *ad interim* irlandês em Madrid ao Secretário-Geral do DEA: Madrid, 20 de Dezembro de 1961[110]

CONFIDENTIAL

SPAIN AND GOA

The invasion by India on the 18th December of Goa has been interpreted in the Spanish press in the worst possible light and the leading articles in this

---

[109] NAI, DEA, 305/271B Part II Goa and other Portuguese enclaves in India, 1960-1968.

[110] NAI, DEA, Embassy Madrid, I.P. 4/51/1, Portugal 1941-1963.

morning's papers blame both the UNO and India for the present situation. "The UNO breaks the peace in Katanga and does not defend it in Goa" proclaims a leader in this morning's "YA", while the monarchist "A.B.C." emphasises the powerlessness of the Organisation to deal with the present situation because of the Soviet veto in the Security Council and the hostile attitude of the Assembly. Much publicity is also given to Mr. Stevenson's statement in the Security Council.

The Spanish Government has not so far condemned the actual invasion but I am forwarding the text of a statement agreed at a meeting of the Government on 15th December condemning the <u>threat</u> by India to use force against Goa and supporting the Portuguese proposal that international advisers be sent there.

According to the statement, the Spanish Government "felt it was its duty" to make public its revulsion towards any act of aggression or of any actions which implied an attack on the territorial sovereignty of a country. It drew attention to the gravity of the situation which would arise if "the international Organisation" showed itself incapable of seeing that the essential object of the United Nations were complied with, the term "United Nations Organisation" is specifically avoided and the reference to "the international Organisation" is, of course, only slightly less cutting than General De Gaulle's "Nations dites Unies" [...]

The text is, of course, nothing more than a re-statement of Spain's traditional support of the Portuguese policy on Goa and a small detail worth mentioning is that the text was circulated by the Foreign Ministry to diplomatic missions here together with a copy of the <u>Portuguese</u> Foreign Ministry's statement of 6th December last. Both countries have consistently refused to transmit information on non-self-governing territories called for in Article 73 on the grounds that these are integral parts of the metropole – though, as you are aware, the Spanish attitude in this respect is not quite as rigid as the Portuguese. Spain in fact, does transmit on official publications about her territories to the UN secretariat (though not to the Trusteeship Council), but makes it clear that it does so only "for enlightenment" and not by reason of any right of the UN to such information.

Aidan Mulloy

290
Carta, Secretário-Geral do DEA ao Encarregado de Negócios português em Dublin: Dublin, 22 de Dezembro de 1961[111]

The Department of External Affairs presents its compliments to the Portuguese Legation and has the honour to acknowledge the Legation's note (Proc. 1,07: N º 898) of 18th December regarding recent events in Goa. The attitude of the Portuguese Government in this matter has been duly noted.

The Department of External Affairs avails itself of this opportunity to renew to the Portuguese Legation the assurance of its highest consideration.

C. C. Cremin

291
Ofício, Ministro Plenipotenciário irlandês em Lisboa ao Secretário-Geral do DEA: Lisboa, 22 de Dezembro de 1961[112]

INDIA AND GOA

While the Portuguese authorities were preparing for the worst in Goa and evacuating women and children to metropolitan Portugal, it was still generally thought and hoped that while the Indians might continue sabre rattling, they would not attack.

2. The attack on and fall of Goa has made no apparent difference to ordinary life in Lisbon. There have, of course, been some repercussions – for example an Art Exhibition under Gulbenkian Foundation auspices which was to have been opened in the presence of the President on the 18th had neither President nor Cabinet Ministers present, and was opened quietly and without speeches; the annual reception by the President of the Diplomatic Corps, scheduled for the 22nd has been cancelled; and a proposed visit to Madeira in the New Year by the

---

[111] NAI, DEA, 305/271B Part II Goa and other Portuguese enclaves in India, 1960-1968.
[112] NAI, DEA, 313/11H Confidential reports from Lisbon Legation, 1961.

President has been postponed. There has been some speculation whether the Indian take-over of Goa would affect the régime, and the possibility of Dr. Salazar retiring and being replaced by an Army nominee has been mentioned – orally, of course – but there seems little likelihood that Metropolitan politics will be affected, although the possibility always exists. In all probability the régime will be strengthened by these occurances [sic] – an opinion which seems to be supported by a huge patriotic-religious rally held here on the evening of the 18th and continuing into the early hours of 19th.

3. How far the events in Goa will affect Portugal's attitude towards NATO and the oldest ally is problematical. So far as UN is concerned any likely change would be for the worse. My impression gained over the past year is that the official attitude here is that the alliance with Britain is the most important of Portugal's international connections [...] It is equally remarkable how, when the Goa incident commenced about a fortnight ago, the British Ambassador was not to be seen and members of his staff all had different stories to account for his absence. I should not be surprised to learn that he had been to London for consultation. The official British attitude that India being a member of the Commonwealth, Britain could not honour her Treaty with Portugal, has not been well received, and this coupled with Britain being charged with looking after Indian interests, has not been offset by Britain's line in the Security Council debate. However, I can see no great deterioration in Portuguese-British relations in the long run. British interests and investments in Portugal are such that neither could afford a cleavage.

4. The preceding paragraphs were written in the fore-noon of the 21st. At lunch time there was a demonstration outside the British and US Embassy chanceries, one of which – the British – I saw. A number of motor-cars bearing anti-British slogans, calling for abolition of the alliance passed in front of the British chancery. There was much noise – car horns and shouting, and a British flag was torn to shreds. There were, according to the local press, other demonstrations in Luanda.

5. The Portuguese people see nothing provocative in their attitude vis-à-vis overseas territories, and events in Goa are not likely to make them change their

"not an inch" attitude. Many to whom I have spoken, while agreeing that such small territories as Goa, Macau, Timor and others were liabilities, maintained that for prestige and on a point of principle Portugal must not yield and must fight to maintain her territories. Nevertheless some thought that ultimately the Portuguese territories might be reduced to Angola and Mozambique, both of which are of importance – but that to lose those would mean the end for Portugal. A stepping up of the recently introduced policy to encourage greater Portuguese emigration to the African territories and the settling there of soldiers now serving in those territories is, I think, to be expected.

J. W. Lennon

292
Ofício, Ministro Plenipotenciário irlandês em Lisboa ao Secretário-Geral do DEA: Lisboa, 27 de Dezembro de 1961[113]

CONFIDENTIAL

The Christmas season coinciding with the fall of Goa has probably helped to soften the blow by providing a counter-attraction. That the blow has been severe is beyond doubt and the already seriously disposed Portuguese people seem to have become quite mournful.

2. A most noteworthy event – or rather a negative event – has been the silence of Dr. Salazar. The only statement by him appearing in the newspapers over the past week is a reprint of an interview given to a FIGARO correspondent, but this interview could have been given ten days ago. His silence has led to speculation of all types – that he was seriously ill, and finally, on St. Stephen's Day, that he had died.

3. The anti-British and US demonstrations of 21st instant were followed by another on 22nd during which an effigy of Nehru and the British and US flags were burnt. Police guards on the chancelleries of these two countries have been

---
[113] NAI, DEA, 313/11H Confidential reports from Lisbon Legation, 1961.

increased. The British community has reacted to the unaccustomed chill they are experiencing, and most of the parties they normally conduct at this time have been cancelled.

4. The latest rumour in Lisbon is that a former Foreign Minister, Dr. Paulo Cunha, has left on a special mission to the Far East. If rumour is to be believed his mission is to make contact with the Communist Chinese with a view to anti--Indian action. Portugal does not recognise the Peking régime, and a Nationalist Minister is still accredited here.

5. Notwithstanding claims still being issued officially that the fighting is still going on in Goa, I have been told that the Ministry of the Army is very dissatisfied with the resistance offered by a small number of Portuguese troops. While it is realised that they had no chance against a much greater and better equipped opposition, it is felt, I understand, that they might have offered greater resistance, and that the officials commanding may be court-martialled for failing to do their duty.

J. W. Lennon

Parte IV
(1962-1970)

A quarta e última parte deste trabalho abre com a reacção à tomada de Goa pela União Indiana e a resultante – de acordo com J. W. Lennon, ainda em Lisboa – quebra de confiança na liderança de Salazar. Uma fonte de informação inesperada, mas importante, foi um dos funcionários da firma de relações públicas George Peabody, que acabara de visitar Goa, e que, embora sob contrato do SNI, disse a Lennon que as forças portuguesas na Índia mal tinham resistido, e que o regime tinha os dias contados: se não seguisse um caminho mais liberal, tudo iria acabar num banho de sangue. É de salientar que Lennon não era inteiramente hostil à política ultramarina portuguesa em geral, embora achasse estranha a escolha de aliados em África: para quem se dizia empenhado em construir uma sociedade multirracial, a Rodésia e a África do Sul eram parceiros inesperados.

Na primavera de 1962, porém, Lennon partiu de Lisboa, sendo substituído por O'Kelly de Gallagh, que assim, pela quarta vez, e aos 72 anos, se encontrou à frente da Legação irlandesa, desta vez até 1967. Assim sendo, a esta missão voltou um defensor de Salazar e da política africana de Portugal (senão do Estado Novo em si). A densidade e qualidade da informação caíram. Em Documentos como os N.º 310, 323, 330, e 341, O'Kelly de Gallagh demonstrou claramente o seu apoio a Portugal contra adversários coloniais e estrangeiros, e frequentemente citou os testemunhos de figuras internacionais que, voltando de África, se mostravam favoráveis aos esforços portugueses. Em Março de 1964, O'Kelly de Gallagh mostrou-se entusiasmado com a iniciativa do Governo português de convidar os chefes de missão acreditados em Lisboa a ir a Angola e Moçambique para investigar *in loco* as condições de vida e a política de integração racial (Documento N.º 340). Apesar da sua defesa deste convite, porém, foi o Encarregado de Negócios irlandês instruído a recusar tal convite, se lho fosse dirigido (Documento N.º 342). O Documento N.º 349, no qual O'Kelly de Gallagh inclui cópia de uma entrevista de Salazar ao jornal francês *Aurore*, em Outubro de 1964, é talvez a mais flagrante demonstração da forma como o Encarregado de Negócios irlandês estava do lado de Salazar – e contra Dublin – em matéria africana.

Quanto à política interna, a análise de O'Kelly de Gallagh não evoluiu: a oposição, cada vez mais forte, era constituída sobretudo por elementos das profissões liberais que, tendo dominado a República, se viam, desde 1926, incapazes de assumir as rédeas do poder, o que desejavam fazer apenas em proveito próprio (Documentos N.º 327, 361). O Encarregado de Negócios irlandês aceitou, sem grandes reservas, a tese oficial sobre o assassinato de Humberto Delgado – que este tinha sido morto pelos seus supostos aliados comunistas, para quem representava um notável embaraço.

No resto da carreira diplomática irlandesa porém, a opinião era bem distinta. Tadgh O'Sullivan, de Nova Iorque, afirmava que uma guerra racial estava agora em curso em Angola (Documento N.º 313); o seu superior, o Embaixador F. H. Boland, descreveu, pouco depois (Documento N.º 317), a crescente preocupação na ONU – e até em Espanha – com a total intransigência portuguesa (isto apesar de alguma admiração pela forma como Franco Nogueira defendia a posição portuguesa – ver o Documento N.º 328). Em 1963, a Irlanda apoiou a resolução sobre os territórios ultramarinos portugueses apresentada pelo grupo africano na Quarta Comissão, completando assim uma transição iniciada com o apoio qualificado a Portugal, em 1956. O Documento N.º 365 mostra que esta posição se foi consolidando; numa declaração de voto perante o Quarto Comité, o delegado irlandês apelidou de "errada e anacrónica" a política colonial portuguesa, explicando que as dúvidas sérias sobre certas expressões contidas na resolução não bastavam para levar o Governo irlandês a mudar o seu voto, já que a prioridade era demonstrar o desagrado irlandês para com o colonialismo português. Mais ainda: o Ministro dos Negócios Estrangeiros e Tánaiste (Vice-Primeiro-Ministro) irlandês, Frank Aiken, via agora com bons olhos a imposição de sanções económicas como forma de forçar o Governo português a mudar de rumo (Documento N.º 366), recusando-se por isso a abster-se, apesar de uma intervenção de última hora do Embaixador português em Dublin (Documentos N.º 367 e 368). A atitude no ano seguinte foi semelhante, e a pressão política para adoptar medidas ainda mais drásticas foi aumentando de ano para ano, com deputados da oposição a perguntar ao Governo por que não rompia as relações diplomáticas com Portugal (28 de Outubro de 1969).

O desagrado irlandês manifestava-se de outras formas. Em 1965, a representação oficial entre os países mantinha-se ainda ao nível de Legação, embora as Embaixadas se tivessem entretanto vulgarizado. Era Dublin a última Legação portuguesa na Europa. Pior ainda, claro está, era o facto de a Legação irlandesa estar entregue de forma permanente a um Encarregado de Negócios interino, se bem que este tivesse a categoria de Ministro Plenipotenciário. No Verão desse ano, Lisboa agiu, com uma *démarche* forte empreendida simultaneamente pelo Ministro em Dublin, Armando de Castro e Abreu, e pelo Secretário-Geral do MNE, José Luís Archer. E se esta acção teve algum sucesso, já que a Legação portuguesa em Dublin foi promovida a Embaixada, a situação em Lisboa continuou na mesma. Quando, em substituição de O´Kelly de Gallagh, foi nomeado Denis B. O'Sullivan,[1] o Secretário-Geral do DEA, Hugh McCann, afirmou que não era ainda possível enviar um Embaixador para Lisboa, devido à falta de funcionários daquela categoria – mas foi forçado a admitir que em breve partiria um novo Embaixador para a Índia (Documento N.º 372).

É interessante notar que foram enviados a O'Sullivan, após a sua primeira conversa com Franco Nogueira, vários documentos explicando a posição oficial irlandesa em relação a Portugal (Documentos N.º 374 e 375). É impossível saber se esta acção foi determinada por um desejo de ver a posição de Dublin sobre a África portuguesa melhor explicada cada vez que as autoridades portuguesas a criticassem, ou pelo receio de ver mais um enviado a Lisboa convencido – mesmo que apenas em parte – pelos argumentos portugueses. Semelhante acção foi necessária após a conversa do Embaixador de Portugal em Dublin, António Alexandre de Rocha Fontes, com o *Taoiseach,* Jack Lynch (Documento N.º 387), que, aos olhos do DEA, não teria frisado suficientemente a posição – e a frustração – irlandesa em relação a Portugal.

Fecham o volume os ofícios lidando com a doença e morte de Salazar, por razões explicadas na Introdução.

---

[1] Denis B.O'Sullivan, nascido em 1921, e educado no University College, Dublin, entrou para o DEA em 1949, vindo do *Office of Public Works*. Foi Vice-Cônsul em São Francisco, Terceiro Secretário em Washington, e Vice-Cônsul-Geral em Nova Iorque. Após a sua estadia em Lisboa (1968-1975) foi ainda Cônsul-Geral em Hamburgo.

1962

293
Ofício, Embaixador irlandês em Washington DC ao Secretário-Geral do DEA: Washington DC, 2 de Janeiro de 1962[2]

CONFIDENTIAL

GOA

In the course of a conversation with Indian Ambassador Nehru, nephew of the Prime Minister, the subject of the Indian action in Goa arose.

I asked him if the incorporation of Goa into India might not mean, at some time, a limitation of the freedom of worship of the Christian Goans. He said that although India is not a Christian country and Portugal is, it is often overlooked that in point of numbers of Christians, India is a bigger Christian country than Portugal. The Christian population of India is 17 millions, more than the total population of Portugal.

India, Ambassador Nehru said, is a multi-racial country and the policy of the Government – he instanced Pondicherry – is to preserve the identity of the varieties of the population. This will happen in Goa. It will continue to preserve its cultural identity. What will not be permitted in Goa, as in the rest of India, is anti-Indian influence attempted by minorities. In India the Christians are a loyal and above-average educated body, proud of the fact that Christianity in India dates from the Christian Apostolic era. But foreign missionary activity is another matter. The experience of colonialism has been that European missionaries are often also European nationalists and they have acted as collaborating agents of imperialist aggrandisement. A distinction therefore is drawn between the fullest freedom of worship and religious education for Indian Christians and the limitation of freedom imposed by India on European countries to send missionaries into India.

---

[2] NAI, DEA, 305/271B Part II Goa and other Portuguese enclaves in India, 1960-1968.

The relics of St. Francis Xavier will be as safely protected in Goa now that it has been recovered to India as when it was administered as a colony by Portugal.

T. J. Kiernan

294
Ofício, Ministro Plenipotenciário irlandês em Lisboa ao Secretário-Geral do DEA: Lisboa, 8 de Janeiro de 1962[3]

CONFIDENTIAL

CURRENT POLITICAL SITUATION IN PORTUGAL

The manner in which the New Year's "Revolution" in Beja has been played up by the foreign press has inflated this incident beyond its actual dimensions and importance. While, if rumour is to be believed, the number of those involved in the attack on the Military Barracks may have been over 100, most of whom escaped, the incident was a repetition on a slightly larger scale of the attack on the Police Station at Almada (a Lisbon working class suburb, just across the Tagus, reputed to be "red" and the recruiting ground of the Beja attack) on 11th November, the eve of the recent "elections", in which one man was killed but which did not receive at all a proportionate publicity.

2. The newspapers likewise exaggerated their reports of the security measures imposed after the Beja incident. On 3rd January I drove through Beja returning from a few days' leave, and the only indications that anything unusual had occurred were that on the Beja side of each town through which I passed two Republican Guardsmen were on duty checking cars passing. As my car has a CD plate I was not, of course, stopped. Then, in Lisbon, the Police Guard normally on duty outside police stations has been provided with steel helmets and sub-machine guns, but so far the concrete shelters seen in France are lacking.

[3] NAI, DEA, 313/11I Confidential reports from Lisbon Legation, 1962.

3. That there has been something boiling under the surface for about ten days past has appeared from a number of incidents such as unexplained shootings of persons who, by their description, could be supporters of the opposition, and by arrests of known leaders of that opposition.

4. Just what the Beja attackers hoped to achieve is doubtful. It may be that they thought that the garrison would support them, which did not happen, or that their action would ultimately result in a snowball action, as in the case of Castro in Cuba, which would finally upset the regime. While this might yet happen, I have great doubts that it will. As already reported, I am of opinion that while the régime has the support of the Army it will be practically impossible to upset it, and the only apparent possibility of a rift occurring in the present system would follow Dr. Salazar's relinquishing the Presidency of the Council, an event which is unlikely to occur of his own volition. In that event there could be great trouble here, as there is no obvious successor and the possibility of contending factions within the armed forces cannot be ruled out.

5. There seems to have been a decline in Dr. Salazar's popularity among the Portuguese public. Criticism – of a mild and discreet kind – is now heard where previously all was praise. In the not unlikely event of the seizure by a powerful neighbour of more of the Overseas Territories – Indonesia and Timor for example – his popularity could decline further, and he might even lose Army support.

6. During the week anti-British and anti-US demonstrations continued – stones and ink were thrown at the British Institute, "anti" posters appeared in the streets – and on 3rd January, when a large demonstration of protest was scheduled but cancelled because of Beja, considerable police forces were stationed in the vicinity of the British Embassy where trouble was expected. Presumably similar precautions were taken as regards the US Embassy but in any event there were no demonstrations.

7. During the week rumours were rife of a pending nationalisation of public utilities at present owned by British finance, e.g. telephones and tramways, and notices demanding such nationalisation have appeared in various parts of Lisbon. A campaign has also started sending, through the post, white feathers to prominent British subjects. One was sent to the British Ambassador's residence.

8. As of to-day, Thursday 4th January, the city appears to have regained its normal calm air, and the possibility of any trouble seems remote.

J. W. Lennon

295
Ofício, Ministro Plenipotenciário irlandês em Lisboa ao Secretário-Geral do DEA: Lisboa, 9 de Janeiro de 1962[4]

CONFIDENTIAL

PORTUGUESE FOREIGN POLICY

The speech delivered on behalf of Dr. Salazar to the National Assembly on 3rd instant (a copy of which is being forwarded separately) is of interest as a statement of current Portuguese foreign policy.

2. While the speech is largely concerned with India and the Goa issue, it treats also of Portugal's attitude towards her overseas territories generally, of her relations with other countries, principally Britain, US, Brazil and Spain, and her future policy vis-à-vis the UN.

3. In regard to the Portuguese overseas territories, Dr. Salazar confirmed that his policy is still of the "not an inch" variety […] Portugal will not negotiate surrender of any part of her possessions, but she is hardly in a position to defend them all – e.g. Timor. This is realised by the Portuguese themselves, and in my view they are reconciled to attacks on and ultimate loss of all territories except Angola and Mozambique. These they will defend to their utmost.

4. The attacks on the US and the hailing of Brazil and Spain, together with other South American states, as friends, are in keeping with the pattern over the past year. However, the attacks on the oldest ally, with particular reference to revision of the alliance, is a new departure. Anti-British feeling in Portugal is high. While the US is given some credit as an idealist, even if a very misguided one, no credit is seen for Britain. How far the anti-British spirit will be allowed proceed is

---

[4] NAI, DEA, 313/11I Confidential reports from Lisbon Legation, 1962.

doubtful. My own view is that British investment and interests in Portugal are such that it won't go too far.

5. The UN policy declaration is also in accord with the general pattern over the past year. Dr. Salazar made it clear that he visualises the Organisation as something which should come to Portugal's assistance, and if it doesn't, he has no use for it. His threat to leave is, I think, genuine, but unless some other country takes the lead, Portugal will probably stay in. His references to Charter revision are very general. I shall try to obtain some information on the type of revision which Portugal has in mind.

6. The final sentence – particularly the final phrase – of the speech has caused much comment and much speculation amongst the people. Just what does Dr. Salazar mean by "that (the Nation) should live on in its heart is small consolation, but consolation nevertheless, for those of us who would wish to die with it"? It has been suggested that he visualises a last stand like that of Nazism in the Berlin bunkers, and that, if his policies don't succeed, he will bring the country down with him.

7. The address has been criticised as being simply a statement of what everyone already knows and having no suggestions or hope for a better future. There would appear to be a marked decline in the popularity of Dr. Salazar amongst the small part of the population politically conscious.

J. W. Lennon

296
Ofício, Ministro Plenipotenciário irlandês em Lisboa ao Secretário-Geral do DEA: Lisboa 18 de Janeiro de 1962[5]

<u>CONFIDENTIAL</u>

<u>POLITICAL SITUATION IN PORTUGAL</u>

A complete calm has descended on Portugal – in any event on Lisbon. The normal political atmosphere has, on the surface, been re-established, but the impression persists that all is not as settled as it seems.

---

[5] NAI, DEA, 313/11I Confidential reports from Lisbon Legation, 1962.

2. The Beja incident has been followed by arrests and refugees seeking asylum in various diplomatic missions. Such events are not reported in the press which incidentally did not refer to General Delgado's statement that he had organised the attack on the Barracks at Beja and had been in the vicinity when it took place. […] It was also heard that the President, Admiral Thomaz, wished to resign. There is some grain of truth in all these rumours, but just how large – or small – it is impossible to fathom. It seems that Dr. Salazar's popularity has received a considerable setback recently, and most people seem to be of opinion that by end of 1962 considerable changes may have occurred. This may be so, but as I have said several times, in my opinion such changes could not take place without Army consent.

[…]

J. W. Lennon

297
Telegrama, Hibernia (Madrid) para Estero: Madrid, 17 de Janeiro de 1962[6]

5. Grateful for direction whether I should accept or attend Indian National Day Reception in view Goa hostile attitude here.

Hibernia

298
Telegrama, Estero para Hibernia: Dublin, 18 de Janeiro de 1962[7]

Your 5. You should accept as attendance does not imply agreement Goa action whereas refusal might imply disagreement.

Estero

---

[6] NAI, DEA, 305/271B Part II Goa and other Portuguese enclaves in India, 1960-1968.
[7] NAI, DEA, 305/271B Part II Goa and other Portuguese enclaves in India, 1960-1968.

299
Carta, Ministro Plenipotenciário irlandês em Lisboa ao Secretário-Geral do DEA: Lisboa, 20 de Janeiro de 1962[8]

CONFIDENTIAL

I have mentioned in previous reports a friend of mine – and Irish-American – Mr. John Reed whose Public Relations firm, George Peabody of New York, is utilised by the Portuguese SNI to advise them on presenting Portugal's aspect of tourism, colonialism, etc to the world. He called on me last evening, and the following is his view of the situation here. In assessing Mr. Reed's opinions it should be remembered that his contacts here are all Cabinet Ministers, heads of Government Departments and of the Armed services, and on occasions, Dr. Salazar himself.

2. Mr Reed was last here just before Christmas, and returned to New York on 15th December. Then came Goa. He was asked by the Portuguese authorities to go to India and if possible to Goa, to assess the position there and report to them. He arrived in India at the beginning of the month and went as far as the Goanese border, but was not admitted. Nevertheless his views on the position are interesting and well-informed. Goa has accepted integration into the Indian Union, and resistance by the Portuguese to the Indian invasion was negligible. While most Goans in Goa would perhaps have preferred the status quo because of better living conditions, there was nevertheless considerable anti-Portuguese feeling where one would least expect to find it – amongst the Goan Catholics. This was attributable to the Portuguese efforts to maintain control of the Church there – for political reasons – by appointing Portuguese bishops (under the Concordat with Rome this was possible), and while 99% of the priests were native Goanese, all bishops were Portuguese. This contrasted with India where the Cardinal is a Goanese. Another anti-Portuguese factor was that there was no education available in Goa in excess of primary school level – deliberate policy – and this forced Goans in search of higher education to go to India where they were

---

[8] NAI, DEA, 313/11I Confidential reports from Lisbon Legation, 1962.

welcomed and indoctrinated. It could be said without fear of contradiction that the many Goanese in India were anti-Portuguese.

3. The non-resistance by the Portuguese troops in Goa had weighed very heavily in Portuguese official circles. It is regarded as the greatest blot ever on Portugal's escutcheon. For more than three weeks past an Inter-Departmental Committee, consisting of the top men of most Departments have been sitting, originally with the objective of finding out what did happen in India, and when this was clarified, trying to decide how to explain the position to the Portuguese people, to whom Dr. Salazar promised a full statement and who had been filled with stories of heroic resistance etc. This Committee is in a dilemma, and the hard core of Salazarists apparently hope to maintain the fiction of resistance. The fate of the 3,000-odd Portuguese troops now prisoners in Goa means nothing to them, and one of their obsessions is that India wants not alone Goa, but also Mozambique.

4. Mr. Reed says that here in Metropolitan Portugal there are three main factions within Government circles. There is firstly the 100% pro-Salazar clique, composed of the representatives of big money, who are now definitely in the saddle and favour repressive measures. This clique has the full support of the 60,000 strong Republican Guard, a semi-military semi-police force, and of the conservative elements of the Army, which numbering about 100,000 has about 25,000 regulars, the balance being conscript. Then there is a liberal army group which attempted the first coup d'état last April, but which does not appear strong enough to achieve anything. The third, and to his mind most hopeful group, consisted of young liberal-minded members of the Government party who were working within that party to secure reform. If they fail, Portugal could be in for a very bad time. The Minister for Overseas Territories, Adriano Moreira, is rumoured as a leader in this group. In fact, according to recent rumour, he was already in prison.

5. Mr. Reed stressed the policy of dividing the armed forces between different Ministries – The Republican Guard with the Ministry of the Interior, the Ministries for Army, Navy and Air Force – and said that the important Ministry was the Ministry of the Interior, which controls also the Secret Police. At the moment the Republican Guard was the most important single item.

6. Asked what he considered to be the next most likely trouble-spot on Portuguese territory, Mr. Reed said that Portuguese circles expected, and hoped, that Guinea would be. Hoped, because they thought they could successfully resist any anti-Portuguese attacks there. They thought that two attacks would come simultaneously – from Senegal and the Republic of Guinea ex-French.

7. On the home front he expects the existing régime to continue for about a year, although the possibility of anti-régime demonstrations on a larger than ever scale in a few weeks' time cannot be discounted. These demonstrations may follow on a decree-law about to be published extending overseas Army duty fom two to four years. The main deciding factor at present was the allegiance of the Republican Guard which was stronger than the home army. However, unless a liberalisation of the régime – and the resignation or removal of Dr. Salazar – followed the efforts of the liberal-minded group at present within the Government – a blood-bath in Portugal could be expected.

8. I have written this report in haste and shall forward it in manuscript with my sons returning to Ireland on 22nd instant. May I ask, in view of apparent lack of security vis-à-vis Portugal that it not be circulated, or if circulation is considered desirable that it be edited in such a way as to ensure that the identity of my contact is kept secret.

J. W. Lennon

300

Ofício, Ministro Plenipotenciário irlandês em Lisboa ao Secretário-Geral do DEA: Lisboa, 2 de Fevereiro de 1962[9]

POLITICAL SITUATION IN PORTUGAL

Apart from a demonstration held in Oporto a few days ago calling for the release of political prisoners, Portugal appears to have relapsed into a state of calm – even apathy. Rumours continue to circulate involving the health of Dr.

---

[9] NAI, DEA, 313/11I Confidential reports from Lisbon Legation, 1962.

Salazar and hinting at liberal tendencies in Government circles which could show themselves at any time.

2. While the agreement reached with India regarding repatriation of prisoners from Goa would appear to be a gain for liberal thought in ruling circles, there is no indication of any change in policy either at home or abroad. "Not an inch" is still the attitude and the UN continues to be the bête noire, derided at every opportunity.

3. The anti-British campaign has died down. No longer does one see the posters presenting the record of British atrocities. An extreme-right journal presented a "poem" featuring the Queen of England which caused a protest by the British Ambassador to the Foreign Minister. The latter is reported to have said that things had gone much further than was intended. During the height of the anti-British campaign, the British Embassy circulated a note to all their citizens here informing them of the British line in the Goa incident and calling on them to follow this line.

4. The reported remark by the Foreign Minister in reply to the British representations reflects the general belief of the origin of such demonstrations. There is little doubt that they are organised officially even though this would be strenuously denied by official circles. About two weeks ago at a lunch for the Lisbon Foreign Press Association the Foreign Minister was asked whether the Government approved of the anti-British anti-American campaign in the newspapers. He replied that the position taken by the press was its own, and not that of the Government. This, in a country where the newspapers carry a statement of the number of pages in each issue and that it was seen by the Censorship Commission.

5. Following their annual meeting towards the end of last month, the Portuguese Episcopacy issued a "note" which, inter-alia, criticised, indirectly, social conditions in Portugal. It said that society must be founded on Truth, Justice, Right, Liberty and Peace, and called on the youth of the country to collaborate in making Portugal richer, more human and more Christian. They should devote themselves to "…the fair distribution of the country's revenue, putting the riches not at the service of only a few, but of all…" "The vast task

which Portugal awaits", it says, in another place, "that is to say economic social, moral, religious and missionary development, demands the union and collaboration of all Portuguese of good will".

6. In conclusion, it is, perhaps, interesting to know that many Portuguese of liberal tendencies regard the UN resolution on Angola as impracticable from many viewpoints. How, for example, could a people as backward as the Angolans be educated in any reasonable period of time to enable them to govern themselves, and how could the Government sponsor in Angola a much more liberal regime than that existing in the Metropole?

J. W. Lennon

301
Ofício, Ministro Plenipotenciário irlandês em Lisboa ao Secretário-Geral do DEA: Lisboa, 13 de Fevereiro de 1962[10]

CONFIDENTIAL

PORTUGAL'S AFRICAN POLICY

The basic factor of Portugal's African policy is to hold on to the African territories – particularly Angola and Mozambique – at no matter what cost. Danger to Portugal's retention of these territories arises, in Portuguese opinion, from two main sources – firstly the "misguided" nationalism-idealism which is typified by the UN and USA, and secondly greed of neighbours leading them to aspire to supplanting Portugal as occupant of these vast and rich territories.

2. To consider first the "nationalist" danger, Portugal denies that there is any native nationalist movement in her territories, that such anti-Portuguese movements as exist are Communist-inspired, and that the Communist aims are being furthered unwillingly by the naïve idealism of the UN and USA. The authorities here will not admit that the natives of these territories have any cause for complaint and deny all charges of oppression, forced labour etc brought

---

[10] NAI, DEA, 313/11I Confidential reports from Lisbon Legation, 1962.

against them, notwithstanding any evidence put forward in support of such charges. They point out, with justification, that Portugal has done as much as any other European power to further the material well-being of their African territories and that if they left, the result would be chaos. They see no condemnation of their policy in the facts that compared with what has been taken out, that which has been put in is extremely small, or that, after over 400 years of Portuguese occupation, the vast majority of the natives are no further advanced than when the Portuguese arrived in Africa.

3. There are, of course, anti-Portuguese irredentist movements in the states bordering Portuguese territory in Africa, due largely to the manner in which Africa was divided between the colonial powers without reference to natural or tribal boundaries, with the result that parts of tribes are now independent while other parts are still under foreign rule. Thus it seems that Portuguese Guinea will almost certainly be absorbed ultimately by either Guiné ex-Française or Senegal – or both. However, it seems that that Portuguese main fear for their African territories, but not in the immediate future, rests in the possibility of India casting her eyes on Mozambique as an outlet for her surplus and growing population. This explains to some extent the strong line being taken in regard to the Indians interned post-Goa in Mozambique and other territories. Portugal is adamant that they must leave [...]

4. Portugal's African policy is leading her into alliances with strange friends having regard to her often-stated multi-racial ideal. Thus the Rhodesia of Sir Roy Welensky and South Africa are rapidly becoming Portugal's strongest – if not only – allies in Africa. This development is showing itself principally in visits to Portugal or to the African territories of Ministers and officials of Rhodesia and South Africa, and to a growing conviction amongst a section of the people that the future of Portugal as an African power rests in an alliance with these two neighbours, even though they see a possibility that ultimately the neighbours might oust Portugal.

[...]

J. W. Lennon

302
Ofício, Ministro Plenipotenciário irlandês em Lisboa ao Secretário-Geral do DEA: Lisboa, 20 de Fevereiro de 1962[11]

Mr. Ronan's letter of 13th instant with enclosed copy of *New York Times* article dated 12th January 1962. [sic]

In my opinion the writer of this article has built his entire case on the rumours current here at the time that the Portuguese authorities were endeavouring to conclude an anti-Indian alliance with China and had despatched a former Foreign Minister, Dr. Paulo Cunha, to the East with that intention [...]

2. The Formosa authorities have paid some attention to the possibility, however. The Chinese Minister here tells me that, on instructions, he approached Dr. Franco Nogueira, the Foreign Minister, in the matter. The letter denied that such an arrangement was a possibility, and the Chinese authorities accept this denial. They see no future for Portugal in recognising the Pekin [sic] régime. The only objective such recognition could have, in their view, is that, as a quid pro quo, Portuguese claims to Macau are recognised by Pekin, and Formosa thinks that, if and when it suits Pekin to take Macau, they will do so, recognition or not. A Portuguese-Pekin anti-Indian alliance over Goa is impossible, according to the Nationalist Chinese, as Pekin had in the past pronounced on many occasions in favour of India taking Goa.

3. The writer of the *New York Times* article refers to Portugal as an overwhelmingly... "Roman Catholic nation". It isn't. Perhaps 20% of the population is Catholic, the rest nothing. In the event of a show-down here, religion would have relatively little say – economic factors would be much more important. As I have stated in several previous reports, the population of Portugal is divided into a small, very wealthy, ruling class, a large poor, or very poor, 90% of the people, and a very small middle class. The "opposition" is made up largely of this middle class, but, while they could be the Mensheviks of Portugal, in the event of a revolution here, the 90%, now largely submerged, would almost certainly

---

[11] NAI, DEA, 313/11I Confidential reports from Lisbon Legation, 1962.

become the Bolsheviks and take over. There is supposed to be a large well organised, but underground Communist Party here, working amongst this 90%. The possibility of there being a Communist-inspired revolution, and ultimately a Communist Government, seems to be admitted by many influential persons here – including the Foreign Minister.

4. In my view, however, a Portuguese Communist Government on its own, independent of events in Spain, is impossible, and this view is prevalent here. It is accepted that Spain, under a Franco-type régime, would intervene in Portugal to prevent Communism being established here.

5. This leads to consideration of another kite being flown in the Foreign Press recently, that of the possibility of an Iberian Federation. This is a more difficult matter to assess. Firstly it must be remembered that historically Portuguese-Spanish relations have been not unlike those between ourselves and Britain. Portugal during the centuries felt her independence menaced by her larger neighbour, in fact was conquered for a period, and has devoted much efforts to insisting on her "non-Spanishness". A Portuguese is quite insulted if mistaken for a Spaniard. Allowing for all this sentiment, there is no doubt that Portuguese-Spanish relations has [sic] become very close in recent years, and are becoming even closer. A new and accelerated phase of development in these relations was marked by the visit to Madrid in November last of the President of Portugal, and the strong support over the past year by Spain for Portugal's position in the UN.

6. […]

7. Nevertheless the impression obtains here that Spain's application for association with the Common Market surprised Portugal. A visit to Madrid last week by Dr. Correia de Oliveira, Minister for State and principal economic adviser to Dr. Salazar, was stated to be for discussions on tourism and television, but it is difficult to accept that a man of the Minister's standing would really interest himself in such matters.

8. In course of a conversation with Dr. Archer, Secretary General of the Foreign Office, I asked him if Spain's application would cause Portugal to move. He replied that Portugal would wait and see how Spain fared – he expected that

her application would have a difficult passage and might be refused, due largely to Belgian Socialist opposition, and this time there was no USA influence to push Spain's application as there had been in the OEEC.

J. W. Lennon

303
Ofício, Ministro Plenipotenciário irlandês em Lisboa ao Secretário-Geral do DEA: Lisboa, 12 de Março de 1962[12]

CONFIDENTIAL

POLITICAL SITUATION IN PORTUGAL

There have been no apparent developments in the situation here in recent weeks – events have followed the well-established, familiar, pattern of political arrests, asylum being sought in foreign diplomatic missions (neither of these is ever reported in the local Press), attacks on the US, the UN, the Indian Union and support of Spanish, South African and Welensky policies.

2. Goa has almost reached the stage of being forgotten, notwithstanding official policy of resurrecting the corpse at every available opportunity – as for example naming three Caravelle planes just purchased by TAP after the Indian territories [...] According to local reports – oral, of course – one prominent internee who will not return is the former Governor of Goa. Instead, as he would, it seems, face a court martial for disobedience of the order to resist, he will seek asylum in Brasil [sic].

3. So far as one can gather, the US is holding off in the matter of the Azores bases, the lease of which expires very soon. Opinion among the greater part of local Americans favours a tough line, on the grounds that Portugal and the Azores need the US more than the US needs them, but they feel that military opinion in Washington will let them down

[...]

J. W. Lennon

---

[12] NAI, DEA, 313/11I Confidential reports from Lisbon Legation, 1962.

304
Ofício, Ministro Plenipotenciário irlandês em Lisboa ao Secretário-Geral do DEA: Lisboa, 22 de Março de 1962[13]

CONFIDENTIAL

The demonstration of 8th instant in Oporto, to which I have already referred, was referred to in the local press but was played down, the impression being given that it was small and a failure. However, I have been informed by a completely reliable eye-witness that it was almost as large as that of 31st January and finished at, after several hours, 10 p.m. only because it was washed out by a violent rain storm. Hundreds of steel-helmeted police and two water-jet tanks were on duty ready to intervene at any moment. Nevertheless the size and duration of the demonstration were not the most significant factors. Priority in significance must be reserved for the fact that the demonstration was, unlike that of 31st January, Communist-sponsored and organised. Several days before the demonstration my informant was notified in a round-about manner by the Communist underground that the demonstration was being organised, that it would be composed largely of women and that the 8th March was selected because that was Woman's Day in the Soviet Union. He discreetly checked this information with the local police authorities, and found that they were aware of the plans and were taking steps to prevent them being implemented. On the day and time scheduled for the demonstration he took an advantageous view-point at the appointed place. Large numbers of police were in evidence, a considerable crowd of spectators but apparently no demonstrators. These, however, in accordance with an obviously well-prepared plan, trickled in small numbers at a given time, later than scheduled – from the spectators and from side streets into the large square fronting the Town Hall, sang the Portuguese national anthem, and commenced to mill around shouting anti-régime slogans and taunting the police. This went on for some time when, again obviously planned, the demonstrators divided into groups and by forcing their way across main traffic

---

[13] NAI, DEA, 313/11I Confidential reports from Lisbon Legation, 1962.

arteries, succeeded in introducing chaos into the city traffic. They then dispersed as quickly as they had assembled before reinforcements of police could arrive. Few arrests were made. The police remained on duty and the atmosphere was tense until the rain storm literally and figuratively dampened things. It seemed that the possibility of violence had not been overlooked by the demonstrators and scattered amongst the spectators on the periphery of the square were groups, who vanished with the demonstrators, that struck my informant as strong-arm men ready to stir up matters if required.

2. My informant has been notified by channels similar to those previously use [sic] that a Communist-led general strike will take place in Porto on 1st May, although strikes are not allowed in Portugal. He thinks that the strike and a demonstration will occur with perhaps fighting with the police, but does not think that this will be the commencement of a Revolution. This latter he thinks might very well come in late autumn.

3. I know that this informant has many friends amongst the non-Communist Opposition and he tells me that they are almost as much perturbed by the developments as are the Government.

J. W. Lennon

[Escrito à mão]: Note for confidential information:

The informant referred to is Mr. J. A. La Freniere, US Consul in Porto, who was stationed in Dublin up to 1957.

305
Ofício, Encarregado de Negócios *ad interim* irlandês em Lisboa ao Secretário-Geral do DEA: Lisboa, 3 de Maio de 1962[14]

CONFIDENTIAL

I have the honour to inform you that on the evening of Tuesday, May 1st, there were street manifestations in Lisbon organised by the Communist forces

---

[14] NAI, DEA, 313/11I Confidential reports from Lisbon Legation, 1962.

against the existing régime. These manifestations had long been expected and the authorities were well prepared for handling them. They began in the lower part of the town at the time of the normal closing of Government and business offices when there would usually be considerable crowds on the city pavements. A number of small groups acting in covert tried to excite the crowd by shouting anti-Salazar slogans and in some cases attacking the police. They indulged in a certain amount of stone throwing and smashing some shop fronts – there was apparently but little looting – and traffic signs. They got no popular support and at no time were the police not in control.

The occasion seems to have been a sort of dress rehearsal trial of strength staged by the local Communists who, for the first time came out into the open. I understand that they threaten a repetition for the 8th.

In the absence of a really free press it is not easy to get exact information on the subject but I gathered from eye witnesses that, on the whole, the manifestations were a fiasco. The police reaction was vigorous, but, I gather, not unduly violent. Indeed, I have heard the opinion that the incidents were a good thing for the police in so far as they showed them just what they might be up against in the future.

The night before the Guarda Nacional Republicana barracks at Aljustrel – near Beja, where there was a similar manifestation some months ago – were attacked with the result that two persons were killed and four wounded. It is all considered part of the same Communist-led plan to overthrow the régime by subverting the military if they can do so.

At the moment there is absolute quiet in Lisbon. I was dining with some friends last night – both Portuguese and foreigners – and the most notable feature of the evening was that not a word was uttered concerning the previous day's incidents, all the guests being genuinely far more interested in the Portuguese football victory over Madrid which gave them the European championship. People in this country are mad about football and I doubt if the attraction of any revolutionary movement would be sufficient to draw the crowds away from the Stadiums.

In view of the recent disturbances in the academic world it is interesting to note that there is no suggestion of the university students having had anything to do with these May Day demonstrations.

O'Kelly de Gallagh

306
Ofício, Encarregado de Negócios *ad interim* irlandês em Lisboa ao Secretário-Geral do DEA: Lisboa, 7 de Maio de 1962[15]

CONFIDENTIAL

Further to my brief report on the Communist disturbance of May 1st, I am now in a position to give you the following somewhat more detailed information:

During the day (May 1st) all large industrial plants in the Lisbon area were heavily guarded in case of trouble – the Sacor refinery was protected by armed men of the "Legião Portuguesa". There was no general strike in Oporto. In the later afternoon and evening Communist-dominated manifestations against the régime took place in Lisbon and Oporto. In both places the authorities has taken plenty of precautions and hundreds of police and Republican Guards were on hand at the principal squares [...] Although at times gun butts had to be used, as well as some tear-gas, and although shots were fired, the main deterrent used were tank-trucks filled with water heavily dyed with aniline blue to enable later identification. Many suits were stained and so were several buildings; quite a number of plate glass windows were smashed, some automobiles and a police patrol car were damaged.

The following day an official note was issued by the Ministry of the Interior saying that the Government had known for a long time about the Communist party's plans to disturb the peace on May 1st – but that, in fact, the intense Communist propaganda did not cause a stoppage of work anywhere [...]

The note says that at one time during the Lisbon manifestations, the authorities were fired upon and thus they had to use their firearms, the result

---

[15] NAI, DEA, 313/11I Confidential reports from Lisbon Legation, 1962.

being one civilian dead and 38 wounded. (S. José Hospital said several of the wounded had been shot through the legs).

[...]

Newspapers reveal that about 100 persons taking part in the Lisbon rioting were arrested by the police; among them are three foreigners (two Belgians, believed tourists, and an American visitor who came down from his hotel room to move his car away from a trouble spot). (Among those wounded by gun butts was an American correspondent, William T. Richards, of TIME AND LIFE. Mr. Richards was given five days to leave Portugal at the end of last March, but twice the authorities have given him an extra thirty days to remain here).

Looking through the list of persons who needed hospital treatment in Lisbon, one finds: an army officer, a guard of the Caxias prison, an agent of the International Police and Sr. Gois Motta, leader of the "Legião Portuguesa".

There were 34 persons wounded in Oporto – the strong display of police there prevented the demonstration from being as big as in Lisbon. It is estimated that not more than 10,000 persons were involved in Lisbon – that is to say formed the crowd. The activists were a very small fraction of that number.

O'Kelly de Gallagh

307
Ofício, Encarregado de Negócios *ad interim* irlandês em Lisboa ao Secretário-Geral do DEA: Lisboa, 5 de Junho de 1962[16]

CONFIDENTIAL

I have the honour to report that, on May 28th, led by General Mário Silva, the Army Minister, the leading officers of the Armed Services and many others (over 1,000), as well as the Ministers of Marine and of Interior, the Secretary for Aeronautics and two Under-Secretaries of State, met in the National Assembly building to pay their compliments and declare their loyalty to Dr. Salazar. This was

---

[16] NAI, DEA, 313/11I Confidential reports from Lisbon Legation, 1962.

done as part of the commemorations of the "National Revolution" of May 28th, 1926, which brought the present regime to power.[17]

G. O'Kelly de Gallagh

308
Ofício, Encarregado de Negócios *ad interim* irlandês em Lisboa ao Secretário-Geral do DEA: Lisboa, 5 de Junho de 1962[18]

CONFIDENTIAL

UNIVERSITY UNREST

I have the honour to report that in the late afternoon of May 31st, students of the Lisbon University tried to gather outside the Ministry of National Education wishing to hand in a manifesto to the Minister. However, they were not allowed near to the building and it is said that they were dispersed without violence. Some scuffling did take place on the side streets leading up to the Campo dos Mártires da Pátria. The manifesto was to request that their situation should be clarified before examinations were due to start the next day, June 1st.

Exams began on June 1st with the exception of the Faculty of Medicine where absenteeism was total. Normal attendance was reported at the other Faculties where exams were scheduled to start on that date. A spokesman of the students told a news agency "this does not mean that students have given up their demands for their rights to meet and to manage their own association." He added:- "It would be against our individual and mutual interests to cause most of the students to lose the better part of a year's work – for some it would mean the destruction of their careers". There are some poorer ones who work their way while attending university courses.

Students of the Faculty of Medicine, however, were inflamed by the attitude of their Council of Professors who strongly protested about the recent Government

---

[17] Inclui resumos dos discursos.
[18] NAI, DEA, 313/11I Confidential reports from Lisbon Legation, 1962.

decree which banned the students' associations and demanded the revoking of the decree. They will, however, be present when called for the second time to sit for their exams.

O'Kelly de Gallagh

309
Ofício, Encarregado de Negócios *ad interim* irlandês em Lisboa ao Secretário-Geral do DEA: Lisboa, 3 de Julho de 1962[19]

CONFIDENTIAL

With reference to Dean Rusk's visit to Lisbon on the 27th ult. I have found it very difficult to get any real line on the conversations he held with either Dr. Salazar or Dr. Franco Nogueira. Everybody who might possibly have been in the know seemed to clam up if the subject was mentioned. The great note of interrogation was, of course, the Azores. Did America ask for a renewal of the "lease"? Did Portugal put up the ante? It's anybody's guess, but my feeling is that, while that particular subject was not discussed in detail, Portugal made no advances and probably let it be understood the American approach to Portuguese issues would require a certain amount of overhauling before Portugal came across with anything. I have no doubt that in the end the two countries will come to an agreement, as it is in both their interests to do so. But a gesture of good will will certainly have to be made on the American side.

[…]

O'Kelly de Gallagh

---

[19] NAI, DEA, 313/11I Confidential reports from Lisbon Legation, 1962.

310
Ofício, Encarregado de Negócios *ad interim* irlandês em Lisboa ao Secretário-Geral do DEA: Lisboa, 10 de Setembro de 1962[20]

CONFIDENTIAL

[...]

The NEW YORK TIMES carried a front page article, with a Thysville-Congo dateline in which the description is given of a military training camp there for terrorists planning to attack Angola. The NEW YORK TIMES article does not reveal exactly where the camp is, but an official note from the Ministry of Foreign Affairs has been published to say the Portuguese Chargé d'Affaires in Leopoldville had seen Mr. Bomboko, the Congolese Minister of Foreign Affairs, about the Thysville military training camp story which first came to the light last week.

Mr. Bomboko stated that his government could not, for the moment, confirm nor deny the story – but he would shortly make an official declaration after the results of an investigation he had ordered were known.

The note says the Portuguese government cannot but find it strange how the Congo government "apparently fights with a lack of information" after so many days have passed and so much has been minutely described in the international press by correspondents who have visited it [...]

Since the above was written the Congo government's reply has been published. It is an amazing document, sidestepping the issue but claiming national sovereignty as a reason for refusing all information on the subject, and adding that the Congo would be betraying the "higher interests of humanity" if it remained neutral in face of the situation in Angola.

O'Kelly de Gallagh

---

[20] NAI, DEA, 313/11I Confidential reports from Lisbon Legation, 1962.

311
Ofício, Encarregado de Negócios *ad interim* irlandês em Lisboa ao Secretário-Geral do DEA: Lisboa, 11 de Setembro de 1962[21]

CONFIDENTIAL

I have the honour to inform you that on August 29th a communiqué was issued by the International Police (PIDE) stating that the so-called Portuguese Communist Party is following up instructions approved by the 22nd Congress of the Communist Party by attempting to maintain a state of permanent agitation in all the national territory.

It is already known, says the communiqué, that Álvaro Cunhal, Mário Pinto de Andrade, Marcelino dos Santos and a representative of Humberto Delgado, have reached an agreement whereby a programme has been worked out which would virtually hand over the Overseas Provinces – with total independence – to the organisations of these Communist elements and would create a popular republic in metropolitan Portugal.

In the course of its duty, the PIDE has recently made some arrests and from the investigations has found out that the Communist party is:

a) trying to establish cells for direct action, notably "patriotic juntas";
b) trying to infiltrate the Armed Forces and public security forces;
c) trying to capture the academic youth movement;
d) trying to induce persons of all tendencies to form a "national front".

The names and occupations of twenty-four persons who have been detained are then given (among them are four women and four students).

[...]

O'Kelly de Gallagh

---

[21] NAI, DEA, 313/11I Confidential reports from Lisbon Legation, 1962.

312
Ofício, Encarregado de Negócios *ad interim* irlandês em Lisboa ao Secretário-Geral do DEA: Lisboa, 26 de Novembro de 1962[22]

CONFIDENTIAL

I have the honour to inform you that I had breakfast this morning with a British Senior F.O. official to talk over his impressions of the six weeks' journey to Mozambique and Angola from which he has just returned.

He was quite cordial when I excused myself for thus coming to pick his brains and answered all my questions with complete frankness.

Though he did not find everything perfect his general impressions were good. He found the Portuguese claim of operating racial equality in their overseas territories substantiated "grosso modo". In what would correspond to our "national schools" there was complete equality, the number of negro children, as was to be expected, far outnumbering the whites. In the secondary schools, though the equality of treatment continued, the numerical ratios were reversed, the whites far outnumbering the blacks, but this must be largely due to the social-economic structure obtaining, most of the negroes not caring to cut off their wage-earning possibilities by prolonging school attendance. Furthermore, there being no university facilities in Angola, it is normally only the whites who would contemplate returning to Portugal to go through the university, for entry into which it would be necessary, as a preliminary, to go through the secondary stage.

In industry, the heads, indeed, the bulk of the foremen were whites. In the army he saw no negro officers though negro non-commissioned officers were far from rare. There are, as was to be expected, a great number of mullatoes. He did not observe any real racial antipathies and all were equal before the law.

In the past decade or so there has been a great social and industrial development and though this may have been stepped up by the impact of recent events it certainly predated them and there is no cause and effect relationship between them.

---

[22] NAI, DEA, 313/11I Confidential reports from Lisbon Legation, 1962.

He found it hard to say what was the extent, or indeed, the nature of the revolt of 1959. To talk of it being an Angolan national revolt is nonsense, because there is no Angolan nation. The tribe is there the social unit and the tribe is not interested in and has no grasp of "nationalism" in the European sense. To call the revolt a racial one of black versus whites might be true, inasmuch that the whole African cauldron is now a racial anti-white revolt. But there would seem to be little evidence of a spontaneous consciously national uprising to throw off the Portuguese yolk. Fairly widespread economic dissatisfaction, fanned and exploited by a fifth column from across the Congo frontier, was probably at the root of the trouble.

The official told me that he met with no suggestion of doubt or hesitation among the Portuguese authorities as to what their course should be in regard to their African territories. "J'y suis j'y reste" describes this attitude of mind and they appear to be utterly unimpressed by the hostility of sections of the United Nations. "Do the United Nations want another Congo in Angola and to create there a vacuum that Moscow would fill? We, at any rate, are not prepared to give it to them."

Their determination seems unshakeable. But they are undoubtedly fighting the present African Zeit Geist. He added, "Perhaps they are right. In ten or fifteen years we should know".

O'Kelly de Gallagh

N.B. The British official mentioned above is the British Ambassador Sir Archibald Ross, but I did not care to use his name in the body of the report as our conversation was obviously confidential and his name should not be mentioned in the matter.

313
Ofício, Primeiro Secretário da Representação Permanente da Irlanda junto das Nações Unidas ao Secretário-Geral do DEA:
Nova Iorque, 5 de Dezembro de 1962[23]

Portuguese Overseas Territories

1. Further to our report of 26 November on the question of the non-compliance of Portugal with Chapter 11 of the Charter and with General Assembly resolution 1542 (XV), the general debate of this subject has concluded in the Fourth Committee. Pending the tabling of a draft resolution it has been decided to take up the next item on the agenda, which consists of five items on Non-Self-Governing Territories appearing in the agenda of the General Assembly as items 49 to 53 inclusive [...]

19. As regards the final operative paragraph, dealing with the Security Council and the possibility of sanctions being adopted against Portugal, you will note that it is couched in qualified and fairly cautious terms.[24] It is considerably milder than the corresponding paragraph of the resolution on Apartheid adopted on 7th November, which "requests the Security Council to take appropriate measures, including sanctions, to secure South Africa's compliance with the resolutions of the General Assembly and of the Security Council on this subject and, if necessary, to consider action under Article 6 of the Charter". It should also be borne in mind that the situation in the Portuguese territories – at least in Angola – is much graver than the situation caused in South Africa by the existence of Apartheid. A racial war of a particularly brutal kind broke out in Angola and was only brought under control – if indeed it has been brought under

---

[23] NAI, DEA, Permanent Mission to the United Nations, X19, Portuguese overseas colonies, 1958-1965.

[24] Non-Compliance of the Government of Portugal with Chapter 11 of the Charter of the United Nations and with General Assembly Resolution 1542 (XV), paragraph 9: Requests the Security Council, in case the Portuguese Government refuses to put into execution the present resolution and former resolutions of the General Assembly, to take all appropriate measures including, if need be, the adoption of sanctions to secure Portugal's compliance with the present resolution.

control – by the adoption of full-scale military measures. Furthermore, it is doubtful if there exists in Portugal the same body of liberal opinion as that found in South Africa, and it is therefore difficult to argue that the adoption of sanctions would make it more difficult for a liberal nucleus to bring about any change for the better in Portuguese policy. For these reasons, and particularly in view of the qualified nature of the paragraph in question, it is submitted that we might consider the possibility of accepting or at least abstaining on that paragraph. As against this, there is the view, which we adopted in formulating our policy on the Apartheid resolution, that Assembly resolutions including provisions for sanctions are strictly speaking contrary to the United Nations Charter, since under the Charter enforcement action is the prerogative of the Security Council.

We shall keep you informed of events in this matter.

Taidgh O'Sullivan
For Permanent Representative

314
Ofício, Encarregado de Negócios *ad interim* irlandês em Lisboa ao Secretário-Geral do DEA: Lisboa, 13 de Dezembro de 1962[25]

CONFIDENTIAL

You will have seen in the press the news of the cabinet reshuffle achieved by Dr. Salazar on the 3rd inst. It is very comparable to the recent reshuffle of the British cabinet achieved by Harold Maxwell, though, from what I understand, the BBC broadcast of the 8th inst. did not seem to advert to the fact.

[…]

Compelling reasons for the changes remain obscure. There would appear to be no question of resignations, but simply of dismissals though the dismissals do not necessarily amount to "disgraces" as is evident by the fact of the high decorations conferred on a least two of the outgoing Ministers – General Mário

---

[25] NAI, DEA, 313/11I Confidential reports from Lisbon Legation, 1962.

Silva, Minister of the Army, and Prof. Adriano Moreira, Minister for Overseas Territories.

[...]

Salazar went on, "It is our conviction that we are defending Europe in the last redoubts where it can still be defended. This thesis may not be universally accepted, but as for ourselves we are in Africa defending what most immediately concerns us, namely Portugal." He spoke about the righs of Portugal and said that only the incongruity, the illogic and the confusion in which we live could explain the speeches made in high assemblies, against these rights. He said that Portugal had paid in blood and tears and treasure for her resistance in Africa and he felt that, as regards the Portuguese problem and the problems of colonialism in general, many are beginning to think again about their first reactions and to revise their judgements as to the manner in which they had first delivered themselves to the world at large. "Our attitude has alerted the general intelligence of civilised peoples and make [sic] them doubt the validity of the stand they first took. When this evolution of World thinking is over and the truth of that for which Portugal is fighting is made manifest – the progress of primitive peoples in the only manner in which such progress can be achieved – then the problem will be solved. The only thing to lament will be that the UN – if its still exists – will no longer be applauding the fiery speeches made against Portugal by many of its orators. Literature will have lost what the peace of the world will have finally gained."

O'Kelly de Gallagh

1963

315
Ofício, Encarregado de Negócios *ad interim* irlandês em Lisboa ao Secretário-Geral do DEA: Lisboa, 25 de Março de 1963[26]

I have the honour to inform you that Francis Cardinal Spellman, of New York, arrived here on the 14th inst. in one of thirteen specially chartered jet-aircraft which brought almost 1,000 American pilgrims for a short visit to Fátima while on their way to Rome. Cardinal Spellman, who was met upon his arrival by the Cardinal Patriarch of Lisbon and the Papal Nuncio, lunched at the American Embassy; he later was received by Dr. Salazar, then he called upon ex-King Humberto of Italy.

O'Kelly de Gallagh

316
Ofício, Encarregado de Negócios *ad interim* irlandês em Lisboa ao Secretário-Geral do DEA: Lisboa, 27 de Março de 1963[27]

CONFIDENTIAL

I have the honour to inform you that late at night on the 21st inst. it was announced a Council of Ministers had approved a report presented by the Minister for National Defence concerning the findings of a Joint Superior Council of the Army and Navy which had been set up to study the circumstances in which Goa was lost to India in December 1961. This Joint Superior Council was formed by eight generals and five admirals and it decided upon the military disciplinary sanctions to be taken and the awards to be conferred as a result of the Goa invasion campaign.

---

[26] NAI, DEA, 313/11J Confidential reports from Lisbon Legation, 1963.
[27] NAI, DEA, 313/11J Confidential reports from Lisbon Legation, 1963.

The decisions taken are:

That eight high-ranking officers of the Army and two officers of the Navy be dismissed from the Armed Services. The Army officers include General Manuel António Vassalo e Silva, the Governor-General of the former Portuguese State of India; Brigadier António José Martins Leitão, the military commander of Goa; Lt. Col. Mário Marques de Andrade, Chief of the High Command of the Headquarters of the Portuguese State of India; Major José Moreira da Silva Rangel de Almeida, group commander; and Major Fernando Alberto da Cunha Baptista de Lucena de Almeida, Governor of Diu. One of the naval officers is Sec. Lt. Manuel José Marques da Silva, commander of the launch SIRIUS. That four Army officers and one Navy officer be compulsorily retired. The Navy officer is Commodore Raul Viegas Ventura, the naval commandant of Goa. That eight Army officers and one Navy officer be placed in inactivity for six months.

All other military personnel are considered legally clear from any responsibility in the loss of Goa, Damão and Diu.

Following the above is a list of military units which are commended, and a long list of military men (Army and Navy) who are either commended, promoted and/or decorated.

O'Kelly de Gallagh

317
Carta, Representante Permanente da Irlanda junto das Nações Unidas ao Secretário-Geral do DEA: Nova Iorque, 26 de Abril de 1963[28]

Mr. O'Sullivan is reporting separately on the recent session of the Security Council held to deal with the dispute between Senegal and Portugal arising out of the firing of aerial rockets or other missiles at a Senegalese border village during recent military exercises in Portuguese Guinea.

---

[28] NAI, DEA, Permanent Mission to the United Nations, X31, Portugal, 1963-1965.

The dispute was to a large extent a storm in a teacup and Portugal has only herself to blame for the fact that the matter was brought before the Security Council at all. Nobody else at the United Nations has the slightest doubt but that the firing did take place, and Portugal was responsible for it. Everybody else agreed similarly that the incident was purely accidental. Portugal took the line, however, of denying the Senegalese charge flatly. She had only to admit the possibility that her planes might have fired at the Senegalese village due to a mistake which Portugal regretted – and the Senegalese case would have collapsed like a pack of cards.

As time goes on, delegations here at the United Nations are becoming more and more concerned at Portugal's intransigence in regard to everything connected with her African territories. The Acting Permanent Representative of Spain, Mr. Pinies, who is Chairman of the Committee on Information regarding Non-Self-Governing Territories, told me last night that his Government was really becoming seriously alarmed as to where Portugal's present policy is leading her. He told me that he had reason to believe that Dr. Salazar's Ministers – including the Foreign Minister, Mr. Nogueira – were becoming increasingly apprehensive, but that Dr. Salazar pays no more attention to the advice of his Ministers than President de Gaulle pays to his. Mr. Pinies told me that, in the hope of laying before Dr. Salazar a factual review of the dangers Portugal is facing and, perhaps, some suggestions as to how they might be averted, he had, with the approval of his Government, suggested to the Portuguese Government that he should pay a visit to Lisbon, in his capacity as Chairman of the Committee on Information, in the course of which he would be received by Dr. Salazar. He had discussed the suggestion beforehand with the African members of the Committee and they supported it strongly. The Portuguese Government, however, turned it down flatly. Mr. Pinies said he knew that the French, British and other Governments were doing their best to persuade Portugal to modify her intransigence, but she remained deaf to all appeals. Mr. Pinies said it seemed to him to be a case of those whom the gods wish to destroy, they first drive mad.

It now seems pretty certain that Portugal's colonial policies will be brought before the Security Council during the month of June when the President of the

Council will be Ambassador Quaison-Sackey of Ghana. The Security Council session is bound to be a very embarrassing one for countries like the United States, Britain and France which, although friendly to Portugal, are anxious to improve their relations with the new States of Africa.

F. H. Boland

318
Ofício, Encarregado de Negócios *ad interim* irlandês em Lisboa ao Secretário-Geral do DEA: Lisboa, 28 de Maio de 1963[29]

SALAZAR-FRANCO TALKS

I have the honour to inform you that at the close of the meeting of the Spanish Head of State and the Portuguese Prime Minister, at Mérida, Spain, on May 14-15 the following joint communiqué was issued:

"In the 24th year of the Peninsular Pact, which has been an instrument for peace, begetting prosperity and progress for Spain and Portugal, the Spanish Head of State, Generalissimo Francisco Franco, and the Portuguese President of the Council, Dr. Oliveira Salazar, met in the town of Mérida on the 14th and 15th of the current month of May. They were accompanied by the Foreign Ministers [...] and by the Ambassadors [...]

In the course of the two-day talks in which the international position was examined and the main problems of interest to Spain and Portugal were analysed, the perfect understanding and the vigorous solidarity of the two Peninsular peoples were again re-affirmed."

The meeting took the public by surprise and it is believed to have been suggested by Generalissimo Franco. Though no details of the conversations were published, the newspapers listed the topics which would necessarily fall under the heading of the main problems of interest to the two countries.

[...]

---

[29] NA, DEA, 313/11J Confidential reports from Lisbon Legation, 1963.

It is difficult to foresee what the more distant future reserves for both Spain and Portugal in relation to their African interests. The immediate future seems very ominous for both, though if the UN should not emerge, or only emerge crippled, from the crisis caused by the Russian financial default, the consequent continent-wide chaos in Africa might well leave Portugal as the only element of stability south of the Mediterranean. How long she could maintain that position would obviously depend on the Western powers and, to an equal extent, on the attitude adopted by the local natives in Mozambique and Angola. There appears, on the face of it, to be a probability of something like the Hundred Years War in Africa, and the ultimate upshot is anybody's guess.

As for the Addis Ababa proposed charter for a United Africa the feeling here is that such a charter is utterly premature, and that, taking into consideration the very varying degrees of immaturity of the various tribal agglomerations – in most cases it would be quite erroneous to speak of "nations" – which at present constitute "Darkest Africa" the implementation of such a charter would result first of all in imposing, through an appalling blood-bath, the Arab-Berber hegemony as in the old black-birding days, and secondly, in extending to the continent as a whole, the sanguinary chaos hitherto happily confined to the Congo – in which case the last state of Africa would be far worse than the first. Consequently it is felt that in all the circumstances the charter will have been still-born.

O'Kelly de Gallagh

319
Ofício, Encarregado de Negócios *ad interim* irlandês em Lisboa ao Secretário-Geral do DEA: Lisboa, 3 de Junho de 1963[30]

CONFIDENCIAL [sic]

I have the honour to inform you that a note has been issued by the International Police (PIDE) stating that since the arrests made at the end of

---

[30] NAI, DEA, Embassy Madrid, I.P. 4/51/1, Portugal 1941-1963.

January of the "Local Committee of the 'so-called' Portuguese Communist Party", it has closely followed investigations into subversive activities. This has resulted in the arrest, by a simultaneous action carried on in various places, of some leading members of the Party. The names of ten persons are given (among them three married couples) and several of them had been detained previously for subversive activities; two had escaped while under detention. Most of them were living with false identity papers.

The principal person arrested appears to be Fernando Augusto da Silva Blanqui Teixeira, a 41-year old chemical engineer, at whose home a considerable number of documents were seized. Some of these documents prove the close understanding between the Communist Party and "other elements of a different formation such as, by the way, the recent meeting which took place in Prague between Delgado and Communist leader Álvaro Cunhal."

In the home of another, some "MPLA" bulletins were discovered which were to be put on sale at Esc.2$50 each to help terrorist movements.

From statements made and the documents found, it has been possible to detain other persons in liberal professions and a civil servant who, because of their occupations, were able to assist the Communist Party without themselves being suspected.

<u>Note.</u> Incidentally, I have been informed by a German newspaper correspondent that ex-Colonel Otto Skorzeny, the man who at Hitler's orders rescued Mussolini in September 1941, from his prison at the Gran Sasso, was living in Spain. Skorzeny would be tracking down communist activities and he has been in Portugal this year.

The same informant stated that at the recent meeting between Franco and Dr. Salazar, they had discussed at length the question of communist infiltration in the Iberian Peninsula – and it would appear to be more serious in Portugal than in Spain. Franco, of course, would much dislike Spain to be threatened with active communism on her western marches. And so Otto Skorzeny may be used for the coordination of the fight against communism in the entire Peninsula.

O'Kelly de Gallagh

320
Ofício, Encarregado de Negócios *ad interim* irlandês em Lisboa ao Secretário-Geral do DEA: Lisboa, 12 de Junho de 1963[31]

CONFIDENTIAL

You will have seem from the British press reports that a suit-case exploded at the London airport some thirty minutes before the departure time of the Lisbon-bound TAP Caravelle on the 6th inst. This suit-case was among the other pieces of luggage about to be loaded onto the aircraft. From the first reports published in the Lisbon newspapers, it was suggested that perhaps a bottle of hair or face lotion had exploded as the suit-case was exposed to the sun. However, when further information became available from the British press, it became clear that some sort of a bomb had exploded in the suit-case. According to airport officials, if the explosion had taken place during flight, the results would have been disastrous. Because of the enquiries which had to be made at the London airport by Scotland Yard officials, the departure of the flight was held up for nearly four hours.

[...]

O'Kelly de Gallagh

321
Ofício, Encarregado de Negócios *ad interim* irlandês em Lisboa ao Secretário-Geral do DEA: Lisboa, 14 de Junho de 1963[32]

I have the honour to inform you that, as I indicated would be the case in the last paragraph of my minute 6/18 of the 11th inst., the Cardinal Patriarch of Lisbon, His Eminence D. Manuel Gonçalves Cerejeira, left Lisbon by air at noon on Monday the 10th. Also, as indicated in the same minute, he was accorded the quite unprecedented homage of the Military honours hitherto exclusively reserved

---
[31] NAI, DEA, 313/11J Confidential reports from Lisbon Legation, 1963.
[32] NAI, DEA, 313/11J Confidential reports from Lisbon Legation, 1963.

for the President of the Republic. He was met at the airport by a representative of the President and a representative of Dr. Salazar, as well as by, inter alia, the Minister of Foreign Affairs and of Justice; and, of course, by the heads of numerous – though not all – diplomatic missions. Among the latter the general opinion was that this new departure from established protocol was not a happy one – indeed that it was unnecessary and pointless. We had never been "mobilised" before on the departure of the Cardinal and the suggestion was tentatively put forward that all this was intended to add to the Cardinal's prestige in Rome for whatever purpose Dr. Salazar may have in mind – such as, for instance, the election of a Sovereign Pontiff who would be sound (from the Portuguese point of view) in African problems – consequently not Montini.

[...]

I append a list published in this morning's paper on the personalities who came to wish him God speed. It is an impressive one and is an evidence of very competent orchestration.

O'Kelly de Gallagh

322
Ofício, Encarregado de Negócios *ad interim* irlandês em Lisboa ao Secretário-Geral do DEA: Lisboa, 3 de Julho de 1963[33]

In the course of a conversation yesterday with Dr. Fragoso, head of the Political Section at the Portuguese Foreign Affairs, President Américo Thomaz's projected visit to Angola in September was mentioned and Dr. Fragoso took the occasion to state that the military position in Angola was well in hand and that the visit should be a great success. A priori, it would certainly seem that things must have quietened down a great deal if the Authorities are prepared to let the President visit the country. In this connexion it is interesting to note the comments

---

[33] NAI, DEA, Permanent Mission to the United Nations, X20, Portuguese Overseas Territories, 1963-1965.

in an editorial article in the *Diário de Notícias* of June 29th captioned "Portugal does not desist". The article says, inter alia, "the conclusion reached – and friend and foes alike must reach it – is simply that Portugal does not desist. We have said time and again, and shall say it as long as it is necessary so that all may hear it: Portugal is also an African country. We are in Africa, we whites from Europe, with the same rights that the Canadians have to occupy Canada, the Americans to occupy the United States and the Australians to occupy Australia". The analogy is perhaps a little laboured and would be more telling if the *Diário de Notícias* were published in Luanda instead of Lisbon.

O'Kelly de Gallagh

323

Ofício, Encarregado de Negócios *ad interim* irlandês em Lisboa ao Secretário-Geral do DEA: Lisboa, 4 de Julho de 1963[34]

CONFIDENTIAL

I have the honour to inform you that I sat next to the Moroccan Chargé d'Affaires at the monthly Heads of Mission lunch to-day.

[...]

II) On the issue of Angola he volunteered the opinion, which I have long held, that there was no real demand for independence in Angola itself. The vast majority of the Angolans were quite indifferent to the question and the whole agitation was manifestly worked up from abroad. To my question as to what he thought would happen should the Portuguese withdraw completely from Angola, he replied that that would mean chaos – another Congo – but that there should be no question of such a total withdrawal on the part of the Portuguese. What the latter should do to conform to present pan-African sentiment, was to accord independence to Angola while remaining very much "present" administratively, economically and even militarily in some such manner as the

---

[34] NAI, DEA, 313/11J Confidential reports from Lisbon Legation, 1963.

French had managed to do in the case of their ex-colonies in Africa. He seemed to think that this was a feasible proposition.

[...]

VI) On the question of training Africans for administrative work – this not in connection with Morocco at all – he estimated that it would take at least fifteen years to create the frame-work of a civil service to carry on the work of Government in countries abandoned by the whites. On my suggesting that it would take very much longer because of the rudimentary degree of civic evolution in the homes and families from which such a civil service would necessarily be recruited – it is a long, long step – several generations long – from tribal absolutism-cum-anarchy to representative democratic Government – he said that of course the spread of popular education was the crux of the matter, and that they had realised that fact so acutely in Morocco, at all events, that education today accounted for some 28% of the Moroccan national budget – a proportion which he claimed to be the highest in the world.

O'Kelly de Gallagh

324
Ofício, Encarregado de Negócios *ad interim* irlandês em Lisboa ao Secretário-Geral do DEA: Lisboa, 5 de Julho de 1963[35]

CONFIDENTIAL

With further reference to the implementation of the anti-Portuguese resolutions of the recent Addis Ababa conference by various African States, I have the honour to inform you – though you will doubtless already have seen it in the Press – that H.E. Ahmadu Abidjo, President of the Republic of the Cameroons [sic] has announced to a Press Conference in Yaunda the decision of his Government

---

[35] NAI, DEA, Permanent Mission to the United Nations, X20, Portuguese Overseas Territories, 1963-1965.

to deny to Portuguese and South African ships and aeroplanes access to Cameroon ports and airfields.

He further announced the severance of diplomatic relations with Portugal and with South Africa and the prohibition of all commercial exchanges with these two countries. He added that his Government desired their expulsion from the UN.

Questioned on the above statement, a spokesman of the Portuguese F.O. commented that there are not now and never have been diplomatic or consular relations between Portugal and the Cameroon Republic:

"There does not now exist, nor has there ever existed and Portuguese Embassy, Legation or Consulate, even honourary, in Cameroon territory. It is therefore difficult to understand how the Cameroon Government proposes to implement its decision.

While it would appear that South African interests in the Cameroons have been confided to France, Portuguese interests in the Cameroons have been confided to nobody for the simple reason that in the Cameroons Portugal has no interests, political, commercial or other.

As for the denial of port and airfield facilities to Portuguese shipping and aeroplanes, there is no record of a Portuguese ship or plane ever touching Cameroon soil – except, of course, in the case of Portuguese ships who may have touched these during the historic epoc [sic] of the "descobrimentos".

It seems clear, therefore, that the Cameroon gesture is one of pure demagogy to give the appearance of implementing resolutions which are unimplementable."

O'Kelly de Gallagh

325
Ofício, Encarregado de Negócios *ad interim* irlandês em Lisboa ao Secretário-Geral do DEA: Lisboa, 11 de Julho de 1963[36]

CONFIDENTIAL

With reference to the severance of diplomatic relations between Portugal and Ethiopia, I have the honour to send you herewith – in translation – the following documents:[37]

A) The Portuguese Foreign Office Communiqué of Saturday the 6th July announcing the severance of diplomatic relations.
B) The letter from the Emperor Hailé Sellassié I to Dr. Salazar, calling upon Portugal to grant immediate independence to Angola and Mozambique.
C) The reply of Dr. Salazar. In places it is involved and obscure, but, as I have said before in a previous report, these two qualities are characteristic of the Doctor's prose, and are even admired.
D) A leading article from the *Diário de Notícias* of the 8th instant dealing with the situation [...]

The Emperor's letter is curious. It is very short and four-fifths of it is devoted to throwing bouquets at Portugal. Indeed it is only in the last paragraph that the tone changes to convey a veritable ultimatum.

In the circumstances Salazar's reply is certainly the soft answer intended to turn away wrath. It failed of its purpose, but is interesting as a declaration of faith by Dr. Salazar and as a résumé of the Portuguese-Ethiopian relations throughout the centuries. It is, factually, completely unanswerable but the ageing Doctor was naïve in not realising, what every budding diplomat could have told him, that it is a mistake to put up an unanswerable case which, by definition, never gets an answer and, of course, he got none.

[...]

O'Kelly de Gallagh

---

[36] NAI, DEA, 313/11J Confidential reports from Lisbon Legation, 1963.
[37] Incluídos com o ofício.

326
Ofício, Encarregado de Negócios *ad interim* irlandês em Lisboa ao Secretário-Geral do DEA: Lisboa, 16 de Julho de 1963[38]

CONFIDENTIAL

I have the honour to inform you that the Ministry of Foreign Affairs issued an official Note to the effect that on June 28th last, the Leopoldville Government had made public its decision not to recognise the Portuguese Government as the legitimate representative of Angola, but to recognise "de jure" a group residing in that city – group led by foreigners and also paid by foreign interests, i.e. non--Africans.

The Portuguese Chargé d'Affaires in Leopoldville was instructed to communicate to the Congolese Prime Minister that the Portuguese Government considered this decision as inadmissible and, in consequence, would be obliged to take such measures as it judged appropriate.

The Chargé d'Affaires was only able to make this communication to the Prime Minister on July 8th, because of the dilatory methods used by the Congolese services.

Following the instructions given him the Portuguese Chargé d'Affaires left Leopoldville on July 9th, having left the chancery building and its administration in the charge of the secretaries on duty there.

The basis upon which the Congolese decision is founded being unacceptable, the Portuguese Government wishes to add – and this was also pointed out to the Congolese Prime Minister – that it finds itself obliged to proceed with a general revision of its attitude towards problems which interest both countries.

Meanwhile, Leopoldville cables report quarrels between different Angola freedom movements […]

O'Kelly de Gallagh

---

[38] NAI, DEA, 313/11J Confidential reports from Lisbon Legation, 1963.

327
Ofício, Encarregado de Negócios *ad interim* irlandês em Lisboa ao Secretário-Geral do DEA: Lisboa, 16 de Julho de 1963[39]

CONFIDENTIAL

I have the honour to inform you that quite a batch of arrests have recently been made here, for reasons which can only be political. I have seen no mention of them in the press. It is believed that twenty-seven persons in all have been detained. I append hereto the names of such as I have been able to ascertain to indicate type of the arrestees.

[...seis médicos; um advogado; um arquitecto; um cientista; um funcionário bancário; um membro da delegação junto da FAO...]

It is striking how many of the disaffected seem to belong to the professional classes – lawyers, doctors etc. In this connexion it is just as well to remember that – other considerations apart – these are the classes who, because of their superior education in a country largely illiterate, more or less ran that country, to their own very pronounced advantage, before the arrival of Salazar on the scene. They still, as a class, consider him an interfering spoil-sport and cannot forgive him for having turned the maggots out of the national cheese.

O'Kelly de Gallagh

328
Encarregado de Negócios *ad interim* da Representação Permanente irlandesa junto das Nações Unidas ao Secretário-Geral do DEA: Nova Iorque, 1 de Agosto de 1963[40]

PORTUGUESE OVERSEAS TERRITORIES

The Security Council yesterday concluded its consideration of the situation in the Portuguese Territories with the adoption of a resolution contained in

---

[39] NAI, DEA, 313/11J Confidential reports from Lisbon Legation, 1963.

[40] NAI, DEA, Permanent Mission to the United Nations, X20, Portuguese Overseas Territories, 1963-1965.

document S/5380 attached thereto. The resolution was adopted by 8 votes to none, with 3 abstentions, Britain, France, and the United States.

The debate was remarkable for the seriousness and moderation displayed by all speakers, with the exception of the Soviet representative, and was in marked contrast to the last debate in the Council on Portuguese colonial problems, the border dispute between Senegal and Portuguese Guinea, which few delegates took seriously and which was regarded by many as a rehearsal for the future discussion of colonial problems in the Council.

The Foreign Ministers of Liberia, Tunisia and Sierra Leone, and the Minister for Finance of Madagascar, presented the African case to the Council after lengthy preparation which had gone on since the Addis Ababa Conference. Since the verbatim record of the meetings has been airmailed to you, I do not propose to attempt to repeat here the views expressed in the debate by any of the speakers. The general impression created by the African speeches was that they were remarkable for their restraint, particularly in view of the history of African action on colonial problems in the Fourth Committee and the Committee on Colonialism during the past two years. The only African statement which tended to be extremist was that of Ambassador Quaison-Sackey of Ghana, who called among other things for the suspension of Portugal. This speech was looked upon as representing the ultimate in the African position, and it was expected that during the negotiations there would be a substantial retreat from that position as set out by Ghana. This in fact proved to be the case.

The statements made by the Portuguese Foreign Minister, Dr. Franco Nogueira, were also remarkable for their reasoned and persuasive tone and attracted a good deal of favourable comment, even among some African representatives. While it was of course realised by everyone that they represented an intransigent policy which offered no hope of negotiation, it was generally acknowledged that, given this position and acknowledging the impassible [sic] gulf between the Portuguese and African positions, Dr. Nogueira had put forward his country's point of view with the utmost moderation and effectiveness. There were many comparisons made between his attitude and that of the South African Foreign Minister, Dr. Loew, and it was generally felt that Dr. Nogueira's method of dealing with the United Nations was far more effective than that of his South African colleague. Apart from the contrast in personalities (which in Dr. Nogueira's case was remarkably illustrated by his personal good relations with the African diplomats) there is of course the contrast between the policies of the two countries. South Africa, in pursuance of its Apartheid policy, inclines more and more towards boycotting UN meetings and is expected eventually to leave the Organization altogether, whereas Portugal still seeks to persuade international opinion of the validity of her policy of setting up a multi-racial society in the "overseas provinces" of Portugal.

Two main points stood out in the policy pursued by the African delegations during the debate: their insistence on the acknowledgement by Portugal of the principle of self-determination in the Portuguese territories and their desire that the supply of armaments to Portugal by her NATO allies should cease. Although NATO, as might be expected, came under heavy fire, the Africans nevertheless refrained from too bitter an attack on the NATO powers in this matter, which to them is the crucial difficulty in liberating the Portuguese colonies, since they feel that the NATO arms supplied to Portugal, even if they are not actually used in the colonies, nevertheless make it possible for Portugal to release other weapons for use against rebels in Angola and Portuguese Guinea. The only full-scale attack on NATO came from the Soviet representative, Mr. Fedorenko, who weakened his case by extending it to an attack on the Common Market. We were told afterwards by African colleagues that this Russian statement was "hardly relevant to the proceedings", and one remarkable feature of the debate as a whole was the lack of lobbying or other diplomatic activity by the Soviet delegation, which took part in no negotiations to our knowledge and had no influence on the final result.

It was clear from the beginning of the proceedings that there was very little hope of any rapprochement of the African and Portuguese positions, and in fact the Portuguese Foreign Minister confined himself to stating his Government's policy and took no part in negotiations. The moderate trend of the African speeches encouraged Western members of the Council, particularly the United States, to work for the adoption of a generally acceptable resolution, and hopes that this might come about were increased when the draft resolution which had been prepared by the African Foreign Ministers were tabled on their behalf by Ghana, Morocco and the Philippines on 26 July. The text, which appears on S/5372, was much more moderate than expected and followed fairly closely the lines of resolution 1807 adopted by the General Assembly at its last session.

[...]

The net effect of the adoption of this resolution is that the Africans have now succeeded in getting the Council to make recommendations to Member States similar to those made by the General Assembly in resolution 1807 (XVII). These recommendations were originally contained in the report made to the Seventeenth Session by the Special Committee on Territories under Portuguese Administration. A comparison of the text of the resolution now adopted with the text of General Assembly Resolution 1807 (XVII) shows that paragraph five of the Council resolution is to all intents and purposes identical with paragraph four of the Assembly resolution, which contained the Committee's recommendations. The same applies to the contents of paragraph six of the Council resolution and paragraph seven of the Assembly resolution, which deal in almost identical terms with the problem of the sale and supply of arms and military equipment to the Portuguese Government.

The Africans have thus achieved a small but definite advance in the direction of UN action against Portugal. Due to their failure to muster seven votes in the Security Council they did not succeed in pushing this advance as far as chapter VII of the Charter. Had they succeeded in getting seven votes, Britain or France, or both, would have exercised their veto.

The result is a matter of some satisfaction on all sides, for very different reasons. The Africans, though many of them deny it, are quite happy about the modest progress achieved. The British delegation has reason for satisfaction in that the United States finally sided with Britain and France in the vote. The Norwegians are particularly happy that the course of the negotiations placed them in a position where their membership of NATO did not prevent them from breaking with Britain, France and the United States and adopting a more liberal attitude in the vote. The present minority Labour Government in Norway depends for support on a left-wing splinter group which has two votes and is in a position to embarrass the Government considerably when Norway votes in the United Nations on NATO lines [...]

Washington's attitude was regarded by many delegates here as a personal blow to Governor Stevenson, who had hoped to move American policy along more liberal lines. His explanation of vote was couched in language which would have been more appropriate from a delegation which had voted for the resolution than from a delegation which had abstained on the vote (see Document S/PB.1049). However, even the British and French representatives in explaining their abstention also made it clear that they favoured the principle of self--determination for the Portuguese territories and that their abstention was essentially due to objections to the language used in certain paragraphs.

The final paragraph in the resolution requests the Secretary General to ensure the implementation of its provisions, to furnish such assistance as he may deem necessary and to report to the Security Council by 31 October 1963. Ambassador Quaison-Sackey of Ghana, whose statements throughout were regarded as an index of African tactical intentions, ended his final statements by a reference to the Secretary General's report in which he said: "we hope that this will be produced before October so that the Council may meet once again if at that time the Government of Portugal has not yet accorded the principle of self--determination to its peoples and its territories."

Since it is highly unlikely that the Government of Portugal will do anything of the kind, and barring any fresh approach to the problem by the Africans, it looks as if the Council will take up this subject again late this year.

The Council, having adopted this resolution, moved on immediately to the even more difficult question of Apartheid [...]

Tadgh O'Sullivan

329
Do Ministro dos Negócios Estrangeiros irlandês ao Secretário-Geral das Nações Unidas (U Thant): Dublin, 25 de Setembro de 1963[41]

The Minister for External Affairs of Ireland presents his compliments to the Secretary-General of the United Nations and has the honour to refer to the Secretary General's Note (TR 300 PORT) of 19 August 1963 regarding the resolution adopted by the Security Council at its 1049th meeting on 31 July 1963 in connection with the situation in the territories under Portuguese administration.

In reply to the Secretary General's request for information on the steps already taken and those proposed to be taken by the Government of Ireland to ensure the implementation of the provisions of operative paragraph 6 of the Resolution mentioned, the Minister for External Affairs has the honour to state that the Government of Ireland has not offered and does not intend to offer the Portuguese Government any assistance which would enable it to continue its repression of the peoples of the territories under its Administration. Furthermore, the Government of Ireland has not permitted and does not intend to permit the sale or supply of arms or military equipment for this purpose to the Portuguese Government.

The Minister for External Affairs of Ireland avails himself of this opportunity to present to the Secretary-General of the United Nations the assurances of his highest consideration.

Frank Aiken

---

[41] NAI, DEA, Permanent Mission to the United Nations, X20, Portuguese Overseas Territories, 1963-1965.

330
Ofício, Encarregado de Negócios *ad interim* irlandês em Lisboa ao Secretário-Geral do DEA: Lisboa, 22 de Outubro de 1963[42]

There is no doubt that the nation – represented on this occasion[43] there by delegations of all the municipalities in the country – gave their President a tremendous welcome. While not possessing an outstanding personality, the Admiral is very close to the people who love him for his simplicity and who feel that he serves this country to the best of his ability. They were genuinely glad to have him back among them again. Indeed the comment was made by various people that the fact of his completely uneventful journey to Angola should be a sufficient proof for any who still doubt that there is no real demand there for separation from Portugal. The comment may be true or not but certainly seems plausible.

[...]

O'Kelly de Gallagh

331
Ofício, Embaixador irlandês em Lagos ao Secretário-Geral do DEA: Lagos, 29 de Outubro de 1963[44]

CONFIDENTIAL

NIGERIA AND PORTUGAL

A serious cabinet crisis is developing here in connection with Nigeria's relations with Portugal. It may lead to the long-expected resignation from the Cabinet of Mr. Jaja Wachuku, Nigeria's undiplomatic Minister of External Affairs. Connected with the Portuguese representation question is the attitude of the

---

[42] NAI, DEA, 313/11J Confidential reports from Lisbon Legation, 1963.

[43] O regresso do Presidente da República da viagem a Angola.

[44] NAI, DEA, Permanent Mission to the United Nations, X20, Portuguese Overseas Territories, 1963-1965.

Minister on the vexed issue of the expulsion from the United Nations of both Portugal and South Africa.

2. Nigeria has never had an accredited Ambassador either from Portugal or South Africa. Early in 1961 the Portuguese sent an Ambassador-designate with letters of credence but after waiting for three months to present them to the Governor--General, he had to return to Portugal. Dr. Nnamdi Azikiwe, the Governor-General, refused to receive him. We can only assume that the Ministry of External Affairs had duly obtained the agrément of the Queen in advance and that the Governor-General (who is now President) was working at cross-purposes with Mr. Wachuku. Otherwise it is difficult to believe that the Ambassador would have come to Lagos.

3. Although the Ambassador-designate had to return home, the Portuguese Government continued to maintain a Second Secretary in Lagos as Chargé d'Affaires a.i. He was given full recognition by the Ministry of External Affairs in the matter of correct placing in the Diplomatic and Consular List, the issue of a "CD" plate for his car, and the usual diplomatic privileges. Although the young diplomat in question, Dr. Carlos Coelho, rarely appears at official functions and is socially rather aloof, there is no doubt about his diplomatic standing. In this connection it will be recalled that the African Summit Conference held at Addis Ababa in May this year called on all African States to sever diplomatic and consular relations with Portugal and South Africa. No action was taken by the Minister of External Affairs, however, to send home Dr. Carlos Coelho.

4. But matters came to an unfortunate head at a dinner party in the evening of Saturday 12th October in the leading hotel in Lagos. The party was given by the Diplomatic Corps collectively in honour of the outgoing Doyen, Viscount Head of Britain, who is leaving for Malasya […] The Corps also invited some of the members of the Department of External Affairs, including Mr. Wachuku's deputy, Dr. Esin, Minister of State. Relations between Mr. Wachuku and almost all the Ministry staff, including Dr. Esin, have steadily deteriorated.

5. Since the Corps as a whole were the hosts in honour of their Doyen, Dr. Coelho of Portugal took his seat at the dinner table. This provoked a reaction from a number of African diplomats. Led by the Ambassadors of Sudan, Ethiopia, Cameroons and Liberia, all the African and Asian representatives walked out in

protest, followed by the representatives of the Nigerian Ministry of External Affairs, and the East Europeans. Only the representatives of Western Europe, and of North and South America and Australia remained to eat the melancholy dinner. My wife and I were not present as we were on our way to Kaduna to present books to the Premier of the Northern Region on behalf of the Cultural Relations Committee. We had, of course, written to Lord Head and to his successor as Doyen, explaining our absence.

6. The action of the representatives of the Ministry in walking out was embarrassing. In effect, they seemed to be criticising their own Government which had not yet broken off relations with Portugal. In the same way, the walk-out by the other diplomats could also be construed as a severe indictment of the host Government. On the following day the Ministry of External Affairs come out with a press communiqué which attacked Portuguese policies in Africa and defended the action of Dr. Esin, Minister of State. Nevertheless, it was not difficult to detect in the communiqué a note of intense embarrassment over the whole incident. In effect, the Ministry seemed to be at cross-purposes with its own Minister.

7. During all this time Mr. Wachuku, the Minister, was at the UN General Assembly and he returned on Saturday last, the 26th October. He was met at Lagos airport by a large contingent of the press who were anxious to see how he wound handle an already delicate situation. His performance, as a responsible Foreign Minister of Africa's greatest nation, was appalling. Sweating profusely and obviously in a foul humour, he denounced the entire Nigerian press and then proceeded to defend the presence of the Portuguese Chargé d'Affaires. He said that the Addis Ababa resolution had no time limit and that he would act on it when he felt like it.

8. Even more serious for his position in the Cabinet, was his handling of questions regarding the expulsion of Portugal and South Africa from the United Nations. Mr. Wachuku argued against their expulsion because they could be subjected to the moral pressure of the Organisation only as long as they are members. While the Minister has considerable logic on his side, it is politically disastrous for him to urge this argument, which is not accepted by other African states. I would be surprised if it is supported by the Government. It was the same

argument which the Nigerian Prime Minister rebutted at the London Commonwealth Conference when he helped to lead the attack on South Africa which resulted in her expulsion from the Commonwealth. Mr. Wachuku also seemed to forget that Chief J. M. Johnson, the Nigerian Minister of Labour, recently relinquished his Chairmanship of the ILO in Geneva and joined other African States in walking out in support of the demand for the expulsion of South Africa. In Rome Chief Dafe, Chairman of Nigerian Airways, recently walked out of the IATA Conference on the same issue. Mr. Wachuku brought the unhappy news conference to a close by shouting at the newsmen: "You let the Government down because you do not know anything. You are ignorant and uninformed. You are not Nigerians."

9. As a result of this performance, Mr. Wachuku has received the most bitter press notices I have ever seen directed at a Nigerian Cabinet Minister, and some Lagos papers demand his resignation today. He has shown a remarkable talent in surviving storms of his own creation during the years I have spent here, but I would be surprised if he weathers this one. His fundamental problem is a contempt for the views of other Africans, and a conviction that he enjoys a monopoly of logic and common sense. On many issues his views are, indeed, logical, sensible and courageous. But Mr. Wachuku ignores at his peril the element of deeply-felt emotion with which political problems are charged in Africa. It would be true to say that there are no more emotional problems on this continent that [sic] the policies of Portugal and South Africa.

E. L Kennedy

332
Ofício, Encarregado de Negócios *ad interim* irlandês em Lisboa ao Secretário-Geral do DEA: Lisboa, 30 de Outubro de 1963[45]

For your information, I have been told that the Portuguese Foreign Minister, Dr. Franco Nogueira, is anxious to obtain the post of Permanent Portuguese Representative at the UN.

---

[45] NAI, DEA, 313/11J Confidential reports from Lisbon Legation, 1963.

He is anxious to get named as soon as possible, but, apparently, Dr. Salazar would prefer to keep him in his present capacity until the autumn and then send him to New York as Permanent Representative when the chips will be really down.

O'Kelly de Gallagh

333
Telegrama, Uneireann a Estero: Nova Iorque, 16 de Novembro de 1963[46]

268 General debate on Portuguese territories is now proceeding in fourth committee and will end on Thursday or Friday next. Question arises whether we should intervene. We did not intervene in general debate in 1961 or 1962, but we participated in questioning of petitioners and in discussion of draft resolutions. At this session we also participated in questioning of petitioners (see A/C.4//SR.1477).

There appears at present to be no pressing reason for an intervention in the general debate on this item. However, if we refrain from doing so, and also refrain from speaking on Oman, we shall have been silent on all major Fourth Committee issues this year, with the exception of a brief intervention on Southern Rhodesia.

Debate is likely to turn on question of use of NATO weapons against African insurgents in Portuguese territories and draft resolution may contain a paragraph referring to this. Unlikely that question of Catholic education, already dealt with in questioning of petitioners, will be an issue. Permrep feels than any intervention should avoid reference to these subjects. If sanctions become an issue, it would be more appropriate to deal with them in discussing the draft resolution or in an explanation of vote, after further consultation with you. Question of expulsion is unlikely to arise.

Suggest that any intervention in general debate be confined to (A) an expression of our continued support for the principle of self-determination and

---

[46] NAI, DEA, Permanent Mission to the United Nations, X20, Portuguese Overseas Territories, 1963-1965.

independence for territories under Portuguese administration and (B) a reference to Portugal's assumption that the grant of independence to her overseas territories would adversely affect her economy (which has been referred to by several speakers). We would argue in this connection that the freeing of subject territories by other European countries, including the smaller colonial powers, has not harmed their economies in any fundamental way, and has in fact sometimes been followed by an economic boom. Portugal might have many advantages to gain from freeing herself from the responsibilities of a colonial power in order to participate more actively in European integration and in European assistance to the emerging nations of Africa.

Would be glad of indication on whether an intervention on these lines is considered desirable.

Uneireann

334
Ofício, Primeiro Secretário da Representação Permanente da Irlanda junto das Nações Unidas ao Secretário-Geral do DEA: Nova Iorque, 20 de Novembro de 1963[47]

PORTUGUESE OVERSEAS TERRITORIES

The general debate in the Fourth Committee on the question of territories under Portuguese administration is to conclude on Thursday or Friday of this week and the question of Oman may therefore be taken up on Monday next. In the absence of a reply to you from my telex N.º 268 it is not proposed to intervene in the debate on Portuguese territories and we have therefore deleted our name from the list of speakers.

Meanwhile, the African group has decided to adopt the same strategy on this item as on Apartheid, and to refer the matter to the Security Council. There is a strong feeling in the Group that the General Assembly has taken these two

---

[47] NAI, DEA, Permanent Mission to the United Nations, X20, Portuguese Overseas Territories, 1963-1965.

items as far as it can go and that an attempt should now be made to have the Security Council take decisions which might result in the effective implementation of previous resolutions on Apartheid and on Portuguese Territories passed both by the Assembly and by the Security Council. This thinking is in line with the general trend towards Security Council action on colonialism to which attention has been drawn in previous reports.

The representative of Ghana yesterday privately circulated the attached draft resolution which would request the Security Council to consider immediately the question of territories under Portuguese administration and to adopt necessary measures to give effect to its own decisions, particularly those contained in its resolution of 31 July 1963 (S/5380). The general reaction among Western delegations to this move is favourable and it is likely that the draft, unless it is substantially modified by the Afro-Asian group, will be passed by an almost unanimous vote. The US delegation has recommended to Washington that it support the draft. The only points on which US representatives tend to have some reservations concern the use of the words "the only means" in the final preambular paragraph and the word "immediately" in operative paragraph 3. It is felt that these words could be interpreted to rule out the possibility of further discussions between representatives of the African Group and representatives of the Portuguese Government similar to those which have taken place since the adoption of the Security Council resolution of 31 July last. We are, however, informed by American colleagues that this point may not be so important as to prevent the US from supporting the draft resolution. The possibility of Security Council action under Chapter VII of the Charter arising out of paragraph 3 of the Ghana draft does not appear to worry the US delegation.

The representative of Ghana, Mr. Yomekpe, suggested to me that we might like to co-sponsor the draft resolution, but I took this remark as being made in jest. He made the same suggestion to the Swedish and Norwegian representatives, who are seriously considering the possibility of co-sponsoring and have sought instructions on the matter. It seems to me that co-sponsorship of Afro-Asian draft resolutions on colonialism is of questionable wisdom, since a Western delegation which becomes closely identified with resolutions however innocuous, puts itself in a position where it might have greater difficulty in opposing or abstaining on other resolutions containing radical provisions.

On the whole, the African decision to refer this matter to the Security Council is a source of some relief to the representatives of NATO member countries on the Fourth Committee, since NATO has been under heavy fire in the debate on the issue of the use of NATO arms by Portuguese forces in Africa and most delegations expected that any resolution passed by the Fourth Committee this year would contain one or more paragraphs criticising NATO for this.

It is recommended that we support a draft resolution on the lines of the enclosed text, unless substantial changes are made in it, but that we refrain from co-sponsorship even if that suggestion is to be made seriously and even if some of the Nordic countries are among the co-sponsors.

For Permanent Representative,

Tadgh O'Sullivan

[incluído com o documento]

DRAFT RESOLUTION Ghana, 19.11.63

Territories under Portuguese Administration

The General Assembly,

Having considered the question of Territories under Portuguese Administration,

Having considered the report on this question submitted by the Special Committee on the situation with regard to the implementation of the Declaration on the granting of independence to colonial countries and peoples (a/5446/ /Add.1 and Corr. 1 and 2),

Having heard the petitioners,

Recalling the Declaration on the granting of independence to colonial countries and peoples contained in General Assembly resolution 1514 (XV) of 14 December 1960,

Recalling General Assembly resolutions 1542 (XV) of 15 December 1960, 1603 (XV) of 20 April 1961, 1699 (XVI) of 19 December 1961, 1742 (XVI) of 30

January 1962, 1807 (XVII) of 14 December 1962 and 1819 (XVII) of 18 December 1962, and Security Council resolutions of 9 June 1961 (S/4835) and of 31 July 1963 (S/5380),

Recalling in particular that the Security Council by its resolution of 31 July 1963 urgently called on Portugal to implement the following:

"(a) The immediate recognition of the right of the peoples of the Territories under its administration to self-determination and independence;

(b) The immediate cessation of all acts of repression and the withdrawal of all military and other forces at present employed for that purpose;

(c) The promulgation of an unconditional political amnesty and the establishment of conditions that will allow the free functioning of political parties;

(d) Negotiations, on the basis of the recognition of the right of self-determination, with the authorized representatives of the political parties within and outside the Territories with a view to the transfer of power to political institutions freely elected and representative of the peoples, in accordance with resolution 1514 (XV);

(e) The granting of independence immediately thereafter to all the Territories under its administration in accordance with the aspirations of the peoples;"

Noting with deep regret and great concern the continued refusal of the Government of Portugal to take any steps to implement the resolutions of the General Assembly and of the Security Council,

Convinced that the implementation of the forementioned resolutions will provide the only means of obtaining a peaceful solution of the question of Territories under Portuguese Administration;

1. Approves the report of the Special Committee, particularly its conclusions and recommendations and expresses its appreciation of the work of the Committee;

2. Deplores the attitude of the Government of Portugal;

3. Requests the Security Council to consider immediately the question of "Territories under Portuguese Administration" and to adopt necessary measures to give effect to its own decisions, particularly those contained in its resolution of 31 July 1963 (S/5380);

4. <u>Requests</u> the Special Committee to continue to keep the situation in the Territories under Portuguese administration under review and to report to the Security Council and to the General Assembly as appropriate, and in any case not later than at the 19th session of the General Assembly.

335
Telegrama, Uneireann para Estero:
Nova Iorque, 22 de Novembro de 1963[48]

283 Reference my report of 20 November on Portuguese territories, general debate has concluded and Fourth Committee will vote today (Friday) on Afro-Asian draft which consists of original Ghana text minus operative paragraphs 1,2 and 4, with a new operative paragraph added. Following is relevant extract:

"Convinced that the implementation of the aforementioned resolutions will provide the only means of obtaining a peaceful solution of the question of territories under Portuguese administration;

1. Requests the Security Council to consider immediately the question of 'Territories under Portuguese administration' and to adopt necessary measures to give effect to its own decisions, particularly those contained in its resolution of 31 July 1963 (S/5380),
2. Decides to maintain the item entitled 'Territories under Portuguese Administration' on the agenda of the eighteenth session of the General Assembly."

Although no delegations had instructions when consulted yesterday, this draft is likely to secure support of Nordics, Australia, New Zealand, Greece, Turkey, Austria and Italy. Netherlands, Canada, US and UK were wavering between support and abstention. We think it likely that former two will support and latter two will abstain, although UK delegation has pointed out to London "disadvantages of abstention" and US delegation has recommended support to Washington.

---

[48] NA, DEA, Permanent Mission to the United Nations, X20, Portuguese Overseas Territories, 1963-1965.

Since resolution is procedural and language is mild, and having regard to attitude of like-minded delegations, we propose to support. We would, however, abstain or vote against if there were separate votes on the words "the only means" in final preambular paragraph and the words following "Administration" in first operative paragraph, since former could exclude all other means of peaceful settlement, including further talks between Africans and Portuguese, and latter could provide for Chapter Seven action.

Uneireann

336
Telegrama, Estero para Uneireann: Dublin, sem data[49]

258 Your 283 Agreed you should support Afro-Asian draft but abstain on the words quote the only means unquote in final preambular and the words following quote Administration unquote in first operative if these put to seperative [sic] votes.

Estero

1964

337
Ofício, Encarregado de Negócios *ad interim* irlandês em Lisboa ao Secretário-Geral do DEA: Lisboa, 14 de Janeiro de 1964[50]

I have the honour to inform you that Dr. Paulo Rodrigues, Under-Secretary of State attached to President Salazar's office, informed a meeting of the National Tourism Council, held last week that approximately 520,000 tourists entered

---

[49] NAI, DEA, Permanent Mission to the United Nations, X20, Portuguese Overseas Territories, 1963-1965.

[50] NAI, DEA, 313/11K Confidential reports from Lisbon Legation, 1964.

Portugal in 1963. Each tourist spent around £45 in the country. The 1962 receipt from the tourist industry was £18 ¼ m. There has been a 360% increase in tourism recorded over the last ten years. In 1962 the tourism income was more than from the country's two most important exports – cork and canned fish. Profits to the national production from the tourist industry are now calculated at Esc. 670,000 for every million invested. He said that 50 m. Escudos (£625,000) had been budgeted for the tourist industry for 1964 [...]

O'Kelly de Gallagh

338
Ofício, Encarregado de Negócios *ad interim* irlandês em Lisboa ao Secretário-Geral do DEA: Lisboa, 24 de Janeiro de 1964[51]

CONFIDENTIAL

With reference to my confidential minute of yesterday, P.R.3/64 [...] I have the honour to inform you that at a dinner last night at which Dr. Archer, the General Secretary of the Portuguese F.O. was present, he stated quite jubilantly, and for all to hear (the party was almost entirely diplomatic) that, now that Communist China had officially accepted the principle that relations could be established with France without the latter having to sever relations with the Formosa Government, the last obstacle was removed for the recognition of Communist China by Portugal. From Dr. Archer's pleased attitude I could gather that recognition may now come sooner than I had thought [...]

O'Kelly de Gallagh

---

[51] NAI, DEA, 313/11K Confidential reports from Lisbon Legation, 1964.

339
Ofício, Encarregado de Negócios *ad interim* irlandês em Lisboa ao Secretário-Geral do DEA: Lisboa, 20 de Fevereiro de 1964[52]

CONFIDENTIAL

I have the honour to inform you that yesterday I attended one of the periodic lunches at the American Men's Luncheon Group. The lunch was presided over by Admiral Anderson, the American Ambassador, and the guest-speaker was Mr. Garin, former Portuguese Ambassador to the UNO and now Ambassador designated to the USA.

Mr. Garin has just returned from a visit to Angola and Mozambique and, in his address, recapitulated for his audience – something over 100 guests, mostly American – his impression of his trip.

I was able to secure from him at the end of the meal the text to which he spoke, copy of which I enclose herewith.[53] He did not limit himself entirely to the text but occasionally developed tangent thoughts.

He made a very good impression on his audience.

O'Kelly de Gallagh

340
Ofício, Encarregado de Negócios *ad interim* irlandês em Lisboa ao Secretário-Geral do DEA: Lisboa, 4 de Março de 1964[54]

CONFIDENTIAL

I have the honour to inform you that the Portuguese Foreign Office has issued individual invitations to most of the Heads of Mission here to visit both the overseas provinces of Angola and Mozambique at dates of their choice for a visit

---

[52] NAI, DEA, Permanent Mission to the United Nations, X20, Portuguese Overseas Territories, 1963-1965.

[53] Incluído com o ofício.

[54] NA, DEA, 313/11K Confidential reports from Lisbon Legation, 1964.

of about four weeks, for the purpose of seeing for themselves the conditions obtaining in these territories. There are, I understand, no strings attached, and the visitors will be free to see and converse with whom they like, when they like, and how they like. While I have not seen any of the actual letters of invitation I understand that all expenses will be paid by the Portuguese Government.

If, as I believe, there are no strings attached, this would, a priori, appear to be a wonderful opportunity for the Heads of Missions accredited to Portugal to form an opinion from investigation on the spot, concerning:

A) the Afro-Asian thesis which seems to have been adopted by the United Nations that the Portuguese régime in Africa is a menace to peace; and

B) the Portuguese claim that it is nothing of the kind but is, on the contrary, the only long-established multi-racial régime in black Africa, and one which has secured for a contented native population a degree of civilisation far in advance of that in the neighbouring territories of the Congo etc.

The truth may lie somewhere in between the two claims but absentee investigation such as practiced by the UN General Secretary and the Afro-Asian bloc does not seem the most efficient method of finding out.

While I do not know definitively on what basis the selection of Heads of Mission has been done it would appear, grosso modo, to have been reserved for Ambassadors. The only Chargé d'Affaires invited so far has been the Uruguayan, who, like myself, is a Minister Plenipotentiary. His Government would not allow him to accept. Most replies have not yet been given. So far as I know the American Ambassador and the Swiss Ambassador are the only ones who have been and have returned. I understand that the Nuncio has accepted.

This move on the part of the Portuguese Government seems shrewd enough. The seekers after objective truth will presumably accept. Those who decline the invitation will be taken as manifesting that such objective truth is not that which they seek.

[…]

O'Kelly de Gallagh

341
Ofício, Encarregado de Negócios *ad interim* irlandês em Lisboa ao Secretário-Geral do DEA: Lisboa, 6 de Março de 1964[55]

I have the honour to enclose herewith a free translation of an article published last month[56] in the "A VOZ", the leading Catholic daily here, over the signature of António d'Eça de Queiroz, son of the dramatist and novelist and formerly head of the Portuguese Broadcasting Corporation.

The article itself is incoherently written. Indeed, it is obviously more a product of emotion than of thought, and its tone is terribly intemperate and hysterical. It is almost impossible to translate it faithfully because of the succession of prodigiously long sentences interspersed with innumerable relative clauses and adjectives by the drove. But its drift is clear enough and I send it to you as an illustration of the reaction of one educated Portuguese to the world attitude to Portugal as illustrated in the world press and, more especially, in the UN. This reaction is characterised by a sense of utter frustration in face of the refusal of the Secretary General of the UN and the African Governments concerned to accept the Portuguese invitation to come and visit Angola and Mozambique and see for themselves the conditions that obtain there.

Whereas the wording of this article is extremely violent and its complete accuracy open to question, I think that the sentiments it expresses are probably fairly representative of those entertained by the country at large. I have seen Mr. Eça de Queiroz since he wrote the article in question, and what makes him just plain stamping mad is the refusal of Mr. U Thant to visit Angola and Mozambique to check for himself the conditions which he proclaims to be a menace to world peace. Mr. Eça de Queiroz claims that the Portuguese African provinces are veritable oases of peace and civilization in the whole chaotic

---

[55] NAI, DEA, Permanent Mission to the United Nations, X20, Portuguese Overseas Territories, 1963-1965.

[56] 7 de Fevereiro de 1964.

continent of Africa. I am inclined to think, grosso modo, the facts – which will never be gleaned from the foreign press – more or less bear him out on this particular point.

O'Kelly de Gallagh

342
Carta, Secretário-Geral do DEA ao Encarregado de Negócios *ad interim* irlandês em Lisboa: Dublin, 11 de Abril de 1964[57]

CONFIDENTIAL

I have consulted the Minister about your minute (6/2A – 6/9) of 4th March on the subject of invitations being issued to Heads of Mission by the Portuguese Foreign Office to visit the overseas provinces of Angola and Mozambique. The Minister feels that if you should receive such an invitation it would be better in all the circumstances that you should refuse it.

Hugh McCann

343
Ofício, Encarregado de Negócios *ad interim* irlandês em Lisboa ao Secretário-Geral do DEA: Lisboa, 16 de Abril de 1964[58]

CONFIDENTIAL

I have the honour to inform you that the Foreign Minister, Dr. Franco Nogueira, gave a press conference on the 9th inst. [...]

Dr. Nogueira said that the American Ambassador had visited him and given his impression of his trip to Angola and Mozambique. I had a conversation myself with the American Ambassador, Admiral Anderson, on the impressions he gained from his African trip. His impressions were distinctly favourable concerning the

---

[57] NAI, DEA, 313/11K Confidential reports from Lisbon Legation, 1964.
[58] NAI, DEA, 313/11K Confidential reports from Lisbon Legation, 1964.

work of Portugal to produce a multi-racial polity, and he said the standard of living in Angola and Mozambique was certainly far higher than in the neighbouring Congo. He said, however, that there remained an awful lot still to do by the Portuguese to achieve their programme. He had seen there some of the best hospitals he had ever seen anywhere, but it was plain that the natives in either Angola or Mozambique were nowhere near fit for full autonomy yet. Incidentally he did not believe that they were ready for it anywhere in Africa, though he would hate to be quoted to that effect.

While very impressed by many things he saw he felt that the Portuguese public relations set-up is still very rudimentary. "Instead of just showing us what they have so far done – which is admittedly very great – it seems to me that their line should be to show the enormous amount that remains to be done and say 'Leave us to get on with the job' ". From my experience here I can confirm the Ambassador's comment. The Portuguese are just simply not Public-Relations minded. They haven't a clue how to handle that problem.

Curiously enough in his replies to my questions the Ambassador seemed as much concerned with the manner in which his trip was organised, for which he had praise, as with the broader issues of Portugal's position in her African territories.

At the conclusion of his press conference, Dr. Franco Nogueira insisted once more that U Thant should accept Portugal's invitation to visit her Overseas Provinces.

O'Kelly de Gallagh

344
Ofício, Encarregado de Negócios *ad interim* irlandês em Lisboa ao Secretário-Geral do DEA: Lisboa, 18 de Agosto de 1964[59]

CONFIDENTIAL

I have the honour to inform you that Mr. Frederic J. Evans, President of the Interamerican Trust Co., gave a press conference recently in Lourenço Marques, in

---

[59] NAI, DEA, 313/11K Confidential reports from Lisbon Legation, 1964.

the course of which he stated that his company was willing to apply "unlimited" capital in Mozambique, and in any case no less than one billion dollars. He said that in Angola the company had financed, among other enterprises, a 260-kilometer road from Luso to Henrique de Carvalho, the factories of the Cellulose Company, and the Craveiro Lopes airport in Luanda. It had also financed the airports of Beja (Portugal), Sal (Cabo Verde Islands) and Funchal (Madeira). The company is now financing Angola's Alto Catumbela power project.

This may be of interest as a manifestation of confidence in the future stability of Portuguese Africa.

O'Kelly de Gallagh

345
Ofício, Encarregado de Negócios *ad interim* irlandês em Lisboa ao Secretário-Geral do DEA: Lisboa, 26 de Agosto de 1964[60]

With oblique reference to President Admiral Thomaz's visit to Mozambique, I have the honour to send you by bag three copies each of the following publications:

A) An Historical Journey. President Américo Thomaz visits Angola;

B) Political Aspects of the New Africa

[…]

The time lag in the issue of both these publications is illustrative of the casualness of the Portuguese propaganda machine – notwithstanding which the documents are worth reading.

O'Kelly de Gallagh

---

[60] NAI, DEA, 313/11K Confidential reports from Lisbon Legation, 1964.

346
Ofício, Encarregado de Negócios *ad interim* irlandês em Lisboa ao Secretário-Geral do DEA: Lisboa, 30 de Setembro de 1964[61]

CONFIDENTIAL

I have the honour to inform you that, on the 23rd inst., on the occasion of the 31st anniversary of the Portuguese Statute of Labour, the Minister of Corporations, Dr. Gonçalves de Proença, announced the promulgation of a new law governing individual labour contracts.

It replaces a more general 1937 law and is, on the whole, favourable to the worker. It defines the mutual responsibilities as well as the guarantees in operation between employer and employee, and has a "favoured-worker clause" which stipulates that in cases of doubt decisions shall be in favour of the worker. The employer must regard his workers as "collaborators", and see that they have just wages, proper working conditions and accident and sickness benefits. Workers must be regular and assiduous in their work and care for their tools, being obedient and loyal to their employers. The law protects the worker from exploitation, from being degraded in his status, having his salary reduced or being transferred against his will. Employers' disciplinary measures are circumscribed, wages and overtime pay are controlled, compulsory holidays and days off stipulated, and a salary scale scheme set forth. Women will receive equal pay with men for equal work under this law, and the minimum working age of minors is fixed at twelve years. The law is operative both for regular salaried workers and for casual labour.

O'Kelly de Gallagh

---

[61] NAI, DEA, 313/11K Confidential reports from Lisbon Legation, 1964.

347
Ofício, Encarregado de Negócios *ad interim* irlandês em Lisboa ao Secretário-Geral do DEA: Lisboa, 15 de Outubro de 1964[62]

CONFIDENTIAL

With reference to the situation in Portuguese Africa, I have the honour to enclose herewith a translation I have been able to obtain through the courtesy of the American Embassy of the speech delivered at the Luanda Chamber of Commerce on the 28th of September by Mr. Franco Nogueira, the Foreign Minister. I think you will find it an interesting document in spite of its length.[63]

O'Kelly de Gallagh

348
Ofício, Encarregado de Negócios *ad interim* irlandês em Lisboa ao Secretário-Geral do DEA: Lisboa, 19 de Outubro de 1964[64]

CONFIDENTIAL

[…][65]

The foregoing is the translation of an ANI message published in the Portuguese press and presumably has the Portuguese slant. On the other hand any Dar-es-Salam messages would appear to me to be even more suspect as most of them seem to fly in the teeth of any ascertainable evidence there is. In this matter I would add my deep conviction that the world press at large is in this case flagrantly guilty of both suppressio veri and suggestion falso [sic].

The Department has probably far more numerous sources of information that have I, but I would suggest great caution in the evaluation of many of the

---

[62] NAI, DEA, 313/11K Confidential reports from Lisbon Legation, 1964.
[63] Incluído com o ofício.
[64] NAI, DEA, 313/11K Confidential reports from Lisbon Legation, 1964.
[65] Refere-se a um artigo sobre o Tanganica no *Diário de Notícias* de 18 de Outubro de 1964.

obviously biased and unsubstantiated paragraphs dealing with Portugal as much, for instance, in the London "TIMES" as in the Paris "MONDE".

The London "TIMES" makes no bones about disliking Portugal and all it stands for and in dealing with people it dislikes, it always runs true to form. It shows no more scruple in verifying its sources of information in the case of Portugal than it did in the case of the Pigott forgeries in 1889 and true to the only tradition it has ever followed, is always prepared to accept and publish as facts any anti-Portuguese rumours it can pick up from basically anti-Portuguese sources. At the same time it took care not to publish a word concerning the five Labour members' recent visit to Portuguese Africa and their favourable report thereon. Or if it did publish anything about it, it was relegated to a back page where I was unable to spot it.

The Paris "MONDE" is little better and quotes as facts rumours "de source authorisée à Dar-es-Salam" – which simply means the propaganda machine of the Dar-es-Salam Government: which Government makes no secret of its hostility to the Mozambique set-up nor of its efforts – hard to reconcile with the UN Charter – to bring it down by direct violence if it can.

O'Kelly de Gallagh

349
Ofício, Encarregado de Negócios *ad interim* irlandês em Lisboa ao Secretário-Geral do DEA: Lisboa, 22 de Outubro de 1964[66]

CONFIDENTIAL

I have the honour to enclose herewith:

A) translation of a commentary in the *Diário da Manhã*[67] (a Government organ) on the interview accorded by Dr. Salazar to the "AURORE" of Paris and published in that paper on the 9th inst.

---

[66] NAI, DEA, 313/11K Confidential reports from Lisbon Legation, 1964.
[67] *Aurore*, 12 de Outubro de 1964:

B) A copy of the "AURORE" which I was able to procure, and on page 11 of which you will find the full text of the interview.[68]

The interview contains statements that no responsible Statesman has yet had the courage to make, but which are, I believe, just simple expressions of the truth. I appreciate that that fact may not render them more palatable to the Afro-Asians.

O'Kelly de Gallagh

---

[68] '—Pour l'Afrique, me dit le président, l'indépandance a été catastrophique. Partout c'est le désordre. La révolte à l'état endémique ou explosif, le retour à la vie primitive des tribus. C'est la lutte au couteau et au pistolet entre les leaders, tandis que les peuples retrouvent la famine, les épidémies, la loi de talion de l'époque précoloniale. Ce n'est pas tout de clamer le droit à la liberté, il faut que les hommes soient aptes à en user. Or, on est obligé de constater qu'en Afrique l'échec a été total, parce que l'on a cru que les Blancs pouvaient être partout remplacés par des Noirs. Or, ce n'est pas vrai. Les Blancs seuls sont capables de planifier une action, d'organiser un travail. Un homme l'avait compris, c'était Tshombé.

Que l'on ne me taxe pas de racisme parce que je dis que les Noirs n'ont pas les mêmes aptitudes que les Blancs: c'est une constatation évidente qui est le fruit de l'éxperience. Les Noirs ont besoin d'être encadrés. J'ai un exemple tout à fait significatif auprès de moi. L'un de mes médecins est un Noir, originaire d'Angola. Il a accompli de très bonnes études à la faculté de Lisbonne avant de s'y fixer. Marié à une Portugaise blanche, dont il a plusieurs enfants, il est reçu partout dans la société. Or, ce médecin me racontait qu'il venait de retourner dans sa terre natale. Après plusieures années, il a revu son frère, qui avait reçu la même éducation que lui, en Suisse. Mais ce frère, également évolué et instruit, au lieu de rester en Europe, s'est installé dans les propriétés paternelles du nord de l'Angola. Et, hors du cadre blanc, il a été repris et asservi aux coutumes tribales. Mon docteur a retrouvé son frère: il vit en concubinage avec plusieurs femmes dont chacune lui avait donné de nombreux enfants, mange avec les doigts et a oublié la civilisation à laquelle it avait était formé...Le cadre européen avait disparu, cela avait suffi à le rendre à la vie primitive.

[…]

Un véritable régime communiste a pris possession de l'Algérie: Là comme à Zanzibar, comme dans les provinces du Congo tenues par les rebelles pro-Chinois, s'organise la subversion qui menace toute l'Afrique. Cette Algérie communiste constitue un danger grave pour l'Europe. La Méditerranée est une mer trop exigüe pour que ses côtes soient partagées entre des nations ennemies. Les Romains avaient dù le constater qui firent les guerres puniques et écrasèrent Carthage pour que règne enfin la paix. Non, on ne peut pas y avoir d'ennemi de part et d'autre du bassin méditerranéen. Or, l'Algérie communiste tend à devenir une base ennemie de l'Europe. Et lorsqu'elle aura fait tomber ses deux ailes, la Tunisie et le Maroc, le Maghreb rouge constituera pour l'Europe la même menace que Cuba pour les Etats-Unis. Pour les Arabes, la tentation sera un jour trop forte de franchir le détroit de Gibraltar et de recommencer l'invasion qui, voilà dix siécles, devait s'arrêter à Poitiers.

[…]

350
Ofício, Encarregado de Negócios *ad interim* irlandês em Lisboa ao Secretário-Geral do DEA: Lisboa, 3 de Novembro de 1964[69]

CONFIDENTIAL

POPE PAUL'S VISIT TO INDIA

I have the honour to give you the following details to fill in the general picture given you in my recent report on the subject.

1) The genesis of the whole thing, it is claimed in Government circles, lies in a phrase in the Holy Father's oration on the occasion of the recent canonisation of some fifty (?) Uganda martyrs, "welcoming the emergence of the African Nations." It is at this phrase that the Portuguese Government took umbrage, considering it an encouragement to rebellion in Angola and Mozambique.

2) It appears that the written comment made from the pulpit by the five young priests alluded to in the above report were to have appeared in identical terms in an editorial of "NOVIDADES" – the leading Catholic paper here. It was suppressed by the censor.

3) In conversation with me the Nuncio described the Portuguese attitude as completely irrational. "They seem to have lost all sense of reality" he said. He has received hundreds of telegrams of solidarity from Portuguese of all classes.

4) The day the Franco Nogueira statement was made the text thereof was sent down to the Emissora Nacional – the Portuguese Broadcasting authority – for publication. The authority concerned thought it dynamite and did not publish it. The result was a peremptory telephone call from Dr. Salazar himself ordering it to be published forthwith.

5) <u>Public opinion</u>. Anybody with whom I have had occasion to speak on the matter was highly critical of the Government's attitude. Indeed it is the first time I have found such unanimity. I would not be surprised if this public reaction should prove to be the "red light" for the Doctor. Let us hope he is not

---

[69] NAI, DEA, 313/11K Confidential reports from Lisbon Legation, 1964.

colour-blind. Incidentally one recalls the old French saying – "Qui mange du Pape en meurt."

6) […]

7) To fill in the personal background of the Minister and of his wife I would say that while Franco Nogueira is not a practising Catholic – I think him completely indifferent on matters religious – he has never, to my knowledge, manifested the slightest hostility to Catholicism. He is not, as far as I know, a mason.
Madame Nogueira, who is half Chinese, is an exemplary practising Catholic. Incidentally, she sings in the Corpo Santo choir every Sunday and is a person universally liked and respected.

8) The question as to whether or not Franco Nogueira agrees with the statement he made is being canvassed. It is suggested in some quarters that it was imposed on him from above. That might possibly be the case, though I would not be prepared to go further. He has proved himself an exceedingly able Foreign Minister. He was, as you are aware, a civil servant, and when I knew him first he was, if I remember rightly, assistant director of the political section of the Portuguese Foreign Office. The suggestion has been made that if he disapproved of the line taken by his Chief the obvious course was to resign. There is no knowing what the effect of such resignation might have been on the public. But, while resignation might have been the ideal course, in such circumstances, it must be remembered that he has no private means; that he has a wife and a young daughter for whom to provide; that if he resigned he would find himself on the pavement with a negligible pension, and that at his time of life he might have great difficulty in obtaining suitable employment outside of the administration, which would, of course, be barred to him. And for him none of the plums in the way of directorship in semi-official concerns that are the reward of the retiring faithful […]

O'Kelly de Gallagh

351

Ofício, Encarregado de Negócios *ad interim* irlandês em Lisboa ao Secretário-Geral do DEA: Lisboa, 27 de Novembro de 1964[70]

Referring to the British Prime Minister's statement in the House of Commons on the 25th inst. in reply to a question by the Labour M.P. Wm. Hamilton, concerning the eventual supplying of arms to Portugal, I have the honour to inform you that a spokesman of the Portuguese Foreign Office has this morning made the following statement to the Press:

"The declaration of the British Prime Minister must be considered as purely theoretical and dictated solely by political considerations. In point of fact the Portuguese Government has not endeavoured nor has it any intention of endeavouring to obtain from Britain arms for its overseas forces. Besides, for a long time past the Portuguese Government has been desirous of avoiding being the cause of the least embarrassment to Her Majesty's Government, and for that reason, even in cases where, as happened not so long ago, that Government offered to sell it armaments – more specifically aeroplanes – the Portuguese Government has declined such offers, feeling incidentally that it could have no guarantee as to the eventual execution of deliveries, and that, furthermore, it could find its requirements elsewhere and more favourable conditions, as was the case recently in the matter of warships and submarines at present being constructed for it in another country.

The British Prime Minister's declaration, therefore, appears to be referring to a request that has never been made, and is, consequently, of no practical import.

The Head of the British Government may rest assured that we shall not place with any British manufacturers or exporters any orders for military equipment."

O'Kelly de Gallagh

---

[70] NAI, DEA, 313/11K Confidential reports from Lisbon Legation, 1964.

352
Ofício, Encarregado de Negócios *ad interim* irlandês em Lisboa ao Secretário-Geral do DEA: Lisboa, 30 de Dezembro de 1964[71]

I have the honour to enclose herewith the text of the Nuncio's address to the President of the Republic on the occasion of the Presidential New Year reception of the Diplomatic Corps – which took place on the 22nd inst.

It is interesting to note that in his reference to Angola and Mozambique the Nuncio is careful to allude to them as "ces grandes provinces d'Outremer". Indeed he seems almost to have gone out of his way to use this term to which, as you are aware, the Portuguese Government attaches so much importance.

O'Kelly de Gallagh

[…Passagem do discurso referido no documento…]:

'…A l'invitation du Gouvernment, de nombreux Chefs de Mission visitèrent les grandes provinces d'Outremer et se rendirent compte des considérables et heureux développements apportés, ces dernières années, à l'évolution sociale, hospitalière, culturelle de ces provinces et à leur essor économique….'

1965

353
Ofício, Encarregado de Negócios *ad interim* irlandês em Lisboa ao Secretário-Geral do DEA: Lisboa, 21 de Janeiro de 1965[72]

CONFIDENTIAL

I have the honour to enclose herewith five copies of an article published in the DIÁRIO DE NOTÍCIAS of the 13th instant over the signature of Augusto de

---
[71] NAI, DEA, 313/11K Confidential reports from Lisbon Legation, 1964.
[72] NAI, DEA, 313/11L Confidential reports from Lisbon Legation, 1965.

Castro, the Director of the paper, one-time Ambassador in Paris, where I knew him, and very close to Salazar. The article, of which I have made a free translation, has received a lot of attention, the Madrid daily "A.B.C." having translated it into Spanish for disseminating in Latin America.

As you will see the UN prestige is low in Portugal and Mr. U Thant is not a popular hero here. It will be observed that in all Mr. de Castro's tirade there is no word of criticism for Indonesia for having slammed the door in the UN. I feel though that the slamming must rather embarrass the Portuguese Government who, while they would doubtless be glad enough to do the same, would prefer to do it in other company than that of an aggressive neighbour to Timor where the UN intervention might yet conceivably be invoked.

O'Kelly de Gallagh

354
Ofício, Encarregado de Negócios *ad interim* irlandês em Lisboa ao Secretário-Geral do DEA: Lisboa, 11 de Fevereiro de 1965[73]

CONFIDENTIAL

DE GAULE'S [sic] PRESS CONFERENCE

I have the honour to enclose translation of an Editorial Comment in the "DIÁRIO DE NOTÍCIAS" of the 8th inst. on de Gaule's [sic] latest press conference. It probably reflects pretty accurately Dr. Salazar's views on the subject.

O'Kelly de Gallagh

---

[73] NAI, DEA, 313/11L Confidential reports from Lisbon Legation, 1965.

355
Ofício, Encarregado de Negócios *ad interim* irlandês em Lisboa ao Secretário-Geral do DEA: Lisboa, 2 de Março de 1965[74]

CONFIDENTIAL

I have the honour to give you hereunder a pretty full English résumé of Dr. Salazar's speech to the "União Nacional" of which he is President, on the occasion of the inauguration of the new executive committee of that body on February 18th. The résumé is taken from the current issue of the "ANGLO-PORTUGUESE NEWS" and is far better done than the official translation issued by the Government and which, I confess, completely defeated me.

As I have had occasion to stress to you on previous occasions, Dr. Salazar's style, while conforming to the strictest Portuguese literary norms, is often terribly involved, not to say obscure, when judged by English norms. The translation achieved by the "ANGLO-PORTUGUESE NEWS" has surmounted this linguistic obstacle and gives a very fair version of Dr. Salazar's thought.

The last paragraph of the translation, in which the new Angelic Doctor calls the Church to order with pastoral solicitude, is not without a certain pontifical piquancy. There are occasions – and this would appear to be one of them – on which Doctor Salazar's homilies savour alarmingly of the encyclical.

O'Kelly de Gallagh

356
Ofício, Encarregado de Negócios *ad interim* irlandês em Lisboa ao Secretário-Geral do DEA: Lisboa, 23 de Março de 1965[75]

CONFIDENTIAL

As you may have seen in the press, Dr. Salazar reshuffled his cabinet on the 18th inst. I append hereto a list of the Government as now constituted. The

---

[74] NAI, DEA, 313/11L Confidential reports from Lisbon Legation, 1965.
[75] NAI, DEA, 313/11L Confidential reports from Lisbon Legation, 1965.

changes affected three ministers, three secretaries and two under-secretaries [...]

No great political importance need be attached to the reshuffle. Indeed it can best be likened to a reshuffle of the domestic staff or a large household where the mistress of the house considers such a shuffle desirable for the better implementing of her domestic ideas. It argues no change in her views.

O'Kelly de Gallagh

357
Ofício, Encarregado de Negócios *ad interim* irlandês em Lisboa ao Secretário-Geral do DEA: Lisboa, 4 de Maio de 1965[76]

CONFIDENTIAL

I have the honour to enclose a summary of the Delgado situation as seen in Portugal. The world press has already given it great publicity with the usual exaggerations, but I think the enclosed account is factual.

O'Kelly de Gallagh

THE DELGADO CASE

The first press message here concerning the discovery of bodies, believed to be those of Humberto Delgado, his Brazilian woman secretary Arajarir Moreira Campos and one other man, came from Madrid and were published in the Portuguese newspapers of April 28th. They stated that the first two bodies had been found by a fifteen-year old boy and his dog, precariously buried under stones, some miles south of Badajoz on the Villanueva road to the Portuguese frontier. The third body was found in the vicinity but may have no connexion with the case. The date given for the discovery was April 27th. Badajoz police went to the spot, but no official communiqué was issued.

On April 29th, messages were published from Rabat and Madrid. Henrique Cerqueira, resident in Rabat, who claimed to be Delgado's representative in Morocco and his political heir, said there was no doubt the bodies were those of Delgado and his secretary. Delgado had been missing since mid-February. In a

---

[76] NAI, DEA, 313/11L Confidential reports from Lisbon Legation, 1965.

communiqué, Cerqueira laid the responsibility for the deaths on the Portuguese Communist Party and the Frente Patriotica de Libertação Nacional (the rival organisation to Delgado's) [...] The "DIÁRIO DA MANHÃ" in an editorial article stated that Delgado had fallen completely into the hands of the Communists both in Brasil [sic] and Prague. His "impulsive exaltation" made him a danger to them. When he left Algiers, his headquarters were assaulted by the rival group. The newspaper recalled the case of Captain Almeida Santos, whose body was found buried on Guincho beach at the time of a plot against the State some years ago, and drew a parallel between the two cases [...]

At first rumours of all sorts were rife as to the authors of the crime. Some sympathisers with the opposition here seemed to try to involve the Portuguese and even the Spanish Government, but now nobody believes that either Government had anything to do with it. Neither had any interest in Delgado's suppression, and insofar as the Portuguese Government is concerned, two arguments were put forward against its possible implication: A) Murder is not in the Salazar tradition and, B) If the Portuguese police had wished to eliminate Delgado they would not have left his corpse, with the identifying ring, in a place where anybody could find it. Furthermore, Delgado was a very irresponsible lightweight and presented no real menace to the régime. As far as can be judged on the little evidence at present available it appears much more likely that he was suppressed by some of his own Communist dissidents [...]

358
Ofício, Encarregado de Negócios *ad interim* irlandês em Lisboa ao Secretário-Geral do DEA: Lisboa, 20 de Maio de 1965[77]

CONFIDENTIAL

I have the honour to enclose herewith translation, in extenso, of the Press Conference given on the 7th inst. by Dr. Franco Nogueira, the Portuguese Foreign Minister [...]

O'Kelly de Gallagh

---

[77] NAI, DEA, 313/11L Confidential reports from Lisbon Legation, 1965.

[...] Q) Can Your Excellency give any more explicit information concerning the case of General Humberto Delgado? A) The Ministry of Foreign Affairs possess no specific information on the subject. As for any information that the Portuguese authorities may have, the matter is evidently a question for the Ministry of the Interior and I can only categorically declare that the Portuguese authorities have absolutely nothing to do with the disappearance and death of this former officer. On the other hand I can add, as indeed, I have already declared to the foreign press, that the possibility of an enquiry into the crime having been mooted in certain international circles and in the international press, the Portuguese Government has not the slightest objection to such an enquiry. It is, however, evident that it is entirely in the competence of the Spanish Government to order an enquiry, and a verification of the facts, as it is, in fact, doing with the utmost diligence [...]

359
Apontamento do Secretário-Geral do DEA sobre uma conversa com o Ministro Plenipotenciário português: Dublin, 26 de Agosto de 1965

NOTE

The Portuguese Minister called to see me this afternoon at his request. The main purpose of the Minister's visit was to convey to me, on his return from Lisbon, the attitude of his Government to our continued reluctance to raise the status of the Portuguese mission to that of Embassy. The Minister spoke with great emotion and the interview was a somewhat difficult one.

The Minister said that he had explained to his Government as conveyed to him by the Tánaiste and that the reaction in Lisbon was very bad. He said that the Portuguese Foreign Minister had reacted with some feeling expressing bewilderment that a Catholic country, like Ireland, should so treat another Catholic country like Portugal – a country which had accepted our refugees in our own dark days. The Portuguese Government could never understand why Ireland should receive with honour Ambassadors from various parts of Africa and

Asia and yet refuse to receive an Ambassador from Portugal. Dr. Salazar himself felt gravely offended when our attitude was conveyed to him.

The Portuguese Minister, speaking very frankly, said that if we could not see our way to receive a Portuguese Ambassador at an early date our relations with Portugal would be bound to deteriorate and he could, from his experience in Lisbon, see bitterness setting in. It might even happen that he would be recalled and replaced by a Chargé d'Affaires [...]

The Portuguese Minister spoke of his personal embarrassment at always being at the end of the queue insofar as Heads of Mission here are concerned. Worse than that he had, on one occasion, been introduced by the Tánaiste to the wife of the Prime Minister of Sierra Leone as the Portuguese Chargé d'Affaires. I immediately assured the Minister that if this did happen it was of course an accidental mistake [...]

At various points in the interview the Portuguese Minister was quivering with emotion and seemed to be experiencing difficulty in restraining himself. He apologised for speaking so frankly but thought that we should know how hurt the Portuguese Government were by our attitude [...]

Hugh McCann

360

Ofício, Encarregado de Negócios *ad interim* irlandês em Lisboa ao Secretário-Geral do DEA: Lisboa, 2 de Setembro de 1965[78]

CONFIDENTIAL

In the course of my recent interview with Ambassador Archer [...] the latter at a given point, leaving the question of the status of the Rhodesian representative, tackled me once more about the status of Irish-Portuguese relations.

He enquired once more when Ireland would consent to receive the Ambassador from Portugal. He stressed the fact that Portugal was a Christian – nay a Catholic – country with whom Ireland had never had the least quarrel, but

---

[78] NAI, DEA, Embassy Lisbon, 6/3 Portuguese Legation in Dublin, 1942-1965.

that Ireland refused to accept a Portuguese Ambassador, for fear, apparently, of giving umbrage to the new African States, while she accepted an Ambassador from non-Christian India, who had recently done Portugal a great wrong, without worrying about the umbrage such a one-sided move might be expected to give in Portugal. His attitude on this question, as it has been all along, is one of wounded bewilderment. He added – a fact which Abreu had already told me in Dublin, and which I reported at the time – that Abreu had asked to be transferred at the end of the year if, in the meantime, he had not been accepted as Ambassador. Archer said that, in fact, he contemplated doing just that, because Abreu was in line for an Embassy and would obviously never get one if he remained in Dublin in the present condition.

Incidentally, Dublin was the only Legation they had in Europe and the prolongation of its functioning on the present basis raised various administrative difficulties for them at headquarters. If, therefore, Abreu should be transferred elsewhere at the end of the year, he – Archer – contemplated replacing him by a Chargé d'Affaires a.i. until such time as the diplomatic relations between the two countries came on to a more formal footing.

I was at the receiving end of this unburdening of Archer's soul and all I could do was to make soothing noises whenever he paused. This was not difficult for me because I understood his position perfectly and am indeed, as you know, basically in sympathy with it. But there was nothing I could really say to him except to manifest great friendship for Portugal – a manifestation which manifestly fell short of what he desired.

You will appreciate that another angle of the situation which periodically causes me embarrassment is the fact that we are ourselves periodically requesting the support of the Portuguese Government for our candidature to various international bodies. The favour traffic does seem a little one--sided, – unless, of course, we receive as many requests from them as they receive from us.

O'Kelly de Gallagh

361
Ofício, Encarregado de Negócios *ad interim* irlandês em Lisboa ao Secretário-Geral do DEA: Lisboa, 3 de Dezembro de 1965[79]

CONFIDENTIAL

With reference to the general elections which took place in Portugal on the 7th of October, I have not so far seen the final figures of the voting, but I give hereunder certain figures culled from press reports.

The poll in Lisbon district reached 187.627 valid votes out of a registered total of 189.765.

In Oporto the turnout was given as 64%. Various of the localities turned in figures varying between 65.4% and 85.7%. In Portuguese Guinea the counting disclosed 90%. In Angola the percentage varied from district to district, running from 68% to 95%, and in Cape Verde it averaged 86%. The above figures are astonishingly high.

Voting appears to have been orderly everywhere. This fact might have been attributed to apathy or indifference was it not for the very high percentage of votes recorded.

The campaigning before polling day was vigorous enough, with manifestos and counter-manifestos succeeding each other daily in the press. There appears to have been reasonable liberty for the publishing of the opposition manifestos but it is to be noted that the editorial comment was very generally hostile.

In the middle of October the Social Democratic Opposition launched their first manifesto calling for self-determination in the African provinces. After some initial hesitation this manifesto was published in most of the press, and the reaction was fatal to the Opposition, rallying, as it did, the country at large around the régime both in Continental Portugal and in Mozambique and Angola.

Whatever hopes the Opposition might originally have had of obtaining a measure of popular support vanished overnight. The indignation caused by their manifesto was perfectly genuine and spontaneous and needed no orchestration.

---
[79] NAI, DEA, 313/11L Confidential reports from Lisbon Legation, 1965.

The Opposition claim that the elections were not free and that all sorts of petty obstacles were put in the way of the Opposition candidates is far from baseless. It is, indeed certain that the dice were loaded against them – though I believe, at this stage, more by the momentum attained over the years by the Government party machine than by any specific orders to-day. It is, however, equally certain that, had the elections been as free as it is possible to get them – as free, as, for instance, at home – the results would have been substantially the same. The great majority of the country would still have backed Dr. Salazar.

It should be remembered that the hard kernel of opposition to him has always been among the "intelligentsia" – the liberal professions etc. [...] But when the issue of Portuguese Africa was raised, even the disgruntled intelligentsia came down flat-footed on the side of the régime. The African question jars a raw nerve in every Portuguese I have ever met. In the circumstances the Opposition manifesto calling for "self-determination" for the African Provinces was a veritable gift from Heaven to Dr. Salazar's régime [...]

O'Kelly de Gallagh

1966

362
Ofício, Encarregado de Negócios *ad interim* irlandês em Lisboa ao Secretário-Geral do DEA: Lisboa, 14 de Abril de 1966[80]

I have the honour to inform you that yesterday Dr. Salazar received a deputation from Angola come to congratulate him on his stand for the freedom of that territory. This morning, contrary to all established usage, I received not only the Portuguese version of his address on that occasion, but also an English translation thereof. This latter document I now forward to you [...] Though there seems to be no weakening in the Portuguese position, it is noteworthy that the

---

[80] NAI, DEA, 313/11M Confidential reports from Lisbon Legation, 1966.

tone of this part of the document[81] is studiously moderate compared with some recent pronouncements [...]

O'Kelly de Gallagh

363
Ofício, Encarregado de Negócios *ad interim* irlandês em Lisboa ao Secretário-Geral do DEA: Lisboa, 1 de Junho de 1966[82]

CONFIDENTIAL

I have the honour to enclose herewith the official translation supplied to the Embassy of the speech made by Dr. Salazar, at Braga, on the 28th of May, on the fortieth anniversary of the National Revolution.

[...]

As you will see there is not the slightest suggestion of his retiring – indeed he proclaims his intention of carrying on – so far as one can judge, indefinitely.

O'Kelly de Gallagh

364
Ofício, Encarregado de Negócios *ad interim* irlandês em Lisboa ao Secretário-Geral do DEA: Lisboa, 15 de Novembro de 1966[83]

CONFIDENTIAL

I have the honour to inform you that Professor Leite Pinto, a former Minister of Education, gave figures of progress in that field during a lecture on the 6th instant, commemorating achievement during the forty years of the New State. He said the Republican Government had achieved little in reducing illiteracy. From 1911-1926 primary school attendance only rose from 272,000 to 331,000.

---

[81] *The Beira imbroglio (Rhodesian blockade)*
[82] NAI, DEA, 313/11M Confidential reports from Lisbon Legation, 1966.
[83] NAI, DEA, 313/11M Confidential reports from Lisbon Legation, 1966.

After the May 28 revolution the increase was faster, and when in 1952 schooling was made compulsory, it was again speeded up. During the last school year, primary school children totalled 900,000 distributed among 21,000 schools and 4,100 teaching centres. At the beginning of the century there were only 7,500 secondary-school children. Now there are some 300,000. There were only fifteen lyceums and technical schools, now there are 160. Overseas figures show a similar rise.

O'Kelly de Gallagh

365
Texto da Declaração de Voto irlandesa em relação ao projecto de Resolução A/C.4/L.842 sobre a questão dos Territórios sob Administração Portuguesa, Quarto Comité, ONU, 5 de Dezembro de 1966[84]

Mr. Chairman:

The Irish delegation will vote in favour of the draft Resolution now before the Committee. We do so in order to place on record our opposition to the colonial policies of the Government of Portugal, which in the second half of the Twentieth Century are mistaken and anachronistic. We did not arrive at this decision without considerable soul searching, and our vote in favour of the resolution is not to be taken as approval of all of its contents.

In particular we cannot support the language contained in operative paragraph 3 of the draft resolution which condemns, as a crime against humanity, the policy of the Government of Portugal in settling foreign immigrants in these territories. The expression "condemns" and the expression "crime against humanity" have very great force in international usage, and we believe that they should not be employed except in circumstances where their use is absolutely essential and unavoidable, and where it represents a carefully considered and sober judgment on the circumstances in question. Where the settlement of foreign immigrants is

---

[84] NAI, DFA/2002/19/11[305/218/13 Pt. IV Political situation in Portuguese Africa June 1966--December 1969].

concerned, we are not satisfied that this is the case. It would be different if it could be proved that the settlement of foreign immigrants in the Portuguese territories has been or is brought about by the uprooting and displacement of the native inhabitants as has too often happened in many parts of the world, including my own country, and still unfortunately occurs in other parts of Africa. The attitude of my delegation to this paragraph would also be more favourable if the language used were confined to the question of the exporting of African workers to South Africa. We are of course absolutely opposed to any forced or coercive migration of labour in any part of the world, and it is this consideration which enables us to abstain on this paragraph rather than a vote against it.

At the 20th Session the Irish delegation was opposed to paragraph 7 of Resolution 2107 (XX) on the grounds that it trespassed on matters which are the prerogative of the Security Council and that it was unrealistic to urge on Governments to implement these measures in the absence of the support of those States whose cooperation is essential for the implementation of a programme of sanctions such as that proposed. The fact that paragraph 7 of the draft resolution now before the Committee consists of a recommendation to the Security Council removes the first of these objections, despite the fact that we still consider it inappropriate for the Assembly to make a recommendation to the Council couched in terms which tend to prejudice the Council's consideration of the matter. It will nevertheless be for the Council in its wisdom to decide whether it is possible and advisable to give binding force to this recommendation, and those States to which I have referred, whose cooperation is necessary if the proposed programme of sanctions is to be successful, will have an opportunity of making their attitude known before the Council.

One very important factor which leads my delegation to have serious doubts about the wisdom of this recommendation to the Security Council is the effect which this sweeping programme of sanctions would have on certain landlocked States, those small neighbours of the Portuguese territories who may have no other source of supply for goods and services than by overland transport through those territories. Here again, the Security Council will give this factor full weight in reaching its decision, but the doubts entertained by my delegation are of such gravity as to cause us to abstain on this paragraph if it is voted on separately.

If despite these reservations my delegation will vote in favour of the draft resolution as a whole, it is, as I stated earlier, in order to record our opposition to the mistaken and anachronistic colonial policies of the Portuguese Government. Ireland and her people are bound to Portugal by many historical ties of friendship and continue to entertain sentiments of affection and admiration for the Portuguese people, whose history has been a glorious one and who have done so much to push back the frontiers of knowledge and to contribute to human progress.

But the subject before us does not concern the friendship of our two peoples, which is inviolable, but the present-day policies of Portugal in her African territories. It is that very friendship which compels us to urge on Portugal the revision of these policies. It is our earnest hope that this noble and enlightened people will before too long yield to the progressive forces which animate the world today, and take the honourable place which awaits them in the new Europe which is fast taking shape on the ruins of the old colonial system. This is a time of trial for the Portuguese people. We wish them well in the difficult decisions which they will have to take in the future.

Thank you, Mr. Chairman.

366
Ofício, Representante Permantente irlandês junto das Nações Unidas ao Secretário-Geral do DEA: Nova Iorque, 6 de Dezembro de 1966[85]

Portuguese Territories

1. After a short discussion at the delegation meeting on the morning of 2nd December concerning the draft Resolution on Portuguese Territories (A/C.4//L.842) the Tánaiste decided, as recorded in the minutes of the meeting, that we

---

[85] NAI, DFA/2002/19/11[305/218/13 Pt. IV Political situation in Portuguese Africa June 1966--December 1969].

should vote for paragraph 7 of the text (sanctions) and for the resolution as a whole. A brief reference was also made to operative paragraph 3, which the Portuguese delegation had suggested to us went much too far, but it was not felt that this paragraph gave rise to any particular difficulties.

2. Subsequent to the delegation meeting, the question of paragraph 7 was again raised with the Tánaiste in the context of a discussion on apartheid [...]

3. It was recognised that this paragraph is more in conformity with our basic view about the application of sanctions than was the corresponding paragraph in last year's resolution, i.e. that it recognises that sanctions are a matter for the Security Council. Furthermore, by calling upon the Security Council to make sanctions obligatory, it would obviate a possible defect in the application of sanctions, viz. that if they are to be effective, they must be applied as a matter of obligation by all countries, subject to eventual deliberate exceptions in favour of countries (e.g. Zambia) whose economy might be jeopardised by the application of sanctions without any compensating impact on the country against which they are directed. Generally speaking, therefore, the paragraph seemed to satisfy the basic requisites of a policy of sanctions.

4. The text, however, did not dispose of one aspect of the question. That is, whether the sanctions mentioned in paragraph 7 of resolution 2107 XX are justified in this particular case. It was pointed out that the sanctions there envisaged did not specifically apply to rail transport, and would not therefore necessarily adversely affect the communications of landlocked countries. Nevertheless it was felt that there was sufficient doubt about the need to apply the sanctions listed to put in question the wisdom of requesting the Security Council to call for their application. The conclusion was therefore reached that it would be better to abstain than to endorse the full content of the paragraph by voting for it.

5. In the course of the discussion, the Tánaiste made it clear that his thinking on sanctions has undergone a certain evolution as compared with a year ago, and that he now thinks that sanctions may be effective, provided however that they are mandatory and, subject to the kind of exception mentioned above, applied by each and every member state.

6. The position reached concerning our attitude towards paragraph 7 was conveyed to Mr. O'Sullivan, and it was suggested that when the vote took place, he should explain our abstention on this paragraph.

7. On the following day (Saturday), Mr. O'Sullivan told me that the resolution might be voted on at the meeting of the Fourth Committee then in progress and that he was preparing notes to explain his vote. We agreed at the same time that he could advise the Portuguese delegate of what he intended to do.

8. When Mr. O'Sullivan told Mr Patrício of how he proposed to vote, the latter asked him what attitude we intended to take on paragraph 3. Mr. O'Sullivan and I discussed this matter thoroughly on Monday morning and agreed that, having regard to the language of the paragraph and the sequence of the argument, it might be better to abstain. The Tánaiste later endorsed this view.[86]

C. C. Cremin

367
Telegrama, Estero a Uneireann: Dublin, 12 de Dezembro de 1966[87]

216 For Tánaiste from Secretary Portuguese Ambassador on instructions from Lisbon made representations this morning regarding our voting on L842. He said there was great surprise in Lisbon that we should vote for a Resolution containing such violent and unreasonable language against Portugal. Lisbon points out that many countries who strongly disapprove Portuguese policies voted against resolution and others such as Denmark Finland Sweden Greece and Malawi abstained. They strongly urge that having made our gesture in Committee we should abstain on resolution as a whole in plenary. They do so on the basis of unwarranted language of the resolution and the disproportionate severity of the measures recommended and having regard to the long standing friendship between

---

[86] Ver *Irish Times*, 6 de Dezembro de 1966; *Irish Press*, 6 de Dezembro de 1966; *Guardian*, 6 de Dezembro de 1966; *Daily Telegraph*, 6 de Dezembro de 1966

[87] NAI, DFA/2002/19/11[305/218/13 Pt. IV Political situation in Portuguese Africa June 1966--December 1969].

Portugal and Ireland. Ambassador expressed personal opinion that a vote in favour in plenary would be very bad indeed for relations with Portugal. Would appreciate having your decision especially in connection with P.Q.

Estero

368

Telegrama, Uneireann para Estero: Nova Iorque, 12 de Dezembro de 1966[88]

For Secretary your 216. Tánaiste has considered démarche but has decided that we should maintain the same position in plenary. Delegate here already informed in that sense. There is of course no question of any lack of friendship for Portugal but Tánaiste is perturbed by complete absence of any kind of movement on her part in matter of overseas territories – an attitude which is now isolated and alone and which is in contrast with attitude even of Spain in recent years.

Uneireann

1967

369

Ofício, Encarregado de Negócios *ad interim* irlandês em Lisboa ao Secretário-Geral do DEA: Lisboa, 21 de Março de 1967[89]

CONFIDENTIAL

You will have seen in the press reports of the visit to Portugal of the Malawi mission which had just been in London for negotiations with the British Government.

The Mission was well received here and has good press mention, generously illustrated with photographs. It was received by Dr. Salazar and by the Ministers

---

[88] NAI, DFA/2002/19/11[305/218/13 Pt. IV Political situation in Portuguese Africa June 1966--December 1969].

[89] NAI, DFA/2002/19/11[305/218/13 Pt. IV Political situation in Portuguese Africa June 1966--December 1969].

of Foreign Affairs and of Overseas, who entertained them to a banquet at the Foreign Office – a courtesy which they returned with a banquet at the Ritz. The impression left in the minds of such of my colleagues as I happened to speak to on the subject was excellent.

I append hereunder translation of the Portuguese Foreign Office Communiqué which has appeared in this morning's press [...]

O'Kelly de Gallagh

370
Ofício, Encarregado de Negócios *ad interim* irlandês em Lisboa ao Secretário-Geral do DEA: Lisboa, 23 de Maio de 1967[90]

I have the honour to inform you that I attended the ceremonies at Fátima on Saturday the 13th inst. in honour of the 50th anniversary of the apparition of Our Lady to the children in the Cova da Iria on May 13, 1917 [...]

The atmosphere in Lisbon during the week immediately preceding the Papal visit was one of keyed-up and very joyful expectancy. During the whole week the front pages of most the press splashed Fátima news to the virtual exclusion of all other items. Fátima and the Pope's visit were the universal topics of conversation [...]

[...] I have never, in my life, seen such a prodigious crowd of people. In the huge asphalt area in front of the Basilica, stretching back, I should say, 6 or 7 hundred meters, there did not, already at that time of the morning, appear to be room for an extra human being. I estimated the multitude in that area and in the adjoining alleys giving access thereto, as probably passing the million and a half. I cannot tell how long most of them had been there, but it must have been for several hours, if not for the entire night. What immediately struck me was the orderliness, the devotion and the good temper manifested [...] The crowd was a popular crowd, mostly country folk, modest folk from the surroundings towns

---

[90] NAI, DEA, 313/11N Confidential reports from Lisbon Legation, 1967-1968.

and villages. I know that there were numerous foreign contingents, including our Blue Army Contingent, but they were lost in the Portuguese crowd.

[…]

At about half past nine there was a movement in the crowd as a great white Caravelle of the TAP bearing Pope and the Papal party, flew over our heads heading for the 25-mile-distant airfield of Monte Real. The whole place resounded to the cries "Viva o Papa" – a cry to be repeated at noon when His Holiness himself drove slowly through the human mass and ascended to the Tribune where we were all awaiting him

[…]

After lunch His Holiness received in audience the President of the Republic and Dr. Salazar – (the paper stated that the latter wept with emotion when he originally greeted the Pope at Monte Real airfield. I was not there so I cannot vouch for it, but though it doesn't seem in character it might be true), the Cardinal Patriarch of Lisbon and various officials and groups

[…] To sum up. This is not the occasion and anyhow it would be presumption on my part to attempt to assess the spiritual results of the Pope's visit. And it would certainly be premature to try to assess the long-term political effects thereof. But it is certain that, on the political plane, the Holy Father showed moral courage of a high order in visiting Portugal – even though it were only to Fátima and as a private pilgrim – at this particular juncture. I had never expected him to do so, though there had been rumours going round for some time. That his visit gave Portugal a big moral boost is undeniable and that the Holy Father was perfectly aware that this would be the case before he ever undertook the journey, seems equally obvious. The exact measure of this boost is as yet hard to compute, though the reaction in the Nordic and English language press, as illustrated by the chagrined and entirely misleading leading article in the TIMES on the 12th, may be taken as a fair indication of how annoyed some of Portugal's chronically hostile allies have been made by what they consider to be a quite uncalled-for "certificat de bonne vie et moeurs" bestowed by the Pope on Portugal. Only time will tell what the ultimate effects will be on world opinion.

[…]

O'Kelly de Gallagh

371
Texto da Declaração de Voto irlandesa em relação ao projecto de Resolução A/C.4/L.872 Rev.1 sobre a questão dos Territórios sob Administração Portuguesa, Quarto Comité, ONU, 10 de Novembro de 1967[91]

Mr. Chairman,

I wish to explain briefly the vote of the Irish delegation on the resolution just approved by this Committee.

At the XXIst Session of the General Assembly, we voted – in this Committee and in Plenary – in favour of the resolution adopted as 2194 (XXI). It was with no feeling of pleasure or satisfaction that we did so, because Portugal is a fellow-European country and one with which we have had a long history of genuine friendship. But we felt it necessary to disassociate ourselves from the colonial policies of the Portuguese Government, which refuses to acknowledge even the principle of the right of the peoples of its overseas territories to freedom and independence.

Unfortunately, we find ourselves again today in the unhappy position of having to vote in favour of a resolution condemning the policies and practices of the Government of Portugal in regard to these territories.

Mr. Chairman, although we voted in favour of the resolution as a whole, there were several aspects of it with which we were not happy. Operative paragraph 4 and the eighteenth preambular paragraph speak of a threat to international peace and security. In the view of my delegation, this is a matter for determination by the Security Council. Also, Sir, we would make a reservation in respect of the use of the words "crime against humanity" in operative paragraph 4. If, therefore, there had been a separate vote on this paragraph and on the eighth preambular, we would have abstained.

With regard to operative paragraph 5, we regard it as a matter of the utmost gravity if the practice of forcible export of African workers to South Africa in fact prevails.

---

[91] NAI, DFA/2002/19/11[305/218/13 Pt. IV Political situation in Portuguese Africa June 1966-December 1969].

We would have voted in favour of operative paragraph 6 and the corresponding ninth preambular paragraph, which deal with the activities of the financial interests operating in the territories. But we would have done so with the very specific qualification that we regard the condemnation as relating solely to those interests which in fact impede the progress of the peoples towards freedom and independence. We do not share the view that foreign investment in a country is necessarily harmful to the well-being of that country. Indeed, it would be illogical for my delegation to accept this view, because my country is very actively engaged in efforts to attract foreign investment. We recognise the need for foreign capital in order to increase employment opportunities for our people, to give them a chance of acquiring new skills and to raise their standard of living.

We would have abstained on operative paragraphs 9 and 10, which seem to my delegation to prejudge matters at present under consideration by the Security Council.

On operative paragraph 11 we would likewise have abstained, as we did last year on a somewhat similar paragraph. We consider it inappropriate for the General Assembly to make a recommendation to the Security Council in terms which tend to prejudice the Council's consideration of the matter.

Nevertheless, despite the reservations I have mentioned, we felt it right to vote for the resolution as a whole.

In conclusion, we would appeal most earnestly to the Government of Portugal to reconsider its attitude in the light of the debate in the Committee and of the resolution just adopted, in the interests both of the Portuguese people and of the peoples of the territories concerned.

Thank you Mr. Chairman

1968

372
Apontamento do Secretário-Geral do DEA sobre uma conversa com o Embaixador português em Dublin: Dublin, 30 de Janeiro de 1968[92]

NOTE

The Portuguese Ambassador came to see me at his own request today.

He said he had transmitted to Lisbon our Note about the appointment of Mr. Denis O'Sullivan to be Chargé d'Affaires ad interim in Portugal. While his authorities were pleased to receive this notification, he had been instructed to express the hope that the appointment of an Ambassador would be made in the near future.

I said I was afraid we could not promise that. As he might be aware, the Department was very short of senior personnel at present and I could not give an indication of when it would be possible for us to appoint an Ambassador to Lisbon. He enquired whether we would be filling other vacancies in the near future. I told him that we would be making an appointment to India [...]

The Portuguese Ambassador referred to the ancient cultural links between Ireland and his country, exemplified by the Dominican community of Corpo Santo and the Convent of the Bom Sucesso, and to the fact that Ireland had not had an accredited Head of Mission in Lisbon since 1963. He feared that his authorities would not take well the prospect of an indefinite prolongation of the position in which the Irish Embassy remained in charge of a Chargé d'Affaires ad interim. He asked me to convey what he had said to the Minister and this I promised to do.

Hugh McCann

---

[92] NAI, DEA, 313/11N Confidential reports from Lisbon Legation, 1967-1968.

373
Ofício, Encarregado de Negócios *ad interim* irlandês em Lisboa ao Secretário-Geral do DEA: Lisboa, 27 de Maio de 1968[93]

With further reference to Mr. O Gallchobhair's minute of 10 May 1968, I wish to report that I called on the Minister for Foreign Affairs, Dr. Alberto Marciano Gorjão Franco Nogueira on Friday evening 24th May, in accordance with the suggestion of the Protocol Section of his Ministry. Dr. Nogueira received me cordially, welcomed me to Portugal and said he hoped I had a pleasant tour of duty here.

He mentioned that he was acquainted with An Tánaiste [...]

In the course of his remarks Dr. Nogueira touched on the fact that the views of the Irish Government on many matters of foreign policy did not coincide with those of the Portuguese Government. He stressed that here he was making an observation, hardly a comment, and certainly not in any way a criticism. No Government could claim or, he thought, would wish to claim infallibility in these matters, nor that they possessed unquestioned wisdom and foresight. He wanted to say, however, that the Portuguese experience was in many ways different from that of the Irish, and because of this they could not accept many things which the Irish Government sincerely accepted. They did not, for instance, agree with the United Nations in many respects nor did they regard the organisation as justifying the support it received, particularly from the small countries, who naturally looked to the UN for support in the midst of big-power rivalry. He appreciated the philosophy of the Irish Government in its attitude to the United Nations, but he felt that perhaps it might be inclined to accept an unduly large part of its information from that source.

The situation in which Portugal found herself was a very complex one, not easily understood by other countries. He hoped that I would have an opportunity to learn more about the Portuguese world and its problems, and I told him I was anxious to do so.

[...]

Denis B. O'Sullivan

---

[93] NAI, DEA, 313/11N Confidential reports from Lisbon Legation, 1967-1968.

374
Comunicação interna do DEA: Dublin, 7 de Junho de 1968[94]

Mr Holmes,

In reference to the attached report of 27th May, 1968, from the Chargé d'Affaires, a.i. at Lisbon, I think it is necessary to send Mr. O'Sullivan a note for his guidance on our attitude towards matters affecting Portugal raised at the UN and elsewhere [...]

Assinatura ilegível

375
Carta, Denis Holmes, DEA, ao Encarregado de Negócios *ad interim* irlandês em Lisboa: Dublin, 8 de Julho de 1968[95]

CONFIDENTIAL

Dear Denis,

Arising out of your report dated 27th May 1968 on your meeting with the Minister for Foreign Affairs, Dr. Nogueira, we have though it might be helpful for you to have some background material concerning our attitude towards Portugal, particularly as it has developed in regard to matters raised at the United Nations and on other international bodies to which both Ireland and Portugal belong.

I am sending you herewith extracts from the Memoranda for the Government concerning "Portuguese Territories" for each of the General Assembly Sessions from 1959 to 1967. This will show the principles which have guided our policy in this matter and the extracts from the Delegation reports which are attached will

---

[94] NAI, DFA/2002/19/11[305/218/13 Pt. IV Political situation in Portuguese Africa June 1966--December 1969].

[95] NAI, DFA/2002/19/11[305/218/13 Pt. IV Political situation in Portuguese Africa June 1966--December 1969].

show how the item was dealt with at the 18th, 20th and 21st Sessions in 1963, 1965 and 1966. The report for 1967 is not yet ready but I am enclosing a copy of the explanation of vote made in the Fourth Committee by our representative (Mr. Power) after voting in favour of the Afro-Asian draft resolution on 10th November, 1967. The texts of this resolution and those of 1966 and 1965 are also enclosed.

[…]

When the questions of South African apartheid and Portuguese colonial territories come up elsewhere than in the United Nations, the general line to be taken is shown in the enclosed extract from instructions which were prepared for the Irish Delegation to the World Health Organisation in 1965. The Portuguese issue has been especially prominent in WHO where, as you will see, Ireland was the only western country to abstain (rather than opposing) on a resolution to suspend Portugal from participation in the WHO Regional Committee for Africa in 1966 and also to suspend technical assistance under WHO to Portugal. We maintained our abstention in 1967 at the 20th WHO Assembly and in the autumn of that year the European Regional Committee of WHO, meeting in Dublin, adopted a resolution intended to ease the administrative difficulties in implementation for the Director-General of WHO and also to make it possible for Portuguese doctors to attend seminars in the European region. The other Regional Committees also made reports (the African one being opposed to any concessions) and at the 21st WHO Assembly last May a resolution emerged noting these differing regional views and deciding (a) that the Director-General should "take into consideration the need not to envisage in WHO programmes any commitment for Portugal until that country renounces the policy of colonial domination"; (b) that provision be made "if necessary in cooperation with other appropriate organisations through special programmes for health activities to the refugees and nationals of countries under colonial domination particularly in regard to the notification of communicable diseases and the professional training of qualified national personnel"; and (c) to ensure "within the limits of his competence the implementation of this resolution and to report periodically to the Regional Committees and to the WHO Assembly." The voting on this resolution was 42 in favour, 9 against and 29 abstentions. The abstentions included the US, Great Britain, the Scandinavians and Latin-Americans as well as Ireland.

No change in the main elements of our policy towards the Portuguese possessions either in the UN or elsewhere is likely to take place and the enclosed material should therefore be of continuing background value. It is of course not to be disclosed or quoted from in any form except where it has already been published as in the case of the Dáil question and explanations of vote in the UN. If there should be any new developments we shall keep you informed.

Yours sincerely,
Denis Holmes

376
Ofício, Encarregado de Negócios *ad interim* irlandês em Lisboa ao Secretário-Geral do DEA: Lisboa, 9 de Setembro de 1968[96]

CONFIDENTIAL

With reference to my cable N.º 19 of today's date I wish to report that Dr. Salazar, President of the Council of Minister, continues to make progress after his operation and no undue anxiety appears to be felt about his condition. Today's bulletins speak confidently of his state and prospects. He was able to take a few steps yesterday assisted by his attendants and to sit in a chair for a quarter of an hour. One of the doctors in attendance told the Press that within ten or twelve days Dr. Salazar would be convalescent (not completely recovered as stated erroneously in the cable).

What gave rise to all this was what seemed to be a minor accident at his summer residence in Estoril. The canvas chair on which he was sitting or about to sit collapsed and his head hit the ground. It was not stated when this occurred, but apart from the bruise there was no other effect until the last few days when headaches and, according to one report, disturbance of his vision and movements,

---

[96] NAI, DEA, 313/11N Confidential reports from Lisbon Legation, 1967-1968.

caused his doctors to carry out various tests and to decide on surgery for, as I understand it, the removal of a clot in the right parietal.

A local anaesthetic was given, and it is stated the operation was quite normal in every way. Dr. Salazar is reported to have been in full possession of his faculties entering the hospital, and there is no indication that his command of affairs lessened at any stage.

[…]

The next several days will no doubt be anxious ones for his doctors lest further clotting occur. At this stage it is impossible to say whether the incident will reduce Dr. Salazar's drive or control of the Government. Undoubtedly it will be some time before he can resume normal activity, and at his age (79 years) it is unlikely that he will be able, or allowed, by his doctors, to undertake as much as before.

The question of succession arises, as it does periodically, but while names have been mentioned I have no information to suggest that an heir apparent has been chosen. As did other members of the Diplomatic Corps, I called at the hospital and left my card.

Denis B. O'Sullivan

377
Ofício, Encarregado de Negócios *ad interim* irlandês em Lisboa ao Secretário-Geral do DEA: Lisboa, 12 de Setembro de 1968[97]

CONFIDENTIAL

With reference to my minute dated 9th inst. about Dr. Salazar, I wish to report that there seems to be no doubt that he is making excellent progress, and the speculation now is when he is likely to leave the hospital. Medical bulletins have discontinued giving particulars of blood pressure, pulse rate etc. and after yesterday's bulletin it is not proposed to issue another until Saturday 14th, at which time there may be some indication of the doctors' plans for their patient.

---

[97] NAI, DEA, 313/11N Confidential reports from Lisbon Legation, 1967-1968.

Dr. Salazar is reported to be sleeping normally and to get up for several hours every day. So far he has had no visitors apart from members of the hospital staff and his housekeeper of many years, who is in attendance to him. Their concern is to see that he gets plenty of rest, although his restricted activity does not seem to tire him – in fact the reporters at the hospital say he has pressed to be allowed to resume some of his reading. As a result, the atmosphere in the hospital is very optimistic.

The hospital lobby continues to be thronged with reporters and visitors (for whose signatures a book has now been provided). Among these have been the Duke of Braganza and his son the Prince of Beira who are the principal members of the Portuguese Royal Family and who have called at the hospital several times. The Prince, aged 23 years, is a lieutenant in the Air Force.

Messages have been received from the Cardinal Secretary of State conveying the paternal wishes and prayers of the Holy Father for Dr. Salazar's recovery, from German Chancellor Kiesinger, from Prime Minister Couve de Murville and from the Deputy Prime Minister of Rhodesia

Denis B. O'Sullivan

378
Ofício, Encarregado de Negócios *ad interim* irlandês em Lisboa ao Secretário-Geral do DEA: Lisboa, 18 de Setembro de 1968[98]

CONFIDENTIAL

With reference to my minute of 12th September regarding Dr. Salazar, I am sure that you have learned from the news reports as much information about his critical state as is available here. The latest medical bulletin stated that Dr. Salazar had maintained the improvement in his condition announced yesterday, "despite some tiring examinations to which he has been subjected". The cardiovascular and neurological conditions were said to have improved. No statement has been

---

[98] NAI, DEA, 313/11N Confidential reports from Lisbon Legation, 1967-1968.

made as to whether there is any paralysis or coma. The general feeling in the city, however, is pessimistic, as it is regarded as certain that if he recovers he would at best be paralysed and unable to carry on as President of the Council of Ministers. For the moment he seems to be under observation by the Portuguese medical team and by the US neurologist Huston Meritt, who was chosen by the Portuguese doctors for that purpose at the invitation of the US Government.

The Council of State was convened yesterday by the President of the Republic. Under the Constitution the Council is obliged, inter alia, to meet whenever the President of the Republic deems it necessary to summon it. No doubt the question of Dr. Salazar's successor was discussed, but no communiqué was issued as to what took place. Appointment of the President of the Council of Ministers is made by the President of the Republic who is also empowered to dismiss him.

In the meantime the strongest candidate to succeed Dr. Salazar is said to be Professor Marcello Caetano, a member of the Council of State and former Minister of State who worked closely with Dr. Salazar until they disagreed some years ago. He is said to be already signing documents at the office of the President of the Council, but no announcement has been made so far.

He was born on 17 August 1906, is married and is a lawyer who was written much on legal administration. He has travelled to France, Italy, Brazil and to Africa. He is said to be a hard worker and a forceful personality.

Denis B. O'Sullivan

379
Ofício, Encarregado de Negócios *ad interim* irlandês em Lisboa ao Secretário-Geral do DEA: Lisboa, 23 de Setembro de 1968[99]

CONFIDENTIAL

Further to my minute dated 20th inst., I wish to state that according to the medical bulletins there appears to have been little change in the condition of

---

[99] NAI, DEA, 313/11N Confidential reports from Lisbon Legation, 1967-1968.

Dr. Salazar in the past week. The latest bulletin (Sunday 8 p.m.) declared that he had "responded slightly and at times with appropriate elementary movements to verbal requests (sensorial reactions)", but, the doctors state that they are still reserving any prognostication. The bulletins also quote his pulse beat, temperature and as far as a layman may judge there is no significant variation in the figures. The patient's breathing is helped, according to the latest bulletin, by an Engström respirator, described by one of the doctors in an interview with reporters, as an "apparatus which breathes for the patient and consequently maintains the phenomenon of breathing so that the sufferer can go on living while his constitution undertakes, with the medication administered him and other therapeutic aids, to recuperate the lesions made." With regard to the sensorial reactions observed, the doctor (Professor Bissaia Barreto) remarked that they were a welcome sign, indicating that Dr. Salazar had "moments of lucidity, of perception and of comprehension". However, Dr. Barreto stated that he was concerned at the patient's temperature (101.66 on 22nd) and was not easy in his mind as regards Dr. Salazar's condition generally.

Meanwhile, no announcement has been made about a substitute or successor at the Office of the President of the Council of Ministers. The President of the Republic, Admiral Américo Thomaz, has been meeting individual members of the Council of State, according to newspaper reports, and indeed must have been very busy as he did not appear at the Red Cross Hospital for the last part of the week until yesterday – that in contrast to his daily and more frequent visits in the early stages of Dr. Salazar's illness.

Denis B. O'Sullivan

380
Telegrama, Hibernia para Estero: Lisboa, 27 de Setembro de 1968[100]

20. NEW PRESIDENT COUNCIL PROFESSOR MARCELLO CAETANO WILL ADDRESS NATION SEVENTEEN HOURS TODAY AFTER FORMAL INVESTING OFFICE

---

[100] NAI, DEA, 313/11N Confidential reports from Lisbon Legation, 1967-1968.

STOP FIVE OTHER MINISTERIAL CHANGES INCLUDING MINISTER STATE ATTACHED COUNCIL PRESIDENTS OFFICE AND MINISTER NATIONAL DEFENCE STOP NO CHANGE MINISTER FOREIGN AFFAIRS STOP

HIBERNIA

381
Ofício, Encarregado de Negócios *ad interim* irlandês em Lisboa ao Secretário-Geral do DEA: Lisboa, 4 de Outubro de 1968[101]

CONFIDENTIAL

With reference to my cable N.º 20 of the 27th inst., I enclose a more or less literal translation of Professor Caetano's speech to the nation when he took over the office of President of the Council of Ministers. Also enclosed is a revised list of the Government Ministers and Secretaries of State.

The new Portuguese Cabinet shows relatively few new names and they do not appear to represent any major changes in policy [...]

Professor Caetano's speech, however, is not that of an unswerving follower of Dr. Salazar. While paying tribute to his predecessor he spoke of the need to change as circumstances might demand, and not merely by the use of formulas or devices adopted by Dr. Salazar. He pleaded for understanding and for time to deal with the country's problems, pointing out that this would involve some sacrifice including certain rights that desirably should be restored. This has been taken to indicate, inter alia, an eventual relaxation of newspaper censorship, and in this connection newspapers here and abroad have noted Professor Caetano's willingness to meet reporters and photographers (although on his own terms).

[...]

Professor Caetano also virtually promised more information to the public and at more frequent intervals, as if to bring the people in closer contact with the making of Government decisions, another departure full of possibilities, even if

---

[101] NAI, DEA, 313/11N Confidential reports from Lisbon Legation, 1967-1968.

unlikely to have much effect immediately; the creation of the new post of Secretary of State for Information and Tourism may be an earnest of the proposal.

However, no great relaxation of controls is expected and in fact, the authorities some days ago refused to admit a correspondent of the GUARDIAN and expelled a Swedish journalist [...]

Denis B. O'Sullivan

382
Ofício, Encarregado de Negócios *ad interim* irlandês em Lisboa ao Secretário-Geral do DEA: Lisboa, 30 de Outubro de 1968[102]

CONFIDENTIAL

With reference to previous reports on the state of health of Dr. Salazar, I wish to state that in an interview given to the Lisbon morning newspaper, DIÁRIO DE NOTÍCIAS, published 30 October 1968, Professor Bissaia Barreto, one of the attending physicians, declared that the patient was taking food (3000 calories) daily, was answering normally questions put to him, and that he was able to bless himself.

Asked whether Dr. Salazar would be paralysed, Professor Barreto replied "No". "From the motor point of view, President Salazar is progressing very well, thanks to the treatment being applied. But apart from that it is notable that the recuperation is due to the uncommon will power with which Dr. Salazar is gifted. This quality is an extraordinary help towards the improvement of his condition".

Professor Barreto would not say when Dr. Salazar might be expected to leave the Red Cross Hospital. "It is a problem which obviously depends on how the process of recuperation continues. And it is really excellent at present."

Dr. Salazar (who was officially given the title of President although no longer in office as President of the Council of Ministers), does not now need special apparatus for breathing. His temperature, blood pressure etc remain normal and

---

[102] NAI, DEA, 313/11N Confidential reports from Lisbon Legation, 1967-1968.

he is gaining some of the weight he lost during the course of his illness. The improvement is remarkable, and, as far as I can judge from colleagues in the Diplomatic Corps, it is also unexpected. In fact at a recent meeting of Heads of Mission there was some discussion about funeral arrangements and the difficulty of getting definite information on certain points from the Protocol at the Ministry of Foreign Affairs.

Denis B. O'Sullivan

383
Ofício, Encarregado de Negócios *ad interim* irlandês em Lisboa ao Secretário-Geral do DEA: Lisboa, 11 de Novembro de 1968[103]

With reference to my minute dated 30th October 1968 about the condition of Dr. Salazar, I wish to state that little change has been reported since the correction of the irregularities of the heart action which occurred over a week ago.

Shortly after this upset a fairly long medical report was published which effectively doused any optimism encouraged by Professor Barreto's earlier commentary. The report stated that the cardio-circulatory function was sufficient for the basic needs of the organism despite the extra-sistolic irregularity. However, there had been an accentuated deterioration of the general condition of the patient during the seven weeks that he had been ill. He was not in a coma but his perception was at a low level. He could only mutter unintelligibly or answer to specific questions and he tired quickly. He was paralysed on the left side, his eye muscles in particular being affected. The absence of significant recuperation over the weeks did not allow a foreseeable amelioration of the injuries to the nervous system.

It is commonly accepted now that he is dying, but the medical bulletins do not say so, nor give any indication as to how long he may linger. The Diplomatic Corps understand that all arrangements have been made by the authorities for the funeral and that there would be a mourning period of two weeks.

---

[103] NAI, DEA, 313/11N Confidential reports from Lisbon Legation, 1967-1968.

In my report of 30 October 1968 I erroneously described Professor Bissaia Barreto as one of the attending physicians [...] He is a long-time friend of Dr. Salazar and has been a regular visitor at his bedside since he entered the hospital.

Denis B. O'Sullivan

1969

384
Ofício, Encarregado de Negócios *ad interim* irlandês em Lisboa ao Secretário-Geral do DEA: Lisboa, 7 de Outubro de 1969[104]

CONFIDENTIAL

Further to my report P.R. 8/69, dated 6th October 1969, about the retirement of Dr. Franco Nogueira, as Minister for Foreign Affairs, to-day's newspapers carry reports of speeches made by him and by the Prime Minister at the ceremonial transfer of office to the latter.

Dr. Nogueira is a candidate of the União Nacional in Lisbon at the election to take place this month, and the remarks made by him and by the Prime Minister were on the subject of the Overseas Territories which have been a main topic of the electoral campaign. Dr. Nogueira stressed that the Territories were part of the country's vital interests and their retention a basic part of foreign policy. There was no equivalence or compensation, as some thought in gaining the goodwill of the United Nations, undermined and passed over, by giving up Angola, Mozambique and Guinea, nor was it worth the effort, as others suggested, to submit or to seek the advice of an organisation in crisis, likened by the Canadian Minister for External Affairs to "a sea of paper" and "swamped in words". Portugal, far from being isolated, has all the contacts she needed in the world, and he instanced the financing of the Cabora-Bassa dam in Africa (without referring to the recent, unpublished, withdrawal of Swedish interests). Was it in her interest to keep the overseas territories or open diplomatic relations with Moscow?

---

[104] NAI, DFA/2002/19/11[305/218/13 Pt. IV Political situation in Portuguese Africa June 1966--December 1969].

Professor Caetano spoke of Dr. Nogueira as "a fighting Minister" and he trusted the electorate would have the good sense to send him to the National Assembly. The change over at the Ministry would not weaken the defence of the overseas territories on the diplomatic front, just as it would not yield on the home front. He then proceeded to examine and criticise opposing viewpoints favouring negotiations with leaders of resistance movements and a cease-fire, to end by affirming that Portugal would not compromise or yield in the struggle, since it was the only genuine road to peace and prosperity.

These remarks must surely be looked on as election speeches, and they indicate how seriously the Government regard the Opposition stands on this matter. In other recent speeches Professor Caetano has put the overseas question as having in effect only two alternatives, the Government stand or chaos and national disgrace. The Opposition have not been able to put forward a sufficiently attractive third alternative, although they seem to have made known a widespread dissatisfaction with the war and its effects. The majority of Portuguese probably support the Government however, and particularly the majority of the electorate, some 1.8 million registered voters.

Denis B. O'Sullivan

385
Apontamento de Denis Holmes, DEA, sobre uma conversa com o Embaixador português em Dublin: Dublin, 11 de Novembro de 1969[105]

The Portuguese Ambassador called to see me this morning at his request. He said that he had just returned from a visit to Lisbon were he was during the general election. The Ambassador stated that in contrast with his predecessor, Mr. Salazar, the present Portuguese leader, Mr. Caetano, is a liberal man. Mr. Caetano is trying to bring in liberal reforms e.g. with a new press law but of course he has to move slowly as he has to have regard to the facts of political life in Portugal.

---

[105] NAI, DFA/2002/19/11[305/218/13 Pt. IV Political situation in Portuguese Africa June 1966--December 1969].

The Ambassador went on to say that high officials in Lisbon with whom he had discussed the situation in the North expressed sympathy with our problem and counselled our emphasising the human rights aspect.

The Ambassador then came to what no doubt was the main purpose of his visit namely to enlist an understanding on our part of Portugal's position in relation to the resolution on Portugal which certain African states will shortly be bringing forward at the United Nations. The Ambassador emphasised that conditions in Angola and Mozambique are not as some Communist elements in those areas would make them out to be. He pointed out that the nearby African state of Malawi are seeking to have normal relations with the authorities in Mozambique. He emphasised that the language used in the resolution put forward by the African states at the UN is not justified by the realities of the situation and he urged that we bear this in mind in considering such resolutions. Finally he made a plea that if we could not see our way to opposing such resolutions we should at least instruct our delegate to abstain on them.

I undertook to enquire into the matter and to convey the Ambassador's request to the Minister.

Denis Holmes

386
Telegrama, Uneireann para Estero: Nova Iorque, 14 de Novembro de 1969[106]

384 FOR HOLMES YOUR 299. RESOLUTION PORTUGUESE TERRITORIES ADOPTED 88 VOTES TO 3 (PORTUGAL SOUTH AFRICA SPAIN) WITH 16 ABSTENTIONS (ARGENTINA AUSTRALIA BELGIUM BRAZIL CUBA FRANCE GREECE ITALY IVORY COAST MALAWI MEXICO NETHERLANDS NEW ZEALAND PERU BRITAIN US). NO SEPARATE VOTING PARAGRAPHS. CONSIDERED UNNECESSARY EXPLAINING VOTE IN VIEW MODIFICATIONS DESCRIBED OUR 374

UNEIREANN

---

[106] NAI, DFA/2002/19/11[305/218/13 Pt. IV Political situation in Portuguese Africa June 1966--December 1969]. O Embaixador português era António Alexandre Rocha Fontes.

387
Carta, Secretário Privado do Taoiseach (Jack Lynch) ao DEA: Dublin, 21 de Novembro de 1969[107]

Office of the Taoiseach

I am desired by the Taoiseach to send you a brief note of his talk with the Portuguese Ambassador who sought an interview with him yesterday.

C. Mefiomáin
Rúnaí Príobháideach

Memo:

Visit of Portuguese Ambassador 20th November, 1969. Spoke in praise of New Prime Minister Mr. Caetano – A man of humble origin – a poor man (still a poor man) wanted to do good but must proceed slowly because Right Wing elements: Communists not taken as a serious threat in Portugal.

Spoke about conditions in Angola – not as Communists etc. allege. Will be another Brazil – new factories etc.

Then he came to position in UN. Ireland the only European country who voted for Resolution last year. Wants us to abstain or not take part this year. This would give Caetano a chance to go ahead with reforms.

The Portuguese support us re N.I. situation etc. I told him I thought that the vote had been taken but he said that this was on the Commission and not yet in General Assembly. I said we always like to take up a definite position and when it came to self determination we were always for. I told him that, not knowing in advance the purpose of his visit, I was not fully up to date on this issue but I would discuss the matter with the Minister for External Affairs.

Earlier on he spoke of the probability of sending an observer to Angola at no expense to us to bring back a first-hand account of conditions there. I did not comment on this.

His English was not fully comprehensible to me so I had some difficulty.

J. L.

---

[107] NAI, DFA/2002/19/11[305/218/13 Pt. IV Political situation in Portuguese Africa June 1966--December 1969].

388
Comunicação interna do DEA endereçada ao Secretário-Geral:
Dublin, 20 de Novembro de 1969[108]

Secretary

The Portuguese Ambassador's call on the Taoiseach took place at very short notice and it seems the Taoiseach may not have had time to study the brief which we prepared very hurriedly for him. There are a few points which should I think be made clear in the light of the Ambassador's remarks:

(1) Mr. Caetano's "new deal". Whatever substance there may be in this concept for domestic Portugal there would seem to be none where her overseas territories are concerned. Our Delegation report for 1968 quoted the Portuguese representative to the effect that "Dr. Salazar's retirement would not mean a change on Portuguese policy on this question as that policy did not depend on one individual or on any government in particular but on the very structure of the Portuguese State." (Page 155 par. 21 of Report on 23rd Session).

(2) Ireland the only European country to vote for the Resolution last year. This is not correct. All the Scandinavians and Canada [sic] supported the 1968 resolution, which had been specially revised by its Afro-Asian sponsors to make it acceptable to them and to us. The final vote was 96 for, 3 against (Brazil, Portugal and South Africa), and 15 abstentions. (Page 156 par. 25 of Report of 23rd Session).

(3) This year's vote in the UN. The Fourth Committee voted on the subject on 14th November 1969 and it was adopted by 88 to 3 with 16 abstentions. Ireland again supported the resolution together with the Scandinavians and Canada. Spain this year voted against while Brazil moved to an abstention. Full particulars are in document A/7768 attached. The subject will of course come up again in the Plenary when it is expected the vote will be similar.

D. H.

---

[108] NAI, DFA/2002/19/11[305/218/13 Pt. IV Political situation in Portuguese Africa June 1966--December 1969].

389
Carta, Encarregado de Negócio *ad interim* irlandês em Lisboa ao DEA: Lisboa, 5 de Dezembro de 1969

Dear Eamonn,

Thank you for sending on the report on the Ambassador's visit to the Taoiseach in connection with the UN vote on the Portuguese Territories.

I have been arranging a bit of a report on Malawi and send it next week.

The point in the Taoiseach's memo about sending an observer to Angola was mentioned by the late Count in a P.R. which I can't quote just now. Several heads of mission here have gone to Angola and Mozambique, and as you probably know there have been visits by various British and I think French parliamentarians. One of the latest visitors was the Dutch Ambassador, and I am told there was some reference in parliament to it – he had been quoted in the Press as saying how impressed he was by schools etc. he had visited, perhaps a natural thing to say at the time, but…

I don't know what value such a trip can be, unless to refute points made by Petitioners at the UN. A three or four-week visit to those vast areas will show only the most obvious things but perhaps that is all the Portuguese want. Countries with trade or cultural interests might want to send an observer but apart from a few Medical Missionaries in Angola I don't think Ireland has any lines to support arguments for an observer (unless CTT move in!).

The press reports on UN votes did not criticise or point up Ireland's vote.

Best wishes.

Yours sincerely,

Denis B. O'Sullivan

---

[109] NAI, DFA/2002/19/11[305/218/13 Pt. IV Political situation in Portuguese Africa June 1966--December 1969].

1970

390
Ofício, Encarregado de Negócios *ad interim* irlandês em Lisboa ao Secretário-Geral do DEA: Lisboa, 20 de Julho de 1970[110]

With reference to previous reports about the health of the former Prime Minister, Dr. Salazar, I wish to state for your information that the kidney infection he developed has been given intensive treatment which, according to the Press, has been immediately effective [...] The medical bulletins had stated his condition was grave, but apparently no crisis was expected, as the President of the Republic, Admiral Thomaz, did not interrupt his sea journey to São Tomé, where he is due on 23rd July on connection with the centenary celebrations of the discovery of the island (1470).

Should a fatal crisis occur, the President would, of course, return. However, the political significance of such an eventuality has lessened very much in view of Professor Caetano's command of the Government and affairs generally.

Denis B. O'Sullivan

391
Ofício, Encarregado de Negócios *ad interim* irlandês em Lisboa ao Secretário-Geral do DEA: Lisboa, 31 de Julho de 1970[111]

With reference to my cable N.º 9 dated July 27th about Dr. Salazar's death I wish to report that the Taoiseach's message of sympathy to Professor Caetano was duly mentioned in the local Press and the text was quoted in at least three of the newspapers.

Among the many photographs published of incidents in the late Premier's life was one showing him with *an tUachtarán* (July 1956) and the late Count O'Kelly de Gallagh on the doorstep of Dr. Salazar's residence in Lisbon – please see enclosed cutting.[112] Dr. Salazar died about 9:30 a.m. on Monday 7th July 1970

---

[110] NAI, DEA, 313/110 Confidential reports from the Lisbon Legation, 1969-1970.
[111] NAI, DEA, 313/110 Confidential reports from the Lisbon Legation, 1969-1970.

following a kidney infection and cardiovascular complications. The event became generally known when the flag in front of his residence and the National Assembly was lowered to half mast about 11:20, after which radio bulletins, and later the television service gave the news.

National mourning was proclaimed from that day until the funeral had taken place on Thursday. Offices, shops and non-essential services were asked to close on Thursday, at least for the duration of the funeral, and in general banks and most offices and shops closed for the day. Radio and television stations replaced their usual programmes with classical or religious music and recordings of Dr. Salazar's speeches, summaries of his life and particular events. All Embassies halfmasted their flags on the day of the funeral, and those which fly them daily had their flags at half mast for the duration.

The lying in state took place on Tuesday and Wednesday at the Jerónimos Monastery (St. Mary of Belém), erected in the 16th century to commemorate the voyages of discovery by Portuguese mariners, a period of exceptional pride and greatness for Portugal to which this entire river area of western Lisbon is dedicated, by means of monuments old and new, squares, and street names.

The Ministry of Foreign Affairs requested the attendance of the Diplomatic Corps (heads of mission) at the lying in state on Tuesday afternoon. There was no procedure for cards, or signing a book, although about five Ambassadors went to the S. Bento residence before the removal of the body. However, it had been arranged that, beginning with members of the Government, groups of about two persons would stand around the (open) coffin, placed in front of the altar; and accordingly at 3 p.m. my wife and I joined the second diplomatic group – the first headed by the Nuncio and senior Ambassadors had attended at 2:30 p.m. Dark, everyday wear, including black tie was specified, and for the ladies short dresses and mantillas.

On Thursday, for the funeral, the Diplomatic Corps were placed near the altar, epistle side, and formal dress (morning coat, black waistcoat) was specified for the men [...] The first seats were reserved for the visiting delegations and foreign

---

[112] Referência ao encontro entre Salazar e de Valera, Presidente da Irlanda (Uachtarán na hÉireann) de 1959 a 1973, embora O'Sullivan se tenha enganado na data do encontro. Ver Documento N°147.

Government representatives – there were delegates from Spain, Brazil, the United States, Great Britain, South Africa, France and Germany; the Belgian and Greek Ambassadors in Lisbon were designated as representatives of their respective governments [...] On the opposite side were relatives of the deceased Premier (one of two surviving sisters, and families, and his two adopted daughters) and his housekeeper of fifty years, who wept silently and uninterruptedly during the service.

The choir of the San Carlos Opera and the National Radio symphony orchestra performed the accompanying music. The Mass including panegyric by a member of the Cathedral Chapter, was presided over by the Cardinal, a fellow student of Salazar's in the early years of the century, who gave the brief Absolution at the end of the ceremony. It began at 10:30 a.m. when the President of the Republic, Admiral Thomáz, arrived (having returned from S. Tomé the previous night) and concluded at 11:45 a.m.

There remained the procession from the Church to an improvised platform on the nearby railway connecting Lisbon to Estoril. The Diplomatic Corps, as well as the official delegations joined the cortège which preceded the heavy coffin shouldered by military bearers.

The coffin was put aboard a train and, escorted by the President, the Prime Minister (Professor Caetano) and other Ministers, relatives and close friends and others, some 400 persons in all, it travelled north from Lisbon to the Salazar birthplace, a village named Santa Comba Dão, near Coimbra, for burial in the local cemetery.

Denis B. O'Sullivan

392

Ofício, Encarregado de Negócios *ad interim* irlandês em Lisboa ao Secretário-Geral do DEA: Lisboa, 3 de Agosto de 1970[113]

[...] I omitted to include the Canadian and Argentine Ambassadors in Lisbon among the group of Governmental Delegations [...]

Denis B. O'Sullivan

---

[113] NAI, DEA, 313/110 Confidential reports from the Lisbon Legation, 1969-1970.

Anexos

Ministros dos Negócios Estrangeiros irlandeses, 1932-1971

[Anexo 1]

Eamon de Valera (Fianna Fáil) Março de 1932 a Fevereiro de 1948
    Em acumulação com o cargo de Taoiseach (Primeiro Ministro)

Séan MacBride (Clann na Poblachta) Fevereiro de 1948 a Junho de 1951

Frank Aiken (Fianna Fáil) Junho de 1951 a Junho de 1954

Liam Cosgrave (Fine Gael) Junho de 1954 a Março de 1957

Frank Aiken (Fianna Fáil) Março de 1957 a Julho de 1969
    Em acumulação com o cargo de Tánaiste (Vice-Primeiro Ministro) a partir de Abril de 1965

Patrick Hillery (Fianna Fáil) Julho de 1969 a Março de 1971

Secretários Gerais (Secretaries) do Department of External Affairs, 1927-1974

[Anexo 2]

Joseph P. Walshe Agosto de 1927 a Maio de 1946

Frederick H. Boland Maio de 1946 a Setembro de 1950

Séan Nunan Setembro de 1950 a Maio de 1955

Séan Murphy Maio de 1955 a Novembro de 1957

Cornelius C. Cremin Dezembro de 1957 a Janeiro de 1963

Hugh McCann Janeiro de 1963 a Abril de 1974

Processos consultados – National Archives of Ireland
[Anexo 3]

EMBASSY LISBON

FILES ABOUT PORTUGAL

6/2	Portugal (Miscellaneous)
6/2	Various enquiries and information regarding conditions, practices, organisations, etc., 1944-1945
6/3	Economic and social conditions in Portugal, 1946
6/3	Portuguese Legation in Dublin, 1943-1965
6/5	Portuguese neutrality in the Second World War
6/6	Cost of living in Portugal
6/7	Portuguese Foreign Office and representatives abroad
6/8	Portugal: Civil aviation, 1944
6/10	Rationing, 1944
6/11	Portugal: Foreign trade, 1945
6/13	Portugal's financial position
6/14	Portuguese Constitution, 1959
6/14	Elections, 1945
6/15	Portugal's economic position, 1949-1965
6/17	Portuguese press, 1947
6/18	Church in Portugal, 1959
6/20	Health services in Portugal, 1959-1963
6/22	United Nations, 1946
6/23	New Year reception by President of the Republic
6/25	Portuguese electoral laws
6/26	Corporate system in Portugal, 1947
6/29	Secret and confidential matters
6/35	Pilgrimages – Fatima, 1958-1962

MISCELLANEOUS FILES

Unnumbered files:

    Visit by Irish officials to Portugal, 1943-44
    Portuguese Red Cross, 1944
    Radio Éireann broadcasts, 1945
    Irish neutrality, 1945
    Confidential communications from Department of External Affairs, 1942-1963

A.7/42	Irish nationals and interests in the war area, 1942
A.8/42	European war 1942: Belligerent nationals in Ireland
1/3/41	Cordell Hull's statement regarding neutrals, 1944
D.1/42	Portuguese press, 1942
D.1/44	Same, 1944
D.2/42	Correspondence unclassified, 1941
D.2/44	Portugal: Conditions, practice, organisation, etc., 1942
D.4/47	Notes to Ministry of Foreign Affairs, 1943
E.1/44	United States request for withdrawal of Axis representatives in Ireland, 1944
F.6/44	Second front restrictions, 1944
F.10/45	Same, 1945

EMBASSY TO THE HOLY SEE

24/104	Fatima, 1951-1967
24/117	Dispute between India and Portugal re. Goa, 1953-1961

EMBASSY MADRID

I.P.4/51/1	Portugal , 1941-1963

PERMANENT MISSION TO THE UNITED NATIONS

X/17	Portugal, 1956-1963
X/19	Portuguese overseas colonies, 1958-1965
X/20	Portuguese overseas territories, 1963-1965
X/31	Portugal, 1963-1965

PRE 100 SERIES

34/303	Establishment of a Council of the Portuguese Colonial Empire, 1935

200 SERIES

206/60/2	Purchase of ships by Irish Shipping Ltd, offer received through Lisbon Legation – Lisbon, 1942-1945
219/81	Confidential reports from Lisbon, 1942-1944
232/46	Corporative organisation of agriculture in Portugal, 1940
232/95	National Congress of Agrarian Science held in Lisbon December 1943, 1944
233/157	Exchange of diplomatic mailbags between Department and Irish Legation Lisbon, 1941-1943
233/157A	Exchange of diplomatic mailbags between Department and Irish Legation Lisbon, 1943-1945
233/176	Telegraphic Communication between Lisbon, Dublin, 1942
233/201	Censorship in Portugal, 1943-1945
233/277	Direct radio telegraphic service between the Vatican State and Portugal, 1944

300 SERIES

305/12/1	Partition, documentation of Lisbon Legation, 1946-1959
305/46/3	Cabinet changes in Portugal , 1950-1959

305/53	Title of Portuguese Head of State
305/137	Speeches of Doctor Salazar, 1950-1960
305/218/13	Portuguese Africa: Political situation, 1962-1965
305/271	Goa and other Portuguese enclaves in India, 1947-1954
305/271A	Goa and other Portuguese enclaves in India, 1954-1955
305/271B	Goa and the other Portuguese enclaves in India, 1955-1958
305/271 Pt II	Goa and the other Portuguese enclaves in India, 1960-1968
305/271/1	Part 1A (transmission of information under Article 73 (E) of the UN Charter (including non-transmission of information from Goa and other Portuguese enclaves), 1957-1959
305/419	"Santa Maria" affair, 1961
313/11	Confidential reports from Lisbon Legation, 1945
313/11A	Confidential reports from Lisbon Legation, 1946-1951
313/11B	Confidential reports from Lisbon Legation, 1952-1954
313/11C	Confidential reports from Lisbon Legation, 1955
313/11D	Confidential reports from Lisbon Legation, 1956-1957
313/11E	Confidential reports from Lisbon Legation, 1958
313/11F	Confidential reports from Lisbon Legation, 1959
313/11G	Confidential reports from Lisbon Legation, 1960
313/11H	Confidential reports from Lisbon Legation, 1961
313/11I	Confidential reports from Lisbon Legation, 1962
313/11J	Confidential reports from Lisbon Legation, 1963
313/11K	Confidential reports from Lisbon Legation, 1964
313/11L	Confidential reports from Lisbon Legation, 1965
313/11M	Confidential reports from Lisbon Legation, 1966
313/11N	Confidential reports from Lisbon Legation, 1967-1968
313/11O	Confidential reports from Lisbon Legation, 1969-1970
314/10/11	Irish-Portuguese trade agreement, 1950-1959
314/44	The Iberian Pact: Treaty of friendship and non-aggression between Spain and Portugal, 1948-1952
317/40	Appointment of a Chargé d'Affaires in Lisbon, 1941-1948
318/79	Establishment of a Portuguese Legation in Dublin and appointment of a Chargé d'Affaires, 1942-1964

321/18	Air services between Lisbon and Foynes, 1945
321/41	Civil aviation in Portugal, 1941-1946
321/79/4	Air agreements between Portugal and other countries, 1946-49
321/80/14	Permission for Portuguese planes to fly over Irish territory, 1947-9
333/7	Exchange of diplomatic bags between the Department and Irish Legation, 1945-48
335/57/10	Order of precedence in Portugal, 1959
338/112	Irish-Portuguese relations: Interview by Dr. Queiroz, Portuguese Chargé d'Affaires, 1948
348/3	Irish-Portuguese trade, 1944-1960

400 SERIES

407/5	Importation of supplies via Lisbon, 1944-1945
407/5A	Procedure re lifting goods at Lisbon, 1945-1946
414/10	Press comments in Portugal re Ireland, 1942-1947
414/10A	Press comments in Portugal re Ireland, 1948-1954
414/23/7	Press of Portugal, 1946

2002 RELEASE

DFA/2002/19/11[305/218/13 Pt. IV Political situation in Portuguese Africa June 1966-December 1969]

SECRETARY'S OFFICE FILES

P SERIES

P12/4	Irish Legation Madrid, 1939-1948
P 12/18	Irish Legation Lisbon (including ref. UN application), 1942-1946